KASHMIR'S TRANSITION TO ISLAM

Kashmir's Transition to Islam

The Role of Muslim Rishis (Fifteenth to Eighteenth Century)

MOHAMMAD ISHAQ KHAN

MANOHAR
2026

First published 1994
Paperback edition 1997
Third edition 2002
Reprinted 2026

ISBN 978-81-7304-199-0

Published by
Ajay Kumar Jain *for*
Manohar Publishers & Distributors
4753/23 Ansari Road, Daryaganj
New Delhi 110 002

Printed and bound in India

Contents

Preface to the Third Edition

Professor Richard Maxwell Eaton has raised some pertinent points regarding *Kashmir's Transition to Islam* and "difficulties inherent in the historical use of Indo-Muslim hagiographies" (*Journal of Islamic Studies*, vol. 10, no. 1, 1999, Oxford). While I am indebted to the learned scholar for his encouraging remarks and insightful comments, nevertheless, some misgivings need to be dispelled.

True, in certain cases, there are "long gaps" between "events discussed and the earliest recorded reference to them"; but it must be borne in mind that such criticism founders on the bedrock of the earliest sources, now extinct, but used by later Persian chroniclers. For instance, Sayyid 'Ali, who wrote his *Tarikh-i Kashmir* in the 1570s, refers to several earliest works which are now not available to us. On the contrary, where contemporary or near contemporary chronicles are available, their authors do not provide any information about an event of crucial significance as eyewitnesses. Thus the intriguing silence of the Sanskrit chroniclers about Lal Ded, Saiyid 'Ali Hamadani and Shaikh Nuruddin Rishi speaks volumes for their hubristic attitudes.

It is also important to note that the terminology of a "conscious missionary" for Shaikh Nuruddin Rishi has been used in a much broader context of invitation to join spiritual and social fellowship (*da'wah*) epitomising the teachings of the Qur'an, *Sunna* and *Tasawwuf* rather than within the perceived narrow confines of the nineteenth-century "Protestant efforts at systematic and bureaucratized proselytization." One wonders why the application of the term "conscious missionary" appears "misleading and quite problematic" to Eaton given a plethora of evidence quoted in this book from Nuruddin's poetry, *tazkira* literature and, also, the latter-day perceptions of his missionary and liberating role in the folk consciousness against the background of the egalitarian teachings of Islam vis-à-vis caste system! One also wonders at Eaton's speculation as to "how ascetics and social recluses could at the same time have been active farmers . . . who conferred dignity on manual labour". Isn't there sufficient evidence in this work itself to show that several Rishis including the prominent ones like Baba Hardi Rishi and Shaikh Daud Batmaloo were also active farmers? For that matter even Nuruddin Rishi is reputed to have once symbolically cultivated a piece of land in order to emphasise the spiritual and social importance of manual labour, abhorrent to the Brahmans. Isn't his poem *Gongal-nama* addressed to the peasants with the main aim of impressing upon them the need for combining asceticism with the agricultural service to God?

Notwithstanding the primary importance of contemporary sources for reconstructing the past, their absence vis-à-vis an event or events in a given case need not, however, prevent an historian from exploring such a challenging historical phenomenon creatively and imaginatively in consonance with the spirit of the time. This point is particularly elaborated in our examination of the advent of Mir Sayyid 'Ali Hamadani in Kashmir in 1384. Although his sojourn in the Valley was an event that had far reaching implications for the future of Brahmanism in Kashmir, yet the Sanskrit chroniclers, viz., Jonaraja and Srivara have not referred to him. In fact, the choice of what events to record and the significance attached to them and what to delete was actually determined by their superior notion of caste (pp. 7-9). Our analysis of the Sanskrit chronicles of the fifteenth century calls in question not only the value of eyewitness accounts, but also the authenticity of historical records against the background of the cherished notions of caste. These contemporary sources cannot always be relied upon as having overriding value, because of their authors' predilections in favour of their own closed ethnocentric cultural environment.

It is heartening to learn on the Internet that Barnes and Nobles have sorted this book as one of the best sellers. My sincere thanks to Manohar for bringing out the third edition. For this edition I have corrected a few errors of fact and print; otherwise, the text remains unchanged.

17 September 2002 MOHAMMAD ISHAQ KHAN

Preface to the Paperback Edition

Nothing, indeed, is dangerously cankerous in societies than ideological intolerance. The mission of the Muslim mystics, the Rishis, of the picturesque Valley of Kashmir was to root out intolerance of every kind in consonance with the ethical spirit of the Quran and the *Sunna*. Kashmiri Muslims should justly feel proud of the glorious heritage that the Sufi masters have bequeathed to them; and, as a researcher, I believe that they will continue to rejoice in cherishing the humanitarian ideals of their spiritual leaders despite the ravages of time and history. Perhaps Napoleon's words best epitomize the lesson that they may learn from the "monumental tragedy" that struck the famous shrine of the revered Sufi, Shaikh Nuruddin Rishi, at Charar-i-Shariff in May, 1994.

> "Tragedy warms the soul, elevates the heart, and
> can and ought to create heroes."

I am grateful to my reviewers in India and Pakistan for emphasizing the usefulness of *Kashmir's Transition to Islam: The Role of Muslim Rishis*. Mr. Mir Abdul Aziz's criticism has enabled me to make a minor correction in this reprint. A word of appreciation for *The Asian Age* for reproducing excerpts from the book in an orderly manner in its "Book of the Week" columns.

I am hopeful that this paperback edition will help scholars and general readers in rediscovering Kashmir as a locus and beacon of what Mohammad Iqbal, the illustrious poet-philosopher of Kashmiri origin, conceptualizes as "spiritual democracy" in his thought-provoking lecture: *The Reconstruction of Religious Thought in Islam.*

Magarmal Bagh, Srinagar
Kashmir, 190001
Febraury 11, 1996

MOHAMMAD ISHAQ KHAN

Preface

Kashmir constitutes a special area in the history of Islam considering the spirited response of its people, living in the Hindu-Buddhist environment, to the egalitarian teachings of the Sufis from Central Asia and Persia who began to pour into the picturesque Valley from the fourteenth century. The response, in fact, first came from Lal Ded, the wandering Saivite woman mystic of the fourteenth century and her spiritual offspring, Nuruddin Rishi, the founder of the indigenous order of Muslim Rishis.

The aim of this book is to enable readers to understand and appreciate what Islam meant to the Rishis and their adherents including even the Sufis of the Kubrawi and Suharwardi orders. Islam, as understood by them, sought to subject the felicity of life on this planet to the norms of morality and of responsibility. Man therefore had to regulate the pattern of human life in such a way as confirmed the truth of the Prophet Muhammad's (Peace of Allah on him) saying: "Religion is indeed man's treatment of his fellows."

What has prompted me, over a period of eight years, to make an in-depth study of the spiritual manhood of the Rishis *vis-a-vis* their social role has been the absence of any serious work which may objectively evaluate the contribution of Kashmir to such a universal movement within the fold of Islam as Sufism. I have endeavoured to bring a new dimension of understanding to the study of Islamic spirituality (Sufism) on careful, critical and empathic analysis of those beliefs, practices, issues, devlopments, and movements that provide some appreciation of that faith which has inspired and informd the lives of Kashmiri Muslims.

There is a direct and fundamental relationship between the evolution of Shaikh Nuruddin's religious career and the gradual development of what may be called the Kashmiri Muslim society. For centuries his mystical poetry has remained the *Weltanschuung* of Kashmiris.

Although I have quoted verses from B.N. Parimoo's English rendering of the Shaikh's poetry wherever necessary, the translations for the most part are entirely my own. I must confess that no translator can reproduce the sublimity and comprehensiveness of the words used by the Shaikh, which mean so much in a single symbol. And this is the reason that at some places I have rendered the meaning of the original in a paraphrase.

It is a matter of great pleasure for me to express grateful thanks to all those who have helped me in the writing of this book: to Abdul Hamid Rather for his assistance at the preliminary stage of the work; to Hakim Abdul Hamid and Sayyid Ausaf Ali for their hospitality during my stay at Jamia Hamdard, New Delhi; to Professor Syed Vahiduddin for useful advice; to Dr. Triloki Nath Ganjoo for drawing my attention to the Sharda manuscript on Shaikh Nuruddin's poetry in his possession; to Professors G.R. Malik and G.M. Shad, Ghulam Rasool Butt, Ex-Munshi of the Research Library, Srinagar, Mir Ghulam Nabi and Ghulam Qadir of Chrar-i Shariff and Dryagam respectively for extending various courtesies; to Professor Mushirul Hasan for seeing the book through the press; and to Mr. Ajay Jain of the Manohar for bringing it out neatly and expeditiously; and, last but not least, especially to Dr. Christian W. Troll, formerly Director and Professor of Islamic Studies at the Vidyajyoti Institute of Religious Studies, Delhi for granting me an easy access to excellent library facilities during his stay in India. It would not be out of place to mention here that during my stay in the United Kingdom (February-September 1992) occasional meetings with Dr. Troll at Oxford and Birmingham made me feel deeply sensitive to such issues of faith, identity, and values as have invigorated my zeal for exploring them in greater depth in times to come.

The tolerance and fortitude of my wife and the love of children have been a great source of strength for me in times of trouble. I dedicate this work to my children with a fervent prayer that they may imbibe universal love, tolerance, altruism and, above all, piety so highly valued by the Rishis as true followers of Islam.

Mohammad Ishaq Khan
Magarmal Bagh, Srinagar
15 February 1993

Introduction

This is a study of people in transition consequent to the advent of the Sufi orders in Kashmir from Central Asia and Persia from the early fourteenth century. Although a gradual process of peaceful penetration by Muslim traders and adventurers had begun in the picturesque Valley centuries before the establishment of the Muslim Sultanate in 1320 by Rinchana, a Buddhist convert to Islam, it was not until the works of philanthropy undertaken by the Sufis, through the organization of the *khanqahs*, that a gradual process of Islamic acculturation began in the caste-ridden Kashmiri society.

But the most distinctive feature of the Kashmiri *khanqah* was (and still is) the devotional fervour with which an invocatory prayer, *Aurad-i Fathiyya*, compiled by Mir Sayyid Ali Hamadani, was recited aloud in chorus by the faithful. Although it is doubtful whether the *Tauhidic Weltanschauung* characterizing the spirit of the prayer was understood by common people in the formative phase of Islam in the Valley, nonetheless, it would not be too bold to assert that their participation in the religious assemblies fulfilled more a social rather than a spiritual function. How these common folk were able to oppose or transcend the Brahmanic society is shown not only by the grave threat felt by the Brahman chroniclers of the fifteenth century on account of the pollution caused by the contact of the local people with the Muslim settlers, but also by the stimulus given by Lal Ded, the wandering Saivite woman mystic of the fourteenth century, against the particularism of the Brahmans. Because of her denunciation of the caste system, idol worship, rituals associated with temple worship and friendliness with Sufis, Lal Ded was ostracized by the highly caste-conscious Brahmans. On the other hand, the folk undergoing the process of Islamic acculturation preserved the memory of the impassioned soul of Lal Ded, not only as a convert to Islam, but above all, as a rebel against the Brahmanic creed. The present work therefore aims at filling a vital gap in the field of historical research that denies to Islam the role of a "religion of social liberation". On a careful examination of the original sources, including hitherto unutilised material in Persian and Kashmiri, I have attempted to show that the Valley of Kashmir constitutes a special zone in the history of Islam, where it not only dealt a severe blow to Brahmanism but simultaneously promoted traditions of tolerance, faith, friendliness and fellow-feeling for members of society. The study's main focus is on the social response of Kashmiris—in the form of emergence of the mystic order of Muslim Rishis—to the egalitarian and philanthropic teachings of Islam as externalised in the Sufis' personality and behaviour.

For over four centuries, the Muslim Rishis, under the influence of their illustrious spiritual preceptor, Shaikh Nuruddin (1378-1439), used the Sufi concept of self-realization not only for ennobling and humanizing social behaviour, but also for galvanising human action for the betterment of society. Islam, in this work, thus ceases to be a dogma of theologians, the 'mysteriously known essence' of the Orientalists, or a political system, but rather unfolds itself as a huge historical movement of eternal spiritual and moral strength, which is by no means independent of life situations.

This work has also tried to show the superficiality of scholarly attempts at cramping the Islamic civilization into pigeon holes of cultural synthesis, syncretism, 'Orthodoxy' versus 'popular religion', the 'Prophetic religion' *vis-a-vis* 'Sufi Islam' and so on. I have therefore also endeavoured to dispel the popular misconceptions about the so-called religious syncretism of the Rishis that both scholars and upholders of 'Islamic Orthodoxy' have allowed to enter their minds. Instead, the thesis that I have tried to build up is that the syncretic tradition has been the necessary concomitant of the process of Islamization rather than its culmination. The fact is that during the centuries of Islamic acculturation, the apparent syncretism of Islamic beliefs and local practices concurrently marked the beginning of a movement for the realisation of the ultimate, if not immediate, objectives of Islam at both the individual and social levels.

Sources

The source material on how Islam entered the Valley of Kashmir is not meagre; but unfortunately, very little work has been done by modern scholars on this subject of vital significance. And whatever little exists lacks any objective analysis in terms of inter-disciplinary approach in Social Sciences, or, for that matter, even in the context of the emerging trend in Islamic studies to study Islam from the standpoint of Islam itself. But before we examine the views of modern scholars about the spread of Islam in Kashmir, it would be worthwhile to evaluate the source material used in the present work.

The biographical account of Mir Sayyid Ali Hamadani given by his disciple, Nuruddin Jafar Badakshi, in *Khulasat al-Manaqib* is the earliest source about the Kubrawi Sufi. Written within a year of Sayyid Ali's death (1385), the work does not contain any information regarding his role in Kashmir beyond a casual reference to his departure for the Valley.[1] Notwithstanding a legendizing tenor in Badakshi's work in describing the miraculous exploits of Sayyid Ali in different parts of the Muslim world, he does not fail to give an objective assessment of his spiritual preceptor's historical role. Thus he quotes Sayyid Ali as saying that his contemporaries were unable to recognize the value of his work and his role and that it would become intelligible only a century after his death.

Jafar Badakshi's silence about Sayyid Ali's activities in Kashmir and his reference to the Sufi's statement raise some suggestive questions in our mind, to which not enough attention has been given in modern writings on the situation of Islam in the Valley in the wake of the Sayyid's death. First, it is doubtful whether the Sayyid visited Kashmir three times; nor does he seem to have really stirred the Valley during his brief visit by securing mass conversions either through miracles or by organizing public sermons in the towns and villages of Kashmir. In Chapter III we have attempted to show that during his sojourn in the Valley the activities of the Sayyid remained confined to the Sultan and a group of neo-converts in Srinagar. And in order to assess the contribution of the Sayyid to Islam in Kashmir we would emphasize the need for understanding his historic role in sociological terms in the light of his prolific writings. Of these, *Aurad-i Fathiyya*, in particular, *Dhakirat al-Muluk*, and a collection of letters, known as *Maktubat* are relevant for our purpose.

The invocatory prayers called *Aurad-i Fathiyya* were vouchsafed to Sayyid Ali Hamadani by the Prophet Muhammad in a state of spiritual experience. "They are the pivot of the order and especially intended for recitation at the group *halqa*."[2] What prompts us to treat an invocatory prayer as an important source of the early history of Kashmir is the pattern of behaviour, reflected by the Muslims of the Valley during its loud recitation. It has been discussed elsewhere[3] that Islam is not merely an abstract ontological category independent of life situations; it is a huge historical movement of very long time periods, a consciousness expressed in the daily life and collectivity of different cultural systems. That this consciousness is also revealed in the centuries-old recitation of *Aurad-i Fathiyya* in a manner undoubtedly suggestive of local influence emboldens us to dispel certain misconceptions about conversions to Islam in Kashmir. Our purpose is not to identify and isolate ritual data for analysis but rather to locate such data within broader historical and cultural matrices in which they occur and find their meaning. (see also Chapter II).

An important work of Sayyid Ali Hamadani is *Dhakhirat al-Muluk.* Its essential purpose is to guide Muslim rulers in the discharge of their duties towards their subjects in the light of the Quran and the *Sunna.* The essence of the Sayyid's admonitions to rulers—inadequately brought home in the modern assessment of his work—is his concern for rendering equitable justice, irrespective of religious differences. While nine chapters of the book mainly focus on religious, social and ethical issues, only one chapter is devoted to the government and its obligations towards the subjects. Yet a modern scholar in his evaluation of *Dhakhirat al-Muluk* seeks to describe Sayyid Ali's mission in Kashmir as a failure since Sultan Qutbuddin did not subscribe to his "political thinking" of imposing "severe discriminatory conditions" of the Sh'afi law upon his non-Muslim subjects.[4]

Although *Dhakhirat al-Muluk* is not a source of the history of Kashmir, yet it is necessary to remove certain misunderstandings about its author's role in Kashmir in view of the above treatment of a passage from it as evidence of his supposed "conflict" with the Sultan for not enforcing the *Shari'a* in his kingdom. In the first place, there is no concrete evidence in the sources to show that the Sayyid ever stood for imposing "discriminatory conditions" on the Kashmiri Sultan's non-Muslim subjects, who were undoubtedly in an overwhelming majority on the eve of his advent in the Valley. Added to this is the fact that the Sayyid notwithstanding his adherence to the Sh'afi school, showed broad-mindedness in allowing a band of local converts and Muslim settlers in Kashmir to follow the Hanafi law. Sayyid Ali's decision seems to have been guided by expediency, since the Hanafi law, as compared to the other three schools of Islamic jurisprudence, is less rigid in regard to the treatment to be meted out to non-Muslims by a Muslim ruler.[5] Likewise, while showing regard for the local religious ethos in allowing neo-Muslims to read *Aurad-i Fathiyya* aloud in chorus, the Sayyid demonstrated a keen sense of practical wisdom and judgement in laying a firm foundation for the gradual assimilation of the folk in Islam.

Thus the view that Sayyid Ali accepted the Caliph Umar's covenant "as a document to be followed universally in all conditions and at all times"[6] does not hold water since the document has been quoted out of context. A careful reading of *Dhakhirat al-Muluk* reveals that the covenant of Umar has the context of the Magi and *Ahl-i Kitab* rather than Kashmir.[7]

Sayyid Ali's letters addressed to the Sultan of Kashmir, Qutbuddin (1373-89), are also revealing. They reflect his tolerant attitude towards the non-Muslims of Kashmir. Had the Sayyid not approved of the "friendly" attitude of the Sultan towards non-Muslims he would have expressed his displeasure, disappointment or disgust in his letters written from Pakhli on the eve of his departure from the Kashmir Valley. On the contrary, the Sayyid seems to have been deeply aware of the implications of his historical mission in Kashmir; and this explains why he enjoined the Sultan to make efforts to popularize the *Shari'a*, but (only) within possible limits. Notwithstanding the Sayyid's *Shari'a* mindedness, neither his letters nor *Dhakhirat al-Muluk* give even the faintest hint that he wanted the Sultan to be unfriendly towards the great majority of his non-Muslim subjects. For him, all subjects of the Sultan were the children of God; hence it was a religious obligation for the Sultan to protect the rights of the weak against the strong.[8]

Sayyid Ali's letter to his close disciple, Sayyid Muhammad Khwarzami, written also from Pakhli, also deserves careful examination. This letter raises serious doubts concerning popular assertions about the radical Islamization of Kashmir brought about by Sayyid Ali in his own lifetime. While the Sayyid's description of Kashmir as a territory of infidels suggests that he did not cause a complete metamorphosis of the social and religious life of Kashmiris, his implicit praise for Sayyid Muhammad Khwarzami for having gained spiritual bliss in such a region[9] is redolent of his mission to ameliorate the malaise of the decadent Brahmanic society through peaceful means. It will be seen that Sayyid Ali's mission in Kashmir was not simply to inspire the local people to a more personal, ecstatic approach to divine love within the ambit of Quran and *Shari'a*, but it was also to make his disciples dedicate themselves to socially useful purposes (Chapter III).

It follows that the chief mission of the Kubrawi Sayyids was not to "uproot infidelity" from Kashmir by imposing the *Shari'a* from above; but it was to make the people still undergoing the process of Islamic acculturation adapt themselves to the *Shari'a*-oriented culture through self-realisation and self-intellection. It is not, therefore, difficult to understand why the Sufis of the Suharwardi order belonging to the sixteenth century, or for that matter, even the Kubrawis and Naqshbandis made genuine attempts at understanding the social roles of the Rishis through intellectual understanding or appreciation. And what has to be borne in mind is that even as standard-bearers of the *Shari'a* they did not fail to make sense of what Islam meant to the Rishis (Chapter VI).

The *Shari'a*, viewed from the long-term perspective, denotes a vitalising challenge and a vivifying force both with regard to its creative originality and ability to communicate in dialogue with other cultures. Strangely enough, the *Shari'a's* role in history has not only been misunderstood, confused and distorted, but even abused by modern scholars, so much so that their misconceptions about it have almost turned into indisputable truths.[11] The ingrained habit of the modern mind in equating the *Shari'a* with either "intolerance" or "orthodoxy" has, indeed, serious implications for the development of Muslim societies in accordance with its universalistic ethical principles. And the great danger in such thinking has not only been the distortion of the *Shari'a*-consciousness by projecting into it inherent prejudices against non-Muslims, but also in over-emphasizing, to a fantastic degree, the significance of the deep-rooted strength of non-Islamic local (even anti-Islamic) beliefs and practices in Muslim societies vis-a-vis the *Shariá*. In such an analysis, the role of the *Shari'a* in moulding societies in a broader framework is relegated to the background; it is the historical and sociological significance of synthesis, syncretism and appropriation that assumes the force of law in historical studies on Islam. Notwithstanding the importance of these concepts in their appropriate socio-historical contexts, we have endeavoured to show that societies exposed to the radiant influences of the *Shariá* have always been characterized by creative and dynamic tension. And it is this tension that has gradually led to the historical evolution of Muslim societies in various parts of the world. This is not to suggest that the process of Islamization as such is an outgrowth of the triumphant pure *Shari'a*; but it is, in reality, a ramification of a process in which individuals or groups adapt themselves to the *Shari'a*-oriented culture by assimilating its values through orderly evolution. The predicament or the tension that has always characterized individuals or groups in Muslim societies is whether to adjust themselves to the cultural boundaries of their geographical environment or mould the ethnocentric environment in consonance with the spirit of their *Tauhidic Weltanschauung.*

The next important source providing us a very useful insight into the early history of Islam in Kashmir is a biography of Sayyid Ali written by Haidar Badakshi, forty years after the death of the saint. Not unlike Jaffar Badakshi, the later biographer is full of praise for the Sayyid's miraculous feats performed during his extensive travels in different parts of the Muslim world. In contrast to his predecessor's account, however, Haidar mentions an important event pertaining to the Sayyid's encounter with a Brahman ascetic (*rahib*) in the heart of Srinagar. No other activity of the Sayyid is recorded in this work beyond the general statement that he brought Islam to Kashmir.

In our investigation of Sayyid Ali Hamadani's encounter with the Brahman priest we shall ask several questions designed to shed some light on the history of worship, culture, and sensibility of Kashmiris and, more particularly, in one of the great centres of their civilization, Srinagar, the city of antiquity. Were the activities of Sayyid Ali in Kashmir directed against the Brahman priest of a temple or a monster (*dev*) or a spirit (*jin*)? Was the triumph of Islam in Kashmir purely a spiritual phenomenon which followed from the conversion of a monster and the miraculous feats of the Sayyid? To what extent do the later embroideries of the hagiographers and chroniclers on the historical fact regarding the conversion of a Brahman ascetic reflect the discontent of the lay strata against the clergy? Why are the near-contemporary Sanskrit chroniclers of Sayyid Ali silent about his role? Why are the Sanskrit chroniclers also silent about the supposed iconoclasm of Sayyid Ali?

Although answers to these questions are not far to seek in this work, it needs to be emphasized here that the sight of Muslims of Srinagar visiting the temple along with their Sultan must have caused a great deal of concern to the Sayyid. However, far from getting the temple demolished the Sayyid was successful in getting a platform (*suffa*) raised near the temple. It was here that he gave a public demonstration of his simple ritualistic practices along with his disciples thereby attracting not only the reigning Sultan but even his Muslim subjects. The Persian chroniclers' euologization of Sayyid Ali's services to Islam in Kashmir needs to be understood in this context.

Although the advent of Sayyid Ali in Kashmir was an event of far reaching significance for the future of Brahmanism in the Valley, yet no Sanskrit chronicler of the Sultanate period has referred to him in his works. In fact, the choice of what events to record and the significance attached to them and what to delete was actually determined by their superior notion of caste. While they describe the conversion of Rinchana to Islam in terms of his failure to get entry into a superior fold of

Brahmanism, not surprisingly, the conversion of a Brahman ascetic of the city at the hands of Sayyid Ali Hamadani was not considered worthy of mention, since it hurt their sense of pride and self-confidence. In the wake of the influx of Muslims from Central Asia and Persia, the Brahmans sensed a grave danger to their caste; this is the reason why, spurred on by the fear of being uprooted from their own original environment, they devised a propagandist strategy to guarantee their declining social structure based on caste. The ideas of the Sanskrit chroniclers were accepted by latter-day Brahmans as unquestioned historical facts. Their whole history now began to be built around a highly venerated tradition, based on the orchestration of two myths:

(i) the heroic resistance put up by the Brahmans to Islam *vis-a-vis* the masses who succumbed to the penetration of alien ideas and practices;

(ii) iconoclasm of Sultan Sikandar (1389-1413) under the influence of the Kubrawi Sayyids.

It should be borne in mind that the Brahmanic order had failed to create institutions based on sound religious philosophy which could have served as a bulwark against the forces of Islamic acculturation. Thus the medieval Kashmiri society was undergoing a crisis of what may be described as 'human sociality' versus Brahmanic particularism. And while the most important dimension of this change was the affirmation of the Brahmanic culture within its own realm, at the same time, Lal Ded's and Shaikh Nuruddin Rishis's assertion of the rights of the under-privileged may be seen as a reaction against a monopolistic and ethnocentric assertion of one single culture. It is not to be wondered at, therefore, that the Brahmans also testified to the historical absurdity of their claims by maintaining a baffling and intriguing silence about these two great Kashmiri mystics in their chronicles.

Ever since the establishment of the Sultanate, the Kashmiri Brahmans were not as concerned over the revival of ethical and spiritual values of Hinduism as they were over the loss of certain privileges which they had been enjoying on account of their proximity to the corridors of power. Even during the early phase of the Sultanate they exercised considerable influence on the Sultans; but it cannot be denied that Sultan Sikandar's reign proved to be the turning-point in their history. During his reign the Brahmans suffered the trauma of dislocation, forced conversion in certain cases, and violence—more due to the ferment created among the people by the conversion of an influential member of the Brahman community, Suha Bhatt, the Finance Minister, to Islam than the supposed iconoclasm of the Sultan. From a careful reading of the Sanskrit sources, it is evident that their anger was directed primarily against Suha Bhatt who had deserted them and the folk who had destroyed the ancient usages of Kashmir (including their loyalty to the Brahmans) as a result of their association with the *yavanas.* The latter were undoubtedly the Kubrawi Sayyids, whose leader Sayyid Muhammad Hamadani, a young boy of eighteen years, did not, because of his qualities of head and heart, fail to elicit the praise of the conservative Brahman chronicler. Thus Jonaraja calls him "the bright moon . . . among the stars"[12] notwithstanding his contempt for the Kubrawi Sayyids in bringing about the Central Asian and Persian orientation of Kashmiri culture.

While in the rest of medieval India, Hinduism seems to have met the challenge of Islam in the restatement of the *bhakti* by the Hindu reformers, the Kashmiri Brahmans remained intent only on manifesting their state of agitated uneasiness and apprehension over the loss of their historic privileges and authority. This is illustrated by the fact that even after Sultan Zain al-Abidin (1420-70) allowed Kashmiris, alleged to have been forcibly converted to Islam during his father's reign, to return to their original faith, the Brahmans evinced no zeal in popularising Hinduism in the Valley on sounder ethical principles of human equality and brotherhood. They considered it beneath their dignity to respond to Lal Ded's teachings in a positive spirit. Consequent upon the Brahmanic indifference towards the Saivite mystic's genuine protests against their ethnocentric beliefs, the common folk, under the influence of Nuruddin Rishi, hailed Lal Ded as their 'avatara'.

A close examination of the Sanskrit chronicles of the fifteenth century thus calls in question not only the value of eye-witness accounts, but also the authenticity of historical records. These contemporary sources cannot be as relied upon as having overriding value, because of their authors' predilections in favour of their own closed ethnocentric cultural environment. In fact, the denunciations and protests of the Brahman chroniclers show their concern for preserving the identity of their community rather than for recording historical facts objectively. Frequent use of such historiographical traditions by even later Persian chroniclers in order to extol the iconoclasm of Sultan Sikandar should not therefore be treated as corroborative evidence, but as a necessary corollary of a distorted tradition.

Historical writings pertaining to the Sultanate period in Kashmir thus need to be read with caution since they involve both learning and imagination, knowing what exists and understanding the complexity of the missing materials within which it exists. An examination of the Persian chronicles, written in Kashmir during the fifteenth and eighteenth centuries, will illustrate the point.

The earliest extant Persian chronicle pertaining to the history of Islam in Kashmir is that of Sayyid Ali. He completed his *Tarikh-i Kashmir* somewhere in the 1570s. The chief merit of his work is his frequent reference to two important earlier works, now extinct, namely Qazi Ibrahim's *Tarikh* and Baba Haji Ibrahim Adhami's treatise entitled *Maqamat*. Among these works, Adhami's work deserves special mention, considering the fact that it was written during a crucial phase of the history of Islam in Kashmir. Adhami is quoted as a friend of Nuruddin Rishi for whom he cherished a deep respect.

Notwithstanding the defective chronology and topography of Sayyid Ali's work, his allusion to an earlier and contemporary source of the Rishi order points to the necessity for establishing its genuineness, and assessing its proper significance in a particular socio-historical context. The very fact that the Sanskrit chroniclers' hubristic concern for preserving the identity of their community has been made the primary source of the history of Islam in Kashmir by almost all modern historians suggests that the essence of Islamization should, after all, be sought in the realm of spiritual anguish and search of the teachers of the folk *vis-a-vis* the caste system. The argument is certainly open to dispute and should therefore be debated. Stereotypical thinking, relying mainly on the Sanskrit works, produced by a social group conscious of its aristocratic status and ethos, is a much grater danger to objectivity than either deficiency of evidence or error in detail. And nothing entrenches a cliche or even a preconceived notion so deep as the somewhat ingrained habits of mind repeating a distorted tradition as an established historical fact in one form or another.

A close scrutiny of Sayyid Ali's *Tarikh* reveals that the truth can be extracted from the evidence by the application of proper principles of criticism involving a precise and basic understanding of the fact that no evidence occurs in isolation. Every textual evidence has a context, and therefore the interaction and interdependence of things calls for imaginative reconstruction and interpretation of an historical event out of 'a congeries of facts and specific details' in which every scientific historian is involved. The asking of relevant questions in order to test the authenticity of a source is therefore a primary task of an historian. Applying these principles to Sayyid Ali's *Tarikh*, we have endeavoured to reduce the uncertainties about the social dimension of Islamization to a minimum.

Among the local chronicles produced during the seventeenth century may be mentioned *Baharistan-i Shahi*[13] of Tahir and two separate works bearing the same title viz., *Tarikh-i Kashmir* of Haidar Malik Chadura and Hasan bin Ali Kashmiri. Notwithstanding their importance as sources of political history, they do not furnish us any detailed information regarding the role of the Rishis in the social life of Kashmiris. The author of *Baharistan-i Shahi* refers to Nuruddin Rishi as one of the noted contemporaries of Sultan Zain al'Abidin. While Hasan occasionally alludes to the Rishis, Haidar Malik's brief description of Nuruddin Rishi helps us to understand the deep impact of mystical poetry on the common folk.

The indigenous Persian chronicles of Kashmir belonging to the eighteenth century are: *Tarikh-i Kashmir, Nawadir al-Akhbar, Tarikh-i Azami* (also known as *Waqi'at-i Kashmir*), *Riyaz al-Islam, Gauhar-i 'Alam, Bagh-i Sulaiman,* being the works of Pandit Narayan Kaul Ajiz, Aba Rafiuddin, Muhammad Azam Diddamari, Abdul Wahab Shaiq, Muhammad Aslam Mun'ami and S'adullah Shahabadi respectively. Among these, works of Muhammad Azam, Shaiq and Shahabadi are particularly important because of their richness of detail and information regarding the role of the Rishis. One common feature of these works is their unbounded praise for the Rishis' social roles.

Muhammad Asiam Mun'ami's *Gauhar-i Alam* deserves special mention in view of its reference to *Nurnama* which the author claims to have consulted for the completion of his work. Although Mun'ami does not throw any fresh light on the Rishis, his claim attests to the popularity of Nuruddin's poetry even in his own times, which was such that Zain al-Abidin's court poet, Mulla Ahmad, rendered it into Persian under the title *Mirat al-Auliya.* True, no other chronicler or hagiographer has referred to this work; but the fact that the repeated renewal of the social content of Nuruddin's poetry—mystical poetry bringing comfort to afflicted souls—was the reason for its abiding influence, can hardly be contested.

Among the Persian chroniclers of the later period whose works exclusively deal with the Rishi movement may be mentioned Mulla Bahauddin Mattu, Baba Kamal and Baba Khalil.

Mattu composed his *Rishinama* in verse in 1832. Based substantially on some earlier *tadhkiras*, especially, *Nurnama* and *Asrar al-Abrar* of Baba Nasib and Baba Daud Mishkati respectively, Mattu's work, nevertheless, adds some more information regarding the activities of the Rishis not found elsewhere.

While Baba Kamal completed his *Rishinama* in 1831, Baba Khalil seems to have written his *Rauzat al-Riyazat* in the earlier phase of the Dogra rule in Kashmir. Baba Kamal frequently refers to his sources which include some earlier hagiographies including those of Baba Daud Khaki, Haidar Tulmuli and Baba Nasib. Even a cursory glance at his work reveals how the author, though himself a Rishi, is keen to emphasize the Islamic dimension of the Rishi movement. Kamal does not ignore the local origin of the movement; and he makes a clear distinction between the verses composed by Nuruddin Rishi during his early career under the influence of the local environment and those which bear the influence of his association with the Kubrawi Sufis. The author quotes Nuruddin's verses profusely; and, in fact, the chief merit of his work lies in sustained attempts at collecting the verses from the scattered sources including the oral repertory to which he had an easy access by virtue of his familial links with the shrine of Chrar-i Shariff.

Baba Khalil's work is a great improvement on Baba Kamal's history of the Rishi movement. He not only corroborates the previous work but even supplements it in several respects. Both Baba Kamal and Baba Khalil, while recording the verses of Lal Ded and Nuruddin, actually reconstitute the nuances in the religious sentiments of the masses and thus testify to the process of Islamic acculturation of the village folk under the influence of their spiritual masters. The abiding merit of their works lies in preserving not only the literary heritage of Lal Ded and Nuruddin but also in the reactions of the folk to their teachings. In fact, the two *Rishinamas* of Chrar-i Shariff draw our attention to the need for renewed scholarly efforts at studying and assessing the way in which the folk themselves created and then disseminated certain forms of feeling, thereby producing a veritable system of emotions and reactions against the Brahmanic supremacy.

Hagiographical Sources

Hagiographical material is found almost everywhere in Muslim societies of South Asia. Notwithstanding the contribution of Khaliq Ahmad Nizami in utilising most of the hagiographies for his research on various aspects of the social, religious and political life in the Delhi Sultanate, much remains to be done in this field. One of the marked characteristics of the biographies of saints is the preponderance of the supernatural. It must however be pointed out that the legends and miracles do not create as great a problem for reconstructing the history of Islam in South Asia as the historians' conventional habit of rejecting them outright as source material. There is no problem as serious as the ingrained habit of making a matter more complex without a genuine attempt at investigating it in depth. And what adds increasingly to the complexity in understanding the true historical nature of hagiographical works is the emphasis in Indian historiography on dividing human affairs into two different compartments of faith and 'reality'. The major problem of modern historical writings on medieval India to our mind is that of confining human endeavour within a single framework. Can any problem of a plural society like India be understood rationally if it is confined within the rationality of a single framework?

Our examination of the hagiographical sources offers too wide a vista, poses problems which are too vast and above all, points to acts of omission and commission on the part of historians in search only of pragmatic and materialist conclusions. This does not imply that our conclusions are not rooted in the problems of society; as a matter of fact, our primary concern has been to recapture and relocate the essence of Kashmir's transition to Islam in the general framework of interaction that a universalist faith sought at the social level. Thus the fundamental paradoxes and contradictions that the hagiographies present acquire a useful content only if the legendary material is studied in respect of the unity of spiritual and temporal life so essential to the unity of Islamic faith and civilisation.

Viewed against our sensitivity to the conjunctures of the spiritual and the temporal in the life of Muslim societies, it would be worthwhile to evaluate the hagiographical literature through the perceptions of the hagiographers rather than the perceptional world of our century. In their world, things do not seem to have preserved their separateness and their identity; they deeply realize in the core of human beings a homogeneity between their individual life-process and the rest of the cosmic order. Thus while turning stones into living beings, elevating dogs to sainthood, making springs pray for the pious and look askance at the wicked, with wild animals bowing before the Rishis, the hagiographers nevertheless do not indulge in fancies, but point symbolically to the unity of man and the world of man as possessing unity in an integrated whole. This unity should not be misconstrued as pantheism; nor should such descriptions move us in the direction of presenting a theocentric view of history. Both history and religion would lose their meaning if either of them is divested of its intrinsic relation to the other. Neither religion nor history can acquire an objective meaning and purpose if they are presented respectively as wholly sacred or wholly profane. Does religion corrupt historical thinking? Or have the so-called secular movements in history corrupted religion? Our purpose in raising such questions is to broaden and deepen our own understanding of the dual and reciprocal function of religion and society in not only generating but also easing inner conflicts and social tensions of the human soul and mind respectively.

The primary hagiographical works, used and analysed for the present study are: *Tadhkirat al-'Arifin* of Mulla 'Ali Raina, *Rishinama*, *Qaisda-i Lamiyya* and *Dastur al-Salikin* of Baba Daud Khaki, *Chilchihat al-'Arifin* of Ishaq Qari, *Rahat al-Talibin* of Hasan Qari, *Hidayat al-Mukhlisin* of Haidar Tulmuli, *Tadhkirat al-Murshidin* of Khwaja Miram Bazaz, *Nurnama* of Baba Nasib, *Asrar al-Abrar* of Baba Daud Mishkati, *Tuhfat al-Fuqara* of Muhammad Murad Teng, *Khawariq al-Salikin* of Mulla Ahmad Sabur and *Fathat-i Kubrawiyya* of Abdul Wahab Nuri.

The hagiographies of Mulla Ali Raina, Miram Bazaz and Muhammad Murad Teng have not been utlised in modern writings on Sufism in Kashmir. While the social significance of the attitudes of the hagiographers has been assessed in detail in Chapters VI and VIII, it will suffice to mention here that our analysis of the hitherto existing material and also of new material primarily stresses the need for widening the horizon of the current methods of investigation in the field of Sufism in South Asia. The reader will notice in our explanation that Sufi literature does not merely hold a fascination for seekers after the Truth because of its appeal to the mind, the senses and the emotions, but in more significant terms, it opens up a broad range of varied but related ideas that form a continuous series in the social drama. The hagiographical literature, replete with legends, miracles, dreams and spiritual experiences, thus helps us to understand Islam not only intuitively, but also rationally and historically.

Accounts of Non-Kashmiris

By the end of the thirteenth century, it would appear from Marco Polo's account, there was a colony of Muslims at Malchmar in Srinagar. However, so insignificant was the population of Muslims in the Valley that even after Rinchana's conversion to Islam in 1320, Kashmir was considered to be the land of 'idol houses'.[14] For Amir Khusrau it was perhaps the *yogis* of the Valley alone who deserved to be mentioned in *Nuh Siphir*.[15] His brief account of the magical powers of the *yogis* helps us in determining the religious atmosphere in the Valley in the thirteenth and early fourteenth centuries.

Mirza Haidar, who wrote his *Tarikh-i Rashidi* in the salubrious climate of Kashmir in 1546, does not fail to mention the characteristics of a 'cultural area' like the Valley in spite of having been ruled by Muslims for over two centuries. And what particularly struck him were the Hindu temples and ancient sites,[16] thereby belying Jonaraja's account of the destruction of numberless temples during Sultan Sikandar's reign. Although the Mirza furnishes some useful information regarding the Nurbakshiyas of Kashmir, it is strange that he does not refer to the Rishis at all. The Rishis carried on their mission through peaceful means and kept themselves aloof from politics. Perhaps that is why they did not attract the attention of the Mirza. Another possibility could be that the Mirza was not able to comprehend the imperceptible change that Kashmiri society had been undergoing under the impact of the Rishis. What gives sustenance to our view is Abul Fazl's brief account of the Rishis in his *Akbarnama*.

While on the one hand Abul Fazl is fully aware of the Rishis' punctiliousness about "the traditional and customary forms of worship"[17] and praises them for their religious tolerance, asceticism, philanthropy, vegetariantism and celibacy, on the other hand he refers to them as Brahmans, in a cryptic manner, thus suggesting that syncretism was a marked characteristic of the Rishis. On a careful examination of Abul Fazl's account and other sources, we have however argued that even after their conversion to Islam the Brahman ascetics were allowed to retreat to caves or meditate on mountain-tops and such other awesome sites of nature, in consonance with the traditions of the Valley of Rishis (*Rishivatika*). While modern scholarship has misunderstood this phenomenon as asceticism in the true manner of the *yogis*, 'coupled with hatred of worldly life,'[18] we see in the ascetic orientation of the Rishi movement a mode of conversion, leading, in the first instance, to the Islamic acculturation of the people rather than the assimilation of Islam in the local culture.

It would therefore be historically absurd to think that Islam totally destroyed ancient Kashmiri culture. However, it would be wrong to separate the evolving Kashmiri Muslim culture from its founding civilisation. One of the touchstones of the Islamic civilisation has been not so much the phenomenon of the so-called 'conversion' as that of 'diffusion". That the Rishis played a significant role in both the diffusion of Islamic civilization and its revitalization is further attested to by the accounts of Amin Ahmad Razi, Jahangir and Mutamid Khan.

The *Haft Iqlim*, completed by Razi in 1594, contains short notices of the Rishis' concern for humanity. Jahangir, unlike Abul Fazl, calls the Rishis by their name in his *Tuzk-i Jahangiri*, and both he and Mutamid Khan, the author of *Iqbalnama-i Jahangiri*, mention the Rishis in glowing terms.

Kashmiri Literature and Folklore

The historical information transmitted by the poetry of Lal Ded and Nuruddin is actually rooted in the concerns of the society they lived in; yet no serious attempt has been made so far to reconstruct the history of Islamization in Kashmir on a careful examination of this category of data. The fact is that the poetry of Lal Ded and Nuruddin belongs to a literature marked by its authoritative and creative tradition. The sociological imagination not only makes their poetry a plausible metaphorical account of a social process but unites it with a larger historical reality which we may describe as rural consciousness. It will be seen that the folks' response to their poetry contains not only "emotion" or "feeling", but also thought permeated with historical incidents, memories and associations. It particularly expresses the cultural style of Islamic civilization in a regional setting and the human spirit that flourished within it. This is why an attempt has also been made to carefully examine the social ramifications of the literary heritage of Lal Ded and Nuruddin in Chapters III, IV and V.

A list of various Kashmiri manuscript collections and published compilations containing the verses of Nuruddin Rishi is given in the bibliography.

Modern Scholarship on Islam in the Field

Modern literature concerning some aspects of the history of Islam in Kashmir is mostly available in Urdu and English, though one cannot ignore contributions of modern Persian chroniclers like Pir Hasan Shah and Haji Muhiuddin Miskin. Hasan's *Asrar al-Akhyar*, translated into Urdu under the title *Tadhkira-i Auliya-i Kashmir*, has been painstakingly compiled and, by and large, it has been extensively used in modern writings on Islam in the Valley. However, one serious drawback of

Hasan's work and that of Miskin's *Tahaif al-Abrar fi dhikr-i Auliya-i Akhyar* is their authors' inability to separate the grain from the chaff. Their treatment of the source material is uncritical. In his zeal to show Sayyid Ali Hamadani as a great protagonist of Islam in the Valley, Hasan even credits him with having demolished the Hindu temples. However, the chief merit of Hasan's and Miskin's works is their detailed description of the Muslim Rishis in a narrative style.

A recent publication by a Pakistani scholar (Muhammad Riyaz, *Ahwal u Athar wa 'Ash'ar Mir Sayyid 'Ali Hamadani*, Islamabad, Pakistan, 1985) extensively deals with the works of Sayyid 'Ali Hamadani. Written in a lucid style and simple Persian, the work also contains a useful discussion on some works attributed to Sayyid 'Ali Hamadani. Riyaz's description of Sayyid 'Ali's role does not contain any fresh insight.

There is a vast bulk of literature available in Urdu on the formative period of Islam in Kashmir in the form of books and innumerable articles. But the historical value of the literary output in Urdu on such a significant theme is rather limited. Very often it is either the Urdu writers' personal beliefs or lack of historical perspective and methodological training that seriously impairs the historical value of their literary output. Although Sayyida Ashraf Zafar has presented a lucid and systematic account of Sayyid 'Ali's life, teachings and works (*Sayyid Mir 'Ali Hamadani*, Delhi 1987), her assessment of the Sayyid's historical role is far from satisfactory.

In recent years, the Jammu and Kashmir Academy of Art, Culture and Languages has brought out a few publications in Kashmiri and Urdu on Lal Ded and Nuruddin Rishi. Unfortunately, some articles contributed to one volume also appear in the same form in another, and constant overlapping and repetition make for unsatisfactory reading. The goal of religious syncretism also finds a strong echo in these official publications though there is also a tendency on the part of some Muslim apologists to Islamize the legendary Rishis of pre-Islamic times to a fantastic degree. Notwithstanding this criticism, some articles appearing in these publications contain useful insights; and, indeed, it is such contributions that have given us the stimulus to explore in depth the richness of the Rishis' creative role in the history of expanding Islamic civilization.

Among modern historians the contributions of G.M.D. Sufi (*Kashir*, 2 vols., Lahore, 1948-49), Mohibbul Hasan (*Kashmir Under the Sultans*, 2nd ed., Srinagar, 1974) and R.K. Parmu (*A History of Muslim Rule in Kashmir*, Delhi 1969) are worthy of mention. While Sufi attempts to write the history of Kashmir from the earliest times to Maharaja Pratap Singh's reign (1885-1925), his presentation has all the defects of a work of a general nature. Despite this fact, Sufi's labours in identifying the Persian manuscript sources pertaining to Kashmir are praiseworthy.

Mohibbul Hasan's *Kashmir Under the Sultans* is the first scholarly attempt at producing a better understanding of the social, economic and particularly, political conditions of Kashmir under the Sultans. His brief analysis of the spread of Islam and its influence on Kashmir is useful. Given the wide scope of the book, the author's generalization about the "influence of Hinduism on Islam"[19] calls for a thoughtful examination rather than outright rejection. The view that "Popular Islam" in Kashmir became "diluted" on account of Sufism's acquiescence in the traditional polytheistic practices is true only to a very limited extent. We have, however, endeavoured to show that the seemingly syncretic beliefs actually provide necessary conditions for the revitalization movements to guide the future of evolving Muslim societies.

R.K. Parmu's *A History of Muslim Rule in Kashmir* has been subjected to a rational analysis by Mohibbul Hasan. Although we have subjected Parmu's view regarding forcible conversion to a critical examination in Chapter III, certain basic contradictions in his argument need to be probed here. On the one hand, he firmly holds the view that "the Hindus accepted Islam simply as security against perpetual harassment. The only people who did not were some very strong-minded Brahmans," but, on the other, Parmu does not seem to be totally unaware of the social nature of conversions of the masses to Islam in the Valley. As he remarks: ". . . it has to be admitted that Islam came to Kashmir as a great riddance. Gradually it restored the moral and social stamina of the people. They were regenerated by a new social order and religion which is simple, intelligible and practical. Islam smashed the age-old divisive and disintegrating social forces. It stabilised, unified and integrated social forces. The philosophy of Islam, in the first instance, awakened the minds of a few; they were the torch bearers. Particularly, the role of the *Rishis* is remarkably unique."[20]

It is unfortunate that a sense of being a worthy descendant of the "strong-minded" Brahmans of the Sultanate period in Kashmir has prevented Parmu from putting his own views to test. While he extensively quotes Jonaraja and Srivara to prove his argument about the Brahmans' resistance to Islam, no attempt has been made in his work to study the response of the common folk to the egalitarianism of Islam. All said and done, Parmu's contribution in provoking our thoughts to fill an important gap in the history of Kashmir cannot be denied.

A.Q. Rafiqi's *Sufism in Kashmir* (Delhi, not dated) is of a different category. It is based on a doctoral thesis approved by the Australian National University; but in spite of the author's claim to have made "a fairly extensive and critical use of all sources available," it is a very disappointing work. There are, indeed, serious problems of misinterpretation, not only of facts concerning the spread of Islam but even of the growth of Sufism in the Valley. Still, as the first work focussed on a significant theme, it merits serious attention.

In the first place, Rafiqi has not consulted an important Persian source on the Suharwardi *silsilah* in Kashmir by Mulla 'Ali Raina. Likewise, he has neither cared to go through the letters of Mir Sayyid 'Ali Hamadani nor examined *Aurad-i Fathiyya* in its socio-historical context of Kashmir to present an integrated picture of the historical role of the Kubrawi Sufis in an important region of the Indian subcontinent. The author's account of the Suharwardi, Naqshbanḍi and Qadiri orders is sketchy and descriptive. While an important Naqshabandi source, *Tuhfat al-Fuqara* of Muhammad Murad Teng, has been completely ignored, no attempt has been made to objectively examine the attitudes of the so-called "Orthodox" Sufi orders towards the "eclectic" order of the Rishis. In his desire to show the Rishis as "liberal" *vis-a-vis* the "Orthodox" Sufis from Central Asia and Persia, Rafiqi immediately jumps to conclusions not borne out by history. Added to this is the poor handling of the insufficient data utilised by him, and a sustained attempt at presenting superficially plausible but actually fallacious arguments supported by wrong reasoning. A few instances will illustrate the point:

Nuruddin "did not concern himself with propagating the faith of Islam"; Sultan Qutbuddin refused to "associate himself" with the "missionary activities' of Sayyid 'Ali Hamadani, "much to the Sayyid's resentment"; "the interests of the state were confused with the demands of orthodox Islam" under the influence of Sayyid Muhammad Hamadani; "Nuruddin's sayings do not tell us anything about his life'; Baba Daud Khaki was "horrified at Rishi practices and *accused* them of violating the laws of *Sharia*" (emphasis mine); the "advent of the Muslim saints was also indirectly responsible for including the non-Muslims to embrace Islam"; "In Srinagar . . . life was definitely and permanently influenced by the Orthodox Persian system; "Akbar was not misled by the representations of Shaikh Yaqub Sarfi to invade Kashmir;" "no earlier Rishi before Rajabuddin is known to have concerned himself with the

Quran"; had Nuruddin Rishi been "a missionary, he would have joined hands with Suha Bhatta, who put some restrictions on him to convert the Hindus to Islam"; in Nuruddin's "recorded remarks there is no mention of (his missionary) zeal"; Jonaraja's "passing reference to Shaikh Nuruddin's harassment by the orthodox Muslims is very informative."

Not only the role of the Kubrawi and Suharwardi Sufis, but also that of the Rishis is lost in the labyrinth of ambiguities, arbitrary, irrational, irreconcilable categories and even loose expressions.

Some writings bearing on Islam in Kashmir which have appeared in learned journals and publications in recent years are also worthy of examination:

Aziz Ahmad's "Conversions to Islam in the Valley of Kashmir" (*Central Asiatique Journal*, vol. xxiii, nos. 1-2, 1979) focusses on "the Great Tradition" represented by the Hamadani mosque and *Khanqah* in a vigoruous style. However, the noted scholar nowhere shows how the "Great Tradition" linked itself to the so-called "Little Tradition" of the Rishis. Thus Aziz Ahmad deprecates the role of the Rishis in the Islamization of Kashmir as compared to the Kubrawi Sayyids. And while attributing the "religious and social transformation' of Kashmir in Sultan Sikandar's reign to the influence of Sayyid 'Ali Hamadani's political ideas, the author inadvertently lends credence to the theory of dramatic and forcible mass conversions. One wonders how, in the absence of any concrete evidence, the "militant Bayhaqi Sayyids" secured conversion to Islam in the Valley. Likewise, it is strange that Aziz Ahmad describes Kashmiri Muslims' 'zealousness' and 'fanaticism' as also leading to conversions in the Valley.

S.A.A. Rizvi's account of the Sufis of Kashmir (*Sufism in India*, 2 vols. New Delhi, 1978-83) is laden with historical inaccuracies. He attributes the conversion of 'many Kashmiris' in the fourteenth century to 'temple demolition' and the use of force by the followers of Sayyid 'Ali Hamadani. In his passion to prove the anti-Hindu attitude of the Kubrawi Sufis, Rizvi has recourse to quoting long passages from *Dhakhirat al-Muluk*. The most glaring naivety underlying Rizvi's assumptions is his emphasis 'on the uprooting of infidelity from Kashmir' as the chief mission of the Kubrawi Sufis. That the author actually accepts the statement of chroniclers on their face value is clearly borne out by our analysis.

Although I have attempted to study the history of Islam in Kashmir from a new angle ("The Impact of Islam on Kashmir in the Sultanate Period, 1320-1586", The *Indian Economic and Social History Review*,

1986; "Islam in Kashmir: An Analysis of Some of its Distinctive Features", *Islam in India*, II, ed., Christian W. Troll, New Delhi, 1985; "Kashmiri Response to Islam", *Islamic Culture*, January 1987), nevertheless, a repetition of certain cliches is also noticeable in my preliminary researches. The present study, therefore, not only seeks to amend the views earlier expressed but also aims at exploring and elaborating them in greater depth on a critical and empathic understanding of the source material.

REFERENCES

1. See Chapter III, note 75.
2. As-Sanusi, *Salsabil*, p. 107 (Quoted in Spencer Trimingham, *Sufi Orders in Islam*, p. 96n)
3. Based on my paper "Towards an Analysis of a Popular Muslim Ritual in the Kashmiri Environment", presented in the international seminar on "New History", India International, New Delhi, February, 1988.
4. Rafiqi, *Sufism in Kashmir*, pp. 83-84.
5. Tritton, *The Caliphs and their Non-Muslim subjects, A Critical Study of the Convenant of Umar*, London, 1970.
6. Rafiqi, *op. cit.*, p. 82.
7. Sayyid 'Ali Hamadani, *Dhakhirat al-Muluk*, Urdu tr. M. Riyaz Qadiri, reprint, New Delhi, 1989, p. 195.
8. *Ibid.*
9. Sayyid Ali Hamadani, *Majmu'a Rasail*, Ms. no. 1966, ff. 26 ab.
10. See my comment on Kenneth Cragg, "Minority Predicament", *Journal: Institute of Muslim Minority Affairs*, Le Vol. XII no. I, Jan 1991, London, pp. 172-74.
11. See particularly Parmu, *A History of Muslim Rule in Kashmir*, pp. 116-130.
12. Jonaraja, *Rajatarangini* (Eng. tr. under the title *Kings of Kashmira*, J.C. Dutt, p. 57).
13. *Baharistan-i Shahi* was written by Tahir, though it has wrongly been described as anonymous.
14. Muhammad bin Tughluq asked Maulana Fakhruddin Zarradi "to go to Kashmir in order to sit in the idol houses of Kashmir and preach Islam there." Quoted in K.A. Nizami, "The Impact of Ibn Taimiyya on South Asia", *Journal of Islamic Studies*, Oxford, I, 1990, p. 132.
15. Amir Khusrau, *Nuh Siphir*, pp. 193-94.
16. Mirza Haidar, *Tarikh-i Rashidi*, p. 426.
17. Abul Fazl, *Ain-i Akbari*, II, p. 354.
18. See Rafiqi, *op. cit.*, preface.
19. Mohibbul Hasan, *Kashmir Under the Sultans.*
20. Parmu, *op. cit.*, p. 432.

CHAPTER I

Conceptual Framework of Conversion to Islam

'Conversion' to Islam in the Indian subcontinent, though a subject of vital importance, has not yet received the scholarly attention it deserves. Among scholars who have rejected the theory of forcible conversion[1] in India may be mentioned Thomas Arnold,[2] Tara Chand,[3] Muhammad Habib,[4] A. B. M. Habibullah,[5] S. M. Ikram,[6] I. H. Qureshi,[7] Khaliq Ahmad Nizami,[8] Aziz Ahmad,[9] Abdul Karim,[10] Momtazur Rahman Tarafdar,[11] and Richard Maxwell Eaton.[12]

The aim of Arnold has been to portray Islam as a peaceful missionary religion similar to missionary Christianity of the nineteenth century. His main conclusion is that a great majority of Indian Muslims are descendants of converts in whose conversion force played no part and in which only the teaching and persuasion of peaceful missionaries, the Sufis, was at work. While Tara Chand describes the process of conversion as a peaceful phenomenon in southern India[13], in the north, he implicitly attributes conversion to the social interaction between Islam and Hinduism. He writes: "The Islamic outlook upon social life was democratic, it set little value upon birth and heredity and its influence quickened in Hinduism the feeling of social equality and intended to break down social barriers."[14]

Although Muhammad Habib treats conversion very indirectly, nonetheless, he regards Islam as "the creed that had come into the world for the elevation of the lower classes."[15] And it is in this context that Habib regards Islam as a revolutionary force *vis-a-vis* the caste ridden social and legal structures of medieval India. His general observation that "face to face with social and economic provisions of the *Shariat* and the Hindu Smritis as practical alternatives, the Indian city-worker preferred the *Shariat*"[16] provides us the key to an explanation of the acceptance of Islam by the Indians.

True, S.M. Ikram attributes conversion to the Islamic concept of equality (*Islami masawat*) and social freedom[17]; but, notwithstanding the role assigned to the Sufis for such conversion, the learned author of the most widely read works[18] stresses that their role in the process of conversion was oblique. The Sufis would feel much happier on seeing a Muslim becoming a good Muslim through their efforts rather than on seeing a non-Muslim becoming a Muslim.[19] Ikram's argument rests solely on a statement of Sayyid Muhammad Gesu Daraz that the obstacles to conversion in India were social rather than spiritual.[20] However, the view that the opposition of the would-be convert's brethern, and the unwillingness to break the extended family and caste ties somewhat aborted the process of conversion in medieval India does not hold good for the Kashmir region. Here, as well shall explain later, Islam offered the prospect of relief for those suffering from what A.B. M. Habibullah characterises in his general statement on the phenomenon of conversion in the thirteenth century northern India as "Brahmanical caste-tyranny".[21]

Habibullah's remarks offer us useful insights into the subject. For him it is not merely the Sufi's "supposed miraculous powers," and "the material prospects" that Islam then "held out" for converts, but, equally important, its "social values" that attracted non-Muslims towards it.[22] We shall also test the authenticity of Habibullah's contention that it was "undeniable that the mysticism of the Sufi furnished Islam's philosophical point of contact with Hinduism. It is through such contacts, fostered by the simplicity and broad humanism of the Sufi that Islam obtained its largest number of converts and it is in this sense that he is considered a missionary."[23]

But, as Peter Hardy rightly observes, Ishtiaq Husain Qureshi presents "the most sophisticated and sustained exposition so far of how peaceful conversion in India probably came about."[24] Qureshi totally rejects forcible conversion and financial pressure, by way of imposing *jizya* upon non-Muslims, as main propellants, and deprecates such inducements as the prospect of official advancement and the retention of landholding rights.[25] Islam as a religion did appeal to people in the subcontinent, but Qureshi argues, "its adherents often made their way to membership of the Muslim community by many bypaths and more as the eventual outcome of a process, perhaps extending over several generations, which began as a loosening, rather than an abandoning, of old religious and social ties and an immediate entering into new ones with a known and established Muslim community."[26] Qureshi thus propounds the thesis of a gradual and indirect conversion through an incomplete change of belief and fellowship.

Qureshi's perceptive remarks, though they refer to Sindh and Bengal,[27] nonetheless, clearly bring home to us the importance of seeing conversion as a gradual process of acculturation and gravitation. And although his thesis is reinforced by Richard M. Eaton's study on the Sufis of Bijapur, unfortunately, the Orientalist misconceptions that the latter has allowed to enter his mind have somewhat marred the quality of his otherwise excellent work. In particular, Eaton's exaggerated emphasis on 'folk Islam'[28] not only tends to dramatize polarity between Islam and Sufism, but is also liable to create a false impression that the followers of the so-called "folk Islam" are not moving eventually in the direction of the *Shari'a*-oriented Islam.

In this study we have attempted to show how Kashmir's transition to Islam took place during a long period of nearly five centuries in terms of a gradual process of acculturation. However, our work goes beyond the limits of studying conversion to Islam as merely a gradual process of acculturation; as a matter of fact, we have endeavoured to explain this process more in terms of the social tension that Islam generated in a caste-ridden society because of its egalitarian spirit. And the interaction that Islam sought at the social level with Hinduism in the Kashmir Valley was not only meaningful and positive but also fruitful; as we shall expound later, Islam did not cause abysmal destruction to ancient Kashmiri culture, but guided the course of its development in such a manner that it eventually emerged out of the narrow waters of Brahmanism into the broad sea of Islamic humanism.

We, therefore, give little weight to the hackneyed argument in most studies on medieval India, that in the course of its expansion in the subcontinent, Islam was conquered by the conquered races. It is true that a considerable number of Muslims in the subcontinent still cling to some social customs and beliefs obnoxious to Islam; but this fact should in no way bring us round the model of religious syncretism, applied by some modern scholars in order to explain the process of conversion to Islam in India.

Asim Roy, for example, concludes: "Islam in Bengal . . . provided an uncommon paradigm of one religion's containing two great traditions juxtaposed to each other, one exogenous and classical, and the other endogenous and syncretistic." He describes "the syncretistic model" as an "orthogenetic" response "of the Bengalis to the challenge of Islam, while the adoption of the classical model represented a 'heterogenetic' response to the same."[29]

Written under the influence of Gustave Von Grunebaum's seminal works,[30] Roy's thesis maintains that the great tradition or the high culture of Islam or, to use his own expression, "Islam in its Perso-Arabic attire" failed to elicit any meaningful response from the masses of Bengali Muslims.[31] But Roy is deluded by his own reasoning when he asserts that the response of Bengalis ranged "between an imitative heterogenetic pattern of total adoption of the foreign model and an orthogenetic pattern of utilizing the external stimulus to generate a momentum of change essentially from within on the basis of indigenous culture.[32] Consequently, the spread of Islam in Bengal is merely described in terms of "syncretistic" and "symbolic forms" rather than on grounds of the meaningful response that Islam itself, as a liberating force, evoked from the Bengalis.

In our study the part played by "syncretistic" and "symbolic forms" in Kashmir's transition to Islam has not been totally ignored. We have not however made a fetish of the misconceived notion that in every Muslim society there has existed a cleavage between the foreign culture and indigenous culture; and that the growth of high culture was aborted by the growth of syncretistic elements within a people who exploited the "external stimulus" to evolve a new pattern of life essentially from within on the foundations of the local culture. Many vague notions of the Orientalists about Islam and the nature of its expansion in different regional environments have centred round the view that while a mere body of *Ulama* represented the 'normative' Islam, the masses, as a whole, followed the Islam of their venerated Sufis. The use of such expressions is common in the Orientalist literature and the purpose behind such orchestration is to show the hostility of the religious reform movements in Islam to Sufism, rather than to its distortions and aberrations. Even a brilliant scholar like Ira Lapidus observes:

> "Muslim communities commonly have two psychological orientations. One derives from the scripturalist form of Islam which stresses the importance of a complete knowledge of the law and the correct performance of ritual and social duties. The other orientation derives from what I shall call, for want of a better term, popular Sufi Islam. As the way of religious salvation, this form of Islam minimizes the importance of knowledge and law, and stresses attachment to the Saint, who is the personal guide,

> the bearer of miraculous and magical powers (*sic*), the intercessor between ordinary men and God."[33]

That Lapidus sees Islam through the perceptions of a Westerner is amply borne out by his application of the Weberian theory[34] to the historical experience of the Muslim people. As he approvingly explicates Weber:

> ". . . the mystical forms of religion yield immediate religious and emotional gratification, but the puritanical forms of religion, or generally, those forms which stress intellectual and emotional discipline, self and communal control of behaviour, inhibit ready emotional release."[35]

This is not, however, to ignore the creative tensions that characterise contemporary Muslim society about what constitutes Islam in its pristine form. And in fact, two belief-systems, with particular social and cultural orientations do exist within Islam in Kashmir as elsewhere, but this fact should, in no way, prompt us to draw a sharp distinction between the "normative" or "official" Islam and the "popular" Islam. Of course, in the Islam of the contemporary social scene a superficial observer may describe the religion as surviving in two forms—Islam as represented by a popular sentiment, in the shrines of the Sufis and Muslim Rishis, and Islam as represented by the two seminal organizations, the Ahl-i-Hadith and the Jamat-i Islami. But it would be nothing short of an intellectual disaster to overemphasize the polarity between these seemingly different belief systems by cramping them into the pigeon holes of modernist scholarship. The empirical fact is that Islam manifests its inherent vitality by keeping alive its great tradition of entering into an endless dialogue with its adherents on questions not only crucial to their personal relationship with the Creator but also to the society they live in.

This work, is, therefore, an attempt to comprehend Islam against the backdrop of the social and cultural context of its adherents rather than merely against the background of the *Tauhidic* universalism. Such an endeavour demands considerable skill in translating, paraphrasing, collating and interpreting texts; it also calls for studying the sources, not only textual but also human, with receptivity and empathy. Capturing the essence of the sources has been the primary aim of this study, and with this objective in mind, we have made a dispassionate attempt to study and understand the meanings that the people of Kashmir have given to their actions in the context of their fundamental religious beliefs.

In examining the sources on how the teachings of a universal religion like Islam were assimilated and, indeed, understood by Kashmiris during the long course of nearly five centuries (fourteenth to eighteenth) we have used the popular concepts of the Orientalist scholarship as points of entry rather than as elements in a rigid scheme. Notwithstanding some historical dimensions to the distinctions between the great tradition and the little tradition and so on, the common denominator in all such distinctions remains intrinsically Islam itself. It is in this sense that we have viewed ideas about Islam and their actual implementation among Muslims as components of a total symbol and action system than as a set of mutually exclusive doctrines. The study of Kashmir's transition to Islam is thus a study of the actual behaviour of mentalities, of responses as much as it is a study of a world religion against the background of its ideal forms rooted essentially in the *Shari'a*. Islam, as we shall see, defines itself not merely by its norms, but also by the acts of the people who profess it. Islam is not only then a matter of theological propositions, but also a historical realization: realizing the Oneness of Allah by total surrender, dedication, service and above all, self-sacrifice.

However, though it may reasonably be argued that Islam is not a coherent social, cultural and historical entity, the fact remains that for a considerable number of Muslims all over the world the achievement of that goal is not a romantic concept. Indeed, for centuries, Muslims have talked and acted in a manner which testifies to the abiding influence of their religious beliefs on their everyday life. It is for this reason that this study attempts to probe deeper into the patterns of Islamic acculturation and assimilation in the most sensitive border state of the Indian Union. And although the importance of the relationship between Islam and society has been discussed at the theoretical level in several scholarly works, very little effort has so far been made to objectively analyse the true dimensions of the societal responses that Islam evoked in its actual historical manifestations. In fact, a serious effort at objective understanding of how Islam is a dimension of a distinctive kind of social experience remains only a desideratum. Therefore, the present work on the interaction between religion and society in the geographical, linguistic and cultural setting of the Kashmir Valley will, it is hoped, be of interest to a wide range of readers, and not merely to specialists.

On the mere textual reading of literary and historical evidence, modern scholars have developed many stereotypes about the spread of Islam in Kashmir which have been accepted in many a publication touching directly or indirectly on the subject. While in some works the Islamization of Kashmir has been attributed to forcible conversions, in much of the literature, Sufis from Central Asia and Persia (notably Sayyid Sharafuddin, Sayyid 'Ali Hamadani and Sayyid Muhammad Hamadani) are credited with having attracted Kashmiris to Islam *en masse*, either through miracles or as a result of their "searing missionary zeal."[36] Our study breaks fresh ground in that it does not treat Islam merely as an ontological phenomenon or, more precisely, as a distinct category independent of the mundane situations of those who assimilated its teachings in their life-styles through centuries. The number of such people was far greater than those sections of Kashmiri society which embraced Islam voluntarily, and this was due to many factors. While we do not entirely rule out political and economic factors behind the entry of certain individuals into Islam, at the same time, there is considerable evidence in the sources which testifies to the conversion of individuals—including even pious Brahman ascetics—to Islam, either out of conviction or through moral suasions of the Sufis.[37] Among them mention may be made of the village watchman (*pasban*), Salat Sanz, who embraced Islam at the hands of the Kubrawi Sufi, Sayyid Husain Simnani (d. 792/1390). Shaikh Salaruddin, as the petty villager came to be known after his conversion to Islam, was fortunate enough to give birth to a son, whom he named Nuruddin.

Nuruddin, also known as Nund, seems to have drunk deep at the fountains of both the Kubrawi and the local mystic traditions from his childhood. It is true that Kashmir had come in contact with Islam long before Nuruddin assumed the role of a missionary, but it was mainly through his mystical poetry, composed in the local dialect, that a dynamic and creative interaction was established between the great tradition of Islam, as represented by the Sufis and the *'Ulama* and the local little tradition of the peasant society. Unlike the saint missionaries from Central Asia and Persia, Nuruddin was capable of entering into a meaningful dialogue with the local people regarding matters ranging from ontology to immediate social concerns. That Islam has always been capable of establishing a vital link between its teachings and society is not only amply borne out by the creative role of Nuruddin as the maker of Kashmiri identity, but simultaneously it is reflected in the social response that his popular mystical poetry generated among the masses.[38]

Our study thus draws attention to the naivety underlying the statements of some Orientalists that Islam merely appealed to the Indians because of their credulous attitude towards its holy personages. The extent to which the superstitious character of the Indian people has been emphasized by modern scholars is amply attested to by the general remark "holy-man Islam" with which even a learned historian of Sufism, Spencer Trimingham, characterizes the spread of Islam in the subcontinent.[39] Notwithstanding the extreme reverence shown by the 'converts' towards their holy personages, it is not correct to say that the 'Indian Islam' at the *khanqah* level is simply a reprehensible innovation (*bida*) or a mass of strange superstitions. The fact of vital social importance is that the *khanqah* and particularly in our case the tombs of the Rishis (*ziyarats* or *asthans*) reveal the dynamics of the saints' role in rural society.

Unfortunately the social dynamics of the saints' role was lost in the latter-day development of the shrines as centres of charlatanism, ignorance, superstition and fatalism. Such a development was bound to provoke long and bitter controversy over the beliefs of the people who held the Sufis in high esteem even to the point of worshipping them. For instance, in Kashmir during the nineteenth century we hear of Ahmad Trali's concern over the cherished belief of the people that it was sacrilegious to visit the shrine of Baba Hardi Rishi (d. 986H) just after eating meat.[40] He even attacked the false belief, perpetuated by the 'converts' themselves, understandably out of extreme reverence for the Rishi, that such visits involved people in great trouble. One wonders whether the solitary concern of an early crusader against superstitions was shared by the *'Ulama*, but the fact remains that it was not until the advent of the Ahl-i Hadith movement towards the close of the last century that the controversy raging round the question of the social behaviour of the people undergoing the process of Islamic acculturation reached its height.

Although the Ahl-i Hadith attacked the un-Islamic practices associated with the visiting of shrines in Kashmir, yet their movement brought to the surface certain vital issues of crucial importance. For them the great majority of the people in the Valley, though Muslims by faith, needed to be converted afresh in view of the dichotomy existing between the normative Islam and Islam as practised by Kashmiris, or for that matter by various other ethnic groups of the subcontinent. In their crusading zeal against the *shirk* associated with the veneration of saints and shrines, the Ahl-i Hadith, however, failed to understand that almost all standards of thought and conduct of the great mass of the unlettered Muslims had been influenced by their ancestral ties with the shrines because of their social and economic importance, apart from the aura of holiness created around the premises of the shrines. Thus lacking sociological perspective, the Ahl-i Hadith, in their vehement criticism of the shrines, helped perpetuate the myth of the religious reform movements' supposed hostility to Sufism.

To the Ahl-i Hadith people visiting the shrines are doing *shirk*. While this is not the place to venture into what is ultimately a theological problem, such a situation is not entirely beyond the realms of sociological analysis. For the Ahl-i Hadith, Islamization means strict adherence to the Quran and Hadith and total break with what they describe as alien elements appended to Islam from Hinduism and Buddhism. Most scholars have mistakenly described the persistence of indigenous practices in the Islam of India as syncretism. In this regard, what has escaped the notice of scholars, notwithstanding the best efforts of some Sufis in reconciling Hinduism and Islam in India, is the fact that even during the formative stage of Islam in India the Sufis had visualized the danger of their religion being swallowed up by the self-confident Hindu culture. Thus as a counterpoise they turned their *khanqahs* into impregnable centres of Islamic culture even in their own times. It was for this reason that the *khanqahs* were not regarded as centres of superstition and ignorance during the formative stage of Islam in the subcontinent.

Khanqahs, indeed, played a significant role in the spread of Islamic values and Islamic elements in the process of acculturation. But this process should not be regarded as 'conversion' or, for that matter, even Islamization in its strict religious sense. In its Biblical sense 'conversion' means the soul's turning to Christ and union with Him in his death and resurrection, which baptism signifies as entering by faith upon a new life. In its Quranic sense, however, 'conversion' is a conscious act on the part of the subject, not an event passively experienced. 'Conversion' to Islam entails intellectual, emotional, and volitional elements, including the basic relationship to or affirmation of the faith in the transcendent Allah, belief in the finality of the prophethood in Muhammad, devotion to the Prophet in personal life, commitment of fellowship to the community of believers (*muminun*), and the ethical transformation of life in accordance with the Quran and the *Sunna*. Viewed against this theoretical formulation, mass 'conversions' of groups to Islam, in a strict religious sense, seems inconceivable.

Mass conversions to Islam in Kashmir at a particular stage in its history and also syncretism in the Islam of Kashmiris are thus misapplied terms. 'Conversion' to Islam, as we shall realise at a later stage, is a development or a social process. As a matter of fact, it is a never-ending process. To describe a great majority of Kashmiri Muslims as *mushriks* in view of their ties to the shrines is not only unwarranted but also tantamount to rejecting the historical and sociological process of a peoples' assimilation in the wider system of Islam. Likewise, to describe the efforts of the Ahl-i Hadith in Islamizing Kashmiri Muslims as a somewhat farfetched dream is to ignore the potential significance of the *Tauhidic* consciousness that they have already generated among the devotees of the shrines. Thus, as an inevitable consequence of the Islamizing process of the Ahl-i Hadith, efforts are afoot in the Kashmir Valley to turn some shrines into dynamic centres of true Islamic learning. Islamization may thus be described as a continuous movement of individuals and groups, departing not only from any form of their traditional ties to the local religious culture, but also as a gradual process towards bringing about a salutary change in the behavioural pattern in accordance with the Quran and the *Sunna.*

Viewed against the background of the foregoing discussion, it would be wrong to weigh, in quantitative terms, what percentage of non-Islamic elements the Kashmiris have carried with them during centuries of their transition to Islam. The fact that they had not gone through the complete process of 'conversion' in the fifteenth century is reflected not only in the verses of Nuruddin, but also in the movement initiated by him and the meaningful response that it generated even from the adherents of various Sufi orders in the Valley. The conviction that the process should be completed at the personal and the social levels is deep-rooted in the very structure of the Quran. Thus the Holy Book enjoins the believers:

وَلْتَكُن مِّنكُمْ أُمَّةٌ يَدْعُونَ إِلَى الْخَيْرِ وَيَأْمُرُونَ بِالْمَعْرُوفِ
وَيَنْهَوْنَ عَنِ الْمُنكَرِ ۚ وَأُولَٰئِكَ هُمُ الْمُفْلِحُونَ ۝

> "Let there arise out of you a community of people who invite to goodness, and enjoin right conduct and forbid what is wrong; such are the ones to achieve happiness."[41]

It would appear that the polarity between the high or great tradition of Islam and the popular Islamic culture or little tradition is no more than a red herring. Islam may not appear to be a concrete concept but in more than one important respect the culture that was born in its bosom influenced and shaped the course of historical development of various Muslim societies. In fact, the cultural dimension of Islam is represented by a system of symbols existing concurrently in scripture, in literature, in art objects, in ceremonies, in festivals, in anniversaries of the saints (*'urses*), in the mentalities of individuals, and above all in the never-ceasing discourses in the mosques and the shrines. The distinguished American anthropologist, Clifford Geertz, though overemphasizing the importance of cultural and symbolic forms in Islam, very pertinently remarks that Islam as a culture by virtue of multiple expressions links high culture to everyday life, and joining the two, allows for variety and individuality.[42] Lapidus, while touching upon the same theme, rightly observes: "As a culture Islam is not something divorced from, above and beyond events. It is precisely a way of conceiving, of articulating, the ordinary issues of worldly experience, whether in moral, family, economic or political matters."[43]

The present work is thus a preliminary attempt at understanding how Islam and historical circumstances have harmoniously blended in the lives of Kashmiris. Islam, indeed, was brought to Kashmir by the Sufis from Central Asia and Persia in the fourteenth century. But how the Kashmiri masses responded to Islam as presented to them in its "Perso-Arabic attire" by the Sufis and the *'Ulama* is a question of great significance and is examined in the subsequent chapters. As we shall see, the response came from Nuruddin, who by assuming the role of a dynamic spiritual leader created an inner conflict in the sensitive souls of a people living in natural surroundings. Under his influence a large number of adherents of his mystic order, *Silsilah-i Rishiyan*, proved themselves to be the subtle force of change by creating conditions for the total assimilation of Kashmiris in Islam. The history of the Rishi movement is actually the history of the changing pattern of social behaviour in relation to the professed religion; and it is this fascinating story that the following chapters have to unfold.

REFERENCES AND NOTES

1. Sir Henry Miers Elliot, W.W. Hunter, Murray Titus and a number of other European historians propagated the view about forcible conversion. According to Hunter "the whole conception of Islam is that of a church either actively militant or conclusively triumphant—forcibly converting the world, for ruling the stiff-necked unbeliever with a rod of iron." *The Imperial Gazetteer of India*, Vol. II, London, 1881, p. 18. See also Sir Henry Elliot, *Appendix to the Arabs in Sindh*, Vol. III, Part I of the *Historians of India* (Cape Town, 1853), p. 1., Murray Titus, *Indian Islam* (London, 1930), p. 312.

2. Thomas Arnold W, *The Preaching of Islam*, London, 1913, pp. 154-93.
3. Tara Chand, *Influence of Islam on Indian Culture*, 2nd ed. Allahabad, 1963.
4. Muhammad Habib, *Sultan Mahmud of Ghaznin*, 2nd ed., 1967, New Delhi; idem, "The Arab Conquest of Sindh", *Islamic Culture*, October 1929. See also Habib's introduction: Khaliq Ahmad Nizami, *infra.*
5. A.B. M. Habibullah, *The Foundation of Muslim Rule in India*, Lahore, 1945.
6. S. M. Ikram, *Ab-i Kawthar*, Seventh Printing, Lahore, 1968.
7. I. H. Qureshi, *The Muslim Community of the Indo-Park Subcontinent* (610-1947), 1st Indian ed. Delhi, 1985.
8. Khaliq Ahmad Nizami, *Some Aspects of Religion and Politics in India During the Thirteenth Century*, reprint, 1978, Delhi; idem, *Tarikh-i Mashaikh-i Chist* Delhi, 1980; idem, *Studies in Medieval Indian History*, Aligarh, 1956.
9. Aziz Ahmad, *Studies in Islamic Culture in the Indian Environment*, Oxford 1964. See also "Conversions to Islam in the Valley of Kashmir", *Central Asiatic Journal*, Vol XXIII, Nos. 1-2, 1979.
10. Abdul Karim, *Social History of the Muslims in Bengal*, Dacca, 1959, pp. 134-139.
11. Momtazur Rahman Tarafdar, *Hussain Shahi Bengal*, Dacca, 1965. I acknowledge my indebtedness to Prof. Tarafdar for presenting me a complimentary copy of his excellent book during my visit to Bangladesh in March, 1980.
12. Richard Maxwell Eaton, *Sufis of Bijapur*, 1300-1700: *Social Role of Sufis in Medieval India*, Princeton, 1978; idem, "Sufi Folk Literature, and the Expansion of Indian Islam," *History of Religions*, No. 14, November, 1974, pp. 117-127.
13. Tara Chand, *op. cit.*, pp. 29-48.
14. *Ibid.*, p. 141.
15. M. Habib, *Sultan Mahmud of Ghaznin*, p. 2.
16. Elliot and Dowson, *History of India as Told by its own Historians*, Vol. II (Revised edition by Habib, S. A. Rashid and K.A. Nizami, Aligarh, 1952), p. 52.
17. Ikram, *op. cit.*, p. 385.
18. Nizami points out that Ikram's three volumes, *Ab-i Kawthar*, *Mauj-i Kawthar* and *Rud-i Kawthar* are "more or less classics". See Nizami, *State and Culture in Medieval India*, New Delhi, 1985, p. 45.
19. *Ibid.*, p. 191.
20. *Ibid.*, p. 195.
21. Habibullah, *op. cit.*, p. 283.
22. *Ibid.*
23. *Ibid.*, p. 282.
24. Peter Hardy, "Modern European and Muslim Explanations of Conversion

to Islam in South Asia: A Preliminary Survey of the Literature", *Conversion to Islam in South Asia*, p. 90. First published in the *Journal of the Royal Asiatic Society*, 1977, No. 2, pp. 177-206. I am thankful to Dr. Peter Hardy for sending me an off-print of his learned article on request.

25. Qureshi, *op. cit.*, pp. 75-78.
26. See Hardy, *op. cit.*, p. 91.
27. Qureshi's brief account of the spread of Islam in Kashmir lacks any analysis and is mainly based on secondary works. See idem, *op. cit.*, pp. 52-57.
28. For Eaton it is not the so called "Orthodox Islam" but "the living tradition of folk Islam", as sustained by the *dargahs* of Sufis, "that has remained responsive to the needs of many". Idem, *op. cit.*, p. 296, also pp. 134-145, 174, 201 and 281. Eaton skilfully endeavours to explain the adhesion of commoners to Islam through "syncretic devotionalism" rather than in terms of their adherence to the Islamic law in one form or the other.
29. Asim Roy, *The Islamic Syncretistic Tradition in Bengal*, Princeton, 1983, p. 250.
30. See Von Grunebaum, "The Concept of Cultural Classicism", in his *Modern Islam: The Search for Cultural Identity*, New York, 1964, pp. 116-22.

    The Morrocan historian and political theorist, Abdullah Laroui has written a serious critique of Grunebaum's views on Islam. See his relevant paper in *The Crisis of the Arab Intellectuals: Traditionalism or Historicism?* (trans. Diarmid Cammell), Berkeley, 1976. Edward Said has also subjected Grunebaum's reductive arguments about Islam to a critical analysis. Here his general remarks about Orientalism are worthy of our attention:

    "The Orientalists from Renan to Goldziher to Macdonald to Von Grunebaum, Gibb and Bernard Lewis saw Islam. . . as a 'cultural synthesis' (the phrase is P.M. Holt's) that could be studied apart from the economics, sociology, and politics of the Islamic peoples." Edward Said, *Orientalism*, London, 1978, p. 105.
31. Asim Roy, *op. cit.*, p. 249.
32. *Ibid.*, p. 250.
33. Ira Lapidus, "Islam and the Historical Experience of Muslim Peoples", *Islamic Studies: A Tradition and its Problems*, California, 1980, p. 97.
34. Max Weber, *The Protestant Ethic and the Spirit of Capitalism*, New York, 1958, pp. 95-154.
35. Ira Lapidus, *op. cit.*, p. 98. For the dichotomy between scripturalist and Sufi movements, see Geertz, *Islam Observed*, New Haven, 1968, pp. 56-89.
36. See Chapter III, "The Social Milieu."
37. See Chapter VII, "The Rishis and Conversion to Islam."
38. See Chapter IV: "Shaikh Nuruddin's Religious Career and its Social Impact."

39. "Indian Islam," observes J. Spencer Trimingham, "seems to have been a holy-man Islam. These (Sufi) migrants in the Hindu environment acquired an aura of holiness; and it was this which attracted Indians to them, rather than formal Islam." *The Sufi Orders in Islam.* Oxford, 1971, p. 22.
40. See Appendix D, "A Note on Risala-i Lahmiyya."
41. The Quran, 3/104.
42. Geertz, *The Interpretation of Cultures,* New York, 1973, pp. 87–125.
43. Ira Lapidus, *op. cit.*, p. 104.

CHAPTER II

The Historical Background of the Rishi Movement

The Rishi movement calls for a word of explanation, if not an apologia, because of the Hindu origin of the term Rishi, which has created a misunderstanding among historians regarding the real historical nature of the movement.[1] True, Rishi merely means a saint or an ascetic in Sanskrit literature,[2] but in the context of the history of Kashmir between the fifteenth and eighteenth centuries, it signifies a movement of indigenous mystics within the fold of Islam, erroneously, called an off-shoot of the Bhakti movement.[3] Kashmiri Muslims, who form nearly ninety-five per-cent of the total population of the Valley,[4] for the most part in the rural areas, owe their entry into Islam to Nuruddin and a host of his disciples and their followers called Rishis, so much so that they take pride in calling their vast mountainous region the *Rishwaer*—the Valley of Rishis.[5]

The term Rishi is undoubtedly of Sanskrit provenance, meaning "a singer of hymns, an inspired poet or sage."[6] According to orthodox Hindu belief, the Rishis "are inspired personages to whom these hymns were revealed, and such an expression as 'the Rishi says' is equivalent to 'so it stands in the sacred text'. In common usage among the Hindus, however, the Rishi meant "a saint or sanctified sage ... an ascetic anchorite."[7]

Kashmir seems to have been the abode of Rishis long before the advent of Islam and for this reason it was known as *Rishi Vatika*.[8] A strong folk tradition still persists, particularly in a number of villages of Kashmir,[9] about the existence of Rishis in very ancient times, and that some forests in the Valley are even named after them[10] gives a certain degree of credence to the oral sources of the Rishi traditions. But it needs to be pointed out that before the coming of Islam to Kashmir the

Rishis were not socially active, since they led a secluded life either in caves or on the tops of mountains.[11] It was not until the emergence of Nuruddin as the founder of an indigenous order of Muslim mystics (Rishi *Silsilah*) that the social significance of the Rishi tradition came to be established for the first time in Kashmir's history. Under his influence the Rishis emerged as a vital social force, so much so that they were found worthy of description by even outside observers of Kashmiri social reality.[12] Kashmiri folk songs, which abound in praise of the Rishis, also testify to their social role.[13]

It may, however, be asked why Nuruddin called his order by a Hindu name and also why his order, in recent years, has been equated with "a new Bhakti movement,"[14] said to have been started by Lal Ded,[15] the Saivite mystic of the fourteenth century. Scholarly approaches to this day have mostly centred round the view that the Rishis were unconcerned about missionary activities, and that having borrowed "elements such as the mortification of the individual soul and hard ascetic exercises" from the *yogis*, they had developed a "hatred of worldly life." They "did not claim any Sufic ancestry and did not hesitate to borrow ideas and practices of the Hindu ascetics, especially those of the Saivites of Kashmir with their emphasis on individual salvation and indifference to the fate of others."[16] The crux of the argument is not merely the fact that the Rishis developed their ideas in Hindu and Buddhist surroundings, but the distorted view that their social behaviour, being in direct contrast to the *Shari'a*-oriented behaviour of the Sufis from Central Asia and Persia, led to the emergence of "two different, broad trends" in Sufism in Kashmir. While the "orthodox" trend was generally followed by immigrant Sufis, "the Rishis, mostly native (sic) practised a broadly-based system of co-existence."[17]

Such stereotypes about the polarity between the Rishis and the Sufis[17a] also rest on the assumption that the Rishi movement was influenced very little by Islam and that it was a reaction against the so-called forcible conversions to Islam secured by Suha Bhatta,[18] the zealous Brahman convert to Islam, who, as the most influential minister of Sultan Sikandar, let loose a reign of terror on the Hindus.[19] While the Sultan's minister has been described as a champion of Islam, Nuruddin Rishi is made to appear as a crusader against "orthodoxy."[20] But the great danger implicit in such a view is that Nuruddin is almost uprooted from the *Shari'a*-oriented environment of the Kubrawi Sufis, by an arbitrary postulation of some misconceived parallelism between different developments characterising medieval society.

Notwithstanding the universal nature of Nuruddin's teaching, it would be pertinent to observe that for a deeper understanding of the impact of the Rishi movement, its cultural, societal and historical aspects constitute the primary and formative categories. No definition of the term Rishi which fails to stress these aspects of Nuruddin's movement will suffice. What is important to the historian is how the Rishi tradition arose at a period of great social crisis consequent upon the advent of Sufis from Central Asia and Persia in Kashmir. And in fact it is against the background of the establishment of the Muslim Sultanate in 1320, the influx of Sufi missionaries and the sense of revolt manifested by Lal Ded[21] against the manifold abuses of the caste-ridden Brahmanic social order, that the social origins of the Rishi movement need to be traced. The Rishi tradition was part and parcel of a new cultural trend; the removal of the Rishi tradition from its socio-historical context would be a form of amputation. To understand the tradition of Muslim Rishis, therefore, it is also necessary to know the culture which gave rise to it.

Baba Daud Mishakati who points to the local origin of the term Rishi writes that before Nuruddin the Rishis were actually ascetics among the Brahmans of Kashmir. But Nuruddin, according to the Suharwardi mystic, renewed the Rishi tradition by doing away with the ways of renunciation of the Hindu ascetics.[22] This view is substantiated by the fact that even during the life time of Nuruddin and many years after his death when the Rishi movement was in full swing there were ascetics among the Brahmans of Kashmir who enjoyed considerable popularity among the unlettered masses.[23] Such men were attracted to the fold of Nuruddin since they seem to have perceived little difference between the goals pursued by them and by the Muslim Rishis.[24] Thus the Rishi movement, though essentially characterized by elements of social protest, also provided the cover under which surviving remnants of the conquered Hindu ascetic tradition could continue to exist in Islam. It is interesting to note that the asceticism of the Brahman saints converted to Islam was particularly suited to provide a framework for the survival of such residues and the assimilation and reinterpretation of elements as were not totally incompatible with the esoteric dimension of Islam.[25] This fact is particularly reflected in the various interpretations of the term Rishi given by hagiographers and Sufis which we shall now try to examine. Mulla 'Ali Raina is the earliest hagiographer to discuss at some length the characteristics of the Rishis which he enumerates as follows:

1. The ultimate aim of the Rishis, the *zahids* and *'abids* of Kashmir, in worshipping God by way of observing continuous fasts is to know the Truth (*Haqq*). With this goal in mind and through observance of various extreme ascetic practices, they are engaged in an incessant struggle against their carnal self. They eat less, talk less and sleep less. Being busy with mystic exercises, they do not like to associate themselves with the people. They fight against none other than their own self (*nafs*). They do not pray in public nor do they ever feel proud of or boast of the prayers they are always secretly engaged in. Having reached the stage of satisfaction (*rida*) their hearts are laden with nothing except the burning desire to seek the countenance of God. Such lovers (*'ashiqan*) and gnostics (*'arifan*) do not like to perform miracles; yet miracles spring from their actions.[26]
2. The secrets of their soul are known to God alone.[27]
3. They resort to extreme frugal eating habits with a view to clean the spirit enmeshed in *nafs-i ammara*.[28]
4. They do not mix with the wordly people (*khalq*); rather they shun their company like wild animals who escape on seeing men. Even if necessity demands their association with them, they do not feel proud of it; but in their hearts are repentant for spending time in the company of such people.[29]
5. No sooner do wordly things reach the Rishis than they distribute these among the needy and the poor.[30]
6. They are so engrossed in their prayers that wordly distractions do not disturb them.[31]
7. A Rishi does not make a mockery of his sincere prayers.[32] His outward actions are in consonance with the spirit of the *Shari'a* while in his inner self he is *tariqa*-oriented.[33] In his *tariqa* there is no scope for transgressing the limits as laid down by *Muhammadiyah*.[34] Such people, known as *'arifan-i Shari'a*, are scarce in this world.[35]

From Ali Raina's description, it appears that while the Suharwardis linked the Rishi order with the Prophet Muhammad, at the same time they did not fail to appreciate the fact that the Rishis subordinated all activity of the individual Muslim, in its exoteric dimension, to the devotion and service of God in strict conformity with the religious law (*Shari'a*). It is not, therefore, surprising that Baba Daud Khaki, a renowned Sufi of the Suharwardi order, eulogized the Rishis and the founder of their order in these words:

The Rishis of this region have been mostly Uwaysis.

Shaikh Nuruddin Rishi, the teacher of all Rishis was greatly devoted to God and had a deep communion with Him.

He led a retired and solitary life, besides observing continuing fasts. He had renounced taking flesh, onions, milk and honey for many years. He was inspired and gifted with miracles and had a fine mode of speech. "He resembled the Uways", says an eloquent speaker.[36]

From Baba Daud Khaki's account, it appears that the word Rishi in the sixteenth century Kashmiri usage meant such particular ascetics as, on account of their extreme devotion to God, abstained from all wordly pleasures.[37] He quotes *Kimiya-i S'adat*[38] to show God's love for such persons for whom He opens the doors of wisdom.[39] Such men, according to Khaki, were the followers of Nuruddin, and did not take meat or even green vegetables.[40] They observed fast almost throughout the year and spent their time in the performance of *dhikr* in their abodes in forests, where they also practised spiritual exercises. While according to Khaki, the Rishis were the followers of Imam Abu Hanifa[41] in the path of *Shari'a*, in *tariqa* or *suluk* they received guidance from their preceptor Nuruddin, who was an Uwaysi.[42]

Baba Daud Mishkati, a close disciple of Baba Daud Khaki, even wrote a treatise in Arabic[43] on the denomination of the word Rishi and the mystic way of life and mode of worship followed by the adherents of this order. A long passage quoted by Mishkati from his hitherto undiscovered source also helps us in understanding the true character of the movement started by Nuruddin. He focusses on the Rishis' austerities, celibacy, self-deprecation, relative seclusion, altruism, deep meditative exercises, supererogatory prayers (*nawafil*) and above all, non-injury even to plants, birds, animals, insects, etc. While some Rishis, according to Mishkati, satisfied their hunger with water or wild vegetables of the forests, others took to trade and cultivation in order to bring their ascetic way of self-discipline and self-denial in consonance with the spirit of the *Shari'a*.[44]

Abdul Wahab Nuri, a Kubrawi hagiographer of the 18th century, says that the Rishi in Kashmiri denotes one devoted to asceticism (*zuhd*) and piety (*taqwa*). The Rishis distinguished themselves for having attained purification of the self (*tazkiya-i nafs*), refinement of heart (*tasfiya-i qalb*) and enlightenment of soul (*tajjali-i ruh*).[45] Although not unaware of the local roots of the movement founded by Nuruddin, Wahab also attempted to give Persian and Arabic orientations to the term. For him Sufis who had wounded hearts deserved to be called Rishis since it was in such a state of quest (*talab*) that they reached the desired goal (*matlub*).[46] And while explaining the Arabic meaning of the word Rishi, Wahab says that it signifies a costly and beautiful dress (*libas-i fakhira jamal*). In other words, the expression is used, in the context of the Qur'an,[47] to imply the dress of piety (*libas-i taqwa*) with which the adherents of Nuruddin's *silsilah* adorned themselves.[48] Thus while describing the Prophet Muhammad as the first Rishi[49] Wahab does not simply Islamize the word Rishi but gives it a much deeper focus.[50]

Besides the Suharwardi and the Kubrawi hagiographers referred to above, the accounts of Muhammad Azam Diddamari,[51] Bahauddin Mattu,[52] Baba Kamal,[53] Baba Khalil,[54] and many others[55] also describe, in more or less the same style, the various dimensions of the word Rishi. From a careful examination of these accounts, it would appear that during the period under discussion the term Rishi was used as a synonym for such Sufis as were wholly dedicated to God. There is, indeed, a temptation to call such men as ascetics; but, as we shall see in the subsequent chapters, their asceticism was qualified in that they chose the life of poverty for the moral good of the needy and the poor living in their social surroundings. The scholarly version of Islam given in the Persian language by a Sufi at a gathering or in his works was beyond the ken of the common man with his average intelligence. It seems, by all accounts, that the poverty and humility of the Rishis and their presence had a magnetic influence, which was far more important than the mere knowledge of the *'Ulama* or the learned Sufis. They made the presence of the divinity more perceptible and closer to the poor. No less an observer than Abul Fazl writes of the two thousand- odd Rishis of his time in glowing terms:

". . . the most respectable class in this country (Kashmir) is that of the (Rishis) who, notwithstanding their need of freedom from the bonds of tradition and custom, are the true worshippers of God. They do not loose the tongue of calumny against those not of their faith, nor beg nor importune. They employ themselves in planting trees, and are generally a source of benefit to the people."[56]

Baba Nasib,[57] a seventeenth century hagiographer, sums up of the impact of the Rishi movement in a long poem. A few lines are worth quoting here:[58]

روشنائیٔ شمع دین از ریشان است
رہنمائیٔ رہ یقین از ریشان است
دل نوازیٔ مردم اهلِ نیاز
از صفائیٔ باطنی دل از ریشان است
خوش سرائیٔ خلد این کشمیر را
خوش رواج از دولت این ریشان است
نورافشان چون اِرم از هر طرف
گوشهٔ هر آستان ریشان است

The candle of religion is lit by the Rishis;
They are the pioneers of the path of belief;
The heart-warming quality of humble souls
Emanates from the inner purity of the hearts of the Rishis;
This vale of Kashmir, that you call a paradise;
Owes a lot of its charm to the traditions set in vogue by the Rishis.

It follows that the Rishi movement, though essentially rooted in the local tradition, became an important aspect or dimension of the Islamic civilization, consequent upon the adoption of cultural traits or social patterns of Muslim immigrants by the Kashmiri rural masses. Given the rural character of the movement, it would be worthwhile to approach the subject from the standpoint suggested by Robert Redfield. A summary of his views would suffice here to make the discussion meaningful.

Redfield's central assumption is that the culture of a peasant society is not autonomous, but an aspect or dimension of a civilization of which it is a part. Since a peasant society is only half a society, peasant culture is a half-culture. It can be fully understood only in relation to the civilization in which it is contained. In order to make intelligible the compound nature of peasant culture, Redfield introduces two important concepts—the Great Tradition and the Little Tradition. In any civilization there is a Great Tradition of the reflective few, and a Little Tradition of the unreflective many. The societal dimensions of these two traditions are the great community and the little community. Thus the Great Tradition is the culture of the great community of priests, theologians and literary men who may not even have seen a village. These two traditions are not mutually exclusive, but interdependent, two currents of thought and action, distinguishable, yet flowing into and out of each other. Thus Redfield assumes that any peasant culture is compounded of empirically and conceptually separable Great and Little Traditions.[59]

Viewed in the context of Redfield's definition, the Little Tradition of Kashmiri peasant society seems to have linked itself with the Great Tradition of Islam through Nuruddin, who, in his numerous verses, seems to have established channels of communication between the two traditions and set up standards of mutual reference and influence. But the dichotomy between these two traditions should not divert our attention from the objective fact that, as a result of its gradual assimilation and absorption in the wider system of Islam, the so-called Little Tradition of the peasant society assumed the form of popular culture. The development of this historical phenomenon was determined by a spontaneous and changing consciousness, expressed, under the influence of Islam, in the people's mode of existence, daily life and collective behaviour. It would seem, then, that the exclusive distinctiveness of the Great Tradition or High Culture *vis-a-vis* the Little Tradition or Popular Culture is meaningless, considering the fact that, under the influence of the Great Tradition, the Little Tradition itself became the vehicle of protest against certain established norms which were inimical to the ethical and spiritual development of the Kashmiri society.[60] It was in this sense that the Rishi movement was, in essence, a popular expression of mounting disagreement, disaffection, tension and conflict generated in the course of time by a particular social order, when it was drawn within the orbit of Islamic civilization. For a fuller appreciation of the argument, it would be necessary to know how Nuruddin himself is at pains to stress the Islamic dimension of the Rishi movement. But before doing so, it seems pertinent to set out certain perimeters for further discussion.

First, a study of the Rishi movement requires a wider focus than is customary for the study of history with its stress on 'pure' or 'autonomous' facts.[61]

Second, a study of the Rishis calls for reflection on the sayings and stories related by men who were either contemporaries or men of integrity and character. This is not to suggest that, from the standpoint of history, there are no subjective elements in the accounts of hagiographers or utterances of the Sufis. What needs to be stressed is that to discover the objective truth concealed in their hyperbolic or symbolic statements we must stretch our imagination much beyond the commonplace canons of historiography.

Third, such a study also involves an understanding in depth of the social relevance of the traditions set in vogue by Nuruddin—their interpretations in later times, their revision in terms of the interests of later generations. Viewed against this background, in the various interpretations of the word Rishi already referred to, we are also able to locate the essential traits of the movement as a social process. It is, therefore, also unnecessary to ask which particular verses of Nuruddin are authentic or original, since an element of interpretation, entering into his words by way of transmission from mouth to mouth through successive generations, makes his poetry a social heritage. In such a debate, then, the historians' conventional readiness to accept the antinomy between history and poetry and also between folklore and history appears to be meaningless and irrelevant.

It follows that the Rishi movement manifests itself as the condition of Islam in Kashmir not only at a given point in its history, but even in changing conditions upto contemporary times. In other words, it is necessary to speak about the dynamics of Islam as a continuing process, an unending march through times towards greater conformity of beliefs, attitudes, or modes of conduct that are generally approved in the *Shari'a.*[62] To learn about the historical manifestation of Islam in the Kashmir region, we shall have to thoughtfully examine Nuruddin's own remarks about the Rishi movement.

It must be pointed out that for Nuruddin the term Rishi is a perspective, a standpoint, an archetype of certain dominant historical personalities and even dominant images to which he wanted his adherents to orient themselves. His use of the term is a way of looking at experience as a whole, a way of interpreting certain elemental features of human existence. Thus in a number of verses,[63] Nuruddin uses a vocabulary and a mystic technique which imbue the word Rishi with something of universal value. He wants to convey something more valuable than an elementary historical definition of the term. However, it should be borne in mind that his attempt is to lodge the material—taken from history and folk traditions—in the human soul, which knows no chronology. It is thus frivolous to argue whether the 'legendary' Rishis mentioned by him in various verses[64] existed or not; what is of importance is to remember that he uses popular figures in the folk consciousness as empty vials into which he could pour his own conceptions. Doubtless, then, his eulogization of the 'legendary' Rishis is not an exact description of a certain band of Rishis but a profound and illuminating portrayal of some living and comprehensible pious men who practised asceticism in their everyday life. A careful analysis of the following verses of Nuruddin on the family tree of the Rishis is, therefore, essential for understanding the most profound dimensions of the subject under reference.

اول ریشی احمدؐ ریشی
دوئم حضرت اویس آو
تریم ریشی زلک ریشی
ژوریم حضرت پلاس آو
پوٗنژیم ریشی رمے ریشی
شیّیم حضرت میران آو
سٕتمِس کرٕہم دشنا ہستی
بہ کُس ریشی مےٚ کیا ناوٚ

The first Rishi was the Prophet Muhammad;
The second in order was Hazrat Uways;
The third Rishi was Zulka Rishi;
The fourth in order was Hazrat Pilas;
The fifth was Rum Rishi;
The sixth in order was Hazrat Miran;
The seventh (me) is miscalled a Rishi;
Do I deserve to be called a Rishi? What is my name?[65]

It will be seen that Nuruddin traces the family tree of the Rishis back to Muhammad and not to any local saint of pre-Islamic times. From the Prophet are descended Uways and the 'legendary'sages of Kashmir, such as Zulka, Miran, Rum and Pilas. Chronologically, Nuruddin is separated from a spiritual master by several centuries. But as one of the leading scholars of Sufism, Henry Corbin remarks, "the events of the soul are themselves the qualitative measure of their own characteristic time. A synchronism impossible in historical time is possible in the *tempus discretum* of the world of the soul or of the *'alam al-mithal.* And this also explains how it is possible, at a distance of several centuries to be the direct synchronous disciple of a master who is chronologically 'in the past'."[66] Nuruddin thus presents a kinship with those Sufis who received guidance in the spiritual path directly from the Prophet Muhammad without having a visible guide (*murshid*) like Uways. The Sufis, known as Uwaysis, owed their name to the first pious ascetic of Islam, Uways al-Qarni of Yemen, a contemporary of the Prophet Muhammad.[67] Viewed against the deeper implications of the term Uwaysi in the history of Sufism,[68] the hagiographers' attempt at tracing the spiritual links of Nuruddin with the Uwaysi Sufis does not seem to be unwarranted.[69]

The earthly existence of Zulka, Miran, Rum and Pilas defies historical analysis, but it may be argued that unless we situate them in the world of analogies (*'alam al-mithal*) we will not be able to arrive at even an approximation of the truth. The fact is that their repeated mention in Nuruddin's verses partakes of a different synchronism, whose peculiar qualitative temporality cannot be doubted. However, nothing would be more dangerous than to apply "objective" historical methods in proving the temporal existence of the 'legendary' Rishis. Nuruddin's main aim in designating by name the dominant images in the folk consciousness seems to have been to show the unchanged significance, authority and universal relevance of the Rishi tradition. Judged by the rules of historical criticism, his claim may seem highly precarious, but its relevance is to another, "transhistoric truth" which, to use the phraseology of Corbin, "cannot be regarded as inferior (because it is of a different order) to the material historical truth whose claim to truth, with the documentation at our disposal, is no less precarious."[70]

Although Nuruddin's eulogization of the 'legendary' Rishis may seem to be incomprehensible to many a rationalist, it is not totally beyond the reach of historical realism or objectivity. True, the Rishis mentioned by him do not fall within quantitative physical time, nor can their supposed one-time existence be measured according to homogenous, uniform units of historical time, but from a strictly historical standpoint, three main points emerge from Nuruddin's attempt at invoking their spiritual ascendency across generations of mankind which obviously culminates in his person:

First, in his recreation of the role of Sufi Shaikh and the founder of a mystic order, Nuruddin defended the social authenticity of the Rishi tradition and its continued capacity to make sense of the world in the face of the challenges posed to it by the Great Tradition of Islam as represented by the *'Ulama.*[71] In order to save the local tradition from going into oblivion, he sought to revivify it by giving it an Islamic content. As a result, the essential elements of ancient popular Kashmiri religious culture, e.g. meditation in the caves, celibacy, vegetarianism, etc., were retained by the Hindu ascetics even after their conversion to Islam. In fact, the inner religious life of a number of Muslim Rishis, as it manifested itself outside the systematic teachings of the *'Ulama*, differed according to the degree of the combination of Islamic elements and existing pre-Islamic traditions and practices. Though rarely capable of acting as an effective organized group, the Rishis still became a framework for associational life within a common social, normative, and ritual order, at a time when the very bases of Kashmiri society were coming under increasingly severe stress consequent upon the advent of Sufi missionaries and the *'Ulama* from Central Asia and Persia. The vital role played by the Rishis in maintaining a balance between the *Shari'a* and *tariqa* on the one hand, and on the other paving the ground for the gradual assimilation and absorption of the local ascetic practices in the wider system of Islam undoubtedly gave their movement enormous authority and social importance.

Second, in his poetry, Nuruddin seems to have given a positive response to the ossification of the *'Ulama* on a spiritual, emotional and social level, wanting to impose a pristine model from above without a thought for the warm, earthy, mystic religion of the Valley.[72] He also seems to have seen in the dogmatic rigidity of the *'Ulama* an inflexibility fatal to the cause of Islam, which was by all accounts still in its infancy during the heyday of his struggle against the caste-ridden Brahmanic society. By making Islam respond to the social mores of the Kashmiri people Nuruddin enabled it to develop a resilient tradition of its own, which of course one still finds deep-rooted in the ties of the Kashmiri peasant society to a great number of the shrines of the Rishis spread in every nook and corner of the Valley.[73]

Third, Nuruddin's verses about the Rishis of yore seem to be definitely rooted in a homogenous body of folk consciousness. His mention of the 'legendary' Rishis does not necessarily point to their Muslim origin, but in extolling their virtues, he reinterprets the old traditions through new points of appreciation. Nuruddin's eulogization also helps us to understand the inexhaustible history of the popular mystic tradition in the Valley which, in spite of having travelled through vast tracts of time, had still kept itself alive. True, it had developed certain dislocations during its long journey as is evident from Nuruddin's condemnation of the false Rishis,[74] but under his inspiring leadership it did restore and invigorate itself, though within a broader framework of Islamic mysticism.

The foregoing discussion should not prompt us to conclude that the Rishi movement was a synthesis of Hindu, Buddhist and Islamic beliefs. Notwithstanding the part played by the Hindu-Buddhist environment in shaping the pantheistic and mystical views of Nuruddin during the early stages of his mystical career, his movement stood in radical contrast to the pre-Islamic concept of a mystic's role in society. The Rishis who lived in Kashmir long before the advent of Islam lived in obscurity as ascetics. Even such *yogi* philosophers of Kashmir Saivism as Vasugupta,[75] Somananda,[76] and Abhinavagupta[77] did not have an appreciable influence on the masses. As a matter of fact, the philosophical treatises of the great Saivite masters of Kashmir were far beyond the reach of the common men.[78] What in fact separated the unlettered folk from the great masters of Saivism was the abstract nature of their philosophical systems[79] and above all, the élitist character of the Sanskrit language in which the mysteries of the man-God relationship were expounded.

The most important preoccupation of the ascetics in pre-Islamic times was not so much human society as its horizons: birth and death, and the vast spiritual cosmos which lay behind the changing outward impressions of this life. They looked upon the society of the *Rishivatika* as though from afar, and disdained it. They were indeed homeless wanderers, spiritual strivers, renouncers of the world and all its fruits. Nuruddin did inherit a wanderlust from the Buddhist and Hindu ascetics, but what is remarkable about him is that even while practising renunciation he did not keep himself aloof from his contemporary society. His greatest contribution lies in making the popular language a vehicle for preaching the faith. His compositions in the popular Kashmiri dialect, particularly addressed to the peasants[80] and artisans, point to the plebeian character of his movement. Although Lal Ded was the first to dissect the claim of the priestly classes, it was her junior contemporary, Nuruddin, who waged a crusade against the Brahmanic pretensions and their claims to possess wisdom and virtue.[81] It is not, therefore, surprising that the conscious feeling that dominates the mind of the authors of *Rishinamas* of Chrar is that Nuruddin's movement opened the path to God for the poor.

Looking at such information as we possess about the social classes affected by the Rishis, we notice that the peasant classes were uniformly involved,[82] though with the gradual success of their movement, petty tradesmen, artisans, sweepers, tanners, *dombs*, *dambel-maets* and men belonging to other down-trodden castes were also influenced in due course.[83] The reason why the peasants in general and men of the other professions rejected conventional Hinduism will become clear at a later stage; here it will suffice to say that in Nuruddin's religious thought the term 'Rishi' began to have deeper social implications than it did within the system of Hindu philosophy. When we pass from the realm of speculative philosophy to the actual history of the Rishi movement during the period covered in this book, we can see the inherent weakness of seeing it only as the off-spring of a marriage between Hinduism and Islam. There were, indeed, both borrowings and innovations. The Rishi concept of 'peace with all'[84] was borrowed from Mahayana Buddhism which flourished in the Valley.[85] The Muslim Rishis also shared with the Hindu-Buddhist ascetics such traits as wanderings in the forests, vegetarianism, controlling the breath, etc. Notwithstanding this, the mystical movements in Islam, Hinduism and Buddhism essentially ran in different directions and had a varying influence on the historical development of their respective societies.

In their scholarly works, however, modern historians have made an admirable attempt in the direction of reducing the differences between Hindu and Muslim mysticism.[86] While such works are of great value in their specific context of serving nationalist goals, nonetheless, they tend to blur the vision of Indian history which is characterized by diversity as well as unity.[87] We are conscious of the fact that a fundamental differentiation would eliminate all possibility of comparisons; yet we believe that notwithstanding certain similarities observed in a comparative study of mysticism in Islam and Hinduism, the history of the Rishi movement will make no sense if it is not understood in the context of Islam's crusading zeal against the division of humankind on the basis of the ties fostered by narrow tribal and racial factors or, by a belief in the inherent superiority of one's own group or culture. Seen in this perspective, the empirical base of our historical research does not remain local or national, but transcends the limits of a region, a nation or a period. The academic rigour of our methodological principle demands that the very notion of a comparison requires identification of both similarities and differences. And when we subject the Rishi movement to an empirical or scientific analysis or even to ordinary canons of intelligibility, it appears as a movement of great historical significance born out of universally accepted human purposes in contrast to the ethnocentricity of the Brahmanic creed. That it is possible to formulate scientific generalizations by observing differences between different occurrences of culture-traits and complexes is amply borne out by a comparative study of the Rishi movement and its parallel in the plains, the Bhakti movement.

Unlike the Bhakti reformers like Kabir and Nanak, the Rishis did not reject the basic elements of Islam. They rejected the idol, yet they did not scorn the Kaba; they condemned the rituals evolved by the Brahmans, yet they were punctilious about the observance of rituals sanctioned by Islam; they loved God to the point of annihilation, yet, even while dead to their selves, they led an active social life for the sake of humanity; they waged a crusade against the social inequalities of the age, yet they endeared themselves to even the die-hard, caste-conscious Brahmans by the nobility of their culture and soundness of their faith in God's mercy for His sincere devotees.

Among such Hindu concepts as run counter to the belief of the Muslim Rishis is the position of *Vedas*, a conception of commands, categorical in nature and external in character without the least suggestion of any commander,[88] and the sacrificial aspect of *Vedic* hymns. Some ecstatic utterances of Nuruddin and other Rishis may tempt us to draw parallels between the Hindu and Muslim mysticism. But on close examination, these similarities prove not to be explicable in terms of imitation. Notwithstanding the close correspondence in form or external appearance, the Upanishadic yearning for self-identification with God is fundamentally different from the type of mental structure and origin of the quest of God of theists like Nuruddin. The interpreters of the *Bhagavad Gita*, belonging to various schools, with their emphasis on the performance of prescribed caste duties, as also "its affirmation of the doctrine of *karma*, and its anthropomorphic belief in the birth of God as man are all opposed to the main trends of sufism in Islam."[89] An attempt to understand the Rishi movement against the devotional aspect of the Bhakti movement, will prove futile when we seek to examine the social implications of Ramanuja's religious attitudes. Thus, according to Ramanuja, Isvara grants emancipation from wordly bonds to those who are recipients of the true knowledge from the study of Hindu scriptures (*Sastras*).[90] Furthermore, his view that Isvara has to be admitted on the authority of the sacred Hindu text,[91] rather than proved by inference,[92] or his acquiescence "in the Hindu scriptural authority on the division of human society into castes,"[93] also presents a contrast to the basic components of Sufism. The notion of *karma* which is the dominant characteristic of the entire Hindu mysticism negates even in its Bhakti aspect in Ramanuja and Nimbarka the Rishi or the Sufi world view.

There is another and more subtle kind of misleading similarity when mystics in two different systems are engaged in similar pursuits: the analysis shows their ends to be completely antithetical and reveals that these systems have arisen in response to absolutely opposite needs. An example of this would be the Buddhist or the *yogic*//Upanishadic meditative practice, which is fundamentally different from those of the Rishis. While in the former one begins by sitting cross-legged with a straight back in some quiet place, in the other the straightness of the back and the folded legs are not required to foster a degree of wakefulness. Among the Rishis awakening was a continuous process which could be obtained not only through the performance of the prescribed prayers, and recitation of *dhikr* but also while devoting oneself to the service of the people. Thus most Rishis devoted themselves to agricultural pursuits and laid out gardens for the general good of society. There is, indeed, considerable evidence to show that the Rishis attached great importance to hard labour and considered it a supreme act of worship.

Furthermore, spiritual awakeness among the Rishis could not be attained through the Buddhist or the *yogic* practice of concentrating on some object, "in some versions at first a physical object but eventually in almost every case a mental image, a single sensation or perhaps a silently repeated sound. In an Upanishadic version one might perhaps have concentrated on the self-dwelling in the heart, 'smaller than a mustard seed and golden (C. III 14). Or in a Buddhist version one might concentrate upon a colour such as blue; or in both a Buddhist and *yogic* meditation on one's breath. The counterpart of this concentration is the strenuous exclusion from the attention of other sensations and indeed of merely adventitious thoughts. One is thereby absorbed in the object of meditation—and indeed some measure of this absorption is experienced by any one who concentrates on some task."[94]

The ultimate aim of the meditative practice in the Buddhist or the *yoga*/Upanishadic systems is the absorption of the individual in a personal deity or God in a spirit of love. Among the Saivites of Kashmir the soul gains knowledge through intense *yogic* contemplation whereby the vision of *Parama Siva*, the Supreme Lord of the Universe, is realized and the individual soul is absorbed in the mystic trance of peace, quiet and joy. In *Pratyabhijna* the soul by its own intuition trained under the instruction of a teacher (*guru*) recognizes itself as God and so rests in the mystic bliss of oneness[95] with God. Whether in ancient times this path of knowledge—led by means of the discipline of *yoga* to the goal by self-illumination and the realization of the oneness of the individual soul with the supreme—was open to the lower castes is a question that needs to be answered satisfactorily, if not convincingly.[96]

The necessity for understanding the historical character of the Rishi movement in a comparative perspective also explains why the Bhakti movement failed to fit into the Kashmiri environment despite the repeated emphasis of the *Bhagavat Purana* on the devotional aspect of Hindu religion. The failure of Hindu mysticism in this respect may be explained in terms of the emphasis it laid on the superiority of caste even within the devotional structure of the Hindu cosmogony. Thus while in the *Bhagavat Purana* low castes are allowed to chant the name of Krishna, they are assigned such a position within the ambit of their caste.[97] True, rituals are considered of secondary importance *vis-a-vis* Bhakti, but, again, the worship of idols and symbols which involves the performance of rituals is not condemned.[98] It is also true that in the *Bhagavat Purana* the monotheistic concept has been clearly defined; God is one and unqualified (*Nirguna*). But then God is also personal and incarnate[99] notwithstanding His oneness. This idea of a personal God or God incarnate which led to the emergence of the concept of *avatara* was diametrically opposed to Islam, though significantly enough, Nuruddin utilized it to the advantage of Islam in Kashmir.[100] By declaring Lal Ded, a Saivite *yogini* of the fourteenth century Kashmir as an *avatara* of Kashmiris, Nuruddin immortalized her name as a rebel against the Brahmanic supremacy. How far the romanticization of Lal Ded in hagiographies and folk consciousness contributed in dispelling the Brahman's false claims of innate spirituality will become clear in the subsequent chapters. Here, suffice it to say that superficial comparisons with limited horizons as outlined in some modern works can hardly lift a veil over the deepening crisis of the power and authority of the Brahmanic belief structure as reflected in the response of the Rishis to the infiltration of Islamic teachings.

The fact is that the Rishis, in spite of their inner preoccupations with God, always found themselves in a relative tension with the social reality. As we shall see later, the problems of the society were an essential part of the Rishis' being; in no sense was the society irrelevant for them since it influenced their thinking and was an important element in the formation of their thought. The Rishis were not totally unaware of the need for struggle in history. They were engaged not merely in a continuous struggle against the carnal desires of their selves, but more importantly, in generating awareness of the social usefulness of living in God's grace by consecrating their lives to His cause. True, the internal dimension of the Rishis was one of love, but in their external manifestation their position was that of responsible members of society as true servants of god.

It would be seen, then, that the similarities between the Rishi and the Bhakti movement are deceptive. Despite the analogous tendencies exhibited by them in some respects, the fact remains that certain precise and original characteristics distinguish the movement of the Muslim Rishis in the Kashmir Valley from that of the *bhaktas* and *yogis* of the Indian plains or, for that matter, even the Hindu-Buddhist ascetics of ancient Kashmir. While in the one the ideas about the man-God relationship remained vague and amorphous, disappearing ultimately among the medley of heterogenous ideas and feelings or culminating in the emergence of religious sects, in the other they blossomed forth and were embodied in the systematic exposition of the *Tauhidic Weltanschauung*, not only in Nuruddin's abundant verses, but also in devotional songs composed in praise of Allah, Muhammad, Sufis and the Rishis, and sung to this day with great fervour in social institutions of great significance in the Kashmir Valley, like the shrines and mosques. The progress and results of these developments in Kashmir through the centuries reveal such pronounced differences of degree that they are almost equivalent to a difference in kind, and in any case are marked by antitheses characteristic of their respective environments. This objective historical situation, which unfolds itself in the following chapters, gives a unique position of strength to Islam in Kashmir.

REFERENCES AND NOTES

1. The question has been superficially discussed in Rizvi, *A History of Sufism in India*, Vol. I, pp. 350–51; Rafiqi, *Sufism in Kashmir*, pp. 134–36. Although K.N. Dhar emphasizes the Islamic dimension of the Rishi

order, he wrongly describes it as a "cult". See *Nund Rishi: a Rosary of Hundred Beads*, p. 6.

2. Monier Williams, *A Sanskrit-English Dictionary*, p. 227.
3. See Ratan Lal Shant, "*Bhagti Tahrik Aur Shaikh Nuruddin Wali*", *Shiraza* (Shaikh al-Alam), Vol. 17, No: 3.3, pp. 88–96.
4. *Census of India*, 1971.
5. Another synonym for *Rishwaer is Pirwaer*. The latter term seems to have been coined during the Sultanate period in Kashmir (1320–1586), when Persian influence permeated almost all aspects of Kashmiri society. For the impact of Persia on Kashmir, see Ishaq Khan "Persian Influences in Kashmir in the Sultanate Period, 1320–1586", *Islamic Culture*, January, 1977.
6. Monier Williams, *op.cit.*, p. 226. In the *Rig* and "*Atharvavedas* 'hym' or 'hymns' of the Rishis are spoken of. It is said, that both the ancient and the recent rishis have generated prayers." See J. Muir, *The Origin of Castes in the Vedic Age*, p. 243.
7. Monier Williams, *op. cit.*, pp. 226–27.
8. According to K.N. Dhar, the term *Rishi-Vatika* suggests "unmistakably ... an order of emancipated recluses rehabilitating man on his lost glory" *op. cit.* p. 6.
9. Interestingly enough, the springs below Verinag, the main source of the river Jehlum, and a hillock in the Islamabad district are named after the Sapta-Rishis. According to Monier Williams, "Seven Rishis or *Sapta rishayah* or *Satarishayah* or *Saptarshayah*, are often mentioned in the Brahmanas and later works as typical representatives of the character and spirit of the pre-historic or mythical period."

   See Monier Williams, *op. cit.*, p. 227. One of these Rishis was Kasyapa who, according to popular tradition, "settled the land of Kashmir" after punishing the demon Jalodbhava (water-born) residing in the lake called *Satisaras*, 'the lake of Sati (Durga)', which occupied the Valley of Kashmir from the beginning of the Kalpa. For details, see Kalhana, *Rajatarangini* (Stein), II, pp. 388–89. Whatever may be the origin of the legend, it cannot be denied that Kashmir has derived its name from Kasyapa Rishi. It is also for this reason that Kashmir has remained, from time immemorial, a land gifted with holy sites and objects of pilgrimages. Kalhana emphasizes this fact when he describes the Valley as a country "where there is not a space as large as a grain of sesamum without a Tirtha". (Kalhana, *op. cit.*, Book, I, V. 38).
10. Dandakvan and Rishivan, for instance, are associated with the 'legendary' Rishis. While Dandakvan was, in olden times, a forest in the Hamal pargana of Kamraj district in the Valley (Pir Hasan Shah, *Tadhkira-i Auliya-i Kashmir*, Urdu tr. p. 105), Rishivan is a mountain in the rear of Safapore (*Ibid.*, p. 108; see also *Bruj-i Nur*, p. 113).

11. Significantly, Amir Khusrau speaks enough of the spiritual powers of the *yogis* of Kashmir who lived in caves and on the tops of the mountains. See *Nuh Siphir*, pp. 193–94.
12. Abul Fazl, *Ain-i Akbari* (Jarret), II, p. 354; Jahangir, *Tuzuk-i Jahangiri*, II, pp. 149–50.
13. *Koshur Luk Baeth*, (ed. Moti Lal Saqi), Vol. IV, pp. 47, 63, 74, 82, 103, 105, 107, 112, 183, Vol V, pp. 15, 31, 43, 54, 59, 64, Vol. VII (ed. Sham Lal Pardesi and Som Nath Sadhu), pp. 96, 103, 130.
14. Rafiqi, *op. cit.*, p. 143. See also Ratan Lal Shant, *op. cit.*
15. For a detailed analysis of Lal Ded's historical role, see Chapter III; also Ishaq Khan, "The Impact of Islam on Kashmir in the Sultanate period, 1320–1586." *The Indian Economic and Social History Review*, Vol. XXIII, No. 2, April–June, 1986, pp. 187–205.
16. Rafiqi, *op. cit.*, Introduction, pp. XVII–XVIII.
17. *Ibid.* Introduction, P. XIV.

17a. Rizvi does not substantiate his argument that there existed "serious differences between the attitude to religion and mysticism of the Kubrawiyya and of Shaikh Nuruddin ..." (*Sufism in India*, I, p. 350). It is, however, significant to note that in one of his verses Nuruddin longs for entry into the paradise through the intercession of the great Kubrawi Sufi, Sayyid Ali Hamadani. See *Kulliyat-i Shaikh al-'Alam*, I, p. 10.

18. *Ibid.*, p. 158.
19. For refutation of this view, see Chapter III.
20. Rafiqi even misrepresents facts in order to prove the crusading zeal of Nuruddin against the alleged persecution of Hindus at the hands of Suha Bhatta. His argument that Suha Bhatta "put restrictions" on Nuruddin for raising his voice against anti-Hindu activities is baseless. Unfortunately Rafiqi takes Mulla Nuruddin of Jonaraja (*Rajatarangini*, ed. Koul, p. 101) for Shaikh Nuruddin. For Mulla Nuruddin, see *Bharistan-i Shahi*, transcript No: 960, f. 26; Ali Yazdi, *Zafar-nama*, II, ed. Moulvi Mohammad Ilahadad, , Bib. Ind., Calcutta, 1855–88, p. 164; *Malfuzat-i Timuri*, A.S.B., 85, f. 319 ab.
21. See Chapter, III; also Ishaq Khan, "The Impact of Islam on Kashmir", *op. cit.*
22. Baba Daud Mishkati, *Asrar al-Abrar*, MS No. 5, ff. 61b, 63b.
23. See Chapter VII, "The Rishis and Conversion to Islam".
24. Baba Nasib, *Nurnama*, ff. 160 ab.
25. See Chapter VI, "The Attitudes of the Sufi Orders Towards the Rishis".
26. Baba Ali Raina, *Tadhirat al-'Arifin*, f. 5 ab.
27. *Ibid.* f. 5b.
28. *Ibid.* The Quran mentions three states or stages as a pre-requisite for the spiritual development of an individual: (i) *Ammara* (Surah 12 : 53) which is inclined to evil, and if not kept under check, will utterly ruin the soul; (ii) *Lawwama* (Surah 5 : 2) which is self-reproaching and

seeks God's grace and pardon after repentance and hopes to reach salvation; (iii) *Mutm'ainna* (Surah 89 : 27), the exalted stage of all, "when it achieves full rest and satisfaction."

29. Ali Raina, *op. cit.*, ff. 5b–6a.
30. *Ibid.* f. 6a.
31. *Ibid.*
32. *Ibid.*
33. Superficially observed, the *Shari'a* (law) and *tariqa* (path) appear to be two categories; in reality, however, they are so intertwined that it is impossible for a true Sufi to follow the one without the other. For an excellent discussion on this question, see Maulana Ashraf Ali Thanwi, *Shari'at-wa-Tariqat*, pp. 17–50.
34. Sayyid Ahmed Barelvi used the appellation *Tariqa-i Muhammadiya* (the way of Muhammad) for the exoteric discipline of Shah Wali Ullah which, though itself based on religious experience, represented a synthesis of the Qadri, the Chisti and the Naqshbandi orders. See for greater details, Gulam Rasul Mihr, *Sayyid Ahmad Shahid*, Lahore, 1952, p. 131; also S.M. Ikram, *Mauj-i Kawthar*, p. 12.
35. 'Ali Raina, *op. cit.*, f. 6a.
36. Khaki, *Rishinama*, f. 39a, 41b, 42a.
37. *Ibid.* 10a.
38. On virtues of asceticism (*zuhd*), see Ghazzali, *Kimiya-i Sadat* (Urdu tr. under the title *Ákseer-i Hidayat*) pp. 505–509.
39. *Ibid.* 10ab.
40. Khaki, *op. cit* f. 39a.
41. *Ibid.*, f. 20a.
42. See *Ibid.*, ff. 38a–41b.
43. It was entitled *Minhaj-ur-Rishiyya*. See Daud Mishkati *op. cit.*, f. 64a.
44. *Ibid.*, ff. 64ab, 65ab.
45. Abdul Wahab Nuri, *Fathat-i Kubrawiyya*, f. 145a.
46. *Ibid.*, f. 145b.
47. "Children of Adam, We have revealed unto you raiment to cover your shame, and splended vesture, but the raiment of restraint from evil, that is best." *The Quran*, VII, v. 26.
48. Wahab, *op. cit.*, f. 145b.
49. *Ibid.*
50. Lacking the Quranic perspective Rafiqi thus fails to understand the context in which Wahab describes the Prophet Muhammad as the founder of the Rishi order. See *op. cit.*, p. 136, see also *Infra*.
51. Muhammad Azam Diddamari, *Waqi'at-i Kashmiri*.
52. *Rishinama*, p. 69.
53. Baba Kamal (*Rishinama*, p. 17) brings the Rishis into the fold of Sufis. According to him each alphabet of the term Rishi is suggestive: 'r' denotes (*riyazat*), 'y' (*yaqin*), 's' (*Shariat*) and 'y' (*yabqa*). Although Baba Kamal's explanation is not etymologically acceptable, it points to

the fact that the Rishi movement was, by all accounts, an integral and not a parallel component of Kashmiri Sufism. The latter view has been casually expressed by Bruce Lawrence in his "Sufism and the History of Religion", *Studies in Islam*, Vol. XVIII, Nos. 3–4, July/October, 1981, p. 139.

54. *Rauzat-al-Riyazat*, pp. 58–63.
55. See also Muhiuddin Miskin, *Tahaif al-Abrar fi dhikr-i Auliya-i Akhyar*, p. 87.
56. *Ain-i Akbari* (Jarret), III, p. 354; also A.A. Razi, *Haft-Iqlim*, f. 156a; Jahangir, *Tuzuk-i Jahangiri*, II, pp. 149–50.
57. For a detailed discussion on Baba Nasib's perception of the Rishi movement, see Chapter VI, "The Attitudes of the Sufi Orders Towards the Rishi Movement."
58. The long poem in praise of the Rishis appears at the end of a brittled manuscript (Nasib, *Nurnama*, R.P.D. No: 3215). The manuscript is not folioed. Other manuscripts in the library are incomplete.
59. Robert Redfield, *Peasant Society and Culture*, p. 72.
60. This is reflected not only in the social protests of Nuruddin, but also to a great extent, in the explicit anger against the Brahmans, exhibited in the hagiographical accounts.
61. See E.H. Carr, *What is History?*, pp. 8–30.
62. Throughout this work the term *Shari'a* has been used in the sense in which it was understood by the great Sufis of Islam, i.e. the moral law, given by Allah and determining the duties of man in relation to God and his fellow beings not only in congruence with the Quran but also with the *Sunna*. The *Shari'a* also comprises the juridical and political obligations as codified in the four schools of Sunni theology; this also explains the fact why occasionally the Rishis urged the rulers to render justice in accordance with its true spirit.
63. *Kulliyat-i Shaikh al-'Alam* (2nd ed.) C.A.P. pp. 33, 77, 149, 152, 187.
64. *Ibid.*, pp. 33; 77, 149, 152.
65. *Ibid.*, p. 33.
66. Henry Corbin, *Creative Imagination in the Sufism of Ibn Arabi*, pp. 66–67.
67. See *infra.*
68. Ishaq Khan, "Sufism in Indian History," *Islam in India* (ed. Christian W. Troll), IV, p. 283.
69. For Mufti Jalaluddin's useful article, "Uwaysiyyat and Rishiyyat", See, *Rishiyyat*, pp. 20–39.
70. Henry Corbin, *op. cit.*, p. 36.
71. For an elaboration of the argument, see Chapter V, "Religious Thought of Shaikh Nuruddin."
72. This is not to suggest that, as a result of Nuruddin's role, Islam was absorbed in the local culture. As a matter of fact, his teachings prepared the ground for the gradual absorption of local culture in Islam. This is

particularly reflected in the changing mood of the people against certain Brahmanic institutions of social exploitation, such as temples, as also against their gradual weaning from the influence of Brahman ascetics masquerading as Rishis.

73. The shrines of the Rishis are innumerable.
74. *Kulliyat-i Shaikh al-'Alam*, pp. 33, 77, 107, 152.
75. In its early phase, Saivism in Kashmir, being based on a number of Tantras, appears to have preached a dualistic doctrine. The characteristics of Saivism, however, began to change from the 8th or 9th century, when it began to preach a sort of idealistic monism based on pure *advaita tatva*. The new doctrine which came to be known as *Trika Sastra* was founded by one Vasugupta who probably lived in the early years of the 9th century. According to J.C. Chatterjee, "Whatever little we know of him is from his pupils, who tell us that he lived in retirement, as a holy sage, in the charming valley of what is now called Harwan stream (the ancient Shadarhad-vana) behind the Shalimar garden near Srinagar." See Chatterjee, *Kashmir Shaivism*, p. 23.
76. He was probably a disciple of Vasugupta who lived towards the end of the 9th century. He supplied philosophical reasonings in support of his master's teachings and thus laid the foundation of the Advaita Saivism or "Trika as a system of philosophy." *Ibid.*, p. 37. See also B.N. Pandit, *Aspects of Kashmir Saivism*, pp. 86–95.
77. Abhinavagupta's (933 – 1015) commentary on *Paratrisika*, a Tantric text, and his composition *Tantraloka* are works of immense value for understanding Kashmiri Saivism. "This school of philosophy recognizes seven systems of *yogic* practice which are the means to shed ignorance and to attain the final realization of self as Siva the absolute. The Trika system has been assigned the highest position among all these seven systems ..." See B.N. Pandit, *op. cit.*, pp. 24–26.
78. Sunil Chandra Ray remarks: "It seems that the idealistic monism of the Trika system being exclusively philosophical and ethical, remained confined to a particular class of learned religious-minded people only. The masses kept themselves attached to their old forms of Siva worship, and perhaps had little to do with the idealistic school." *Early History and Culture of Kashmir*, p. 174.
79. Although Kalhana's *Rajatarangini* is replete with references to Saiva establishments in the Valley, it does not hint at the *Trika* system at all.
80. *Kulliyat-i Shaikh al-'Alam*, pp. 81, 160, 163, 189.
81. See Chapters V and VII.
82. Not only do the strong ties of the peasants with the shrines of the Rishis testify to this fact, but even as late as the beginning of this century "every cultivator in Kashmir set apart a small share of his rice crops as an offering to the shrine" of Nuruddin. Even "one walnut tree in every village was donated to some saint." Lawrence, *The Valley of Kashmir*, p. 289.

83. Nuruddin undoubtedly emerges as a champion of the down-trodden sections of the Kashmiri society against the caste-ridden Brahmanic social order. This is reflected in his various verses in condemnation of the caste system. See *Kulliyat-i Shaikh al-'Alam*, pp, 86, 90, 91, 112, 170–171, etc. See also Chapter V and VII.
84. See Ishaq Khan, "The Mystical Career and Poetry of Nuruddin Rishi Kashmiri: Socio-Historical Dimensions," *Studies in Islam*, Vol. XIX, Nos. 1–2, January-April, 1982, pp. 113, 116–17.
85. Buddhism flourished in Kashmir during the reign of the Kusanas (Ist to 3rd century A.D.) when great scholars of this faith lived there. One of them was the Bodhisattva, Nagarjuna, who resided in a forest at Sadarhadvana (modern Harwan). See Kalhana, *Rajatarangini*, Book I, V, 173. Besides the Kusana kings, Kashmir rulers also seem to have promoted the cause of Buddhism in the early centuries of the Christian era. Meghavahana, for instance, imposed a ban on the slaughter of animals in his kingdom. He also prohibited the killing of animals in sacrifice. *Ibid.*, Book, II, Vs 6 and 7.
86. See Tarachand, *Influence of Islam on Indian Culture.*
87. See also Ishaq Khan, "Sufism in Indian History," *op. cit.*, p. 282; see also Dasgupta, *History of Indian Philosophy*, II, pp. 438, 520.
88. Dasgupta, *Hindu Mysticism*, p. 8.
89. *Ibid.*
90. Dasgupta, *History of Indian Philosophy*, III, pp. 160–61.
91. *Ibid.*, III, p. 158.
92. In an illuminating discussion with a Brahman, Nuruddin explained the existence and omnipotence of God in rational terms. See Baba Khalil, *Rauzat-al-Riyazat*, p. 855.
93. Dasgupta, *History of Indian Philosophy*, II, p. 441.
94. Michael Carrithers, *The Buddha*, p. 31.
95. Pratyabhijna, though intrinsically a philosophical system, is also known as 'Kashmir Saivism'. For an excellent discussion on this system, see R.K. Kaw, "A compendium of Pratyabhijna Philosophy of Kashmir," *Research Biannual*, Vol. I, No. II, pp. 4–14.
96. B.N. Pandit's view (*op. cit*, p. 36) that "Kashmir Saivism accepts no restrictions based on caste" is a wild generalization rather than a social fact.
97. True, the "devotional religion of the *Bhagawata Purana* opened the way for the spiritual emancipation of the individual," but as Tara Chand remarks, "it did not remove the chains of social slavery; it still demanded that the followers of *Bhagawata* forsaking all desires should act in consonance with their caste." *Influence of Islam on Indian Culture*, p. 134. Ramananda "recognized and endorsed the caste system" notwithstanding the fact that he enrolled the low castes as his disciples. Aziz Ahmad, *op. cit.*, p. 142. In his *Anand Bhashya*, in the chapter on Sudras, he did not recognize the right of a Sudra to read the *Vedas*. And

in matters of social concern, he could not be expected to cast off the sense of superiority of a Hindu over a Mohammadan and of belonging to the regenerate classes (*dwijas*) over Sudra" (Italics mine). See Bartheval, *The Nirguna School of Hindu Poetry*, p. 14. That Ramananda even "enjoined strict segregation and perfect privacy in the matter of food" shows that he did not stand for "social equality" in the real sense. Yusuf Husain, *Glimpses of Medieval Indian Culture*, p. 12.

98. Tara Chand, *op. cit.*, p. 134.
99. *Ibid.*, p. 133.
100. See the next chapter.

CHAPTER III

Socio-Religious Milieu of Shaikh Nuruddin Rishi

Some six centuries preceding the foundation of the Sultanate in Kashmir in 1320, a gradual process of peaceful penetration by Muslim traders and adventurers had already begun in the Valley. According to Kalhana, "Varjraditya, the son and successor of Raja Lalitaditya (A.D. 724–61) sold many men to *mlecchas*, and introduced into the country practices which befitted the *mlecchas*."[1] Harsha (1089–1101) is said to have recruited Turkish soldiers and even introduced, under Muslim influence, some refinements in dress and ornaments.[2] Again, in the reign of Bhiksacara (1120–21), Muslim soldiers were employed and deputed to attack Sussala in Lahora.[3] By the end of the thirteenth century, it would appear that there was a colony of Muslims in Kashmir.[4] This is evidenced by Marco Polo who writes that the inhabitants of the Valley did not kill animals; instead, they sought the services of the 'Saracens' who lived among them as butchers.[5] Marco Polo evidently refers to the Turks (the 'Turuskas' of Kalhana),[6] whose services were sought by the Hindu rulers of Kashmir not merely as soldiers, but sometimes even as artists.[7] Thus Islam did not make its way into Kashmir by "forcible conquest," but, as Stein observes, "by gradual conversion, for which the influx of foreign adventurers both from the south and from Central Asia had prepared the ground."[8]

The most prominent among the early Muslim immigrants from Central Asia to Kashmir was Sayyid Sharafuddin, a Sufi of the Suharwardi order.[9] He was a disciple of Shah Ni'matullah Farsi[10] and is reported to have come to Kashmir in the reign of the King Suhadeva (1301–20)[11] from Turkistan.[12] About his missionary activities very little is known beyond the fact that he converted Rinchana to Islam.[13]

Rinchana was the son of a Ladakhi chief, Lha-Chen-denyos-grub (Lhachen d Ngos-grub), who ruled Ladakh from 1290 to 1320.[14] The unfavourable political circumstances prevailing in Ladakh following his father's death drove him to Kashmir along with his followers. The political instability in the Valley, caused by Zulju's invasion of Kashmir in 1320 and the ravages caused by the Mongol invaders for eight months afforded him an opportunity to occupy the throne of Kashmir by the end of 1320. Although the circumstances leading to the rise of the Buddhist prince to political power have been discussed elsewhere,[15] his subsequent conversion to Islam is important from the viewpoint of the history of Kashmir.

Besides being a soldier of fortune, Rinchana, like other Buddhists of the medieval period, was fond of taking part in religious discussions.[16] Even as a king he is reputed to have spent sleepless nights in the quest for truth.[17] It was his 'spiritual cravings' which prompted him to hold a religious discussion with Devaswami, a Brahman priest, who lived in the city of Srinagar. Disgusted with the spiritual pretensions and the caste-consciousness of the Brahman, Rinchana rejected Saivism.[18] Soon after, he happened to meet Sharfuddin[19] who explained to the inquisitive seeker after the truth the simplicity of his faith. Rinchana seems to have been impressed by the personality of the Sufi, who embodied both human and divine love. Thus Rinchana accepted Islam under the influence of Sharafuddin. He adopted the Muslim name of Sadruddin on the advice of the Sufi.[20]

There is little doubt that Rinchana accepted Islam at the behest of Sharfuddin. Not only are the Persian sources unanimous in regard to his association with the Sufi[21] but the subsequent facts of his conversion also testify to his spiritual affiliation with the saint. The very name Sadruddin (The leader of religion) given by the Suharwardi Sufi to the convert suggests that the saint wanted to make him conscious about his duties as the first Muslim ruler of Kashmir. The establishment of a *khanqah* by Rinchana—the first of its kind in Srinagar, the nerve-centre of the Kashmiri Brahmans—must have contributed to the diffusion of Islamic culture. The hospice was maintained through endowments of villages, and its income was utilized for the comfort of the travellers and the poor. A mosque was also built near the hospice by the Sultan where he offered congregational prayers at appointed times.[22] So close were Rinchana and Sharafuddin to each other that the Ladakhi tradition preserved in the 'Song of Bodro Masjid' speaks of the Sufi as a friend of the Buddhist prince.[23] The traders from Ladakh to the *khanqah* of

Sharafuddin must have preserved the memory of friendship between the two remarkable personalities from Turkistan and Ladakh.

The conversion of Rinchana should not be treated as an isolated case; nor was it merely a matter of political expediency.[24] In medieval times it was the personal decision of the chiefs that usually determined the collective action of groups or clans. It can be safely inferred that a considerable number of the Buddhist followers of Rinchana who accompanied him from Ladakh to Kashmir must also have embraced Islam after their chief's assumption of political power and his subsequent conversion. Rawanchandra, Rinchana's brother-in-law, for instance, accepted Islam immediately after the king's conversion.[25] It was also partly due to the support of his devoted Ladakhi followers that Rinchana was able to rule, though not without trouble, for a brief period of three years, from 1320 to 1323.

After Rinchana's death in 1323, Islam does not seem to have received official patronage owing to internecine political conflicts in Kashmir. In 1339, Shah Mir,[26] trusted counsellor of Rinchana, ascended the throne after defeating Kota Rani at Andarkoat.[27] The founder of the new ruling dynasty and his successors, Jamshed (1342–43) and 'Alauddin (1343–54), were more concerned with restoring law and order in Kashmir than devoting themselves to the religious affairs of a small number of their Muslim subjects living peacefully in Hindu-Buddhist surroundings. Sultan Shihabuddin (1354–73) was so tolerant towards his non-Muslim subjects that he turned down the suggestion of his Hindu minister, Udayasri, to melt the brass image of Buddha for coining it into money. The Sultan was so angry with the minister that, according to the Brahman chronicler, Jonaraja, he remarked: "Past generations have set up images to obtain fame and even merit, and you propose to demolish them. Some have obtained renown by setting up images of gods, others by worshipping them, some by duly maintaining them, and some by demolishing them. How great is the enormity of such a deed."[28]

Shihabuddin was the first Sultan who opened a number of *madrasas* in Kashmir where the Quran, *hadith* and *fiqh* were taught.[29] Perhaps the Sultan did so because of his association with two Sufis of the Kubrawi order, Sayyid Tajuddin and Sayyid Husain Simnani. These Sufis were deputed by Sayyid 'Ali Hamadani to Kashmir so that they could see for themselves the religious conditions prevailing there.[30] The first to enter Srinagar was Tajuddin who was given a warm welcome by the Sultan.[31] But Sayyid Husain Simnani joined his brother in 775 A.H. after staying in India[32] for some time. The Sultan also received Sayyid Husain Simnani cordially and helped him through a state grant to maintain a kitchen[33] at Kulgam.[34] Husain Simnani settled in the village permanently and through his philanthropic activities was able to attract the residents of the area and the nearby villages towards Islam.[35]

Among the non-Muslims who accepted Islam at the hands of Sayyid Husain Simnani was the village watchman, Salat Sanz, the father of Nuruddin Rishi. Although his conversion has not been mentioned in the earlier sources,[36] fortunately Nuruddin himself refers to it in a verse.[37] He is reputed to have adopted the name of Shaikh Salar after his conversion.[38] But despite the assumption of a Muslim name by Salat Sanz, the tribal name was retained in his family. This is evidenced by the name Nanda Sanz, given to his illustrious son by Shaikh Salar himself. In his verses Nuruddin invariably refers to himself by the family name.[39]

It is significant that Nuruddin not only testifies to the social role played by Husain Simnani but also that of the latter's cousin Haider,[40] who is reputed to have spent most of his time in serving the visitors to the *khanqah*.[41] One *kharwar*[42] of rice was cooked daily in the kitchen maintained by Husain Simnani,[43] and it was served along with a variety of dishes to visitors belonging to different sections of society.[44] All this emboldens us to infer that the *khanqah* must have become a magnet, attracting the poor sections of the village society.

Nuruddin was 12 years old at the time of Sayyid Husain Simnani's death in A.H. 792/1390.[45] During his childhood he seems to have kept the company of the Kubrawi Sufi owing to the paternal links of the family with the saint. Furthermore, the ancestral home of Nuruddin was situated within the sphere of Husain Simnani's radiating influence.[46] Hence it would be wrong to rule out the possible influence of the Kubrawi Sufi on Nuruddin's mind even at the formative stage of the development of his religious career.

There is yet another important element among the sources of Nuruddin's thought. While the influence of Lal Ded on Nuruddin can hardly be denied,[47] the association of the *yogini* with Husain Simnani[48] must have induced him to seek inspiration from both. This also explains the fact that in the sources both Simnani and Lal Ded are described as the earliest preceptors of Nuruddin.[49] Before we examine the influence of Lal Ded on Nuruddin, it would be useful to discuss at some length the role of her contemporary, Mir Sayyid Ali Hamadani,[50] in the history of Islam in Kashmir.

Sayyid 'Ali came to Kashmir in 783/1384 along with a large number of his followers.[51] The reigning Sultan, Qutubuddin (1773–89) and his officials are said to have given a warm welcome to Sayyid 'Ali on his arrival in Srinagar. It was at an inn in the newly founded part of the city, 'Alauddinpura, that Sayyid 'Ali took up his residence.[52] A raised floor (*suffa*) was constructed there for the purpose of prayers which were also joined by the Sultan.[53]

At the advent of Sayyid 'Ali the number of Muslims in Kashmir seems to have been insignificant as compared to the great majority of Hindus. This is testified to not only by the sources[54] but also by the fact that a large number of non-Muslims formed the main prop of the government.[55] Islam, in fact, had not yet gained a firm foothold even in the capital city of Kashmir. Thus the small number of Muslims living in Srinagar continued to cling to their ancestral customs.[56] For instance, in the newly founded 'Alauddinpura,[57] evidently a Muslim locality, there existed a temple to which both the Sultan and his Muslim subjects flocked every morning.[58] The Sultan even participated in the *yagna* ceremony once so as to avert a famine. On this occasion the Brahmans received gifts from the Sultan.[59] What is more reprehensible from the viewpoint of the *Shari'a* was that the Sultan kept two sisters as his wives.[60]

Sayyid Ali thus addressed himself to the task of first reforming the Sultan, rather than converting his non-Muslim subjects who were separated from a scholar like him by the barriers of language. He made Qutubuddin conscious of his obligations towards fulfilling the requirements of *Shari'a* in his personal life; and it was on his advice that the Sultan divorced the eldest of his wives. The Sultan was also advised to discard the Hindu dress and, instead, wear the dress which was in vogue in Muslim countries.[61] Gradually, other Muslim subjects of the Sultan also adapted themselves to the Muslim way of life.[62]

Sayyid 'Ali's historic role in Kashmir needs to be understood on a careful examination of the source material which, in our view, includes not only Persian chronicles, but also the hitherto unutilized letters[63] and invocatory prayers[64] compiled by him. Without making use of these sources and relying mainly on the textual reading of the Persian chronicles, modern historians have popularised certain stereotypes about the great Kubrawi Sufi. Of these the most popular is the view that he converted thousands of Kashmiris to Islam.[65] Another view tends to create the impression that Sayyid 'Ali's mission was not a success as he failed to make the Sultan enforce the Islamic law in his kingdom. Thus Rafiqi wants us to believe that Sayyid 'Ali left Kashmir in disgust on account of his dissatisfaction "with the Sultan's response to his teachings." It is amazing to find Rafiqi making out a case against the Sayyid for his alleged differences with the Sultan on the question of the position of non-Muslim subjects in the state. Since the Sultan was on friendly terms with them, contends Rafiqi, there arose a "conflict" between him and the Sayyid.[66]

A closer examination of the views referred to above reveals the oversimplified nature of such assumptions. Our study of the sources, including those not available to Rafiqi, shows that it would be a grave error to suppose that Sayyid 'Ali's relations with the Sultan were strained on account of the latter's friendly attitude towards the Hindus. True, in the *Dhakhirat al-muluk* Sayyid 'Ali instructs the Muslim rulers to impose various kinds of taxes on non-Muslim subjects, but there is no conclusive evidence in the sources to show that he wanted Sultan Qutubuddin to make Kashmir a practical ground for the implementation of the Islamic theoretical principles.[67] Notwithstanding Sayyid Ali's emphasis on following the *Shari'a*, he also seems to have allowed practical wisdom and expediency to guide him in his attitude towards the Sultan's non-Muslim subjects in Kashmir rather than the model he had chosen in his general work for a Muslim Sultan to follow. How a different social milieu mellowed the attitude of Sayyid 'Ali towards non-Muslims is particularly reflected in a letter he wrote to the Kashmir Sultan from Pakhli[68] in the wake of his departure from the Valley. The humility of the Kubrawi Sufi and his respect for a true Brahman devotee of God are revealed in the following verses contained in the letter under reference:

گر برہمن حالِ من بیند بر اندازد دَرم
زانکہ چوں من بدکنش را پیش. بُت ہم بار نیست

If the Brahman peeps into my (inner) condition,
he will turn me out of his sight;
In that he would not allow a wicked man like me to present myself before the idol.[69]

In another letter sent to the Sultan from Pakhli, Sayyid 'Ali urged him to leave no stone unturned in popularizing the *Shari'a*, but only within the possible limits.[70] Notwithstanding his *Shari'a*-mindedness, these letters nowhere give even hint that Sayyid 'Ali wanted the Sultan to be unfriendly towards the great majority of his non-Muslim subjects.

On the contrary, he advises the Sultan to render equitable justice to the privileged (*khas*) and the common men (*'am*). For him all the subjects of the Sultan were the children of God; hence it was obligatory on him to protect the rights of the weak against the strong.[71]

In many ways, Sayyid Áli's attitude towards the non-Muslims was tolerant, respectful and above all, realistic. But for his tolerance and saintly wisdom, he would not have been able to attract them towards Islam. The popular view that Sayyid 'Ali converted the masses to Islam, either through miracles or by his extensive travels in the valley, is subject to the following qualifications:

1. It is difficult to determine the dates of Sayyid 'Ali's stay in Kashmir in view of the conflicting evidence furnished by the earlier available sources concerning his arrival in the Valley. Thus while the author of *Tarikh-i Kashmir* gives 786/1384–85 as the date of his arrival, at the same time he refers to a chronogram (*maqdam sharif baju*) of Sayyid Muhammad Khawari which gives the date of the Sufi's arrival as 785/1383–84.[72] It would be seen that in either case Sayyid Ali stayed in the Valley for one year or 40 days.[73]
2. In a letter to his favourite disciple, Maulana Muhammad Khwarzami, sent to him from Pakhli after returning from Kashmir, Sayyid 'Ali praised his close companion for having gained spiritual bliss in a reign of infidels.[74]
3. Nuruddin J'afar Badkshi, a disciple of Sayyid 'Ali, who wrote a biography on his spiritual mentor, nowhere refers to the latter's activities in Kashmir.[75] The intriguing silence of this important source shows that the miraculous feats of Sayyid 'Ali in Kashmir, as described in the later Kashmir sources, are mere latter-day concoctions.
4. Another biographer of Sayyid 'Ali refers to only one encounter of the Sayyid with a Brahman ascetic (*rahib*) in Srinagar whom he converted to Islam.[76] No other activity of Sayyid 'Ali is recorded beyond the general statement that he brought Islam to Kashmir.[77]

It seems that Sayyid 'Ali's stay in Kashmir was brief, not extending beyond one year. During this period he remained the royal guest and, as such, his activities remained mainly confined to royal circles. He imparted lessons to the Sultan on God's commands about the good works (*ma'ruf*) and evil (*munkar*).[78] Besides engaging in some missionary activities in Alauddinpura and around the capital, he does not seem to have established any mass contacts. One wonders how, in view of the language barrier, a Sufi scholar like Sayyid 'Ali, would have made the esoteric as well as the exoteric version of Islam, as given by him in a plethora of works, intelligible to the Kashmiri masses. As a matter of fact, the Sayyid is himself reported to have said that it was beyond the ken of his contemporaries to understand the esoteric message of Islam as contained in his works and that its worth would be recognized only a century after his death.[79] That Sayyid 'Ali's influence, in the first instance, remained confined to the royal court is evidenced by the verses[80] composed by Sultan Qutbuddin himself in honour of his spiritual mentor:

جانم فدای بر قدم خاک تو بادا یا امیر　　روحم فدای بر شرف نام تو بادا یا امیر
از آمدنت مشرف اسلام گشته ام　　اسمم فدای بر آمدن تو بادا یا امیر
چون آمد آن شه از ملک ولایت　　گرفت کشمیر از اسلام رایت
بگفتند از که یافت ترتیب این ملک　　گفتم که "از آن شاه هدایت"

Before the departure of Sayyid 'Ali from Kashmir, the Sultan tried to persuade him to extend his stay in the Valley, but the Sayyid refused. However, he asked his disciple Maulana Muhammad Balkhi[81] to guide the Sultan in matters pertaining to the *Shari'a*.[82] Sayyid 'Ali also gifted his cap to the Sultan which he always wore under his own cap. In this reverential practice Qutbuddin was followed by his successors until the death of Sultan Fateh Shah (1486–93) when, according to the latter's will, the cap was buried along with his dead body.[83]

The foregoing discussion, however, should not delude us into believing that Sayyid 'Ali's role in the religious history of Kashmir was negligible. Islam, in no small measure, owes its success to his remarkable role which was distinguished by his tolerance towards the Kashmiris' penchant for singing hymns aloud in temples. The sight of a small number of people professing faith in Islam and simultaneously going to temples must have caused a great deal of concern to Sayyid 'Ali. But it goes to his credit that instead of taking a narrow view of the religious situation in Kashmir, he showed an actute discernment and a keen practical sense in grasping the essential elements of popular Kashmiri religious culture and ethos, and gave creative expression to these in enjoining his followers in the Valley to recite *Aurad-i Fathiyya* aloud in a chorus in mosques.[84] Such a simple practice of invoking God's help did not call for either animal sacrifice or the beating of drums. That the drummers of temples, in due course, realized the futility of flattering the vanity of the Brahman priests is reflected in the anguish of the Brahman chroniclers over the local peoples' growing laxity in the performance of prescribed ceremonies. Even a conservative chronicler like Srivara seems to have been so impressed by the novelty of God being praised in chorus by the rich and the poor together that he could not conceal his feelings about the loud prayers of the faithful in the Jam'a mosque of Srinagar. Thus writes he: "It was here that the *yavanas* (Muslims) chanted mantras and looked graceful like the thousand lotuses with humming bees".[85]

The fact that Kashmiri Muslims have always regarded *Aurad-i Fathiyya* as a parting gift of Sayyid 'Ali Hamadani to them is still emphasized by the *mullahs* in the mosques and shrines of the Valley. It is in the context of the unique chanting of this invocatory prayer in the mosques and shrines of Kashmir even in our own times that we consider it necessary to record below the mystical experience of a Suharwardi Sufi in Kashmir.

It is said that Sayyid Ahmad Kirmani who came to Kashmir in the sixteenth century was distressed, like the leaders of the modern Ahl-i Hadith movement, to see the Muslims reciting the *aurad* loudly in the mosques. As he considered this practice to be against the *Shari'a* he did not approve of it. Thus, after preaching to the people to refrain from repeating the *aurad* in chorus, Ahmad Kirmani decided to leave Kashmir for good. However, while forbidding such a practice the Suharwardi Sufi had not realized the importance of the creative role played by Sayyid 'Ali in making the oneness of God comprehensible to the Kashmiris, through the loud recitation of the *aurad* in a congregation, in the formative period of Islam in the Valley. Curiously enough, the significance of reciting the *aurad* aloud in the mosques was revealed to him in a state of contemplation (*muraqaba*) at Iblihag Marg, situated in the district of Baramulla. In the meditative experience he saw Sayyid 'Ali Hamadani in an angry mood. When he enquired from Sayyid 'Ali about the cause of his anger, the latter expressed his dissatisfaction over the fact of forbidding the Kashmiris to recite the *aurad*. Sayyid 'Ali told him in the spiritual encounter that it was owing to *Aurad-i Fathiyya* that Islam was understood by the common man in Kashmir. No sooner did Kirmani return from his mystic experience than he rushed back to Srinagar to relate to the people his spiritual experience. He went from street to street and from mosque to mosque urging the people to recite the *aurad* after morning and evening prayers.[86]

The modern reasoning mind may not lend credence to the anecdote recorded in the Persian chronicles and hagiographies. On close examination, however, one finds a subtle fact in the anecdote which is also attested to by the religious behaviour of contemporary Kashmiri Muslims. The truth is that modern historians, with their stereotypes about conversions, have yet to realise the importance of *aurad* literature in the day-to-day life of Kashmiri Muslims, not to speak of the hold exercised by it over the medieval mind.[87] Even now the repetition of the *aurad* in mosques and shrines with folded hands in a state of spiritual ecstasy is noticeable to a keen observer. Such a practice, which speaks eloquently of the assimilation of the local mode of worship in the Islam of Kashmiris, is abhorrent to the Ahl-i Hadith. However, a careful analysis of Kashmiri Muslims' religious traditions reveals that Islam's victory in the Valley was effected more by the Kashmiri's urge to experience the Divine in terms of love and not as a mere abstraction. In other words, Islam developed a resilient tradition of its own in Kashmir,[88] first under the guidance of Sayyid 'Ali Hamadani and later, as we shall see in the subsequent chapters, under Nuruddin Rishi.

A brief reference made earlier to Lal Ded, the Saivite *yogini* of the fourteenth century, now needs to be elaborated in its proper historical context.

Little is known about Lalla's life, though according to a popular tradition, based on Muslim sources, she was a contemporary of Sayyid Hussain Simnani and Sayyid 'Ali Hamadani. The tradition of her association with both these Sufis is so strong that not only has Lalla always been remembered as a Muslim but even as a great apostle of Islam by Kashmiri Muslims. Mulla 'Ali Raina, who was the first to mention her, says that she was a chosen disciple of Sayyid Husain Simnani.[89] It was at the latter's command that Lalla took spiritual charge of Nuruddin just after his birth. 'Ali Raina also refers to Lalla's meetings with Sayyid Jalaluddin Makhdum Jahaniyan (1308–1383)[89a] and Sayyid 'Ali Hamadani.[90] Raina was also the first to euologize Lalla as Maryam-i Makani and Rabia Thani.[91] Haidar Tulmuli, a contemporary of 'Ali Raina, also refers to Lalla's association with Simnani and her guidance to Nuruddin.[92] Although from the viewpoint of history, Tulmuli's eye-witness account of Lalla's presence before Shaikh Hamza Makhdum[93] in spiritual terms deserves little credence, the hagiographer, nonetheless testifies to the high esteem in which Lalla was held even in the

Suharwardi circles. So dominant was the influence of Lalla on the Muslim mind that, in Tulmuli's opinion, save the disciples of Hamza Makhdum, none could attain her spiritual status.[94]

Lalla was also described in glowing terms by Sufis like Baba Nasibuddin Ghazi[95] and Baba Daud Mishkati.[96] The account of her family life, given for the first time by Baba Nasib, was later corroborated by Baba Daud Miskati, Aba Rafi'uddin,[97] Muhammad Azam Diddamari,[98] Abdul Wahab Nuri,[99] S'adullah Shahabadi[100] and the authors of the *Rishinamas* of Chrar.[101] A Pandit writer of the early nineteenth century who regarded Lalla as a Hindu, nonetheless, based his account of the *yogini's* early life on Muslim sources.[102] At the same time he attests to the hagiographers' account of Lalla's encounter with Sayyid 'Ali Hamadani[103] which, shorn of its supernatural halo, speaks of the force of the tradition regarding the *yogini's* association with the Sufi.

Although scholarly attempts in this century have centred round describing Lalla as an exponent of Saivism,[104] much of what has been written about her ignores the earlier evidence which surrounds her name in the hagiographical accounts. Such evidence which gives a clear idea of Lalla's personality and testifies to the estimation in which she was held by Muslims is worthy of examination, particularly due to the significance of the data itself. The question which needs to be fully examined is why, besides Mulla Raina—himself a close disciple and the brother of Shaikh Hamza Makhdum—other prominent adherents of the Suharwardi order granted a pre-eminent position to her. How is it that other living *Saivite* mystics of Lalla's time did not attract the attention of the hagiographers? Much of what hagiographers tell us of Lalla's association with the Sufis may not be true; yet behind these legends there exists a substratum of truth about her friendliness with Islam.

An attempt has been made in recent years to study Lalla against the background of the Bhakti movement that characterised northern India between the fifteenth and seventeenth centuries.[106] It is true that seeking God within oneself was the common goal of both Lalla and the Bhakti saints. However, on such an analogy the basic difference in the approach of Lalla and the Bhakti saints towards the problems of their respective societies cannot be ignored. Added to this is the fact that the attitude of the Bhakti saints towards Islam was fundamentally different from that of Lalla. Unlike the Bhakti reformers, like Kabir and Nanak, Lalla was not critical of Islamic rituals. For Kabir particularly, Muslim rituals like *Haj*, *namaz*, fasting and circumcision were irrational and obscured the reality of the oneness of God. These 'superficialities' were for Kabir the cause of Hindu-Muslim conflict. In his criticism of contemporary Muslim society, Kabir even assigned a secondary place to the Quran as compared to the direct knowledge or *anubhava jnana*.[107]

It is also tempting to draw a comparison between Lalla and the Bhakti reformers on the ground that both crusaded against caste, the Brahmanic supremacy and idol worship. However, such an analogy appears illusory on closer examination of the historical impact of the Bhakti reformers and Lalla within their regional environments. What needs to be emphasized is the reformatory character of the Bhakti movement which, in a way, aborted the process of Islamic acculturation that had set in among the low-caste Hindus of northern Indian plains long before the establishment of the Delhi Sultanate in 1206. Although the Bhakti movement did not emerge as a challenge to Islam, it nonetheless may be conceived as an attempt at raising the social status of the low-caste Hindus. Such an attempt on the part of the Bhakti reformers also included the inculcation of Hindu beliefs and practices among the lower sections of society.[108] But unlike the Bhakti reformers, Lalla's teachings did not either reform or revitalize the Kashmiri Hindu society. Nor did Lalla give a strong impetus to the new religious movement in Kashmiri Saivism. As a matter of fact, the popular form of Saivism, since the fourteenth century, has centred round the external rituals and practices, decried so vehemently by Lalla. Many of her ideas, voicing dissent against the existing institutions and values, were not echoed by even a single Saivite who can be named during her lifetime or after her death.

Nor did Lalla's mystical poetry, like the *sakhi* and *sabad* of Kabir and Nanak and *caupai* and *doha* of Tulsi, achieve an honour which normally would be accorded to such Hindu scriptures as the *Vedas* and *Upanishads*. The importance of her songs, unlike those of the Bhakti reformers, does not lie in inculcating Hindu beliefs and practices among the lower sections of society. In fact, Lalla did not give a "systematic expose of Saivism on the lines laid down by the theologians who preceded her;" on the other hand, her songs illustrate "a picture of the actual hopes and fears of the common folk that nominally followed the teachings of those wise men whom they had accepted as their guides."[109]

It may be argued that Lalla's verses, in view of their Sanskritised form, belie the influence of Islam on her thought. But to talk in such terms is tantamount to uprooting Lalla from her environment, which was undoubtedly exposed to Islamic influences centuries before the establishment of the Muslim Sultanate. One wonders how a wandering mystic like Lalla who did not have a closed mind could have shut her eyes to the presence of her contemporaries like Sayyid Husain Simnani, Sayyid Tajuddin an Sayyid 'Ali Hamadani. Such an environment for a woman, ostracised from her group by the caste-conscious Brahmans, predicated three options: to embrace Islam, to reform the Hindu society, or to revolt against the caste-ridden social order. As to the first option, hagiographers and chroniclers do not furnish us with any conclusive evidence.[110] The presumption that she wanted to reform the Hindu society flounders on the bedrock of her seminal historical role which speaks more of her association with Islam than with Saivism. There is, however, considerable evidence to show that the protesting trend in Lalla's verses against the social and spiritual pretensions of the Brahmans set in motion new forces rejecting the latter's cherished idea that social status was determined by caste. An important development in this direction was the flowering of the idea of the dignity and the fundamental equality of man, so trenchantly espoused by her younger contemporary, Nuruddin Rishi.

It would, therefore, be unreasonable to suggest that Lalla remained immune from Islamic influence. From Islam, at least, she imbibed a critical attitude towards the many abuses of the caste-ridden social order. It may be true that Islam did not directly contribute to her thought, but it certainly proved to be an important influence on the manner of her expression.[111] Lalla's verses against Brahmanic supremacy in particular, uttered under conditions ripe for resistance as well as for emulative movement, seem to have been taken as her 'conversion' to Islam by the Hindu masses, who were undergoing a process of Islamic acculturation—a fact attested to by strong documentary evidence. So deep-rooted was the halo of Lalla's 'conversion' in the folk consciousness that even Nuruddin Rishi's verses affirming his faith in Islam were attributed to her.[112]

Although Lalla's mystical verses are marked by the denunciation of the exploitation of the masses by the Brahmans, the Sanskrit chroniclers of the Sultanate period have maintained an intriguing silence about her. Birbal Kachru, who completed his narrative in the Sikh period (1819–46), was the first Pandit chronicler to refer to her.[113] One clear inference to be drawn from the silence of the *Ahl-i Qalam*[113a] regarding Lalla is that she must have been considered a renegade by the high-caste Brahmans. This explains why Lalla's greatest eulogists have been Muslim hagiographers and Persian chroniclers, so much so that the memory of

Lalla proved to be no less a force than the Sufis and the Rishis in bringing the bulk of Hindus in Kashmir closer to the monotheistic faith of Islam. It is doubtful that Lalla would have thought of causing sacrilege to idols while entering a temple, but the fact that an argument of this form could be propounded in a subtle way in the hagiological literature points to a substantial change in the intellectual climate.[114] For now, not only was the Brahmanical view challenged but also those two qualities, wisdom and virtue, which were considered to be their monopoly.[115] In fact, Lalla did not preach Islam, but her *vaakh* which was not in conflict with the ontological teachings of the Sufis, served the cause of Islam in Kashmir. While Sayyid 'Ali Hamadani's works dealt more exclusively with mysticism proper and were generally intended for use by the author's fellow Sufis,[116] Lalla, on the other hand, propagated the mystic idea of divine unity in simple language which had a deep and direct appeal to the common man. For her, true devotion did not imply various rituals and practices evolved by the Brahman but meant seeking God within oneself, and also in the routine of daily life:

> "Siva abides in all that is, everywhere
> Then do not discriminate between a Hindu and a Musalman.
> If thou art wise, know thyself
> That is true knowledge of the Lord."[117]

Lalla's approach to religion, based on mysticism, was fundamentally humanistic and individualistic. By rejecting formal and organized religion which was based on the supreme authority of the Brahman, she helped the common man accept the Sufi ideas of equality and the brotherhood of man:

> "I renounced fraud, untruth, deceit,
> I taught my mind to see the one in all my follow-men,
> How could I then discriminate between man and man,
> And not accept the food offered to me by brother man."[118]

The worship of idols was vehemently criticised by Lalla:

> "The idol is but stone,
> The temple is but stone,
> From top to bottom all is stone."[119]

In her criticism of the ritualistic practices of the Brahmans, Lalla remarked:

"He does not need the kusa grass, nor sesame seed,
Flowers and water He does not need,
He who, in honest faith, accepts his Guru's word,
On Siva meditates constantly,
He, full of joy, from action freed, will not be born again."[120]

Again, castigating the Brahman's greed for making animal sacrifices obligatory, Lalla remarked:

"It covers your shame,
Saves you from cold,
It's food and drink,
Mere water and grass,
Who counselled you, O Brahmin,
To slaughter a living sheep as a sacrifice,
Unto a lifeless stone."[121]

Lalla was, indeed, disgusted by the hypocrisy of the Brahman and thus exposed his pride for claiming himself to be the learned:

"The thoughtless read the holy books
As parrots, in their cage, recite Ram, Ram,
Their reading is like churning water,
Fruitless effort, ridiculous conceit."[122]

Lalla's spirit of revolt against the social inequalities of her age is manifest in these verses:

"When can I break the bonds of shame?
When I am indifferent to jibes and jeers.
When can I discard the robe of dignity?
When desires cease to nag my mind."[123]

Some verses of Lalla have been translated literally to describe her semi-nude condition.[124] In fact, these verses have been read and interpreted out of the social context. The historical term of reference to such a context is the sense of revolt generated in her mind by the iniquitious social order and, above all, by her spiritual preceptor, Sayyid Husain Simnani:

"The Guru gave me only one word;
Enter into thyself from the outer world;
The guru's precept came to me as God's word;
That's why I started dancing nude."[125]

There is a strong folk tradition about Lalla's nude wanderings until her meeting with Sayyid 'Ali Hamadani. When asked why she violated the established norms of decency and culture, she is reported to have remarked that there was no 'man' about, but one day on seeing Sayyid 'Ali Hamadani in the distance she cried out "I have seen a man', and in order to cover herself fled. Seeing a baker's shop nearby she jumped into the burning oven. The baker closed the lid out of sheer frustration fearing punishment for murder. But he was wonderstruck when he suddenly found Lalla coming out of the oven clad in celestial clothes of emerald green, greeting warmly the distinguished saint from Hamadan, who had followed her to the baker's shop.[126]

There is little doubt that Lalla's ascetic self-discipline must have inspired not only Nuruddin in the days of his youth, but also some women who became the latter's disciples.[127] True, she was critical of penance and fasting,[127a] but her exhortations for choosing the life of poverty had certainly its desired effect on the group of people who called themselves Rishis:

"In life I sought neither wealth nor power;
Nor ran after the pleasures of sense;
Moderate in food and drink, I lived a controlled life;
And loved my God."[128]

Unlike the Brahmans of Kashmir, Lalla did not like meat. We have already referred to her denunciation of sacrificing a sheep before the idol. The example of her vegetarianism must have also influenced the Rishis:

"Whether they killed a large sheep or a small one,
Lalla had her round stone (as her usual fare)."[129]

As a true precursor of the Rishis, Lalla was a wandering ascetic engrossed in God-consciousness, yearning to see God everywhere (*Shiv tshorun thali thale*).[130] The prevalent caste taboos about food and a drink did not impress her (*anas khyanas kyah chum dvesh*);[131] nor was she bothered about the performance of the ceremonial rites[131a] which to this day have remained part and parcel of an average Kashmiri Pandit.

The Rishi tradition, thus, arose at a period of great social crisis; in fact the tradition came to be modelled after a cultural pattern which was in direct conflict with the decadent Brahmanic order, its agents and its doctrines. It would, therefore, be a form of amputation to study the Rishi tradition outside the context of the new cultural trend.

It is also necessary to expound the importance of the historical role of Lalla in the context of her elevation to *avatarhood* by no less a person than the founder of the Rishi order. As Nuruddin remarks in one of his popular verses:

> That Lalla of Padmanpore
> Who had drunk to her fill the nectar
> She was an *avatar* of ours
> O God, grant me the same spiritual power.[132]

Undoubtedly, Lalla gave a unique orientation to the evolution of a new cultural pattern in Kashmir. The influence of her *vaakh* was deep on Nuruddin during the formative stage of his mystical career; likewise the impact of her revolt against social and religious discrimination was tremendous on the folk for whom, even from the point of view of Hindu scriptures, she was the saviour in 'the hour of calamity and enslavement.' Lalla actually shot into prominence in an age of social ferment when Hinduism in Kashmir, as a result of its declining strength,[133] was exposed to the radiant influence of Islam through the egalitarian spirit of the Sufis. That Lalla herself presents a dismal picture of the collapse of *dharma* is amply borne out by the foregoing discussion. That Lalla, as an ardent lover of Siva, succeeded in reviving Saivism is an argument belied by the very silence of our Saivite chroniclers and poets of her near-contemporary and later times. What is, however, of significance to remember from the viewpoint of social history is the historical dimension of her elevation to *avatar* by a devout Muslim like Nuruddin.

According to the Hindu scriptures, *avatars* are born for the purpose of re-establishing *dharma*, but as *Bhagavat Purana* repeatedly stresses they also emerge on the social scene "for teaching the mortals the wisdoms of the ages. They have taught and given right perspectives and direction to human beings. They have set through their lives an example of right conduct and instilled hope and courage."[134] It is obvious, then, why Nuruddin described Lalla as an *avatar*, since Lalla, in a true spirit of an *avatar*, assumed the role befitting the situational demands, and reshaped anomalies and derangements into a progressive adjustment and harmony. Briefly speaking, Lalla wanted that man should become "more of a man" and swim across darkness into light.

The impact of Lalla's eulogization as an *avatar* of Kashmiris must have also contributed a great deal to her romanticization, so much so that a Suharwardi Sufi of the seventeenth century, himself influenced by the Rishi movement, extolled her in the following terms:

"Passion for God set fire to all she had,
And from her heart rose clouds of smoke,
Having had a draught of *ahd-e-alast*,[135]
Intoxicated and drunk with joy was she,
One cup of this God-intoxicating drink,
Shatters reason into bits,
A little drowsiness from it is headier than
Intoxication from a hundred jars of wine."[135a]

Significantly, Lalla was well aware of the success of her role in contemporary society:

"Whatever I uttered with my tongue, became a *mantra*".[136]
Again:
"I burnt the foulness of my soul;
I slew my heart, its passions all;
I spread my garments, hem and sat;
Just there, on bended knees,
In utter surrender unto Him;
My fame as Lalla spread afar."[137]

The aural value of Lalla's verses and their profound impact on Kashmiri society is not simply illustrated by Nuruddin's and the hagiographers' eulogization of her role, but also by the fact that her teachings were translated into action by the socially oppressed people rather than by the Brahmans. The very interpolations in Lalla's verses suggests that each word that she uttered became a precept, a maxim of conduct for her Muslim followers with their roots in the local culture. Although most modern writers have been at pains to emphasize interpolations in both Lalla's and Nuruddin's mystical poetry,[138] unfortunately, they have failed to grasp the similarity of the context in which these verses were produced. In fact, the language which Nuruddin spoke was not an individual inheritance but a social acquisition from the environment in which he grew up. The poetry of Lalla and Nuruddin came to be the daily bread of many Kashmiris of the period, who formed their *Weltanschauung* in accordance with the picture presented to them by their two spiritual teachers. The importance of mystical poetry and literature to an average Kashmiri is evident even today to an observer of contemporary society in the Valley.[139]

Some Important questions are bound to arise when we consider the evidence regarding the elevation of Lalla to Rabia Thani, Arifa, Maryam-i Makani, Majnun-i Aqila, etc., in the mystic literature. Did she accept Islam? What was Lalla's position in her contemporary society?

It should be borne in mind that Lalla was disowned, not only in her own times, but for the greater part of Kashmiri history, by the Hindu élite on account of her hostility to the Brahman creed. The admirable attempts of some Pandit scholars[140] in recent times to resuscitate Lalla are, therefore, paradoxical. True, Lalla's poetry nowhere gives any proof of her having embraced Islam, but the evidence of some later sources regarding her close association with Sayyid Husain Simnani[141] should not be dismissed as a figment of the imagination of medieval writers. This evidence suggests that Lalla did not live in a historical vacuum, isolated from the lower strata of society of the time and, more importantly, from the succeeding generations of her people. It is reasonable to assume that the focal point of her supposed meeting with the Sufis and the living tradition of calling her Lal Ded, Lal Mouj (Lalla, the Mother) by Kashmiri Muslims, particularly, by the rural folk, must contain a kernel of truth about her association with Islam. In any case, such evidence indicates the important place occupied by Lalla in the lives of the various strata of the Kashmiri people as well as her role in the formation of a regional culture. Such a culture drew its essential vitality from a conflict, a division, a turmoil and struggle created in the individual psyche by the challenges posed to the social order by Lalla and the Sufi missionaries.[142]

It would appear from the foregoing discussion that the social conditions in Kashmir offered a fertile ground for the zealous Sufi missionaries like Mir Muhammad Hamadani, the son of Mir Sayyid 'Ali Hamadani, and a number of his disciples, to preach the doctrines of Islam. Thus the subsequent role of Muhammad Hamadani needs to be studied not merely in the context of his missionary zeal to win converts but, more importantly, in the context of his deep concern for the enforcement of the Islamic law in a land where the norms of the *Shari'a* were violated by the new 'converts'; in fact, his aim was not only to 'convert' afresh, but to consolidate the foothold already gained by Sayyid Husain Simnani and Sayyid 'Ali Hamadani.

Sayyid Muhammad Hamadani arrived in Kashmir in 796/1393 at the age of twenty-two.[143] His visit was understandably inspired by the will of his father who is reputed to have written two documents for his son.[144] According to the testament of his father, Sayyid Muhammad Hamadani embarked on his travels after completing his education. In fact, Sayyid 'Ali regarded travel as the best education.[145]

Muhammad Hamadani was given a royal reception on his arrival in Kashmir.[146] It is said that he was accompanied by three hundred scholars and saints, some of whom settled permanently in the Valley owing to the patronage extended to them by the reigning Sultan.[147] Jonaraja writes: "The king had a fondness for the Yavanas (Muslims) ... Many Yavanas left other sovereigns and took shelter under this king who was renowned for charity. As the bright moon is among the stars as was Muhammad of Mera country (Mir Muhammad Hamadani) among the Yavanas; and although he was a boy he became their chief by learning."[148]

Sultan Sikandar constructed a *khanqah* for Muhammad Hamadani in Srinagar on the site where his father had sojourned during his visit to the Valley. The *khanqah* was maintained out of the revenues of two *parganas* granted by the Sultan to Muhammad Hamadani. In addition, through a state grant, the revenues of a separate *pargana* were exclusively put at the disposal of the Sayyid for his personal use.[149]

The initial gain secured by Muhammad Hamadani was the conversion of Suha Bhatta, the Sultan's chief minister and commander-in-chief, whom he named Saifuddin. The latter gave his daughter in marriage to Sayyid Muhammad after the death of his first wife, Bibi Taj Khatun, the daughter of Sayyid Husain Baihaqi.[150]

The conversion of Suha Bhatta to Islam must have come as a bolt from the blue to the Brahmans of Srinagar who undoubtedly felt an imminent threat to their pre-eminent position. It is not unlikely that the conversion of an influential minister also induced his fellow countrymen to accept Islam. This explains the fact that Jonaraja gives a hyperbolic account of the measures taken by the Sultan, on the advice of Suha Bhatta, to force the Hindus to accept Islam. While the destruction caused to some temples and images during Sikandar's reign[151] cannot be denied—more as a result of the abetment on the part of the zealous, high-ranking convert to Islam—at the same time, contemporary evidence regarding the construction of a Siva temple with a golden *linga* by the Sultan's Hindu wife, Shoba Devi, should not be lost sight of.[152]

It would, therefore, be absurd to accept at its face value Jonaraja's statement about the alleged wholesale destruction of temples in the villages and towns as a result of Sikandar's anti-Hindu policy. Far from giving an objective account of the religious ferment caused by the bold protest of Lalla and the activities of the Kubrawi Sufis, Jonaraja takes pride in highlighting only the reaction of his own community against the onslaughts of such forces as, in his view, sounded the doom of ancient Kashmiri culture. In order to prove the superiority of his own

Fig. 1(a)

Fig. 1(b) Within dotted border and flowery background, the coin issued by the Afghan Governor, Atta Muhammad Khan, in honour of Shaikh Nuruddin Rishi. The translation of the couplet inscribed on the coin is:

"The coin became bright through Nuruddin
It became current through the revered chief of the pious."

Fig. 2(a) Pilgrims at the shrine of Nuruddin in Chrar-i-Shariff looking reverentially at the relics of the Rishia being exhibited on the eve of his anniversary. See Figs. 2(b c) also.

Fig. 2(b)

Fig. 2(c)

Fig. 3 Baba Bamuddin's shrine at Bamzu.

Fig. 4 Folk dancers at the shrine of Baba Nasibuddin Ghazi.

Fig. 5 Pilgrims with their offerings at the shrine of Baba Rishi.

social group, the chronicler does not fail to extol his caste to the skies for rejecting Islam. He also talks about the sacrifices of the Brahmans, understandably, in terms of their migration to the Indian plains and the payment of *jizya*. According to Jonaraja, it was the Brahmans alone who put up a somewhat heroic resistance, while the rest of the population by their pusillanimity gave a long rope to the immigrant Muslims to pollute the 'kingdom of Kashmir'. However, by lamenting in the same breath the powerlessness of the Brahmans and the *avatars* and the inefficacy of their *mantras* in such a situation, the chronicler reduces the credibility of his own statement about the sufferings and sacrifices of his community. The *avatars* who had hitherto demonstrated their strength are now relegated to the background mainly because of the "sins" of Kashmiris. It is not, therefore, surprising that out of sheer arrogance Jonaraja even makes the *avatars* feel concerned over the terrible fate of Kashmiris in general and that of his community in particular.[153]

A careful analysis of Jonaraja's lamentations in depicting the sad plight of the Brahmans also shows his concern for the preservation of his community's identity, which was threatened more by the growing process of Islamic acculturation than by Sultan Sikandar's alleged vandalism. It is small wonder that the acceptance of the values of an alien culture by the non-privileged sections of Kashmiri society was denounced as an unpardonable "sin" by the caste-conscious Brahman chronicler out of his religious ethnocentrism. We, however, see in the misconceived "sins of Kashmiris" of Jonaraja's time elements of social protest against the Brahmanic supremacy. It must be pointed out that there did not take place a total destruction of the ancient usages of Kashmir as a result of the alleged iconoclasm of Sultan Sikandar and the influx of Muhammad Hamadani's disciples into Kashmir. It needs to be stressed again that some temples seem to have been razed to the ground by zealous 'converts' themselves; and it is not unlikely that Lalla's popular verses regarding the denunciation of idol-worship and temple sanctity also bestirred them into action against some centres of social exploitation.[154]

Notwithstanding the popular movement against the Brahmans for turning temples and idols into agencies of exploitation in the name of faith, the Kashmiris did not totally reject their ancestral belief in the efficacy of temples and shrines (*asthapans*). That is the reason why in the newly constructed mosques and shrines (*ziyarats* or *asthans*) certain features of the Hindu and the Buddhist monastic life were retained to a marked degree. Even now one notices bells fastened to the gates of some *ziyarats* in the Valley, belonging to the medieval period.[155] The preservation of the relics of the Sufis, particularly, those of the Rishis, in their tombs and their public exhibition on special occasions speak of the assimilation of the local Hindu-Buddhist practices in the Islam of Kashmir.[156] It is also not be wondered at, therefore, that a mere sight of the relics at congregations specially on the eve of *'Urs*, causes the devotees to recite litanies and *munajat* in chorus. A special characteristic of the Kashmiri Muslims' social behaviour at such gatherings is the focus on the object of veneration with folded hands, which undoubtedly suggests local influence on their mode of prayer. From the architectural point of view too, the medieval *ziyarats* are representative of a curious blending of Hindu, Buddhist and Islamic art styles.

It should also be borne in mind that Jonaraja has not merely magnified the iconoclastic activities of the converted Brahman minister of Sultan Sikandar, but even concocted the story of the Brahman resistance to the activities of the Sufi missionaries. That the purpose behind this orchestration seems to have been to perpetuate the myth of forcible conversion is amply borne out by the tacit approval given by modern scholars[157] and journalists[158] to Jonaraja's tendentious writings. However, it is a pity that Jonaraja either seems to have been unable to comprehend or deliberately ignored the basic fact that the decadent Brahmanic order had failed to create sufficiently strong institutions, based on a sound religious philosophy, which could have worked as an effective bulwark against the forces of Islamic acculturation. From Lalla's verses and other sources, it becomes clear that the common man groaned under the weight of various social evils promoted by the corrupt priests. Even the Brahman ascetics, *rahibs* of the Persian chroniclers and hagiographers, used to resort to sorcery in order to overawe their innocent followers.[159] In such a social environment the miracles woven around the personalities of the Sufis by their disciples must have also contributed their share to the weakening of the authority of the Brahmans.[160] No less a part was played by the credulous devotees of the shrines themselves in miracle-mongering, so that according to the current popular belief among Kashmiri Muslims, Islam spread in the Valley mainly owing to the supernatural feats of the Sufis and the Rishis against the Brahman *rahibs* and various deities.

There is yet another side to the picture. The Persian chroniclers, in their zeal to present both Muhammad Hamadani and Sultan Sikandar as champions of Islam in the Valley, generally state that infidelity was uprooted from the Valley because of their influence. This view has recently been uncritically accepted by some modern scholars who describe them as adherents of "Islamic orthodoxy."[161] R.K. Parmu even goes to the extent of saying that Muhammad Hamadani employed "all those militant methods which are associated with the title *ghazi*" for the spread of Islam.[162] On a careful analysis, however, even Muhammad Hamadani, like his illustrious father, seems to have been realistic in his approach towards the religious susceptibilities of the local people. This is amply borne out by his attitude towards Nuruddin Rishi who was criticised by Muhammad Hamadani's close disciples, the Sayyids, for following the Hindu way of life.[163] It is significant that the leader of the Sayyids gave due recognition to Nuruddin's spiritual status by describing the Rishi as a perfect *Wali*, thereby declaring his humility before his *Shari'a*-minded followers. Although Nuruddin enrolled himself as the *zahiri* disciple of Muhammad Hamadani, what is of importance to remember is that he was entrusted the task of popularising the Rishi order in the Valley by the Sayyid himself.[164]

Nuruddin was thus a spiritual heir not only to Lalla, but to the Kubrawi order as well. In fact, his verses in praise of Sayyid Husain Simnani[165] and Sayyid Muhammad Hamadani[166] testify to the influence of the Kubrawi order on the development of his unique personality in the galaxy of the Sufis. Although Muhammad Hamadani spent seventeen years in the Valley, he seems to have expressed the desire to meet Nuruddin towards the end of his sojourn in Kashmir, and that too, only after hearing about the popularity of the Rishi among the commoners. It is significant that his decision to pay a personal visit to the Rishi was not liked by some of his Sayyid followers mainly due to two reasons. First, as already stated, the asceticism of Nuruddin was repugnant to their *Shari'a*-oriented life style,[167] and second, contrary to the *Sunna* the Sayyids were highly conscious of their pedigrees.[168] However, when Muhammad Hamadani set off to meet Nuruddin, the latter came out of his abode to greet the distinguished guest.[169] The popular verse in which Nuruddin seems to have hailed Muhammad Hamadani's visit[170] is important for two reasons from the strictly historical point of view. First, it corresponds with the date of Muhammad Hamadani's arrival in Kashmir in terms of *abjad*; second, in describing the Sayyid as the spiritual preceptor of the Kashmiris Nuruddin bears witness to the fruits of his experience as an ascetic and mystic, the experience of one who had trodden the mystic way and knew what it was to have attained the goal. Nuruddin's denunciation of extreme asceticism at the later stage of his life and his exhortations to his followers to follow the *Shari'a* and the *Sunna* ought to be studied against the background of Muhammad Hamadani's influence on him. In fact, Nuruddin maintained close contacts with the Kubrawi Sufis, who by all accounts were leaders of the spiritual life even after the departure of Muhammad Hamadani from Kashmir. Among these must be mentioned Shaikh Bahauddin Ganj Baksh, Shaikh Sultan and Haji Ibrahim Adham.

Shaikh Bahauddin Ganj Baksh was a disciple of Khwaja Ishaq Khatlani, one of the most distinguished disciples of Sayyid 'Ali Hamadani. Although he lived in seclusion, he was able to attract even Sultan Zain al-'Abidin to his abode under Zaina Kadal. According to Baba 'Uthman and Uchap Ganai, Ganj Baksh was held in high esteem by Nuruddin.[171]

Shaikh Sultan had obtained *sanad* to guide his people in the mystic path from Khawaja Ishaq Khatlani and Shaikh Nuruddin Badakshi. It was at Drugjan in Srinagar that he built a *khanqah* for the benefit of the people. Towards the end of his life, he settled in Pakhli at the request of its ruler, Sultan Muhammad Khan.[172]

Haji Ibrahim Adham was a disciple of the Kubrawi Sufi, Shaikh Ahmad. The original home of Ibrahim Adham was Balkh. His extensive travels in the Muslim world finally brought him to Srinagar during the reign of Sultan Sikandar. Although himself a Sufi, he was a great admirer of Nuruddin Rishi with whom he entered into a dialogue on spiritual matters.[173] It is unfortunate that his compilation, *Maqamat*, the earliest source on Sufism in Kashmir, is not extant. Sayyid 'Ali often alludes to Adhami's work in his description of Nuruddin's role in the history of Sufism in Kashmir. Significantly, the author of *Maqamat* is popularly known as Baba Adhami, understandably for his association with the founder of the Rishi order.

In spite of his illiteracy, Nuruddin Rishi had a wide range of sources to draw upon. There was enough spiritual inspiration in the Valley for an earnest seeker after the truth like him to have an opportunity for gaining knowledge of a faith which had posed an imminent threat to the belief structure of his own social environment. His verses bear eloquent testimony to the discussions with those who differed from him as well as those whose views were similar to his. It was not by meditation and penance in the cave and the forests alone, but also through extensive discussions during the long course of his travels in different parts of the Valley[174] with the Hindu ascetics,[175] the Brahmans,[176] the theologians,[177] the commoners,[178] including even peasant girls,[179] and, above all, Sufis like Muhammad Hamadani, Shaikh Sultan, Sultan Ganj Baksh and a Sufi scholar like Haji Adhami that Nuruddin was able to quench his thirst for a knowledge which would lead to the solution of the difficulties and problems of his faith. Small wonder, then, that Nuruddin, in spite of his humble origin earned titles such as the leader of the world, (*Shaikh al-'Alam*) and the upholder of the banner of Kashmir (*'Alamdar-i Kashmir*).

REFERENCES AND NOTES

1. Kalhana, *Rajatarangini* (tr. stein), Book 4, No. 379.
2. *Ibid.* Book 7, No. 1149; *Ibid.*, Book I, Introduction, p. 112.
3. *Ibid.* Book 8, Nos. 885–86.
4. In all probability, the earliest Muslim settlers in Kashmir inhabited the present locality of Malchmar which, undoubtedly, is one of the oldest sites in the city of Srinagar. While 'malch' is a derivative of *mleccha*, the term 'Mar' used for foreigners in olden times denotes 'place' in Kashmiri. While writing about the importance of the study of English place-name, A.L. Rowse very rightly observes: "So much of the documentation of our early history has perished: the place-names themselves are the most reliable documents that remain". See Rowse, *The Use of History*, p. 188.
5. *The Travels of Marco Polo* (Ed. and trans. by Ronald Lathan), p. 79.
6. See Kalhana, *op. cit.*, Book 7, No: 1149, Book 8, Nos. 885–886, 919, 923.
7. When King Kalasa (1063–89) "wished to put a gilt parasol over the Kalasesa (temple of Siva), there came to him an artist from the Turuska country,' *Ibid.*, Book, 7 No. 528.
8. *Ibid.*, Book, I, p. 130.
9. *Baharistan-i Shahi*, f. 14b, Aba Rafi'uddin, *Nawadir al-Akhbar*, f. 13a, Muhammad Aslam, *Gawhar-i 'Alam*, f. 101b.
10. Little is known about Shah Niam'atullah Farsi beyond the fact that he was a disciple of Shaikh Shihabuddin Suharwardi (1144–1234). The latter popularised the Suharwardi order, founded by his nephew, Ziauddin Abul Suharwardi (d. 1167), the author of the well known Sufi treatise, *Adab al-Muridin*.
11. Baba Daud Mishkati, *Asrar al-Abrar*, f. 45a; Muhammad Azam Diddamari, *Waqi'at-i Kashmir*, p. 30; Pir Hasan, *Asrar al-Akhyar*, (Urdu. tr. under the title, *Tarikh-i Auliya-i Kashmir*, Vol. III, p. 4).
12. Mishkati, *op. cit.*, f. 44a.
13. See *Infra.*
14. Francke, *Antiquities of Indian Tibet*, II, p. 98. Also *Indian Antiquary*, July, 1908, p. 187.
15. See for greater details; Mohibbul Hasan, *Kashmir Under the Sultans*, pp. 34–39.
16. As late as Husain Shah's reign (1563–70) we hear of the discussions between the Sultan and the Buddhist priests living in his kingdom. Haidar Malik, *Tarikh-i Kashmir* f. 159b.

17. *Baharistan-i Shahi*, f. 14a; Hasan bin Ali, *Tarikh-i Kashmir*, f. 98a, Haidar Malik, *op. cit.*, ff. 101b–202a.
18. Jonaraja writes that Rinchana wanted to become a Saivite (see Srikanth Kaul, *Rajatarangini of Jonaraja*, Intro. p. 72). But his version that the Brahman Devasvami did not consider it proper to convert a Buddhist into Hinduism is open to doubt. First, conversions from Buddhism into Hinduism and vice-versa were common in ancient and medieval times and, second, conversion of a king to Hinduism would have been welcomed by the Brahmans of Srinagar, in that it would have tightened their grip over their credulous devotees. It is certain that Rinchana did not accept Saivism in view of the abuses which had crept into it because of the corrupt practices of the Brahmans. Thus it was also out of rancour that Jonaraja not only gave a distorted picture of the circumstances that led Rinchana to reject Saivism, but even deliberately omitted to mention his conversion to Islam. Mohibbul Hasan is nearer the point when he remarks: "In reality the reason why Rinchana did not embrace Saivism was that it could not satisfy his spiritual cravings." (*op. cit.*, p. 40n.)
19. *Baharistan-i Shahi*, f. 14b; Baba Nasib, *Majmu'a dar Ansab Mashaikh-i Kashmir*, f. 106; Mishkati, *op. cit.*, f. 44b; Aba Refi'uddin, *op. cit.*, f. 13a; Diddamari, *op. cit.*, pp. 29–30.
20. Persian chroniclers (Hasan bin Ali, *op. cit.*, ff. 99b–100a; Haidar Malik, *op. cit.*, ff. 102–103a) say that while Hindu and Buddhist priests did not satisfy the spiritual quest of Rinchana, he finally decided to accept the faith of the first person whom he would see the next morning. And on seeing Sayyid Sharafuddin offering prayers near his palace the same morning, the king, after entering into a dialogue with the Sufi, became a Muslim. The patent fact about Rinchana's conversion, though described in supernatural terms by the chroniclers, nontheless, bears an elaborate testimony to the historic role of the first Suharwardi Sufi during the formative phase of Islam in Kashmir.
21. *Ibid.*
22. *Baharistan-i Shahi*, f. 15ab; Hasan bin Ali, *op. cit.*, ff. 100b–101a; Haidar Malik, *op. cit.* f. 103ab.
23. Francke, *op. cit.*, p. 98.
24. Rafiqi, (*Sufism in Kashmir*, pp. 9–10) and Rizvi (*Sufism in India*, I, p. 290 & n) attribute Rinchāna's conversion to Islam to his political ambitions and association with Shah Mir. This view is solely based on the false reasoning of Abul Fazl (*Ain-i Akbari* II, p. 184) rather than on patent facts, furnished by local chronicles, about Rinchana's association with Sayyid Sharafuddin. What further negates the view attributing Rinchana's conversion to Islam to the political factor is the fact that he assumed the reins of government in his hands as a Buddhist prince rather than as a convert to Islam. It is also hard to find any valid justification for this view on the ground that even as a king Rinchana

held discussions with the Brahman priest of Srinagar who, as noted before, failed to provide a panacea for the troubles of his soul.

25. *Baharistan-i Shahi*, f. 15a; Haidar Malik, *op. cit.*, f. 84a; Hasan bin 'Ali, *op. cit.*, f. 102a; Mishkati, *op. cit.*, f. 50a; Aba Rafiuddin, *op. cit.*, f. 17b; Diddamari, *op. cit.* p. 30.
26. For different views about his ancestry, see N.K. Zutshi, *Sultan-Zain-ul Abidin of Kashmir*, pp. 5–7.
27. For details, see Mohibbul Hasan, *op. cit.*, pp. 43–48.
28. Jonaraja, *Rajatarangini*, (tr. Dutt), p. 44.
29. Aba Rafiuddin, *op. cit.*, ff. 23a; Mohammad Aslam, *op. cit.*, f. 110b. See also Sayyid 'Ali, *Tarikh-i Kashmir*, p. 10.
30. Sayyid 'Ali, *op. cit.*, f. 1a; Diddamari, *op. cit.*, p. 38; Wahab, *op. cit.*, f. 69; Mohammad Aslam, *op. cit.*, f. 116ab.
31. Sayyid Ali, *op. cit.* f. 2b; Rafi'uddin, *op. cit.*, f. 23b, Wahab, *op. cit.*, f. 69b.
32. Mishkati, *op. cit.* f. 33a; Diddamari, *op. cit.*, pp. 35, 38; Wahab, *op. cit.*, f. 69a.
33. Sayyid 'Ali, *op. cit.* f. 1a; Wahab, *op. cit.*, f. 69b.
34. It is situated at a distance of 34 miles to the southwest of Srinagar.
35. See Mishkati, *op. cit.*, f. 33ab; Diddamari, *op. cit.*, p. 38; Wahab, *op. cit.*, f. 69a.
36. Baba Nasibuddin Ghazi traces the genealogy (*nisba*) of Nuruddin to the tribe of watchmen (*qabila-i pasban*). See Baba Nasib, *Nurnama*, f. 2b.
37. *Kulliyat-i Shaikh-al 'Alam*, p. 22.
38. Nuruddin describes his father as a man of 'pious deeds' who remained steadfast in performing his religious duties after embracing Islam, *Ibid.*, p. 172.
39. See *Ibid.*, pp. 148, 150, 153, 155, 160, 163, 164, 167, 171–72, 174, 190, 192, 197, 201, 204–7.
40. *Ibid.*, p. 22.
41. Pir Hasan, *op. cit.*, III, p. 10.
42. "The kharwar, or ass's load, has been from centuries past the standard weight in Kashmir." One *kharwar* is equivalent to 177 lbs. See Walter Lawrence, *The Valley of Kashmir*, pp. 242–43.
43. Pir Hasan, *op. cit.*, p. 10.
44. *Ibid.*, Mishkati, *op. cit.*, f. 33ab Wahab, *op. cit.* f. 69b.
45. Pir Hasan, *op. cit.*, p. 10.
46. The village of Kaimuh or ancient Katimusa (*Rajatarangini*, tr. Stein, II, 55, and n), is famous for being the birth-place of Nuruddin. From here, the shrine of Sayyid Husain Simnani is situated at a distance of about seven kilometres. It was also at Kaimuh that the Shaikh resorted to seclusion in a cave for 12 years during the earlier stage of his mystical career.
47. See also Ishaq Khan, "The Mystical Career and Poetry of Nuruddin

Rishi Kashmiri: Socio-Historical Dimensions", *Studies in Islam*, Jan/ April, 1982, pp. 101–02.

48. Mulla 'Ali Raina, *Tadhkirat-al-Arifin*, f. 37a, 38ab, 41b; Haidar Tulmuli, *Hidyat al-Mukhlisin*, ff. 188ab.
49. Raina, *op. cit.*, f. 41b; S'adullah Shahabadi, *Bagh-i Sulaiman*, ff. 72ab.
50. For detailed biographical information, see Sayyida Ashraf Zafar, *Sayyid Mir 'Ali Hamadani*, Delhi, 1987; Muhammad Riyaz, *Ahwal-u-athār-wa-ash'ar Mir Sayyid 'Ali Hamadani*, Islamabad (Pakistan), 1985.
51. Rafiqi, *op. cit*, pp. 35–36.
52. Sayyid Ali, *op. cit.*, f. 3b; Diddamari, *op. cit.*, p. 36; Wahab, *op. cit.*, f. 58b.
53. *Baharistan-i Shahi*, f. 24a; Hasan bin 'Ali, *op. cit.*, ff. 109b–110a. See also *Waqfnama* (quoted in Pir Hasan, *Tarikh-i Hasan*, I, p. 332).
54. Baba Nasib, *op. cit.*, f. 205a. See also Mohibbul Hasan, *op. cit.*, p. 56.
55. Sultan Shihabudddin (1354–73) reposed great trust in his Hindu ministers, Udayasri and Kota Bhatt. Jonaraja, *op. cit.*, p. 41. *Baharistan-i Shahi*, f. 21a. The Persian chroniclers call Udayasri by the name of Udshahrawal.
56. *Ibid.*, p. 53; a also Srivara, *op. cit.*, p. 142.
57. It presently occupies the site of the Khanqah-i Mu'alla and its neighbourhood.
58. Sayyid 'Ali, *op. cit.*, f. 4b; Wahab, *op. cit.*, f. 115a.
59. Jonaraja, *op. cit.*, p. 53.
60. Wahab, *op. cit.*, f. 147b.
61. *Ibid*, ff. 147b–48b; Hasan bin 'Ali, *op. cit.* f. 108b; Haidar Malik Chadura, *op. cit.*, f. 110b.
62. Under the influence of Islam the change in the pattern of social life of commoners is reflected in the protests of the Brahman chroniclers. See Jonaraja, *op. cit.*, pp. 57, 59; Srivara, op. cit., pp. 235, 319, 320; also Ishaq Khan, "The Impact of Islam on Kashmir in the Sultanate Period, 1320–1586", *Indian Economic and Social History Review*, Vol. XXIII, No. 2, 1986.
63. Sayyid Ali Hamadani, *Majmu'a Rasail*, also called *Maktubat*. See also Muhammad Riyaz, *op. cit.*, pp. 54, 143–44.
64. *Aurad-i Fathiyya* of Sayyid Ali Hamadani has run into several popular editions. There is hardly a mosque in Kashmir, excepting of course that of the Ahl-i Hadith, which does not possess several copies of this age-old invocatory prayer for the use of such Muslims as have not committed it to memory. For the Urdu translation of and commentary on the *aurad*, see Assadullah Shah Dawarki, *Tafhim al-Aurad*. n.d. Lahore. See also *Aurad-i Fathyyia* (Urdu tr. by Moulvi Muhammad Ibrahim), Srinagar.
65. G.M.D. Sufi, *Kashir*, I, p. 81; Mohibbul Hasan, *op. cit.*, p. 235. See also Sayyida Ashraf Zafar, *op. cit.*, p. 127.
66. Rafiqi, *op. cit.*, p. 39.

67. Rafiqi mistakenly creates the impression that Sayyid Ali's attitude towards the Hindus of Kashmir was discriminatory. See. Rafiqi, *op. cit.*, pp. 82, 84. Unfortunately his views are based on the Sayyid's theoretical formulations in *Dhakhirat al-Muluk* rather than on the saint's historical role in Kashmir which was guided both by expediency and saintly wisdom.
68. Pakhli is described as consisting of the whole of the territory between Kashmir in the east and the Indus in the west, including the lower Valley of the Kishanganga and the Valley of streams which flow into the latter. Stein, "Memoir on the Ancient Geography of Kashmir" in Kalhana, *op. cit.*, II, p. 434.
69. Sayyid Áli Hamadani, *Majmu'a-Rasail*, f. 26b. See also *Risala-i 'Uqbat* (quoted in Riyaz, *op. cit.* p. 54).
70. *Ibid.*
71. *Ibid.* Even in *Dhakhirat al-Muluk* the Sayyid instructs the Muslim sultans to protect the rights of their non-Muslim subjects.
72. Sayyid 'Ali, *Tarikh-i Kashmir*, ff. 2a, 3a.
73. Amir Ahmad Razi (*Haft Iqlim*, f. 93a) who refers to only one visit of Sayyid 'Ali Hamadani to Kashmir, interestingly enough, is the only author to state that the Sayyid stayed in the Valley for forty days (*Chihal rouz tawaquf kard*), *Ibid.*
74. Sayyid 'Ali Hamadani, *Rasail*, ff. 26ab.
75. It is, however, wrong to say the Jafar Badakshi does not refer to Kashmir at all; as a matter of fact, the expression, *'ba taraf-i mahshar raft'* (*khulasat al-Manaqib*, f. 129) has inadvertently been written by most scribes instead of *ba taraf-i Kashmir raft.*
76. Haidar Badakshi, *Manqabat al-Jawahir*, f. 75a.
77. In a poetical composition Sultan Qutubuddin pays tributes to Sayyid 'Ali Hamadani not only for bringing him close to Islam, but even Kashmir (*girift Kashmir az Islam rayat*). *Ibid.*
78. That the Sultan considered Sayyid 'Ali his spiritual guide is not only borne out by the sources, but also by the title "Shah-i Hidayat" which Qutubuddin gave to the Sayyid. *Ibid.*
79. Jafar Badakshi, *op. cit.*, f. 20b.
80. Haidar Badakshi, *op. cit.*, f. 75a.
81. He is popularly known in Kashmir as Pir Haji Muhammad. See Pir Hasan, *Asrar al-Akhyar* (Urdu. tr.), p. 20.
82. Wahab, *op. cit.*, f. 151b; Hasan 'Ali, *op. cit.*, ff. 110b. *Majmu'a dar Ansab Mashaikh-i Kashmir*, f. 111b.
83. Hasan bin 'Ali, *op. cit.*, f. 110a; Haidar Malik, *op. cit.*, f. 111a.
84. The *dhikr* was the major activity of the Kubrawi order in Kashmir; so much so that regular attendance at the Khanqah-i Mu'alla seems to have become, for practical purposes, the best index of membership. The social aspect of the *dhikr* was of fundamental significance. For the

importance of *dhikr*, see *The Quran*. s. 18: v. 24; s. 33: v. 41; s. 39: v. 22; s. 43: v. 36; s. 63; v. 9 and elsewhere.

85. Srivara, *op. cit.*, p. 235.
86. Sayyid Ali, *op. cit.* f, 31a; Wahab, *op. cit.*, f. 105a.
87. Bruce Lawrence rightly points out that the invocatory prayers have not been studied by the scholars. See Lawrence, *Notes from a Distant Flute: The Extant Literature of Pre-Mughal Indian Sufism*, Tehran, 1978.
88. See also Ishaq Khan, "Islam in Kashmir: Historical Analysis of its Distinctive Features", *Islam in India* (ed. Christian W. Troll), pp. 94–5; also the author's paper "Towards an Analysis of a Popular Muslim Ritual in the Kashmiri Environment", presented in the International Seminar on "New History" organized by Jawaharlal Nehru University at the India International Centre in New Delhi in February, 1988.
89. 'Ali Raina, *op. cit.*, 37a, 41b.

89a. *Ibid.*, ff. 36ab–38a. For a brief information about Makhdum-i Jahanian see Afif, *Tarikh-i Firuz Shahi*, pp. 514–516. See also K.A. Nizami, *Some Aspects of Religion and Politics in India*, p. 225n.

90. 'Ali Raina, *op. cit.*, ff. 37ab–38a.
91. *Ibid.*
92. Haidar Tulmuli, *Hidayat al-Mukhlisin*, ff. 188ab.
93. *Ibid.*
94. *Ibid.*, 189a.
95. Baba Nasib, *op. cit.*, ff. 83ab–84ab.
96. Mishkati, *op. cit.*, ff. 320ab–324a.
97. *Ibid.*
98. Diddamari, *op. cit.*, MS. No. 1843; f. 29; MS. No. 100; ff. 20ab.
99. Wahab, *op. cit.*, ff. 151b; 164b–166a.
100. Shahabadi, *op. cit.*, ff. 90ab.
101. Baba Kamal, *Rishinama*, pp. 353–55; Baba Khalil, *Rauzat-al-Riyazat*, pp. 832–46.
102. Birbal Kachru, *Majmu'a al-Tawarikh*, ff. 73b, 74b–75ab, 76ab.
103. *Ibid.*, ff. 76ab.
104. See B.N. Parimoo, *The Ascent of Self*, Delhi, 1978; Jayalal Kaul, *Lal Ded*, Sahitya Akademi, 1973.
105. Ali Raina, *op. cit.*, ff. 37ab–38a, 41b.
106. Mohindar Raina, "Lal Ded aur Bhakti Marg, "*Shiraza*", VI, 18, Nov. – Dec., 1979, No. 7, 8, pp. 171–83.
107. For a critical appraisal of Kabir's views on Islam, see Aziz Ahmad, *Studies in Islamic Culture in the Indian Environment*, pp. 143–47.
108. S.C. Malik, *Indian Movements : Some Aspects of Dissent, Protest and Reform*, Simla, 1978, pp. 46–48; 51, 55–58, 114–116 and 118–20.
109. Grierson and Barnett, *Lalla-Vakyani*, preface, V-VI.
110. This is also the reason that earlier hagiographers nowhere make any reference to the tomb or shrine of Lalla. Although there is a folk tradition

that Lal Ded was buried in Bijbehara, her supposed grave situated in the vicinity of Baba Nasib's shrine seems to me of a later date.

111. Rafiqi has thus commited an abysmal error of studying Lal Ded as an isolated figure who has no connection whatsoever with Islam. See Rafiqi, *op. cit.*, p. 145.
112. Birbal Kachru speaks of her as 'a saintly, chaste and pure-of-heart woman from the community of Hindus (who) had stepped up the dais of Divine manifestation.' See Kachru *op. cit.*, f.99b.
113. The Kashmiri Pandits were very proud of their literary traditions and, therefore, styled themselves as the *Ahl-i Qalam.*
114. Baba Nasib is the first to relate the incredible story of Lal Ded's entry into a temple for purposes of easing herself; nonetheless, the dialogues attributed by him to the Brahman priest, Lalla and Nuruddin clearly reflect the protestant trend in the religious situation of Kashmir in the seventeenth century. See Baba Nasib, *op. cit.*, f. 84a.
115. *Ibid.*
116. For detailed information on the works of Sayyid 'Ali Hamadani, see Muhammad Riyaz, *op. cit.*
117. Jayalal Kaul, *op. cit.*, p. 107.
118. *Ibid.*
119. *Ibid.* p. 16.
120. *Ibid.* p. 110.
121. *Ibid.*
122. *Ibid.*, p. 104.
123. *Ibid.*, p. 103.
124. *Ibid.*, pp. 12–13; Parimoo concludes that "dancing nude' is a metaphorical way of saying that her joy knew no bounds, on obtaining the 'key' to the treasures of mystical knowledge." *op. cit.*, p. 63.
125. Parimoo, *op. cit.*, p. 59.
126. Grierson and Barnett, *op. cit.*, pp. 1–3, 121–22.
127. See Appendix: "Woman Saints of Kashmir."
127a. Jayalal Kaul, *op. cit.*, p. 99.
128. *Ibid.*, p. 98.
129. Parimoo, *op. cit.*, p. 7. The verse has been understood by Parimoo as Lal Ded's expression of resentment against her cruel mother-in-law who is alleged to have been in the habit of putting a round stone in her eating bowl. But it is unthinkable that Lal Ded would have protested on account of "poor food". What, however, is reasonable to suggest is the mystic's supreme effort in disciplining herself through extreme ascetic exercise.
130. Abdul Ahad Azad, *Kashmiri Zuban Aur Sha'iri*, II, p. 113.
131. Jayalal Kaul, *op. cit.*, p. 47.
131a. Jayalal Kaul and Nandlal Talib, *Lal Ded* (3rd ed.), pp. 41, 43, 110, 112, 136–41.

132. *Kulliyat*, p. 21.
133. The extent to which Hinduism had declined in Kashmir is amply borne out by Lal Ded's and Nuruddin's protests against the Brahman priests and ascetics in their verses.
134. Quoted in R.K. Pandey, *The Concept of Avatars*, pp. 8–9.
135. "*Alastu birabikum, qalu bala*" (Am I not your Lord? asked Allah, 'yes', answered they). See the covenant between Allah and human souls, *The Quran*, s. VII, v. 172.
135a. Jayalal Kaul, *op. cit*, pp 1–2.
136. *Ibid.*, p. 59.
137. *Ibid.*, p. 117.
138. Baba Khalil discusses at some length the sayings of Lal Ded, although he is conscious of the fact that many of these are in the Sanskrit language. See Khalil, *op. cit.*, p. 846.
139. Rafiqi's statement that "either the followers of Nuruddin wrongly attributed to him some of Lalla's savings in order to prove him superior or Pandit Dharun Dasa recited to Grierson some of Nuruddin's sayings believing or pretending that they were Lalla's" (Rafiqi, *op. cit.*, p. 151) fails to take into account, in sociological terms, the Kashmiris' reluctance to walk away from their cultural inheritance which they believe to be their own even after rejecting Brahmanism.
140. Jayalal Kaul, *op. cit.*, Parimoo, *op. cit.*
141. 'Ali Raina, *op. cit.*, ff. 37a, 41b.
142. Ishaq Khan, "The Impact of Islam on Kashmir", *op. cit.*, p. 199.
143. Sayyid 'Ali, *op. cit.*, f. 9b; *Baharistan-i Shahi*, f. 26a; Mishkati, *op. cit.*, f. 37b; Diddamari, *op. cit.*, p. 42.
144. Wahab, *op. cit.*, f. 162a.
145. *Ibid.* f. 155b.
146. *Baharistan-i Shahi*, ff. 25b, 26; Haidar Malik, *op. cit.*, Diddamari, *op. cit.*, p. 37; Mishkati, *op. cit.*, f. 45a.
147. Diddamari, *op. cit.*, p. 42; Wahab, *op. cit.*, f. 62b.
148. Jonaraja, *op. cit.*, p. 57.
149. Sayyid 'Ali, *op. cit.*, ff. 10a, 12ab, 35ab–36ab; Mishkati, *op. cit.*, f. 38a; Diddamari, *op. cit.*, p. 42; Wahab, *op. cit.*, f. 62b.
150. For the role of the Baihaqi Sayyids in Kashmir, see Mohibbul Hasan, *op. cit.*, pp. 107–08; 162–74; 220; 286n.
151. Mirza Haidar Dughlat writes in about 1546: "First and foremost among the wonders of Kashmir stand her idol temples. In and around Kashmir there are more than 150 temples... In the rest of the world there is not to be seen, or heard of, one building like this. How wonderful that there should be (here) a hundred and fifty of them." *Tarikh-i Rashidi*, p. 426, Abul Fazl (Ain-i Akbari II, p. 124. and Jahangir, (*Tuzuk-i Jahangiri*), II, p. 150 also testify to the existence of 'lofty idol temples' in the Valley.

152. Jonaraja (See Kaul, *op. cit.* St. 544). The following dedicatory note in Sharda script on a sculpture found at Ganesh temple raises doubts about the Sultan's alleged inconoclasm: "(Sak) 85 Sri Sakandar Saha Rajya Samgha Pati Rahwa Kastava ka ta tha" (Quoted in an unpublished paper of J.L. Bhan, Reader, Centre of Central Asian Studies, Kashmir University).
153. Jonaraja, *op. cit.*, p. 59.
154. Baba Nasib, *Supra.*
155. See, for example, the famous mosque named after Shah Hamdan in Srinagar.
156. See photograph No. 1.
157. See Parmu, *A History of Muslim Rule in Kashmir*, pp. 129–130.
158. Gawashlal Kaul's book, *Kashmir Through the Ages*, has enjoyed so much popularity that it has so far run into several editions.
159. Haidar Badakshi's account (*op. cit.*, ff. 75a) clearly suggests that the terms *rahib* (ascetic) and *dev* (monster or demon) have been used for the priests of the temple rather than for any superhuman. No wonder, therefore, Lal Ded was very critical of the magical powers of the priests masquerading as ascetics:

  "To stop a flowing stream, to cool a raging fire,
  To walk on one's feet in the sky,
  To labour at milking a wooden cow—
  All these, in the end, are but base jugglery."

  See Grierson and Barnett, *op. cit.*, p. 58.
160. See Chapter VIII, "The Societal Dimensions of Miracles."
161. Both Rizvi and Rafiqi describe the Kubrawi Sufis as 'Orthodox'. 'Rafiqi wrongly states that "their main concern appears to have been to help the administration, and make it an instrument in propagating Islam." *op. cit.*, p. XIVI; also Wahab, *op. cit.*, ff. 163a–164b.
162. Parmu, *op. cit.*, p. 118.
163. Sayyid 'Ali, *op. cit.*, f. 34a.
164. See Khat- irshad, *Appendix.*
165. *Kulliyat*, pp. 22–23.
166. In one of his verses Nuruddin longs for entry into paradise through the intercession of Sayyid 'Ali Hamadani, *Ibid.*, p. 36.
167. Sayyid 'Ali, *op. cit.*, ff. 340b.
168. See Chapter VI, "The Attitudes of the Sufi Orders Towards the Rishis."
169. Wahab, *op. cit.*, ff. 160b–162b.
170. *Koishern-pir aaw* (the spiritual leader of Kashmiris has come), See *Ibid.*, f. 109b.
171. Sayyid 'Ali, *op. cit.*, ff. 19b, 32a.
172. *Ibid.*
173. *Ibid.*

174. *Kulliyat*, p. 75. See also, p. 105.
175. Sayyid 'Ali, *op. cit*, ff. 37b–38ab; Baba Nasib, *op. cit.*, ff. 99ab; Shahabadi, *op. cit.*, ff. 106ab; Wahab, *op. cit.*, ff. 167b–168b; Baba Kamal, *op. cit.*, pp. 73–87.
176. Baba Nasib, *op. cit.*, ff. 45b–48ab; 53b–54a, 59b–60ab; 99ab–103ab; Baba Kamal, *op. cit.*, pp. 90–91, 107, 142.
177. Baba Nasib, *op. cit.*, ff. 48b–50a; Shahabadi, *op. cit.*, f. 103a; Baba Kamal, *op. cit.*, ff. 150–54, 176–79.
178. Baba Nasib, *op. cit.*, ff. 27b, 56b–57a; Wahab, *op. cit.*, ff. 158b–160ab; Baba Kamal, *op. cit.*, pp. 104–05, 108–09; Wahab, *op. cit.*, ff. 156ab.
179. Baba Nasib, *op. cit.*, f. 27b; Shahabadi, *op. cit.*, ff. 100ab; Bahauddin Mattu, *Rishinama*, pp. 188–89.

CHAPTER IV

Shaikh Nuruddin's Religious Career and its Social Impact

There is a direct and fundamental relationship between the evolution of Shaikh Nuruddin's religious career and the gradual development of what may be called the Kashmiri Muslim society. The fact is that during the Shaikh's period the Muslim population of the Valley was a minority[1] or perhaps a very small majority of the entire population of the Kashmir region. From a careful analysis of his verses, it would appear that the society of the Kashmir Valley was not purely Islamic in form, nor did it have a radical transformation overnight on its contact with the Great Tradition of Islam. Indeed the Shaikh's verses represent not only certain basic facts about the gradual transition of Kashmir to Islam, but also something of the crisis through which he was himself passing and its impact on the social norms and meaning of Islam in the regional context. So central is the new sense of crisis and self-awareness evident in his verses that his poetry assumes the pervasiveness of a vital tradition.

Religion for the Shaikh was a matter of experience; it was 'real' rather than merely 'notional'. In Kantian terms his knowledge began with experience that arose out of experience. An understanding of Islam's historical manifestation in Kashmir, therefore, requires a prior understanding of the man who influenced the Kashmiri mind more profoundly than any other religious leader.[2] It is not merely the mystic Nuruddin whom we seek to discover in this chapter but also the maker of Kashmiri Muslim identity, and the eloquent protagonist of Islamic human values whose balanced religious enthusiasm, tolerance and, above all, *Tauhidic* universalism continue to dominate the attitudes and beliefs of contemporary Kashmir. The history of Islam in Kashmir is, in fact, bound up integrally with the mystical, moral and aesthetic sensibilities and even philosophic insights of Nuruddin; it goes without saying that he influenced the course of Islamic development in the Valley by coordinating it and giving it direction through language and communication.

It must be explained that ours is a study to discover not only the Shaikh of history but also that of legend and faith. An objective understanding of the Shaikh, therefore, demands a careful and minute examination of the traditions stemming from his historical role. These traditions, both oral and written, testify to the great extent of religious consciousness generated among the common folk through their transmission by repetition.

Traditions which are the collective representation of past events remarks the celebrated anthropologist, E.E. Evans-Pritchard, form part of the study of the society to which they belong.[3] Every tradition is a historical fact. Whether or not the tradition is true, the repeated transmission of the tradition is itself a 'tremendous fact' and worthy of serious examination. At least, traditions reveal the mind and imagination of the transmitter, about the society he lived in, about the cultural realities to which the 'legend' was considered to be relevant and which were reflected in the details of the 'legend'. The historical hermeneutic has seldom liberated the sources from its straitjacket with its emphasis on the so-called "original source". True, one cannot rely on legends alone as a source of history, but the historians' somewhat ingrained habit of rejecting legendary evidence without using it judiciously seldom render historical narrative objective. We can hardly make sense of the life of the rural people in pre-modern times by an outright rejection of legends and folklore which are the lungs of rural culture.[4]

The folk traditions about Nuruddin's mystical life need to be studied in the light of the significant contribution his poetical verses have, through centuries, made in influencing the tone and attitudes of a people living in the particular geographical environment of the Kashmir Valley. As we shall see, his poetry not only became the cultural heritage of a linguistic group, but besides being the direct outcome of the growth of Islamic civilisation in the Kashmir Valley, it also became identified with its expanding frontier. In assessing the value of his verses as source material, we must, however, remember that their psychological function and aesthetic qualities have not distorted the historical facts contained in them. The kind of historical information transmitted by his poetry was actually germane to the concerns of the society he lived in.

His poetry is, therefore, not merely a historical source but it also conveys the attitudes and behaviour patterns which influenced a number of the adherents of his mystic order in a period of great social crises in Kashmir's history. The Shaikh's poetry is not a survival of something hackneyed and socially irrelevant but something of abiding value. In the following account an attempt will be made to bring crude historical realism and 'legends' into an effective relationship, claiming them both as indistinguishable aspects of a whole experience.

According to a tradition, quoted in several hagiological works, for three days after his birth in 779/1378 A.D.[5] Nuruddin did not take milk from his mother. But, then, Lal Ded visited the house of Salar Ganai, the father of the newly-born, and addressed the latter:

> Thou wast not ashamed of being born; why then art thou ashamed of sucking (at the mother's breast).[6]

The baby started taking milk and thereafter Lal Ded's visits to the parental house of Nuruddin continued. It was Lal Ded, indeed, who was the earliest source of inspiration for Nuruddin.

The popular tradition about Lal Ded's influence on Nuruddin, though enveloped in legendary material, contains a kernel of historical truth. It not only conveys some information about the early influence on the Shaikh's mind, but also reveals the dynamic relationship, a creative tension that existed between the local and the Islamic mystic traditions. There is thus a need to understand clearly the formative influence exercised by Lal Ded on Nuruddin. And, like Ibn 'Arabi's veneration for Fatima of Cordova, who was a spiritual mother to him,[7] Nuruddin also speaks with devotion of Lal Ded's teachings, oriented towards a life of intimacy with God.[8] No wonder, therefore, the general theme of the verses composed by the young Nuruddin under the influence of Lal Ded is mainly the necessity of a period of asceticism during which an aspirant can wean himself from the world. The Shaikh, as will be seen later, also says much about himself in relation to the virtues of asceticism of other local saints,[9] though never in an arrogant strain.

Nuruddin's religious career falls into three main stages: the first is that of an orphan struggling to eke out his mundane existence; the second is that of an ascetic who withdraws himself from wordly affairs in order to know the religious truth; and in the third and final stage he gives up the life of a recluse to advocate ethics of a dynamic and positive nature. This division has in it the inevitable limitations of a generalization, but simultaneously it helps us to perceive in a clearer light the shifts and changes which are natural to the evolution of the career of a mystic such as Nuruddin.

Some unfortunate circumstances seem to have moulded Nuruddin's outlook towards worldly affairs during the earlier phase of his religious career. He became an orphan at an early age; besides, the death of Lal Ded and Sayyid Husain Simnani deprived the young Nuruddin of their spiritual care. The Sanz family seems to have lived in abject poverty after the death of Shaikh Salar, as is evidenced by the thefts committed by Nuruddin's brothers in order to survive. Nuruddin is also reported to have been asked by his two brothers, Shesh and Kundar, to help in a burglary but he did not come up to their expectations since he showed an abhorrence for the life of a thief. When he entered a village hut in order to commit a theft he "came out empty handed" and ran away after throwing his own blanket over the poverty-stricken inmates of the house. On another occasion he was asked by his brothers to take care of a cow they had stolen. While driving the cow he heard a dog bark, *wow, wow.* Suddenly Nuruddin was overcome with a sense of guilt. *Wow* means 'sow' in Kashmir. Thinking that the dog was reminding him that what he sowed in this world would be reaped by him in the Hereafter, he let loose the cow;[10]

> The dog is calling from the courtyard,
> My brothers pay heed to (what he says)
> He who sows here shall reap there
> The dog is urging *sow*, or *sow.*

Emphasizing the same point the Shaikh remarks in the poem:

> When an assessment is made of your good deeds and sins;
> Brothers, the thought of the Day of Judgement should be uppermost in your minds.
> See, whether your nobler actions can overweigh your sins;
> The dog is urging, *sow* or *sow.*[12]

Another interesting anecdote regarding the Shaikh's early life is narrated by him in a verse. He was sent to learn the craft of weaving by his mother, but he could not become an apprentice since the tools of the weaver inspired his muse:[13]

> One instrument holds my rapt attention.
> The other teaches me renounce the world;
> The paddle points down to the grave;
> This is the craft to which my parents have apprenticed me.[14]

A conversation between the Shaikh and the weaver recorded in the hagiological literature is worthy of notice. The Shaikh is reported to have been dissatisfied with the commonplace answer of the weaver when asked to explain the movement of the shuttle "through the tangle of threads." In the weaver's explanation that the cloth was woven because of the to and fro movement of the thread through the shuttle, the Shaikh found an inner meaning. His explanation was that the movement of the shuttle was symbolic of two doors of the world, the one through which we enter (birth) and the other through which we leave (death). The shuttle thus resembles man who carrying the thread of his destiny, tosses to and fro in this world, and departs when the thread is exhausted.[15]

The other-worldliness of the Shaikh did not permit him to learn the weaver's craft. This is why he deprecated the importance of living in the world.

> "Why did I not listen to Death, the friend,
> Who can propitiate him, the great Destroyer?
> Few are my pieties but piled up the sins;
> Little have I gained by my birth in the world.[16]

The Shaikh retired to a cave at Kaimuh,[17] the place of his birth. He gave various excuses to his mother when she insisted on his returning home. He talks about the insolent riches of the world, human desires, anger and ego, which preoccupy the human mind. He draws lurid pictures of the Day of Judgement and hell to impress upon his mother the futility of paddling one's own canoe in the material world:

> This life is a hollow bubble;
> We are just a drop in its vast ocean,
> An ass like me is unable to bear its brunt,
> Having deserted home, why should I care to live?[18]

Nuruddin himself expounds as to why he took to the jungle early in life, in the true spirit of the rishis:

> In the pursuit of mundane affairs my desires became limitless;
> So I retired to the jungle, early in life,
> May the Lord saturate the Rishi's mind with longing for Thee;
> For I remember with gratitude how kind Thou art.[19]

Nuruddin's decision to lead an ascetic's life which marks the beginning of the second stage in his religious career, seems to have been voluntary. It was influenced by his craving for seeking the truth.[20]

The path of renunciation followed by the rishis preceding him and their extreme ascetic habits must have also played an important part in shaping his outlook on wordly life.[21] It is unlikely that the penance in the cave was undertaken at the command of any saint.

> The company of saints I did not keep,
> Till right moment and youth slipped by,
> Wrongly did I attach (myself) to the world;
> Have thy play and let's go home.[22]

It is certain that the Shaikh chose the 'legendary' rishis as the earliest models of holiness. This is borne out by the unqualified praise for them in his poetry:

> Zulka Rishi of Dandakvan[23]
> Who subsisted on (wild) fruit of shrubs,
> Was a true lover to attain salvation,
> May God grant me the same spiritual power.[24]

What inspires the Shaikh about the lives of the rishis is not only their penance, meditation, abstemious habits, but above all, their devotion to God and burning love for the Creator:

> Miran Rishi of Reshivan[25]
> Who lived for a thousand lunar months
> In a state of union with God did he leave for his heavenly abode.
> May God grant me the same spiritual power.[26]

Other rishis of yore to whom the Shaikh looks for inspiration are Rum Rishi[27] and Pilas Rishi.[28]

The rishis are, undoubtedly, Nuruddin's refuge at the earlier stage of his mystical career. He frequently refers to the term *rishi* whose meaning was familiar to the common folk; but it meant to him not merely an ascetic of this world, as in common parlance, but the good. The company of such men was sought by him, since he thought it was like heaven. The term was used by him for all believers with some quality more rarefied, designating a special state of grace. All his references to the local Hindu saints in the days of his youth indicate a generally understood social environment; it is not the rishis as such that are essential for Nuruddin, but the presence of the Creator that they make possible for the earnest seeker even in an oppressive Brahmanic society. The ultimate object of Nuruddin is, therefore, to follow the rishis of yore, and he expresses a longing to rise to the heights of their spiritual glory by means of fervent prayers.

Nuruddin's exaltation of the 'legendary rishis' is neither a sentimental expression nor a romantic idealization; it is a genuine and healthy appreciation, in the absence of any contemporary documentary evidence on the rishis of olden days, and a corrective to such purely rational perceptions as deny their existence. Such phenomena also need to be studied as objective facts and behaviour patterns. What is worth investigating is how a large number of Muslim Rishis modelled their lives upon those of 'legendary' Hindu and Buddhist Rishis. This development, it may be argued, occurred only in a particular social context, as part of a culture, in a milieu. As a matter of fact, the impact of the historical role of the so-called 'legendary' rishis on the rural consciousness has yet to be assessed by historians. The Shaikh's longing for an ordered rhythm in the life of the Rishis is the kind of longing which enables us to use the mystic matrix as a simulacrum of the social and moral attitudes of the Rishis.

Having thus secluded himself in the cave in the manner of the rishis, the Shaikh combined the daunting series of recitations of God's name with extremes of asceticism, self-mortification, long fasts, and sexual abstinence. In order to discipline his soul, he followed extreme ascetic practices to free himself from his sensual self. The Shaikh subsisted on wild vegetables and did not touch meat.[29] He considered *vopalhak*[30] and chicory to be the favourite dish of the chosen of God.[31] He wore ragged garments but used the *kangri*[32] to protect himself against the rigours of cold.[33]

The ethics of asceticism finds a systematic exposition in the conversations which the Shaikh had with his mother and wife in the cave. The doctrine of negation of the wordly life is emphasized when his mother urges him to return home:

> Mother do not pester me;
> Nund has already buried himself,
> Mother the world is mortal;
> Therefore, I have retired to the cave.[34]

Reacting to his mother's insistence on his taking enough food, the Shaikh remarks:

> How can (good) food satiate (my spiritual thirst), mother?
> Give it to a dog or a Brahman[35]

Can't I crush my ego?
Having renounced home, why should I care to live.[36]

And when Zai Ded implores her husband to give up the path of renunciation, the Shaikh says:

Zai, have love for the next world;
Groping in the dark will lead you nowhere.[37]

It must also be explained that most of the verses composed by the Shaikh in the cave bear an indelible mark of Saivite philosophy. According to *Sivadaita* or the *Trika* philosophy of Kashmir, the *atman*, meaning the true and innermost self, is present everywhere and is in every being. It "is a changeless reality of the nature of a purely experiencing principle, as distinguished from whatever may *assume the form* of either the experience or the means of experience."[38] There is no room for a second Reality in the philosophy of the Trinity (*Siva-Sakti-Anu*). As B. N. Parimoo observes, "The experiencing principles, the means of experience and the object of experience, are in essence modes of one and the same Truth. The experiencer, the medium of experience and the object of experience are different aspects of the same all-pervading *Siva* in as much as it is He who assumes the forms simultaneously of the Experiencer and Experienced."[39]

Thus, while withdrawing his mind from all objective activities, the Shaikh turned towards the subject, that is, the real self, and gradually got wholly absorbed into it.

Having forsaken all I sought You,
While searching You the prime of my youth passed away,
When I found You within my own self.
I remained in safety because of Your luminations.[40]

Ascetic training is thus the prerequisite for the achievement of any higher mystical state. The following verse is also typical of the Saivite way of renunciation:

He is near me I am near Him,
I found solace in His nearness,
In vain did I seek Him elsewhere,
Lo : I found the Beloved within my own consciousness.[41]

The unitive experience leading to intuitive realization of the real self is called *Parama-Siva* or consciousness in Saiva philosophy. The phenomenal universe which exists in *Parama-Siva* in the form of pure consciousness, "is nothing but an objective manifestation of His divine powers."[42] Thus, the Shaikh, after establishing a personal relation between himself and incarnate god through ascetic training remarks:

> The universe is the objective manifestation of the essence of Siva,
> If you realise it through annihilation of self, you will get merged into Him,
> What will you find after death, if you do not recognize Him in this world?
> Search Him in yourself and give me keen hearing.[43]

Although elements in the Shaikh's verses are compatible with the Saivite aspiration after self-identification with God, the influence of ontological monism of Sufism on his inquisitive mind cannot be ruled out. The Shaikh does not draw formal and verbal parallels between Hindu and Muslim ideas of unitive experience but he elaborates fully the spirit that animates the mystical movements in Hinduism and Islam.

> "What qualities hast thou found in the world?
> To allow thy body a free, loose rope?
> The Musalman and Hindu sail in the same boat.
> Have thy play and let's us go home."[44]

And while transcending the barriers of theological ethnocentrism the Shaikh remarks:

> Among the brothers of the same parents.
> Why did you create a barrier?
> Muslims and Hindus are one.
> When will God be kind to His servants?[45]

The Shaikh warns that the worldly pleasures should not detract our attention from God, "who is our home." Life can become meaningful only when "We are able to 'ascend back' into His presence."[46] He brings to light the piercing longing of his soul seeking direct intervention of divine action to sanctify the human creature through a love that transfigures, not only the soul, but also the body through constant prayer.

> Thou existed and Thou (alone) will exist.
> Continue to remember Thou, none, but Thou.
> Thou alone will assuage the anguish (of thy soul).
> O my soul, recognize thyself.[47]

In the following verses in particular the Shaikh exhibits a trenchant religious impulse, inspired by Hindu as well as Muslim sources, and fervently prays for the vision of the transcendent yet immanent God:

> Nirguna,[48] manifest thyself unto me.
> Thy name (alone) have I been chanting;
> Lord help me reach the acme of my spiritual desires,
> I do remember gratefully how kind Thou art.
> Thou removed all veils between thyself and the Prophet.
> And Thou revealed Quran unto him.
> Lord the one (Prophet) who remained steadfast in Thy way.
> I do remember gratefully; how kind Thou art.[49]

It follows that in the prime of his youth the socio-cultural tradition represented by Nuruddin was purely mystical rather than of this world. His conception of the universe and things around him was such as could have led to a separation of himself from these phenomena. The self-image of man, according to such a view, was that of a quasi-divine being whose only aim was to attain a mystical union with God. How the norms of the material worlds which lead to the realization of substantive modes of relationship between man and his environment and between man and man emerged in the Shaikh's thought is an important question requiring examination.

In fact, the crystallization of such a process began when Nuruddin came in contact with Sayyid Muhammad Hamadani, who is reputed to have played an important role in the spread of Islamic teachings in Kashmir along with a number of his disciples. That the Sayyid became the spiritual preceptor of the Shaikh when the latter was in his early thirties is attested to not only by documentary evidence,[50] but also by a new trend in his thought which we shall discuss at some length in the next chapter. Here it will suffice to say that from now on, the mystic Nuruddin addressed himself to the task of reforming society by becoming a conscious missionary. He toured different parts of the Valley in the hope of teaching Islam to the unlettered folk. Although it is difficult to say whether the Shaikh fully succeeded in imparting the tenets of Islam to the commoners in his lifetime, it can hardly be denied that for generations after his death his teachings remained the *Weltanschauung* of the common folk. And it is chiefly for this reason that he is remembered to this day, not only as a Sufi but also as the greatest local teacher of Islam in Kashmir. So indelible has been the influence of the Shaikh on Kashmiri society that the people have preserved to this day not only the memory of his visits in every nook and corner of the

Valley, but have turned the habitats of the Shaikh in several villages into places of venerations. It is also significant that many a proverb reflecting the attitude of the Shaikh towards the responses of the rural folk to his teachings are said to have gained currency in the aftermath of his visits. The fact is that the Kashmiri peasants' life has been closely interwoven with the Shaikh's teachings and their impact on the development of a new cultural trend.

In view of the role of a conscious Muslim missionary assumed by the mystic Nuruddin, it is not difficult to understand why his speech did not remain Sanskritized during the last phase of his religious career. In fact it was his association with the Kubrawi Sufis that led to a great change in his thought. To suppose, therefore, that the Sanskritised verses alone are the authentic verses of the Shaikh is tantamount to confining the influences on his dynamic personality to an infinitesimal number of Brahman ascetics, which certainly was not the case. The preponderance of Arabic and Persian words in his verses was inevitable both from historical and etymological points of view consequent to his close association with the Sufis of the Kubrawi order, and that too, when Sayyid Muhammad Hamadani had delegated to him the authority of guiding his countrymen on the right path. This also explains the fact that the Shaikh's poetry reveals a language that flows effortlessly; a succinct demonstration that he had instilled into his mind and heart the mystic doctrines he had learnt through his association with the Kubrawi Sufis, and having been imbued completely with those doctrines, translated his thoughts into his mother tongue, of which he was a unique master. In the period before the Shaikh, we know of no instance of Kashmiri compositions such as the Shaikh's, and in the period following his death, there has hardly been any notable composer of such mystical verse.

The Arabic and Persian words used by the Shaikh seem to have become an integral part of the Kashmiri language even during his lifetime. But for this, he would not have become the best and greatest representative of Kashmiri Sufism. His selection of key words from *tasawwuf*, intended for the common folk, presupposes full knowledge of the Quran, full comprehension of its meaning structure and full participation in its linguistic consciousness. This explains why he was able to impart a clear exposition of the Quranic verses. That he also plunged into the depths of the Quran's emotional currents, was at home with its reasoning and felt his way into its symbols explain why he earned the title of *Shaikh al-'Alam*.[51]

An important question which also needs some explanation is how Nuruddin's oral verses were transmitted. In fact such mass seem to have been transmitted and preserved first by the hundreds of his followers and then, by the pervasive didactic element characterizing most of his verses composed after the absorption of his Kashmiri identity into Islam. For fervent Muslims (theoretically every Muslim is a potential missionary), they were a vehicle for the propagation of Islamic values. It is significant that there are still some unlettered folk in the villages who remember by heart the verses of their Shaikh.

The verses of Nuruddin had an intrinsic attraction even to a non-zealot listener like the average Kashmiri peasant. Most of the verses of the Shaikh, depicting the miseries of the oppressed sections of society in simple terms, must have led to their preservation and dissemination among the common men. Significantly, our study of various manuscripts reveals that the versions are not so divergent as would lead us to doubt their authenticity. There is, undoubtedly, sufficient written information about these verses to enable the historian to estimate their value as historical evidence, which of course, is also corroborated by the oral traditions preserved in the collective consciousness of the common people. Nuruddin's verses are not simply anonymous oral traditions sharing the common characteristic of being transmitted spontaneously from one person to another; but rather they were transmitted from the residents of one locality to another. There is hardly a verse of Nuruddin which has not a social, cultural, and more importantly, topographical context.

Another point to be borne in mind is that his poetry belongs to a literature marked for its authoritative and creative tradition. It is indeed rooted in a homogenous body of common experience that cuts across academic compartments of knowledge. The sociological imagination not only makes it a plausible metaphorical account of social process but unites it with a larger historical reality which we may describe as rural consciousness. As we shall see in the next chapter, the relation between rural history and the Shaikh's verses is not only thematic or referential but also genetic and organic. The Shaikh's poetry, in the ultimate analysis, is social history as poetry.

In the transmission of the Shaikh's verses were involved not only the Rishis, but significantly, at a later stage, the theologians and *imams* of the mosques as well.[52] Interpolations were thus bound to occur in his popular verses. But we should not devalue the significance of such verses on that account. Interpolations, as a distinguished French anthropologist remarks, "always tend to provide some explanation of the phenomena described and amount to being an interpretation of the original tradition."[53] In other words, interpolation in the Shaikh's verses is itself a piece of documentary evidence about the historical development of Kashmiri society and culture. Every interpolation as such is an example of how a tradition was not only carried on but even made to serve the theological and polemical needs of a later generation. Of course, some of the Shaikh's verses seem to have been eroded as a result of interpolations and accretions *en route* but it is not difficult to separate such verses, considering that the method of expression is quite unlike that of the Shaikh and was only employed in later days. Clearly this kind of idiom was employed because some words had become unintelligible to the informants who recited the verses. With the spread of Islamic teachings, archaic words contained in Nuruddin's verses began to be replaced by Persian and Arabic words. This is not to suggest that these verses are necessarily different from the original compositions; on the contrary, the changes in the idiom merely suggest the growth of Kashmiri language into literature on reaching the age of awareness. As such, Kashmiri owes a great deal to Nuruddin since it was through his compositions that it articulated the expanding complex of impulses and responses, and orchestrated the music of consciousness. Kashmiri, in the ultimate analysis, is the verbal correlative of people's genius; it symbolises, to use the expression of Wittgenstein, a way of life.

It follows that Nuruddin's poetry expresses the cultural style of the Islamic civilization in a regional setting and the quality of human spirit that flourishes within it. Our study shows that it would be a grave error to disembody and to divorce language and religion from the historical context in which cultural forms make themselves manifest. It further attests to the indelible influence of language and religion upon the identity of cultural groups. So deep-rooted has been the impact of Nuruddin's mystical ideas on the formation of Kashmiri language that litterateurs of the contemporary social scene in Kashmir continue to resist attempts at obliterating their religious and cultural identity. The mundane situations and Islam thus seem to coalesce rather than conflict in the ongoing social drama in Kashmir.

REFERENCES AND NOTES

1. Baba Nasib, *Nurnama*, f. 205a.
2. The titles given to Sayyid 'Ali Hamadani and Shaikh Nuruddin by Kashmiris have profound meaning. The epithet, "Alamdar-i Kashmir", by which the latter is popularly known is significant for two reasons:

first, it elevates Nuruddin to the position of the upholder of the banner of Kashmiri identity. Second, it signifies that his role has been much more important in the religious and cultural history of Kashmiri rural masses than that of Sayyid 'Ali popularly known as "Shah-i Hamdan". The latter title suggests that Kashmiri Muslim masses never regarded the pious missionary from Hamadan as more than a venerated saint or a religious preacher who left Kashmir for good after securing a firm basis for further development of Islam in the Valley.

3. Evans Pritchard, "Social Anthropology: Past and Present", *Man*, 1950, Vol. 198, pp. 118-124.
4. Generally speaking, historians' approach to the source material, particularly the hagiographical literature, has remained far from objective. If on the one hand, they consider chronicles and hagiographies to be primary sources, on the other, the material contained in these works about miracles of the saints is treated with utter disdain by them. The manner in which historians generally reject legendary evidence is wholly unscientific and subjective. Applying modern standards purely within the bounds of their limited reason and failing to enter into the attitudes and minds of the medieval times empathically, modern historians abysmally ignore the social context of popular traditions within the purview of their rational analysis. The ineluctable conclusion to which they are driven is that material 'facts' alone are worthy of attention. However, the variety of facts available on such a sensitive theme as the history of Sufism demand not only rational analysis but, more importantly, the ability to understand the multiple dimensions of the strong Sufic traditions. In the present work, therefore, our aim is to study, more seriously, questions related to religion and society within a meaningful and creative relationship rather than in watertight compartments of faith and material fact.
5. Baba Nasib, *op. cit.*, f. 3a; Wahab, *Fathh-i Kubrawiyya*, f. 145a, Shahabadi, *Bagh-i Sulaiman*, f. 90b, Bahauddin Mattu, *Rishinama*, p. 73.
6. Bahauddin Mattu, *op. cit.*, p. 73.
7. Henry Corbin, *Creative Imagination in the Philosophy of Ibn Arabi*, p. 40.
8. *Kulliyat*, p. 21; also note on p. 148.
9. *Ibid.*, pp. 148-50, 152.
10. Nasib, *op. cit.*, ff. 9ab-10ab; Mishkati, *op. cit.*, ff. 70b-71a; Wahab, *op. cit.*, ff. 152ab; Shahabadi, *op. cit.*, ff. 91b-92ab.
11. Nasib, *op. cit.*, f 9b; Shahabadi, *op. cit.*, f. 92b; Khalil, *op. cit.*, p. 136.
12. *Kulliyat* II (1st. ed.), p. 62.
13. Nasib, *op. cit.*, ff. 11ab; Mishkati, *op. cit.*, f. 72b; Wahab, *op. cit.*, f. 152b; Shahabadi, *op. cit.*, ff. 92b-93a.
14. Some uncommon words which have crept into a few manuscripts owing to the carelessness of the scribes need careful examination. Parimoo (*Nand Rishi: Unity in Diversity*, p. 34) translates *ota* as 'reed'. However, the original word seems to have been *ouk* (one), since it is a rhyme for

mouk (other), but wrongly translated as shuttle by the learned scholar. In these verses the Shaikh actually refers to the one and not the tools of the weaver.

15. Nasib, *op. cit.*, ff. 11ab-12a; Wahab, *op. cit.*, ff. 152-153a.
16. Parimoo, *op. cit.*, p. 144.
17. It is situated at a distance of 48 kilometres to the south of Srinagar.
18. Translated from Parimoo's (*op. cit.*, pp. 53-4) transliteration. Compare *Kulliyat*, (2nd ed.), p. 167.
19. *Kulliyat*, (2nd. ed.), p. 144.
20. *Ibid.*, pp. 165–67.
21. *Ibid.*, II (1st ed.) pp. 26-28, 32-33.
22. *Ibid*, p. 132.
23. See Chatper II "The Historical Background of the Rishi Movement" n. 10.
24. *Kulliyat*, II, 1st ed. p. 26.
25. See Chapter II, "The Historical Background of the Rishi Movement", n. 10.
26. *Kulliyat*, II, 1st ed., p. 26.
27. *Ibid*, pp. 27, 31.
28. *Ibid*, p. 32.
29. From Baba Nasib's account it appears that Nuruddin had tasted meat before taking to asceticism. See Nasib, *op. cit.*, f. 50a.
30. Nuruddin and a good number of his followers lived on the wild *vopalhak* (*dispsacus inermis*) and other herbs of the forest.
31. *Kulliyat* I, pp. 50, 65. II, p. 153.
32. *Kangri* is a portable earthenware bowl, covered with a frame of wicker work. Kashmiris put hot embers into the bowl for keeping themselves warm during the winter. Usually the *kangri* is kept under a long, loose-wrapper (*pheran*) or a blanket. See for more details on *kangri*, Ishaq Khan, *Hitory of Srinagar. A Study in Socio-Cultural Change*, pp. 85-86.
33. *Kulliyat*, I, p. 26.
34. Translated from the Shaikh's verses reproduced by Ghulam Muhammad Ajir in his article, "Rishiyat ki Nafsiyati Tawil", *Rishiyat*, p. 116.
35. The Shaikh's tolerant attitude towards the Hindus is well known; but, under the influence of Lal Ded, he left no stone unturned in exposing the Brahmans. In this verse the Brahman is described as symbolising the insatiable hunger of the dog.
36. *Kulliyat*, II, p. 63.
37. *Bruj-i Nur*, p. 65.
38. J.C. Chatterji, *Kashmir Shaivism*, p. 43.
39. B. N. Parimoo, *The Ascent of the Self*, p. xix.
40. I have translated these verses from those reproduced in *Shams al-'Arifin*, p. 52.
41. *Kulliyat*, I, p. 74.

42. B. N. Pandit, *Aspects of Kashmir Saivism*, p. 36.
43. *Kulliyat*, I. p. 28.
44. Parimoo, *op. cit.*, p. 90.
45. *Kulliyat*, II, pp. 33-34.
46. Parimoo, *op. cit.*, p. 89.
47. *Kulliyat*, II, p. 79.
48. According to Saivite philosophy of Kashmir, God is formless, (*Nirguna*) as well as a qualified being (*Saguna*).
49. Translated from the verses as quoted in *Shams al-'Arifin*, pp. 67-68.
50. Wahab, *op. cit.*, f. 145a; *Sabur, Khawariq al-Salikin*, f. 30ab. Khalil, *op.cit.*, pp. 529-36.
51. The epithet first occurs in Baba Nasib, *op. cit.*, f. 88a.
52. It is important to remember that the Shaikh's poetry captivated both the Kubrawis and the Suharwardis. Hardly a century after the death of the Shaikh, the chronicler Sayyid Ali remarked about the popularity of his verses in glowing terms: "His absorbing verses have carved a place of their own in every heart." *Tarikh-i Kashmir*, f. 33b.
53. Jan Vansina, *Oral Tradition: A Study in Historical Methodology* (ts. from the French by H.M. Wright), p. 45.

CHAPTER V

Religious Thought of Shaikh Nuruddin

"Religious thought among the Indian Muslims never became a philosophy of religion," rightly observes Muhammad Mujeeb, "it was the search for the true spirit of the *Shari'ah*, and basically an intellectual and emotional vindication and affirmation of accepted belief."[1] Although the *'Ulama* had clearly defined functions and social roles as the literate guardians of the *Shari'a*, they were generally criticised in explicit terms by the Sufis for their inability to invigorate religious life by a harmonious coordination of belief and practice. True, the *'Ulama* had come to be accepted as descendants of the Prophet's family; but even having secured a dominant position for themselves with such descent as a banner of legitimacy, they could not come upto the expectations of the Sufis. For the *'Ulama* the *Shari'a* contained juridical and political obligations (*muamalat*) in addition to the duties to be performed by Muslims in relation to God and fellow beings. The Sufis, who did not disagree with the *'Ulama* on this account, nevertheless, stole a march over the latter as true exemplars of Islamic belief and conduct—and this they did by making personal fulfilment of religious duties the sole aim of their life. Religious thought of the Sufis and the *'Ulama* emanated from the same source; yet it was not the *'Ulama* but the Sufis who made their mark in history as the stable embodiments of the *Shari'a* in terms of their strict adherence to it in everyday life.

Nuruddin, like many Sufis of Islam was severe in his condemnation of the *'Ulama* of contemporary society; but this fact should not lead one to conclude that he was against the elaborate structure of consensus, custom and law that the distinguished *'Ulama* of the four schools of Islamic thought had constructed. There is no evidence to warrant the assertion that the *'Ulama*, mistakenly supposed to be the standard-bearers of "orthodoxy", were attacked by him on that ground. Significantly, they were made the butt of ridicule for their deviations from practising the true spirit of the *Shari'a* in daily life. It was, in fact, the *'Ulamas'* failure to bring exoteric (*zahir*) and esoteric (*batin*) aspects of religious life into a harmonious, balanced relationship that determined Nuruddin's attitude towards them. Their malicious mind,[2] arrogance,[3] hypocrisy[4] and pursuit of material gains[5] at the cost of spiritual benefits were so horrifying to him that he even urged his followers to seek the refuge of Allah at the mere sight of an *'alim.*[6] In his view there was no more horrifying and utterly convincing representation of deadly evil than the *'Ulama* with factious spirit emanating from their false learning and pride.[7] Addressing such *'Ulama* in the severest terms, Nuruddin warned that none of them would obtain salvation on the Day of Judgement.[8] The knowledge of such *'Ulama* was not based on the true spirit of the *Shari'a*;[9] in his view it amounted to nothing short of a religious catastrophe. Thus, while rebuking an *'alim* for his false pride in learning, Nuruddin remarked:

> The true spirit of *Al-Hamud,*[9a] *Qul-hu-Wa'allah*[9b] and *Attahiyat,*[9c]
> If practised in everyday life, is equivalent to learning the Quran;
> See, is not it futile to learn like the Satan;
> Who was doomed despite his learning.[10]

Given the ossification of the *'Ulama* at both the social and spiritual levels, the significance of Nuruddin's verses as an important vehicle in the spread of Islamic teachings can hardly be denied. He visited the greater part of the Kashmir Valley,[11] and that a number of villages still preserve the tradition of his visit or sojourn in one form or another testifies to his missionary role. It was, indeed, easier for the common man to understand the true spirit of the *Shari'a*—submission, dependence on God, obedience, contemplation, repentance, endeavour, dedication, altriusm and a fulfilment of the duties of fellowship—through Nuruddin's popular verses than through the scholarly works of the Sufi missionaries.[12] It seems that the poverty and humility of Nuruddin and a number of the adherents of his order and, by all accounts, their very presence had a magnetic influence,[13] which was far more important than the mere knowledge of the *'Ulama* or even the learned Sufis. The mission of Nuruddin was essentially to make Islam comprehensible to the non-literate, who were mostly agriculturists. Consequently, Kashmiri peasant society, though already drawn within the orbit of Islamic civilization, linked itself with the high culture of Islam through Nuruddin's teachings, who undoubtedly established channels of communication between the two traditions and set up standards of mutual reference and influence.

What radically distinguishes Nuruddin from his contemporary Sufis was his ability to reason out things with his fellowmen in a courageous and straightforward manner. What he felt intuitively was made public through intelligent expression in an arguable form. True, at the earlier stage of his mystical career he encouraged pietistic quietism, mystic contemplation and ecstasy for the return to God, but on returning from the repose of unitive experience he entered the sweep of history with a view to controlling its forces. Following the Prophetic tradition, he returned to the world from the cave with renewed vigour and faith:

> Thou hast caused me to move in the right direction,
> In the jungle did I seek Thy shelter.
> I shall bow before Thee five times a day;
> I do gratefully remember how kind Thou art.[14]

Unlike the Hindu ascetics, Nuruddin did not ignore society altogether. The former, while seeking union with God, placed themselves outside the historical process, which rests upon social cooperation and mutual understanding between men. Even after their return from periods of withdrawal and contemplation the Hindu mystics remained highly individualistic in their approach to religion.[15] And while leading secluded lives they seldom felt the need to direct or guide the society of which they were a part. Nuruddin, on the other hand, made his intuitive faculty serve contemporary society by the argument of word and deed. In his verses there is an element of a dynamic inner worldly asceticism seeking to achieve mastery not only over his individual self but also over the world around him:

> O Supreme God, Thou art to be held in highest esteem.
> Since it was in seeking Thou that I was freed from the delusion of self.
> Be kind enough to make me a powerful instrument of Thy innate devotion;
> I do gratefully remember how kind Thou art.[16]

The verses of Nuruddin give evidence of his belief in both the transcendence and the immanence of God. Here it is necessary to remember that although he looks on the divine reality beyond concept and image, nonetheless he expresses himself in the language of love not unlike those of Sufi masters like Mansur al-Hallaj and Jalauddin Rumi. Significantly, he invariably uses the local term *Bhugi,*[17] the derivative of Bhagwan, for Allah. In so doing, he attempts to make the Quran accessible to the commoners in their own medium. However, for understanding the message of the Quran he urges men to create a desire in their heart and mind. In his opinion the divine reality is, first of all, the limitless object of desire:

> The Prophet's longing (for Thee) was satiated.
> When Thou vouchsafed Quran unto him.
> Lord: the one (the Prophet) who remained steadfast in Thy way.
> I do gratefully remember how kind Thou art.[18]

Again:

> Who will kindle in this life;
> The lamp of knowledge and religion;
> Who will renounce fraud and adopt true knowledge;
> The essence of all knowledge is *alif, lam* and *mim.*[19]

The particular letters, *alif, lam* and *mim* are prefixed to the six chapters (*suras*) of the Quran.[20] A great deal has been written about these, but most writers recognise them as mystic symbols. While for some each letter represents an attribute of God, the most popular interpretation is that "these letters are the initial, the final and the middle (or again the initial) letter of three names: Allah, Jibril and Muhammad—the source of revelation, the heavenly messenger who brought it and the human messenger through whom it was translated into speech."[21]

Nuruddin thus attempted to bring home the principle of close correspondence between the esoteric and exoteric elements of religious life. In his view the surest means of approach to Allah is the recitation of the Quran which unites the created with the Creator.[22] This unity has to be understood in both emotional and intellectual terms. In fact, in his thought a certain equilibrium of the emotional and intellectual attitudes is noticeable. For Nuruddin, love is born spontaneously when the divine reality is felt or contemplated while reading the Quran. In a true Quranic spirit he considers the thoughtless reading of the Holy Book to be an exercise in futility. Although he regards inculcation of divine love in the heart as a key to the understanding of the Quran, it also involves in his view a metaphysical view of things, the Quranic *taffakur,*[23] a relationship in which the divine presence manifests itself as grace to the individual.

While reciting (the Quran) I proclaimed His Majesty.
In contemplating Him I became speechless.
In the depths of my heart and mind.
Was revealed the meaning of His Presence.[24]

Contemplation on the verses of the Quran is the recurring theme in Nuruddin's message to his followers;[24a] it takes unquestioned precedence over all forms of spiritual life, particularly emotional love. Doubtless the heart will become illuminated, love will become perfect, and actions will become purposeful only through the radiance of knowledge gained in contemplation.[25] Love and the actions of the adherents of his order were thus an integral part of their Shaikh's knowledge of Quranic universalism. As we shall see later, love and social actions of the Rishis actually sprang from their identification of knowledge with its object, the divine reality.

Although Nuruddin loved Allah to the point of annihilating himself, his longing, unlike Hallaj, did not put him into a hypnotic trance. In these verses he speaks of seeking to be drowned in the verses of the Quran in the true manner of Hallaj:

The reading of the Quran should have broken the fleshly talisman of your life.
In reading the Quran Mansur annihilated himself,
Of what avail is your purposeless existence even after reading the Quran[26]?

It should not be supposed that Nuruddin demanded of a Muslim the denial of Mansur al-Hallaj,[27] but an alert, rationally controlled patterning of life according to the *Shari'a*. Not unlike some great Sufis of Islam he offered a fascinating explanation of *ana al-Haqq*. Significantly, he seems to have understood Mansur from the standpoint of the *Wahdat al-Shuhud*.[28] In his perception of the death of Mansur we see a sublime example of Allah's transcendence. For him Mansur was a true lover of Allah; the one who had understood fully the inner meaning of the Quran. Not only did Mansur, in his view, follow the letter and spirit of the Quran, but he even sacrificed his life in proclaiming the truth of the Quran. True, he did not approve of the way in which Mansur revealed the inner secret, but even then not unlike Shibli[28a] he calimed to be a follower of Mansur's line:

Who has separated me from Mansur?
He and myself pursued the same goal;

He slipped in saying "I"
But blessed was he when "I" became grace.[29]

Dwelling upon the theme of *ana al-Haqq*, Jalaluddin Rumi had almost offered a similar explanation:

"To say "I" in due time is Divine grace;
To say "I" in undue time is a curse.
The "I" of Mansur became grace;
That of Pharaoh became a curse."[30]

That Nuruddin ranks among one of the few leading Sufis of Islam in understanding the mystic ideas of Hallaj is shown by the fact that, not unlike 'Abdul Qadir Gilani (d. 1166), he believed that it was the intoxication of Mansur's heart, *ana al-Haqq* and the way he revealed the great mysteries of divine love and union, that brought him death.[31]

Mansur revealed the inner secret,
He should not have made it public,
He ought to have borne the brunt of love,
Despite the pangs of his soul.[32]

Again:

When the Beloved manifested Himself,
Unto Mansur was His vision vouchsafed,
For He made him drunk with His love,
Lo : His death was a price for His yearning.[33]

In touching upon the theme of *ana al-Haqq* Nuruddin seems to have been concerned over maintaining a balance between the *Shari'a* and *tariqa*,[34] the interrelated truths deep-rooted in the very structure of the Quran itself. For him *tariqa* was the path and the *Shari'a* the guide;[35] the latter was also a warning against the pitfalls in the path. Mansur followed both, but while in union with the ultimate reality, he lost himself in the ocean of His love and grace;[36] instead of living in it he perferred to die rather than live in His presence. So overcome was Mansur with the experience of living in His Presence that he could not but openly proclaim the hidden truth of God's mercy bestowed on him. Nuruddin's message to the devotees, therefore, was only to feel comfort in Allah's presence without effacing the human identity.[37] The meaning of the unity of inner experience was to be felt and understood in consonance with the *Shari'a*.[38] A seeker after the Truth was not merely a lover but also a man of conspicuous social activity. To live within the grace of the Infinite was, in his view, bound to create in a seeker an intuitive and spiritual awareness of the Reality.[39] That this awareness of the Reality grew in proportion to the spiritual growth and receptivity of a seeker is abundantly expounded by Nuruddin in his verses.

No less noteworthy are Nuruddin's wisdom as a spiritual guide, his emotional balance, and sensitivity as seen in his verses. In most of his verses he emphasises a virtual distinction of 'knower' from 'known.'[39a] That he assigns each thing its proper measure is particularly brought out in the following verses,[40] in which his journey of the soul to God culminates in the experience of *tauhid*:

I owned the *Kalima*
"There is no deity but Allah"[41]
And consumed myself in the fire that it generates;
Realising the mirage of existential unity,
I found the Eternal.[42]
So I transcended space.[43]

The Shaikh, indeed is not satisfied with the mere recitation of the *kalima* for the profession of faith in Islam. According to him, its real force lies in the conscious acceptance of *tauhid* and its stipulations and complete conformity to it in practical life:

The meaning of *kalima* is the source of all knowledge;
The good actions spring from self-restraint (in accordance with its spirit).
The source of void[44] is known to Him alone;
His Infiniteness knows no bounds.[45]

The real meaning of *tauhid* becomes clear when a man fully realizes that in the whole of universe there is absolutely no being worthy of adoration beside Allah. Emphasizing the importance of the sincere act of professing faith in His oneness for a meaningful and purposeful existence, the Shaikh also frequently has recourse to the concept of *pun* and *pap*[45a] for the dissemination of Islam among the common folk:

And when the Lord will ignite the fire of Hell;
On that day will be weighed (your) virtuous acts (*pun*)
But if you finally grasp the meaning of *kalima*.
So will you attain salvation here and the Hereafter.[45b]

The Shaikh also impressed upon the people that the more they learnt about the deeper content of the *kalima*, the more they would become conscious of the sin of worshipping a multiplicity of deities. It was in this context that while criticising the animistic beliefs of his compatriots, even though undergoing the process of Islamic acculturation, the Shaikh remarked:

> O Pandit, the brother : O Pandits :
> How long will you remain wedded to the worship of stones and springs?[46]
> Your thoughtless search did not bear any fruit;
> Submit yourselves to the Lord and His messenger;
> Aren't you solicitous of (spiritual and worldly) success?[47]

The recital of the *kalima* also demands firm faith in the finality of the Prophethood of Muhammad. In the Shaikh's view the message of Muhammad was not meant for any particular people, place or period. His message was universal in that he completed the mission of the prophets sent before for the guidance of mankind. In most of his verses, he respects the "orthodox" argument that Muhammad was "a blessing for all (the people) of the world"[48] by virtue of his humane approach to the mundane issues of a universal nature.[48a] Following in the footsteps of Muhammad was, therefore, in his view an easy way of reaching the truth.[49]

According to the Quran the Prophet was possessed not only of the *kitab*, the written 'book, but also of the *hikma*, the 'wisdom'[50] by which ultimate principles can be applied to the details and episodes of ordinary life. Consequently, both the sayings (*hadith*) and actions (*Sunna*) of the Prophet, which were in strict conformity with divine revelations, constituted the *Shari'a*. Far from being a formal code, the *Shari'a* was a synonym for obligations of the human being towards the Creator and His creatures. Nuruddin, therefore, urged men to act within the scope of what he called *Shar'a-i Muhammad*.[51]

> "Little will he weary who does pious deeds,
> Observing the religious law at each step;
> Humble he remains despite his substance;
> And sits very low on the wheel of life."[52]

In an attempt to make the *Shari'a*-structured social relationship intelligible to the unlettered folk, Nuruddin integrated the early success of Islam with the unbounded faith and undaunted spirit of the four illustrious companions of the Prophet. For him they were not merely sublime examples of living faith, but in his verses, they are presented as truly dynamic individuals. Each of them evokes the praise of Nuruddin for his human qualities: Abu Bakr for his lovable nature and friendship, Uthman who while compiling the Quran enabled men to distinguish between right and wrong (*furqan*), Umar for his courageous spirit in subduing the snares of the ego and Ali for his generosity and compassion in treating the hungry as his guests.[53]

Little wonder, therefore, that the Shaikh repeatedly exhorts men to cultivate the virtues of the four companions of the Prophet.[53a] At one place he even yearns to pass over the bridge across the infernal fire (*pul-i sirat*)[53b] with the four pious Caliphs. Elsewhere they are extolled in these terms:

> Salute to the four companions;
> Who bowed before Thee;
> They are the mainstay of the four worlds
> I do gratefully remember how kind Thou art.[53c]

The four worlds (*Chour Alam*) referred to in the verse are *nasut, malakut, jabarut* and *lahut*. The first is the world of humanity, perceived through the physical senses. This is the mundane or phenomenal world, described by Ghazzali as *'Alam al-mulk-wa-shahada.* Even within the sphere of his existence (*nasut*) a human being is capable of rising to the heights of angels not only through spiritual faculties, but also through the development of such ethical qualities in his personality as are called angelic, in common parlance. *Malakut* does not merely signify the invisible spiritual or angelic world, as commonly understood, but a human ability to perceive through action and insight what is beyond the reach of average men engrossed in mundane affairs. The third gradation of existence is that in which a human being is further capable of perceiving the Majesty of Allah through contemplating His Names and Attributes. This sphere is, indeed, 'the world of power' or 'the celestial world' in which a Sufi feels comfort in living under the pervasive influence of the power of the Almighty. But the last sphere of existence, "the world of the Godhead", is beyond perception. It is the indescribable world of unity, though erroneously defined as a stage in which human identity absorbs in 'timeless unicity'. The fact, however, is that human nature (*nasut*) is not identical or interchangeable with the divine (*lahut*). The only union that one can think of between the Creator and the created can be best described within the framework of the *Shari'a*; and in this sense *nasut, malakut, jabarut* and *lahut* merely represent the mystic idea of four spheres of existence (*maratib-i wujud*) rather than any definite stages in Sufism.[53d] Even the great Sufis of Islam who had reached the understanding of *lahut* never claimed divinity for themselves. And although Allah vouchsafed them merely a slight understanding of the *'Alam al-Ghaib*, the (uncreated) world of the mystery, they continued to derive greatest solace in remaining His humble servants (*'ubud*). Nuruddin who had fully realised this mystic truth (*Haqiqa*) within the ambit of the *Tauhid-Shari'a* structured relationship therefore repeatedly refers to the way and the practice of the four companions. The purpose was to re-affirm the mystic truth that Allah's commands to servants were never annulled; in reality, the words: "And serve thy Lord till the inevitable (i.e., death) come unto thee"[53e] point to the same fact. Thus it is not difficult to understand the sense in which Nuruddin described the pious Caliphs not only as the living embodiments of the *Shari'a*, but, also, as the earliest followers in the *tariqa* of Muhammad who bridged the four spheres of existence.

It follows that the mission of Nuruddin was to preserve both the spiritual and social sense of the divine revelation. Like Sufis of the main orders he was concerned with the equation *tauhid-Shari'a-haqiqa* but he distinguished himself among his contemporaries and the succeeding generations both as a mystic and a social being. His role was undoubtedly marked off from most Sufis by his social concerns, over and above his spiritual pre-occupations. In fact, his whole concept of man's social role is based on the *Shari'a*; for him it exists to regulate mankind and enjoins obedience to what is ordained. Man can unite himself with Allah by serving His creatures; the *Shari'a* exists for the service of mankind. It is the firm belief of the Shaikh that unerring faith in and strict adherence to the *Shari'a* alone can lead to the experience of the truth (*Haqiqa*) and that all the three constitute the world's foundation and its subsistence. Even in being profoundly conscious of the nothingness of human existence he urges the human being to eliminate the element of non-being by consecrating himself to His cause. Thus union with Allah is possible along the lines of Islamic insight:

> You will reach the *'arsh*[54] by the load of your (nobler) actions.[55]
> So shall the grace of the Omnipotent[56] embrace you.[57]

From an examination of the Shaikh's innumerable verses, it is crystal clear that he was the greatest Kashmiri exponent of Allah's Oneness. Whenever he talks of *tauhid* his frame of reference is the Quran. Conscious of the futility of speculations about this essential question, he repeatedly emphasizes the significance of ritual prayer, an obligatory act, through which an earnest seeker after the truth finds his desire transformed into conformity with the will of Allah. The more man contemplates Him, the more he is able to learn about the virtues of obsequiousness to the Lord. And during the hours of seclusion, instead of losing one's self in the ocean of Allah, a seeker becomes aware of the true nature of his relations with Him. But even in moments of mystic ecstasy the Shaikh stresses both the spiritual and social sense of the praise (*alhamud*) to Allah and the greetings (*attahiyat*) to Him, the Prophet and His righteous servants, recited during the course of ritual prayers. Such a seeker, in his estimation, not unlike the teachings of the Naqshbandis, returns to the world a changed person with a mission to ameliorate it according to Allah's will.

> He will reach the goal;[58]
> Who has committed to heart,
> *Alhamud, Qulhu-Allah, Attahiyat*
> Realise Your essence, my soul.[59]

The concept of *tauhid* thus not only affirms that Allah created man in the best of forms for obeying His commands, but it also lays upon him certain obligations. *Tauhid*, in fact, encompasses the whole universe. As Ismail Raji al-Faruqi observes, "All mankind is object of man's moral action, all earth and sky are his theater, his material. He is responsible for all that takes place in the universe, in every one of its remotest corners. For man's *taklif* or obligation is universal, cosmic. It comes to an end only on the Day of Judgement."[60]

There is ample evidence to show that Nuruddin's thoughts throbbed with *tauhidic* humanism and universalism. This is illustrated not only by the fact that in his verses the content of the Quran is couched in metaphors drawn from the social environment, but also by the imagery of flowers and foliage,[61] of mountains and landscape,[62] of birds[62a] and animals,[62b] of fish[63] and fowl,[64] of seasons and weather,[65] of rivers and springs.[66] In fact, he regarded the act of observing natural phenomena as essential for understanding the purpose of creation. Though constituted of matter, nature was neither evil nor hostile to man or God. In a way he considered the natural and the material to be divinely constituted, because they are God's creation.[67] But it may be pointed out that for him nature was only worthy of contemplation rather than adoration. This view was intrinsically based on the Quran which enjoins men to make full use of their senses and utilise the energies latent in nature for their benefit. The Quran directs men to awaken their dormant faculties by observation of the natural phenomena, for they are signs or "portents" of God.[68]

For Nuruddin, therefore, each and every detail of the world was suffused with meaning, having what Cassirer refers to as "symbolic pregnance."[69] He saw the world as a text, a system of symbols for ever unfolding. The exegesis of this text was itself a mode of worship. But profound meditation on the nature of reality (metaphysics and cosmology) in the context of Quranic exhortations was also a mode of intellectual knowledge or gnosis (*ma 'arifah*) for him; it was a special mode of access to ontological truth and in particular a "taste" of Unity. This kind of knowledge enabled him to reach the transcendent which is beyond discursive reason (*'aql*). In agreement with the Quranic concept of personal integration and harmony between the individual and the cosmos he was able to give a lucid explanation of the Quranic verses and their implications for life (ethics in the broadest sense). Thus while exhorting his followers to devote themselves to understanding the meaning of *Surat al-Ikhlas*, he actually directed them to mould the quality of personal life in accordance with the letter and spirit of the Quran. In the language of religious ethics as developed by him, *Ikhlas* did not merely mean an effort on the part of the believer to come nearer to God through its mere recitation in every prayer (*namaz*), but a sustained effort at keeping the ideal of serving God's creatures above all other thoughts. *Ikhlas* demanded selflessness with regard to both word and deed. The culmination of one's *Ikhlas* was the disappearance of the thought of divine reward in this or the next world.[70]

Nuruddin's teachings are, undoubtedly, grounded in the Quranic ethics of humanism and reciprocal love. The ethics of non-violence that he advocates is of an activistic and positive nature; it aims at rendering positive good to human beings in the hour of their adversity. Unlike the Hindu ascetics, he did not merely associate the norm of non-violence with ascetic self-denial. Influenced as he was by the virtue of moderation as extolled in the Quran, he did not carry his asceticism to the extent to which we find it in Jainism, Buddhism and Hinduism. True, in his emphasis on non-injury to all living creatures his ideas bear close resemblance to Hindu and Buddhist ascetic philosophy. But it would be pertinent to point out that although the ethic of universal love is ordained in the Quran, it could not develop into the ethic of non-killing and non-injury to all living creatures. The fact is that the ethical system of Islam remained mostly oriented towards the non-cosmic love of nature and the anthropocentric ethics both at the political and sociological levels, as a result of theological emphasis on theocentric ethnocentrism. In Nuruddin's thought, however, it was the cosmic love of nature which constituted the pivotal point, crucial to the understanding of the ethics of Quranic universalism. It was also in this context that he attempted to explain during his conversations with peasant girls the importance of thoughtful living. In taunting the girls for cutting the green grass as fodder for their cows, Nuruddin did not express his disapproval of the act, but actually wanted to explain to his would-be disciples the social injustice in allegorical terms:

> "Life it has, so why should it be cut
> Never shouldst thou feed life on life;
> However, who can undo the writ of Fate?
> All that I wanted to find was the pious motive."[71]

One of the girls was quick to reply that the cow fulfilled the needs of human beings. She said:

> "May be milk and ghee will cool someone's fire father;
> So did I come with a sickle in my waist"[72]

Nuruddin was so pleased with the Hindu girl's reply that he called her a hidden jewel (*ratna mani*).[73] He also admitted her among his disciples, at her own request.[74]

Evidently, love for Nuruddin did not merely signify a mystical union with God, but an active and sympathetic attitude towards all living creatures. True, he was no exception to some form of religious ethnocentrism, but, in his view, this particularism did not sanction discrimination, considering the Quranic emphasis on Islam as a religion of love. His faith in the acceptance of equality of all creatures in the kingdom of God[75] is actually an attempt at expounding the Islamic ethics as contained in the Quran.[76] Taking into consideration his emphasis— in the context of Quran—on help to the poor and the needy, mercy and kindness towards all[77] and condemnation of lust (*lobh*),[78] pride (*ahankar*)[79] and anger (*krodh*),[80] it can be safely said that the value system of non-violence as contained in Nuruddin's thought illustrates not only his adherence to the Quranic emphasis on mercy, but it also shows the richness and positive commitment of the Rishis to the traditions of non-violence.

The characteristics laid down for a true believer of God have been described at length by Nuruddin, the chief among the virtues being righteousness and love in dealings with fellow beings.

According to him, the hallmarks of a true Muslim are virtues such as forgiveness, kindness, tolerance, mercy, generosity, compassion, patience, humility[81] and above all, the earnest desire to earn an honest living.[82] He condemns such negative norms of behaviour as anger, jealousy, intolerance, and vindictiveness.[83] Although the retributive form of justice is sanctioned in the Quran, Nuruddin does not advocate it. On the contrary, he lays stress on the wider Quranic context which enjoins the Muslim to give up the right of retribution for such an act raises his status both in the eyes of God and man.[84] That he gives mercy and kindness the place of supremacy in the ethical system of the Quran can hardly be overstressed.[85]

It would thus be seen that Nuruddin disliked tyranny and violence to fellow human beings for one's own gain. True, he regarded the gap between the rich and the poor as ordained in the existing social system,[86] but it will not be too much to say that in Nuruddin's thought the concept of justice is treated as the *sine qua non* of a stable social order. For him kindness is a form of non-violence at the personal level of which justice is the expression at the social level.[87] Thus, in contrast to the ascetic value-orientation of the Hindu tradition, Nuruddin gave a humanistic and life-affirming content to the concept of non-violence. The long poem in which he extols the virtues of a true Muslim reflects his sincere desire to mediate Islam to the common folk through the agency of their own medium. In order to understand fully how Nuruddin made this mediating capacity manifest among the unlettered, it would not be out of place of reproduce a few extracts from his poem:

> One who does not neglect one's daily duties,
> Who longs to live by the sweat of one's brow,
> Who controls the bestial anger of one's mind,
> Who shows fortitude in provocation,
> May truly be called a Muslim.[88]

> He will be among the people of paradise
> Who shares meals with the hungry,
> (who) is obsessed with the idea of removing hunger,
> Who humbly bows (in prayers) in all sincerity,
> Who scorns anger, greed, illusion, arrogance and self-conceit,
> May truly be called a Muslim.[89]

> One who beautifully expounds (the truth) for others,
> Who makes his inner soul affirm the truth,
> Who does not covet another's property,
> Whose soul does not run amuck at the mere sight of wealth,
> Follows the right path steadfastly in accordance with the *Sharia*,
> May truly be called a Muslim.[90]

Travelling around to learn from experience,
Consecrating life to the search for Truth,
Tightens the belly to learn (the virtues of) patience,
Gives up his ego;
Contemplates Him in seclusion,
May truly be called a Muslim.[91]

We shall now turn to Nuruddin's evaluation of the social and economic institutions of his time against the background of the Quranic injunctions.

The most important issue that troubled Nuruddin was the institution of priesthood that created a division between the Brahman clergy and the laity mainly on the basis of caste. The doctrine of caste struck at the root of human equality and was responsible for various tyrannies. But Nuruddin made a clean sweep of such a doctrine and threw open the door to spiritual opportunity for one and all by expounding the Quranic concept of the dignity of man in a number of verses. Man's pedigree was not to be esteemed since it generated pride not worthy of a true servant of God. Nobility of birth did not guarantee nobility of mind; on the contrary, it goaded the wretched and even fools to covet honour[92] not by their own virtue but only because of the merits of their ancestors. Nuruddin's contribution to the evolution of the concept of the dignity of man in a caste-ridden society can be better appreciated against the Quranic verses proclaiming all men descended from one and the same pair.[93]

It is of no consequence of what parents a man is born since the origin of all mankind is the same. Here man is asked to be ambitious of true honour and of the real glory and perfection of his common origin:

Adam is the progenitor of the human race,
The Mother Eve has the same primordiality,
(So) from where have the 'low-castes' descended?
How can a 'high born' deride his own ancestry?[94]

The contempt in which the common man was held by the Brahmans must have touched the sensitive soul of Nuruddin. In order to tame the ferocity of their pride he challenged the concept of purity of the Brahman's birth in terms of the *tauhidic* humanism and universalism. It was a Muslim's commitment to an ethic of action which was valued by Nuruddin *vis-a-vis* the unethical egocentrism of the Brahman:

One who harps proudly upon one's caste,
Is bereft of reason and wisdom,
Here the good alone can claim noble descent;
In the Hereafter 'caste' will be extinct,
Were you to imbibe the essence of Islam,
Then no one would be purer than you.[95]

Furthermore, 'excellence in the deed' (*falah*), or 'felicity through works', in terms of which the Quran describes the purpose of creation as a whole, finds a powerful echo in the following verses of Nuruddin:

The distinguished ancestry will not ennoble and unite (people);[96]
The nobility of birth is not decreed.
(Beware), lest the thought of noble ancestry should stupefy you;
Conform to righteousness; nay, noble descent is a sham.[97]

The call and mission of Nuruddin was thus addressed to reason, seeking to convince people of the primacy of action over birth and his message was by no means beyond the comprehension of even the unlettered masses. Even his concept of death was born out of the ethical teachings of the Quran. His verses concerning the end of human life should not be described as an emotional expression of the fear of death; rather, they seem to have functioned as an effective medium of satire and social commentary on inequality, injustice and repression in the masterly use of metaphor and allegory. Some of these verses are worth quoting:

"[By] displaying the caste in the world,
What will thou gain?
Into dust will turn the bones,
When the earth envelopes the body:
To utter disgrace will he come
Who, forgetting himself, jeers at others."[98]

From the viewpoint of social history, Nuruddin's description of the social inequalities[99] existing in the contemporary society is important. Apart from the caste system, his criticism of the rich is also rooted in the social ethics of the Quran.[100] Not only do his verses graphically depict the hoarding of grain in the rich families[101] but in these is also reflected the plight of small children in a permanent state of hunger.[102] He regarded hunger as the most degrading of adversities.[103] According to him true blessedness consists in satisfying the subsistence needs of the poor.[104] The exploitation and sufferings of the weak at the hands of the strong is evidenced by his verses.[105] He refers to rich men who owned big houses[106] jewels, horses and elephants.[107] While they enjoyed musical concerts in their homes, the Shaikh, however, is pained to note that some poor persons were condemned to be cruelly treated at their gates.[108]

Nuruddin's criticism of the entertainments enjoyed by the rich sprang from his concern over their negligence of social responsibilities. The Quran which values the personal character of responsibility nevertheless emphasizes the social implications of moral actions for the future of mankind.[109] Viewed from the standpoint of the Quran, Nuruddin's disapproval of the amusements of the rich was not wholly unjustified, for these actually dissipated every serious thought from their minds.

> One amuses oneself by organising a musical concert,
> Although aware, yet pretends innocence (about human sufferings),
> (While) the other is being scourged,
> (Has) God Himself willed it so?[110]

It follows that in the Shaikh's view the rich who lived only to entertain themselves could seldom show sympathy to man in distress. He did not even approve of musical concerts organized by the rich in honour of a saint.[111] He was very critical of such *darwishes* as asserted the prerogative of virtue on such occasions.

It is then evident that Nuruddin was greatly moved by the abject poverty of his countrymen. Remarkably, however, he did not regard poverty as an absolute category, but rather as a stage in man's spiritual and social development. It was in essence a state of life in the transitory world for the cultivation of virtues of contentment, patience, fortitude, prudence and resignation.[112]

Undoubtedly, he made a clear distinction between pauperism and poverty; the former was despicable since it made people dependent on others for their existence, and not on their own exertions.[113] Not unlike Dryden, he thought that "the daring of the soul" proceeded from such virtues of poverty as are least understood. In fact, poverty was esteemed by Nuruddin not only by virtue of its being the pride of the prophets,[114] but also because of its being a spur rather than a clog. It was disgraceful only when it stifled the noblest thoughts in a poor man. It would not be unrealistic to assume that Nuruddin's aim in painting social exploitation was to make the rich feel ashamed of their conduct in acquiring wealth by unlawful means.[115]

Although there is no evidence to suggest that Nuruddin wanted the poor to rise against the rich, his exaltation of the poor man's pride points to social tensions affecting even a mystic' life. He was mindful of the indignities to which human beings were subjected on account of their wretched conditions; he attempted to change their despair into resolution. Doubtless in the given social system the best way for a mystic was to make poverty look respectable, compared with the miseries that awaited the covetous rich, not only in the Hereafter but even in this world.

But it would be wrong to infer from the foregoing account that Nuruddin taught the poor and the discontented to remain satisfied with their lot. In fact, he desired them to live honourably, virtuously and above all spiritually in the depths of the poverty of the prophets:

> Poverty is a shield against Hell,
> Poverty is the virtue of Prophets,
> Poverty is the wealth of this and the next world,
> Poverty is sweet and fragrant,
> One who is steadfast in the path of poverty,
> So will be honoured here and the Hereafter.[116]

The inference is that Nuruddin did not like the life of pomp and show and, therefore, urged his followers to live in an entire abnegation of all worldly enjoyments. He taught his disciples with a wealthy background that *faqr* or self-imposed poverty was endurance in the world of want and distress.

> He will feel his inner self awakened,
> Who will curb anger, spite and enmity,
> He will be honoured among men,
> Who will imbibe the Prophet's simplicity.[117]

Little wonder that among the Rishis, *jihad* against the baser self of man became internalised, the function of a supreme effort, apparently having no relation to this world, but directed intrinsically to the world to come. Life for Nuruddin was not a sport; it was a thoughtful and purposeful living in the true manner of the prophets. It was movement, activity, striving and struggling against the odds of a probationary period. Spiritual virtue was thus necessarily a social virtue in a direct sense. And, indeed, by wearing poor and tattered garments,[118] he did not show contempt for the world, but rather affirmed his inner attitude towards the wants of the needy. His humility lay not in his extinction of the self but more importantly in the vindication of glory which lies in the hard labour of the toiling masses.[119] It is not therefore difficult to understand why among the Muslim Rishis the importance attached to manual labour was unparalleled[120] while to the Hindu ascetics it was taboo. While for the former asceticism was only a means to an end, for the latter it was the end itself.

Nuruddin's verses in praise of manual labour should be studied against the Brahmanic tradition which looked down on all forms of manual work as servile, in contrast to purely intellectual activities.[121] It would not be an exaggeration to say that the diffusion of the basic Islamic precepts about the dignity of labour among Kashmiri artisans was the product of his teachings. In some of his verses these precepts are reinforced by parallels and metaphors drawn between them and the implements of the potter.[122] For him, labour had its place in the world. He insisted on the proper carrying out of one's occupation. He himself continued in his work.[123] His example to his followers, therefore, was clear: work has a positive value in maintaining a reasonable material condition of the believer. However, he considered labour to be worthless if it was performed in society chiefly to sustain physical existence. Subsistence and physical well-being have their importance; in one sense he regarded them as the necessary goals of human effort, since without them the purpose of creation would be defeated. Yet, even though necessary, they are still the least of man's goals. Thus he made a clear distinction between the struggle for existence of both man and animal. Man's distinctive dignity lies in his capacity to think for his own good and that of mankind.[124]

It is significant to note that Nuruddin linked the dignity of manual labour with the holiness of learning. He held that manual labour of the agriculturists was man's divinely appointed task in this world and, in his verses, emphasized the importance of cultivation of both the soil and the mind. As to the more specific question about the spiritual value of working the land, he admired the idyllic quality of rural life as against the corruption and artificiality of urban civilization. In his popular poem *Gongalnama*[125] he comes near to describing the toilers of the soil as "the chosen people of God" since in his view their activities are not only necessary for a sound social order but also contain certain spiritual truths for the thoughtful. The cardinal point emerging in his exhortations to the peasant is that his life symbolises the only honest way, wherein he reaps the fruit of the seed sown in the ground from God as a reward for his virtuous industry. Vice can hardly find time to contaminate the innocent life of the peasant since the virtues of honesty, fear of God, humility, patience, industriousness and self-reliance cultivated in his mind through the labour of love and hope bring God perpetually before his view, thereby invigorating his mind and heart with the most exalted notions of supreme power, and the most endearing view of the divine benignity.

There can be no gainsaying the fact that the rudiments of Muslim rituals were learnt by the unlettered folk through the mystical verses contained in *Gongalnama.* In the following verses images taken from the peasants' life are described in such a manner that various aspects of their work while tilling the soil are elevated to symbols of spiritual activities:

> "The plough share is thy bath and ablutions;
> perform them well:
> The yoke is thy conscience: abandon the thoughts of family or tribe;
> Tilling the land is reading the Quran: read it correctly;
> One who celebrates the Gongal, will surely celebrate the krav."[126]

The different evaluations placed on pride and humility in the Quran are many. Prayer (*salat*) at appointed times is emphasized not only in terms of its ritual character, but more importantly, for its ethical value. Man's social activity often brings him into conflict with members of the society of which he is a part. There is hardly a human being whose ego is not touched by some offence. Quite often, the hurt ego finds expression in such negative forms of social behaviour as anger, revenge, rancour, pride and conflict. Man is thus prone to sink to the lowest depths of pride, arrogance and greed. It is for curbing these feelings in human beings apart from other reasons that prostration before God was made obligatory at least five times a day in the Quran. Thus while addressing the village folk, Nuruddin reiterates the ethical importance of *salat* and other rituals in the following verses:

> "In all humility bend thou in prayers;
> Weed out the field (mind) and throw them away,
> Do perform well: *Roza, Namaz, Haj* and *Zakath*
> One who celebrates the Gongal will surely celebrate the krav."[127]

And while emphasizing the importance of fasting (*saum*) for inculcating the virtues of tolerance and resignation, Nuruddin remarks:

> "Yoke to the plough the bullock of thy ego;
> Goad him on with the birch of fasting;
> Thus will he start tugging at the plough;
> One who celebrates the Gongal, will surely celebrate the krav."[128]

It is important to note here that a link between the practices of Sufis and the common folk was supplied by Nuruddin's verses. Significantly, he even employed indigenous themes and imagery for the popularisation of such highly valued Sufi practices as *makhfi chahar zarb*[129] and *habs-i dam.*[130]

> "Memorising holy verses and meditation on God are grainy years.
> Honest devotion is "the Mukhfi Chahar Zarb",
> Listen, Superior to all is the control of mind:
> One who celebrates the Gongal, will surely celebrate the krav."[131]

It is an established fact that the folk verses composed by Nuruddin were indeed sung by the toiling masses, and but for their oral transmission the *Rishinamas* of Chrar and innumerable other compilations of the Shaikh's verses would not have been possible. The "*Gongalnama*" must have won popularity since it appealed especially to the village men and women who for centuries did the tilling, ploughing, sowing and harvesting. It also had a popular appeal not only because it extolled the activities performed by the peasants but also because its content was permeated with imagery especially meaningful to their sensitive souls. The dominant theme of the poem is that spring is the time to build up ones habits, hopes and faiths. But the strength and safety of the peasantry consists not only in hope and faith but also in enterprise and energy. The spring season was, indeed, a continual source of intoxication for the Shaikh;[132] he often refers to the sad spectacle of his own youth, idling away the spring time of his existence in jungles and caves.[133] In his imagery of the spring season, therefore, the purpose was to give an *élan* to the peasants by the ethical affirmativeness of the Islamic precepts.

> Come out of your ignorance, the son of Adam:
> Whatever you have sown here will bear fruit in the Hereafter;
> Your sins and noble needs will be weighed there,
> (So) one who realises early will (surely) strive
> (in His way).[134]

There is a popular belief among many a devotee of the Prophet Muhammad that he is a living intercessor for them at the throne of Allah, but the Ahl-i Hadith, deriving their authority from the Quran and the *Sunna*, contend that the Prophet would intercede only on the Day of Judgement by the permission (*izn*) of Allah, and that the question of intercession for sins does not arise at all until that day.[135] Although Nuruddin's verses echo the general belief about the Prophet's right to seek the mercy of Allah for the sinners on the last day, nonetheless, he emphasises that the intercession will be especially for meritorious acts of the believers in the mundane world rather than for the sins committed by them. At one place he even implores Muslims not to cause embarrassment to their beloved Prophet before Allah on the Day of Judgement for the sins committed by them in this world.[136] Thus, as an exemplar of inward piety and good conduct, Nuruddin kindled an invigorating spirit among the people for combining social action with the highest spiritual goal, i.e., doing good in this world in the hope of being bestowed the *shaf'ah* of Muhammad for righteousness rather than licentiousness.

The Prophet will plead in your behalf,
Entrust your case to him;
(For) Nund Rishi fully knows the worth of the cultivators' labour.
One who realises early will (surely) strive
(in His way).[137]

Thus Nuruddin's view was that if the world is to bear its fruit, it must be cultivated. It would not be incorrect to say that in the *Gongalnama*, to use the literary expression of Ismail Raji al-Faruqi, the Shaikh "recrystallized the ancient Mesopotamian principle of agricultural service to God as the general transformation of the earth into the orchard wherein man is to his nourishment and pleasure."[138] Although conscious of the transience of the world, he attempted to make people equally aware of its splendour and glory. So strong is his rejection of world-denial, in conformity with the ethical limits set by the *Shari'a* for its realization, that it would not be superflous to reproduce below a few more verses to reject the misconceived notion that self-solace was the only goal of the founder of the Rishi order of the Muslim mystics in the Valley.[139]

Perform your duties from *Zeth*[140]
Bearing in mind (the sequel to) the Autumn,
Magh,[141] is the period of fecundity; be thoughtful,
One who realises early, will (surely) strive (in His way).[142]

Realize early that spring bubbles over,
'Make hay while the sun shines'
(Beware) of falling behind, spring is a 'trap" (for the thoughtless);
One who realises early, will (surely) strive (in His Way).[143]

The value of crops will be determined on ripening;
And each product will be named according to its quality;
The fate of the depraved will be sealed;
One who realises early will (surely) strive (in His Way).[144]

Life has come to its ultimate end steathily;
Realise, O thoughtless, the (sad) end of your life;
While exploiting (others) see, you (actually) robbed yourself,
One who realises early, will (surely) strive (in His Way).[145]

Do'nt be enchanted by palatial houses[146]
You will be answerable there (for robbing others)[147]
Is an ignoramous ready enough to heed the warning?
(But) one who realises early, will (surely) strive (in His Way).[148]

The religious thought which the verses of Nuruddin unfold has both the precision of a treatise and the coherence of a system. Although doctrinal and philosophical to a certain extent, it does not concern itself with abstract speculations. More precisely, he set forth in simple and uncomplicated language such principles and maxims as bear directly on the religious life and are the fruit of a dearly-bought experience. As we read, we seem to hear the voice of the teacher addressing his disciples and expounding for their benefit the truths that he has learnt through introspection. Thus, after spending twelve years in the cave, the Shaikh realized that physical seclusion associated with asceticism, however useful it may be in the inculcation of self-discipline, does not make up its essence. Rather, it lies in emulating the example of the Prophet Muhammad:

There are jackals and monkeys in the forests;
The caves are infested with rats;
Those who offer prayers five times a day to wash off the dirt of their heart;
Those who lead a family life, they are privileged[149]
A dutiful householder will be crowned (with success on the Day of Judgement);
The messenger of Allah (Muhammad) led a marital life and won the Divine grace.[150]

Social obligations towards children, the wife and other members of a family thus appear in the Shaikh's thought as the most important manifestations of the religious duties enshrined in the *Shari'a* of Muhammad. His denunciation of his own wanderings in the jungles during his early days points to the cardinal feature of his thought that basic social obligations are not to be neglected even after a complete surrender to divine obligations. While addressing his disciple, Nasr Baba, the Shaikh recollects an earlier time of spiritual ebb and flow, when his love was not perfect, and how he sought to assuage his anguish by retiring to the cave:

> Nasr Baba, it did not behove me to retire to the jungle,
> I thought it was a supreme act of worship:
> Lo: it was an ignominy;
> But the truth was revealed only after instrospection.[151]

It is obvious that in the Shaikh's view, the essence of the *Shari'a* lies not only in transmitting acts of worship to the faithful but also in self-examination. Action was thus a *leit-motif* in the teachings of the Shaikh. The value of work resides in using it as a means to help others and to sustain a way of life that furnishes one with the essentials of existence, no more and no less. For ultimately work is devoted to God and founded on love, and without that devotion and that foundation it is neither meaningful nor intelligible. The concept of world thus finally appears as an integral part of the divine synthesis in Nuruddin's thought. Its true significance resides only in so far as it relates to the next world. The social actions of individuals in this world are only a preparation for what is to come. The world is neither intrinsically evil nor an abode of darkness; its main function is to serve as a prolegomenon to the world to come. The cleaning of the heart of vices and passions through the recitation of *dhikr* is not enough; what is required is cleaning it of excessive love of the world which clogs the average mind.

Nuruddin was not opposed to the world and its social system but rather moved within the social order so qualitatively informing his personal relations with men as to enter into the contentment of God. True, he was indifferent to political institutions, but even so his greatest achievement lay in ennobling the conduct of the reigning Sultan, Zain al-'Abidin, who richly deserved the title of the 'Great King' or *Badshah*. The policy of religious tolerance for which Zain al-Abidin is famous in history undoubtedly bears the stamp of Nuruddin's influence on the Sultan's mind. It is remarkable that when *Badshah* first sought the guidance of the Shaikh, he was advised to make sustained efforts for administering justice in his kingdom.[152]

Conclusion

It goes without saying that Shaikh Nuruddin played a central role within the framework of a cognitive moral and social order. He redefined and reordered the life-world of the followers of the Rishi order, requiring of them not only devotion to God but patterns of social behaviour in congruity with the norms of the *Shari'a*. The key principles central to this order were: trusting in Allah in what is open or revealed; following the essence of the *Shari'a* of Muhammad in word and deed; giving a wide berth to vain and rich peoples' company; being content with Allah in living in the depths of poverty of the prophets sent for the guidance of mankind; spending money earned by hard labour for the relief of the poor and the distressed; and thus returning to Him in happiness. Little wonder, therefore, that the Shaikh's teachings created an intense solidarity of communion among the host of his followers. As Troeltsch writes in the context of the social role of the Christian churches, the absolute individualism coming from the religious idea of a pure-hearted love of God, leads only to an equally absolute fellowship among those united in God.[153] Although by definition the Kashmiri masses were excluded from the highest reaches of the mystical path that was accessible only to the spiritual *élite*, yet they joined together in emulating the example of the founder of the Rishi order, forming a society in which the value system derived sustenance entirely from the Shaikh's interpretation of existence in conformity with the true spirit of the *Shari'a*. This fellowship the foundations of whose inter-relations was love and fraternity, sought as a collectivity to experience an awareness of the created in the *Shari'a*-structured relationship. It attempted by the corporate repetition of the names of God, and in the concentrated emotion of the ritual, to escape from the finite world of ugly want, and to participate, to whatever degree, in the Infinite. Thus what the worldly *'Ulama* failed to provide as a result of the crisis in their belief and practice, the richly personal and social ethics of Nuruddin and his followers offered in abundance.

REFERENCES AND NOTES

1. Mohammad Mujeeb, *Indian Muslims*, p. 97.
2. *Kulliyat-i Shaikh al-'Alam*, pp. 94, 126-27.
3. *Ibid.*, p. 127.
4. *Ibid.*, pp. 94-95, 127.
5. *Ibid.*, pp. 126-27; Baba Nasib, *Nurnama*, f. 49ab.
6. *Kulliyat*, pp. 128-29; see also Baba Kamal, *Rishinama*, p. 178.

7. *Kulliyat*, p. 127.
8. *Ibid.*
9. As we shall see in the text of this chapter, Nuruddin attempted to explain the Sufi ideal of the *Sharia* as prefigured in the Quran, namely, surrender (Islam), faith (*iman*) and doing everything 'as beautifully as possible' (*ihsan*). The fulfilment of this ideal required not only 'the interiorization of ritual acts' but also a constant endeavour to produce a model of peaceful domestic and social life worthy of imitation.

9a. *Al-Hamud* meaning praise is another title of the first chapter (*surah*) of the Quran called *Fatihah*. This *surah* is recited in every ritual prayer (*namaz*).

9b. Here the reference is to the 112th chapter of the Quran entitled *Al-Ikhlas*. The term means sincerity. In other words, through the repeated recitation of this chapter in the daily prayer, a Muslim affirms his faith in all sincerity in Allah. The social meaning of the term denotes that a Muslim performs his obligation in the sight of Allah alone.

9c. *Attahiyat* means 'greetings'. The adorations (i.e. *attahiyatu*) which are part of the daily prayers are for Allah, "and also of the body and of alms-giving. Peace be on thee, O Prophet, with the mercy of Allah and His blessing. Peace be upon us, and upon Allah's righteous servants."

10. Baba Nasib, *op. cit.*, f. 49a; see also Baba Kamal, *op. cit.*, p. 177; Baba Khalil, *Rauzat-al-Riyazat*, pp. 540-547; *Kulliyat*, p. 37.
11. Baba Kamal, *op. cit.*, p. 167; Baba Khalil, *op. cit.*, p. 524. *Kulliyat*, p. 75; also p. 105.
12. Baba Khalil's poem in praise of Nuruddin typifies the sentiments of latter-day Rishis for their spiritual preceptor's contribution in popularising the *Shari'a* of Muhammad among the commoners (*khalq*). See Khalil, *op. cit.*, p. 299; see also Baba Kamal, *op. cit.*, pp. 224-25.
13. A number of Kashmiri poems extolling the poverty of the Rishis attest to the indelible influence exercised by their exemplary behaviour on the commoners.
14. *Kulliyat*, p. 143.
15. The chief aim of renouncers in Hinduism was to gain liberation from earthly existence (*moksa*). See Patrick Olivelle, *Renunciation in Hinduism: A Medieval Debate*, Vol. I, Vienna, 1986.
16. *Kulliyat*, p. 144.
17. *Ibid.*, pp. 38, 48, 59, 143, 182, etc.
18. *Ibid.*, p. 143.
19. *Guldasta: Kalam-i Shaikh al-'Alam*, p. 80.
20. *The Quran*, Surahs: 2, 3, 29, 30, 31, 32.
21. *Ibid.*, (Eng. Tr. by Abdullah Yusuf Ali), Vol. I, p. 17n.
22. *Kulliyat*, pp. 37, 64, 156.
23. The Quran repeatedly states that the righteous are those who ponder the creation of the heavens and the earth and affirm, "Our Lord, You have not created this creation in vain." See *The Quran*, 3/191; 21/16.

24. *Guldasta-i Kalam-i Shaikh al-'Alam*, p. 286. In this verse the Shaikh quotes the Quranic verse "Withersoever you turn, there is the Face of God." *The Quran.*, 2/115. According to the Quran, the real servants of Allah are those who remember Him morning, noon, and night, and who do not hanker after worldly gain, but seek His "Face." The word "Face" (*Wajh*) implies striving to live in the presence of God which is the main aim of spiritual aspiration. The words "Face of God" and "His Face" occur in the Quran in an appropriate signification in each place. See *Ibid*,, 2/115; 6/52; 18/28.

24a. "Listen to the verses (*shruks*) of the Holy Quran", exhorts the Shaikh. See *Kulliyat*, p. 42; also p. 54. The term *shruk* is the derivative of the Sanskrit *sloka*. At another place he instructs the believer to read the Quran daily so that he is enlightened by the Presence (*Hazrat*) of the Lord. *Ibid.*, p. 156.

25. *Ibid.*, p. 41. The Shaikh invariably uses *dhyan* and *fikr* for profound religious contemplation.

26. *Ibid.*, p. 37; Baba Kamal, *op. cit.*, p. 177.

27. For a detailed study of his life and thought, see Louis Massignon, *The Passion of Hallaj.* Notwithstanding Massignon's outstanding literary contribution and the great influence exercised by him in softening the attitude of Western scholars towards Islam, his study of Hallaj is not free from serious defects. Among these must be mentioned his emphasis, to the point of error, on Hallaj's fight against the doctrinal system of Islam. Hallaj did not dare pesonalize Islam as dramatized by Massignon; but it was his inflamed love rather than any preconceived battle against "orthodoxy" that made him the darling of many Sufis of Islam. This fact has been clearly brought home by Nuruddin in his eulogization of Mansur Hallaj whose death, according to him, not only kindled the fire of longing for God among lovers (*'ashaqan*) and gnostics (*'arifs*), but even elevated them. See *Kulliyat*, p. 90.

28. On the use and abuse of *Wahdat al-Wujud* and *Wahadat al-Shuhud*, see Ishaq Khan, "Sufism in Indian History", *Muslim Shrines in India*, Vol. IV, pp 275-291.

28a. Abu Bakr b. Dulaf b. Jahdar al-shibli, a disciple of Janaid Bhagdadi, "had a blameless spiritual life." See Ali Uthman al-Hujwiri, *The Kashf al-Mahjub*, (tr. Nicholson), p. 155. "Al-Hallaj and I are of one belief," remarked Shibli, "but my madness saved me, while his intelligence destroyed him." Although Hujwiri approvingly quotes the remarks of Shibli to prove Hallaj's faith in Islam and his own abundant love for the mystic, yet he firmly holds that "his 'path' is not soundly established on any principle, and his state is not fixed in any position, and his experiences are largely mingled with error." See *Ibid.*, p. 151-52.

29. *Kulliyat*, p. 78.

30. See A. Schimmel, "Mystic Impact of Hallaj" in Hafeez Malik, *Poet Philosopher of Pakistan.* ed., Columbia 1971, p. 316.

31. *Ibid., Passim.*
32. Baba Kamal, *op. cit.*, p. 56; *Kulliyat*, p. 76.
33. *Kulliyat*, p. 67; also *Rishinama* (Taus Banihali),p. 146.
34. While the *Shari'a* has been the starting point or guide of all Sufi orders in Islam, *tariqa* indicates the path, way. or the branch adopted by the followers of the *Sharia* in order to reach near a truer understanding of the Truth (*Haqiqa*). Most prominent Sufis who represented these three stages ultimately distinguished themselves as true embodiments of the *Shari'a*.
35. The term *Sharia* occurs in this sense frequently in Nuruddin's verses. See *Kuliyat*, pp. 46, 78-79, 90, 176, etc.
36. *Ibid.* p. 78.
37. *Ibid.*, p. 76; see also *Infra*, n. 39a.
38. *Ibid.*, p. 90.
39. *Ibid.*, p. 91; see also pp. 29, 41, 48, 51.
39a. "You are my Lord, and myself is your humble servant", *Ibid.*, p. 48.
40. At another place the Shaikh echoes the same sentiment: "I am His humble servant, He is my Lord," *Ibid.*, p. 91.
41. '*La ilaha illa' llah*' is the article of faith that every Muslim is required to recite with sincerity.
42. Nuruddin uses the term *wujud* implying thereby the 'intoxicated' state of a mystic in which the latter deludes himself into believing that 'Everything is He'. This stage of mystic eperience, popularly known as *Wahdat al-Wujud*, is only a personal experience and by no means an objective reality. In fact, the objective truth, 'Everything is from Him' (*Wahdat al-Shuhud*) or 'Unity of Vision', is realized by the mystic only after annihilating himself in the experience of His Oneness. When the mystic reaches this final stage of spiritual path he returns to himself so as to live in the abiding grace of His everlasting Oneness or Presence.
43. "So I reached *la makan*," is the expression used by the Shaikh. Interestingly enough, this verse is also attributed to Lal Ded. See *Kulliyat*, p. 29. At another place the Shaikh remarks that the one who controls one's *nafs* will reach *la makan*. *Ibid.* p. 88.
44. Here the Shaikh's use of the Sanskrit term *shunya* (void) closely corresponds to *la makan*.
45. *Kulliyat*, p. 49.
45a. See *Ibid.*, pp. 107, 112, 145-47, 157, 163, 165, etc.
45b. *Ibid.*, p. 107.
46. For Baba Daud Khaki's views about the springs, see Chapter VI, "The Attitudes of the Sufi Orders Towards the Rishis".
47. *Kulliyat*, pp. 109-110.
48. The Quran, 21/107. At another place the Quran states: "We have not sent thee but as a universal (Messenger) to men, giving them glad tidings, and warning them (against sin), but most men understand not." *Ibid.*, 34/28.

48a. *Ibid.*, p. 35.
49. *Ibid.*, pp. 30, 35, 37, 51, 78, 143, etc.
50. *The Quran.*
51. *Kulliyat*, pp. 46, 78-79, 90.
52. Parimoo, *Unity in Diversity*, pp. 202-203.
53. *Kulliyat*, p. 36.
53a. *Ibid.*, pp. 30, 57.
53b. *Ibid.*, pp. 118; see also, p. 97.
The world *sirat* occurs in the Quran thirty-eight times. Although it denotes the "right way" (*Sirat al-Mustaqim*) in almost all verses of the Holy Book, in several works on Muslim traditions and Sufism, it is generally used for the bridge across the infernal fire 'which is described as finer than a hair and sharper than a sword, and is beset on each side with briars and hooked thorns.' In many verses Nuruddin repeats the popular tradition that the righteous (*nundaen*) will pass over it with 'the swiftness of lightning' but the depraved, after quickly missing their steps, will fall·into the fire of hell.
53c. *Kulliyat*, p. 143.
53d. Eager to prove the synthesis of Hindu and Islamic mystic traditions, Athar Abbas Rizvi remarks: "Yogic obstacles and stages correspond with those along the Sufi path. They are numbered differently; the four stages of the Sufi journey are *nasut*, *malakut*, *jabarut* and *lahut*. According to the Sufis of Ibn al-Arabi's school, *nasut* (human nature) is like a vessel which contains the *lahut* (Divine nature)." See Rizvi, *op. cit.*, I, p. 369. Rizvi gives tacit approval to the misconception that the "*lahut* in the heart was identified with *anahata-cakra* of the Yogis." *Ibid.*, p. 353. Tara Chand's views are also misconceived: ". . . The absolute God in His divinity (*lahut*) became in Adam God in Humanity (*nasut*). Mansur conceived of the relation of God with man as the infusion of the divine into the human soul; in Hindu terms, the illumination of *buddhi* by *Purusa*." *Influence of Islam on India Culture*, pp. 70-71.
53e. *The Quran*, 15/99.
54. '*Arsh* denotes the throne of Allah. "He is the Lord of the mighty throne." *Quran*, 11/129.
55. The Shaikh emphasizes the importance of performing ritual prayers by the frequent use of the Sanskrit term *kiriya* or *kirya*. The word has also been employed in several verses to impress upon the unlettered folk the strict observance of religious duties for the development of a stable social order.
56. Here the attribute Omnipotent or the Great has been appropriately used out of the most Beautiful Names (*Asma al-Husna*) or attributes of Allah. See *the Quran*, 39/23.
57. *Suhbat thavi panay Jabbar* (*Kulliyat*, p. 135), if literally translated, means that the Absolute will Himself vouchsafe you His companionship.

58. In this verse the Shaikh repeats the words *velu, velu*, emphasizing thereby the importance of time (*vela*).
59. *Kulliyat*, p. 173.
60. Ismail Raji al Faruqi, *Tawhid: Its Implications for Thought and Life*, p. 71.
61. *Kulliyat*, pp. 75, 76, 99, 105, 137.
62. In some verses the Shaikh praises God for endowing the world with the inexhaustible wealth of nature in order to enable man to gain His knowledge (*m'arifa*). *Kulliyat*, pp. 31, 48.
62a. *Ibid.*, pp. 33, 41, 66, 104, 108.
53. *Ibid.*, p. 90.
64. Parimoo, *op. cit.*, p. 226; see also *Kulliyat*, p. 137.
65. *Kulliyat*, pp. 81, 87, 96.
66. *Ibid.*, pp. 33, 74, 82.
67. Parimoo, *op. cit.*, p. 158.
68. The *Quran*, 2 164; 3 190; 6 95-99; 17 12; 10 5-6; 30 20-27; 45 3-6; 36 37-40; and 41 39-40.
69. See E. Cassirer, *The Philosophy of Symbolic Forms*, Vol. I. (tr. Mannheim), New York and London, Yale Univesity Press, 1953.
70. See *supra*.
71. Parimoo, *op. cit.*, p. 275.
72. *Ibid.*, p. 276.
73. *Ibid.*, pp. 276-77.
74. *Ibid.*, pp. 278-79.
75. Quran says: *Laqad karamna bani Adam*, "We have made all the children of Adam (i.e. all human beings) respectable and dignified." *The Quran:* 17/70. Again it declares: 'Surely the noblest of you in the sight of Allah is one who is most pious, most mindful of his duty'. *Ibid.*, 49/13. The Prophet Muhammad's well-known address on the eve of the Farewell pilgrimage is also worth quoting here: "O people verily your Lord is one and your father is one. All of you belong to Adam and Adam was made of clay. There is no superiority for an Arab over a non-Arab nor for a non-Arab over an Arab; nor for a white-coloured over a black-coloured; nor for a black-skinned on a white-skinned except in piety. Verily the noblest among you is he who is the most pious."
76. See also *Infra*, n: 93.
77. *Kulliyat*, pp. 175-76, 180. The Shaikh greatly valued *ihsan*. *Ibid.*,p. 203.
78. See *Ibid.*, pp. 39, 46, 50, 60, 74, 92, 98, 103, 117, 138, etc.
79. *Ibid.*, pp. 50, 74, 130, etc.
80. *Ibid.*, pp. 35, 50-51, 138-39, 156-57.
81. *Ibid.*, pp. 175-76.
82. *Ibid.*, pp. 170-80.
83. 'Anger (*krodh*) does not behove a Muslim,' is the theme of many verses of the Shaikh, *Ibid.*, pp. 156-57.
84. *The Quran*, s. 23, v. 96; s. 41, v. 34; s. 42, v. 37, 40, 43, s. 45, v. 14.

85. *Kulliyat*, pp. 35, 51, 55, 175-76, 156-57, 180, etc.
86. *Ibid.*, pp. 181-82.
87. See *Supra.*
88. *Ibid.*, p. 175.
89. *Ibid.*
90. *Ibid.*, p. 176.
91. *Ibid.*
92. *Ibid.*, p. 97.
93. "O mankind! Be careful of your duty to your Lord who created you from a single soul and from it created its mate and from them twain hath spread abroad a multitude of men and women. Be careful of your duty towards Allah in whom ye claim (your rights) of one another and towards the womb (that bore you). Lo! Allah hath been a watcher over you." *The Quran*, 4/1. Again "O mankind, we created you from a single (pair) of male and female; and made you into nations and tribes, that ye may know each other (not that ye may despise each other). Verily the most honoured of you in the sight of Allah is (he who is) the most righteous of you." *Ibid.*, 49 13, See also *Ibid.*, 39/6.
94. *Kulliyat*, p. 206.
95. *Ibid.*, p. 86.
96. Parimoo is not correct in saying that the term *sangan* in the verse 'does not suit the context." See Parimoo, *op. cit.*, p. 156n. In reality, the Shaikh clearly impresses upon men that noble birth (*kaval* or *kaula*) is not a badge or a colour or a symbol that can foster unity (*sangan* or *sang*) among people.
97. *Kulliyat*, p. 104.
98. Parimoo, *op. cit.*, p. 226.
99. *Kulliyat*, pp. 97, 98, 113.
100. *The Quran* repeatedly enjoins upon the wealthy to take due care of the needs of the poor. "In their wealth the needy, the beggar and the destitute have their due." *The Quran*, 51/19. The wealthy or those who take pleasure in squandering their wealth have been described as brothers of the devil. See *Ibid.*
101. *Kulliyat*, p. 182.
102. *Ibid.*
103. *Ibid.*, pp. 106-07.
104. *Ibid.*, pp. 175, 180.
105. *Ibid.*, pp. 65, 163.
106. *Ibid.*, pp. 65, 163.
107. *Ibid.*, p. 183. Parimoo, *op. cit.*, p. 117.
108. *Kulliyat*, p. 182.
109. "The righteous shall inherit the earth." *The Quran* 21/105.
110. *Kulliyat*, p. 181.
111. *Ibid.* p. 106.
112. *Ibid.*, p. 66.

113. *Ibid.*, pp. 70-71; also 106-7.
114. *Faqr* or poverty was the ideal or the quality of the Prophet Muhammad who claimed that it was his pride. It was also the ideal of the Sufis both in the sense of not possessing anything in this world and not be possessed by anything.
115. See *Kulliyat*, pp. 110-111.
116. *Ibid.*, p. 46.
117. *Ibid.*, p. 100.
118. *Ibid.*, pp. 40, See also 51, 66.
119. See *Infra.*
120. See Baba Nasib, *op. cit.*, ff. 157b; Khaki, *Rishinama*, ff. 58a, 110a; Teng, *Tuhfat al-Fuqara*, ff. 43ab; Mishkati, *op. cit.*, 101a, 110b, 104a, 111a, 118ab.
121. The Kashmiri Pandits' contempt for manual labour has continued into more recent times. See Ishaq Khan: "The Impact of Islam on Kashmir in the Sultanate Period, 1320-1586," *The Indian Economic and Social History Review*, April-June, 1986, p. 192. Huxley, visiting Kashmir in the 1920s, remarks: "The Kashmiri Pandit has a more than Spanish objection to manual labour." Quoted in T.N. Madan, *Family and Kinship*, Bombay, 1965, p. 25.
122. *Kulliyat*, p. 131.
123. Nuruddin is also reputed to have once cultivated a piece of land which came to be known as *Shaikh-i Nari*. See Baba Kamal, *op. cit.*, pp. 51-53.
124. Mishkati, *op. cit.*, ff. 81b, 83ab.
125. *Kulliyat*, pp. 160-63. 'Gongal' is a ceremony observed in the villages on the eve of spring. Rice and walnuts are distributed among children to mark the occasion of the beginning of farming in the New Year.
126. Parimoo, *op. cit.*, p. 193.
127. *Ibid.*, pp. 193-94.
128. *Ibid.*, p. 192.
129. A particular method of glorifying God by the constant repetition of His name, by rhythmic breathing either mentally (*dhikr-i khafi*) or aloud (*dhikr-i jali* or *jahri*). This practice which was specially adopted by the Suharwardis also seems to have been popularised by Nuruddin. For more details on *dhikr-i chahar zarb*, see Khaki, *Dastur al-Salikin*, ff. 78a; 142b.
130. *Habs-i dam* means 'holding of breath.' Abu Yazid al-Bistami (d. A.D. 874) is reported to have remarked, "For gnostics, worship is observance of the breath," and Abu Bakr ash-Shibli (d. A.D. 945) as saying that "*Tasawwuf* is control of the faculties and observance of the breath." See Faridud-Din Attar, *Tazkirat al-auliya*, text & tr. given by R.A. Nicholson, "The Origin and Development of Sufism", *Journal of Royal Asiatic Society*, 1906, p. 344. Nuruddin makes the importance of the practice of *dhikr-i khafi* abundantly clear in a verse in which he urges

the seeker to keep the tongue pressed against the roof of his mouth, his lips and teeth firmly shut, and hold his breath (*dhikr-i Haqq par zev dith talas*). See Parimoo, *op. cit.*, p. 129. The Naqshbandi Sufis firmly believed in this practice.

131. Parimoo, *op. cit.*
132. See also *Kulliyat.*
133. *Ibid.*, p. 174.
134. *Ibid.*, p. 134. My translation of the Shaikh's verses is different from that of Parimoo.
135. Although the right of intercession primarily belongs to the Prophet Muhammad (see also Nawab Sidique Hasan Khan, *Ikhlas al-Tauhid lil-Hamid al-Majid*, 1305 A.H. p. 50), the Quran, nonetheless, also grants this right to men of piety. Pointing to such exalted individuals the Quran repeatedly states that they will have no fear on the Day of Judgement. See *The Quran*, s. 20: v. 109, also s. 10: v. 3; s. 19: v. 87; s. 53: v. 26.
136. *Guldasta-i Kalam-i Shaikh al-'Alam*, p. 201.
137. *Ibid.* p. 163. It may be argued that, Nuruddin's views bear some semblance to the Mu'tazilla who were of the opinion that the intercession of the Prophet 'is for the increase of merit, and not for the prevention of punishment.' Hughes, *Dictionary of Islam*, p. 215.
138. al-Faruqi, *op. cit.*, p. 96.
139. Nuruddin uses the best possible imagery to emphasize the supreme significance of combining exoteric and esoteric facets of the truly spiritual life.
140. The second Hindu month (corresponding to May-June).
141. Name of the tenth Hindu month (corresponding to January-February), the full moon of which is near the constellation of *Magha* or a Leonis (Regulus).
142. *Kulliyat*, p. 160.
143. *Ibid.*, p. 160.
144. *Ibid.*, p. 162; Afaqi, *op. cit.*, p. 113; Ashraf, *op. cit.*, p. 143; Parimoo, *op. cit.*, p. 196.
145. *Kulliyat*, p. 162.
146. In this verse the Shaikh evidently refers to the balconies (*zali-dab*) and the grand drawing rooms (*robkhana*) of the big Srinagar houses.
147. "Fear the day wherein no soul shall pay recompense for another soul. Nor shall intercession be accepted for it, nor shall compensation be taken from it, nor shall they be helped." *The Quran*. s. 2: v. 45.
148. *Kulliyat*, p. 163.
149. *Ibid.* pp. 86-87, 205; see also Afaqi, *op. cit.*, p. 167.
150. *Afaqi*, *op. cit.*, p. 167.
151. *Kulliyat*, p. 174.
152. Baba Nasib, *op. cit.* f. 63b-64a.
153. E. Troeltsch, *The Social Teachings of the Christian Churches*, p. 56.

CHAPTER VI

The Attitudes of the Sufi Orders Towards the Rishi Movement

So important was the Rishi movement in the traditional Kashmiri society that an attempt should be made here to bring out aspects of its social and religious significance as reflected in the responses of the hagiographers. Most of them, though also venerated as Sufis of the Suharwardi order in the Valley,[1] were greatly influenced by the popularity of the Rishis and the hold exercised by them in their regional environment. Consequently, through their writings, the dynamic tension between Islam and the regional culture found expression in the remarkable assimilation of a variety of elements of the popular culture in Islam. Since the aim of the hagiographers was to help Kashmiris assimilate Islam into their lives, this important goal was gradually accomplished without distorting its essential precepts. In fact, the assimilation of Islam was no easy task, which explains why the hagiographers, while not considering the environment to be antagonistic to their faith, gradually paved the way for drawing the common folk into the legal and social orbit of Islam. The hagiographers also represented the literate aspect of Islam, as living reminders that the Rishis had blended into the new human environment, local forms and beliefs—extreme ascetic discipline, celibacy, and vegetarianism—but by juxtaposition rather than fusion, the old and the new existing in parallel to each other. In this chapter, therefore, we shall particularly focus on the works of the Suharwardis, though an attempt will also be made to examine the attitudes of the Kubrawis and the Naqshbandis in order to gauge the influence the Rishis had on the evolution of Kashmiri Muslim society.

Suharwardi Attitude Towards the Rishis

Until the reign of Sultan Zain al-'Abidin no Sufi of the Suharwardi order save Sayyid Sharafuddin made his presence felt in the Valley.[2] During the fifteenth and the first half of sixteenth century, Sayyid Muhammad Isfhani,[3] Sayyid Ahmad Kirmani[4] and Jamaluddin Bukhari[5] came to Kashmir. All of them traced their spiritual lineage to Sayyid Jalaluddin Bukhari (1308-84) of Uchh popularly known as Makhdum Jahaniyan-i Jahan Gasht.[6] In contrast to the active participation of the Suharwardis of Uchh and Multan in the politics of northern India,[7] the immigrant Sufis of this order in Kashmir lived in relative seclusion. Sayyid Muhammad retired to the village of Khanpur[8] in order to avoid contact with the people who came in numbers to seek his blessings in Srinagar. For his extreme ascetic practices he earned the title of *Janbaz.*[9] While we have already referred to the acquiescence of Sayyid Ahmad Kirmani in the local ethos, his disciple Baba Masud, preferred asceticism to worldly life. Before coming into contact with Sayyid Ahmad, Baba Masud was known for his riches.[10]

Sayyid Jamaluddin, who stayed in Kashmir for only six months, also laid emphasis on asceticism. He advised his disciples to shun *'Ulama-i Zahiri* for their want of esoteric knowledge.[11] It was also by stressing the virtues of reciting *dhikr*[12] that he was able to attract a considerable number of local people towards his order among whom was Shaikh Hamza Makhdum,[13] through whose influence the Suharwardi order gained considerable popularity in the Valley.

Hamza Makhdum was originally rooted in the Kubrawi tradition. He received his early education from Shaikh Fath Ullah,[14] the son of Shaikh Ismail Kubrawi.[15] He was also conversant with some works of Sayyid 'Ali Hamadani.[16] In the true spirit of the local Kubrawi and Suharwardi traditions, Hamza Makhdum emphasized the importance of the continuous recitation of *dhikr* so much so that he regarded it as a remedy for the troubles of the heart.[17] Being a son of the soil, Hamza Makhdum was able to establish a meaningful contact with the people through a number of visits to the rural areas.[18] Not only did he influence the Rishi movement by enrolling some Rishis as his disciples,[19] but at the same time, by undertaking a pilgrimage to the tomb of Nuruddin[20] he extended the sphere of influence of the Rishis even to the Suharwardi circles. Small wonder, therefore, that his prominent disciples recorded the activities of the Rishis with reverence in their hagiographies. Among these must be mentioned Baba 'Ali Raina, Baba Daud Khaki, Khwaja

Ishaq Qari, Khawaja Hasan Qari and Baba Haidar Tulmuli. In their works, the disciple of Baba Daud Khaki, Baba Nasibuddin Ghazi, and the latter's disciple, Baba Daud Mishkati, discuss at great length the role of the Rishis. But before we evaluate the importance of their works for understanding the Suharwardi attitude towards the Rishis, it would be necessary to examine in this context the attitude of the immediate disciples of Hamza Makdum.

Baba 'Ali Raina furnishes some important evidence about the esteem in which the Rishis were held by his brother and *murshid*, Hamza Makhdum. Before his enrolment in the Suharwardi order, Ali Raina was advised by Hamza Makhdum to visit the tomb of Nuruddin Rishi.[21] While staying there for a night, 'Ali Raina had the spiritual experience of seeing Nuruddin in a dream, who drew the pilgrim's attention to the abject poverty of the custodians of his tomb. Overwhelmed by the mystical experience and by the Shaikh's concern for the poor, Ali Raina distributed some coins as *bakshish* among the *mujawirs.* Thus the practice of doling out coins to the *mujawirs* of the shrine of Nuruddin was legitimized by no less a person than the Surharwardi Sufi himself.[22]

Although 'Ali Raina was greatly impressed by the merit and popularity of the mystical poetry of Nuruddin, he did not record any verse of the Shaikh in his *tadhkira*. Nor did he attempt to describe the activities of Nuruddin and his *khalifas* at any length. However, his eulogization of Nuruddin[23] enables us to understand the influence that the Rishi movement had come to wield on the thought processes of even the noted Suharwardis. 'Ali Raina particularly extolled to the skies the spirituality of Hardi Rishi,[24] the most celebrated Rishi of his time, whose possession of supra-normal powers captivated all other well known disciples of Hamza Makkdum. So deep was the impact of Hardi Rishi's personality on the mind of the Suharwardi that 'Ali Raina is even eager to convince his readers about the authenticity of the miracles attributed to the Rishi to which he says he was himself an eye witness.[25]

Even as an infant, Hardi Rishi is said to have refused to take milk during the ember days (*Ramadan*) at the appointed time of the fast.[26] So enamoured was 'Ali Raina of the Rishi that he not only calls him a born friend of Allah (*Wali-i madarzad*) but even dexterously uses the Quranic verses[27] to impress upon his readers the truth of his argument and conviction. Thus he remarks:

> And if all trees in the earth were pens, and the sea, with all seas to help it were ink, the words of Hardi Rishi could not be exhausted.[27a]

The world in which the Sufis and their hagiographers lived may not be fathomed by a reasoning mind of our age. But for understanding the phenomenon of the religious life of the Sufis, it is necessary for us to project ourselves into their world.[28] For them the supernatural is an ever-present reality. It is in this context that we consider it of some value to carry ourselves into realms which, though trans-historical, reveal states of mind that conditioned the life of people in the medieval period. In this respect we do not consider the anecdote analyzed below to be without social significance.

According to 'Ali Raina, Hardi Rishi received esoteric guidance from both Uways-i Qarni and the Prophet Khizr.[29] But it was the command (*amr*) of the Prophet Muhammad which was the decisive point in Hardi Rishi's initiation in the Suharwardi order.[30] Significantly, however, Hamza Makhdum is reported to have condescended to come to the Rishi's house in order to enrol him as his disciple.[31] As Hardi Rishi came to know through secret knowledge about the visit of the most venerated Suharwardi Sufi of Kashmir he made arrangements for serving a feast to the distinguished guest. Despite the known aversion of Hardi Rishi to causing harm to living creatures, an animal was slaughtered to celebrate the occasion. The Rishi was asked by Hamza Makhdum to partake of the non-vegetarian food, which he tasted, for the only time in his life,[32] in order to conform his behaviour to the *Sunna*. But what is of equal importance to remember from our viewpoint is that Hamza Makhdum himself, in deference to the Rishi's attitude towards living creatures, allowed him to practice vegetarianism[33] thereby dispelling the false notion that the vegetarianism of the Rishis was distasteful to the Suharwardis in view of its local origin.

Our examination of the account of Khawaja Miram Bazaz, a less known disciple of Hamza Makhdum, will show how emotions can shape the contours of thought. The structure of the human psyche, if analysed dispassionately, can lift the veil from the reality of the spiritual life, which is man's response to his supernatural surroundings, and reveal the material conditions of the saints' existence, and the quality of their life.

According to Miram Bazaz, Hardi Rishi refused to taste meat when Hamza Makhdum asked him to share food with him. What prevented the Rishi from touching meat were the exhortations of Khizr, Christ, Moses, Idris and Ilyas who were spiritually present on the occasion. Asked as to why he was hesitant to taste meat, Hardi Rishi told the guest about his spiritual experience. Thereupon, the Suharwardi Sufi impressed upon the Rishi that it was the command of the Prophet Muhammad that he should share food with him. And, in order to dispel the Rishi's doubt, Hamza Makhdum invoked the help of the Prophet Muhammad whose spiritual presence finally caused the Rishi to share the non-vegetarian meal with the Suharwardi Sufi.[34]

Mir Bazaz's account, of course, is riddled with supernatural events; but behind these habits of mind common to all hagiographers, we see a patent objective reality, though turned into a supramundane event by the structure of human emotions in order to impress upon readers the spirituality of Hamza Makhdum. On a careful examination of Miram Bazaz's account, in conjunction with other contemporary sources,[35] it would appear that the Suharwardi Sufi's main concern was to show that the Rishi did not unswervingly follow a course opposed to the *Sunna*. This is why he did not make a fetish of the *Sunna* once Hardi Rishi willingly shared non-vegetarian food with Hamza Makhdum. Moreover, the purpose behind Hamza Makhdum's meaningful meeting with Hardi Rishi was not only to confirm the supremacy of the *Sunna* in Sufism but it was also to legitimise the social behaviour of the Rishis, which though in consonance with local conditions, did not amount to a flagrant violation of the *Sunna*. But for this reason, Hamza Makhdum would not have allowed Hardi Rishi to follow the path of the Rishis even after initiating him in the Suharwardi order. Not only did Miram Bazaz testify to this fact,[36] but what gives further support to our view is that Hamza Makhdum himself contributed a great deal to giving a wider social focus and authenticity to the Rishi movement by gifting his cap (*kulah*) and turban (*'amama*) to Hardi Rishi.[37] The empathic attitude of the celebrated Suharwardi saint towards Hardi Rishi, in fact, gave a fillip to both the Rishis and the Suharwardis for perfecting the process of Islamic acculturation of the masses within the bounds of the spiritual and legal structure of Islam.

Hasan Qari,[38] Haidar Tulmuli and Ishaq Qari have also spoken highly of Hardi Rishi. Haidar Tulmuli particularly corroborates 'Ali Raina regarding the exalted status of Hardi Rishi among the *auliya*. In spite of being a disciple of Hamza Makhdum, Haidar Tulmuli calls Hardi Rishi the King of saints (*Sultan al-Auliya*).[39] Even the experienced Sufis are said to have taken lessons from Hardi Rishi in *suluk*. We are told that many people from 'Hindustan' and some more distant lands flocked to Hardi Rishi and sought his discipleship.[40] Haidar Tulmuli refers to the four *darwishes* of Hind who joined the Rishi order on seeing Hardi Rishi.[41]

In fact, the accounts of Suharwardis are full of Hardi Rishi's miraculous exploits. Ishaq Qari even credits Hardi Rishi with having saved one of his *murids* from the punishments of the grave for having died a debtor. The Rishi is said to have turned a heap of dung into money in order to liquidate the debt which his deceased disciple owed to people.[42] Even God is said to have been in correspondence with Hardi Rishi. According to an eye-witness account, furnished by Ishaq Qari, once he saw a visitor with a letter in his hand entering the house of Hardi Rishi. Ishaq Qari, who himself opened the letter, tells us that it was sent from Heaven, and contained a message of forgiveness (*magfirat*) for Hardi Rishi's disciples and *zahids.*[43] A number of people are said to have attained to the status of *Qutb*[44] and *Ghauth*[45] at the mere look of Hardi Rishi.[46]

Although the credibility of the miracles[47] attributed to Hardi Rishi is open to serious questions even from the viewpoint of the *Shari'a*, it would be nothing short of a blunder to treat these accounts with disdain, considering the relative neutrality of their compilers as adherents of the Suharwardi order. At least, these accounts speak of the towering personality of Hardi Rishi who was able to captivate even the closest disciples of Hamza Makhdum.

One is particularly struck by Baba Daud Khaki's unbounded praise for Hardi Rishi in his *Qasida-i Lamiyya* and, in its extended form the *Rishinama.* Khaki was undoubtedly the most distinguished disciple of Hamza Makdum under whose care he devoted himself to practising *tasawuuf.* He served his preceptor with great humility and, consequently, was appointed his *khalifa* by Hamza Makhdum even during his life time.[48]

The important feature of Khaki's works[49] is his praise for most (*aksar*) Rishis of Kashmir. His eulogization is however qualified; in it a conscious attempt has been made to portray the Rishis as followers of the *Ahl-i Sunnat wa Jam'a.*[50] While Khaki describes the contemplative life of Hardi Rishi as based on *pas-i anfas*[51] the practice of remembering God through *khilwat dar anjuman* and *hosh dar dam*, at the same time he praises the Rishi for the Kubrawi practice of reciting *Aurad-i Fathiyya* regularly.[52] Khaki does not mince his words in relating the purpose behind his unlimited praise for Hardi Rishi in following the Naqshbandi and the Kubrawi practices; as he points out, it was to impress upon his readers the unwavering faith of the Rishis in *'aqida-i Sunniya.* Furthermore, his object was also to testify to the abundant love that the Rishis had for the Prophet Muhammad, his companions and the *Ahl-i bait.*[53]

Khaki's eulogy of the Rishis also dispels the misconceived notion that the Suharwardis were hostile towards the Shias.[54] Remarkably, influenced by the Rishis, Khaki seems to have been keen to bridge the differences between the Shias and the Sunnis, though from his own standpoint. In this regard, a careful reading of his *Dastur al-Salikin* in conjunction with other works authored by him, viz., *Qasida-i Lamiyya*, *Rishinama* and *Qasida-i Gusl-i Yusuf Shahi* reveals a salutary change in his tone and attitude towards the Shias; and this was due to his association with the Rishis, particularly, Hardi Rishi. There is little doubt that Hardi Rishi was largely responsible for mellowing Khaki's attitude towards the Shias. This fact is particularly reflected in Khaki's account of Hardi Rishi's views about the Shias. Hardi Rishi is reported to have said, while referring to the Shias, that the Rishis did not feel jealousy towards any human being. It was not worthy of the pious to nurse malice against any person, he observed. And while urging his followers not to dissipate their time in mutual bickering, he also advised them to make the best use of time in seeking the countenance of God.[55] But for fully appreciating the influence of Rishis even on a prominent Suharwardi Sufi like Khaki it is important to understand the content of a dream related to Khaki by Hardi Rishi himself. Our attempt should not be misconstrued as entering into the realm of the supernatural; in reality, it is centred round the study of an entirely different dimension of the spiritual life, unlikely to be appreciated by such readers of this book as are living in an entirely different atmosphere from that of the Sufis. In questioning the authenticity of the vision experienced by Hardi Rishi we would be liable to distort our historical prespective, and betray a lack of spiritual awareness. Even from the empirical point of view, understanding the structure and meaning of mystical experiences for various Sufi orders calls for a total view of the subject with which we are concerned, in order to render our analysis objective.[56]

Once Hardi Rishi saw Caliph Ali in a vision. Answering the Rishi's question about the fate of the Shias, Ali is said to have expressed his displeasure over their harbouring spite against other companions of the Prophet Muhammad.[57] Significantly in contrast to *Dastur al-Salikin*, Khaki's criticism of the Shias in the *Rishinama* seems to be based more on reason, than on the much talked about hatred of the Suharwardis for the Shias. Although he sticks to the use of the appellation *rawafiz*[58] for the Shias, Hardi Rishi is quoted as calling them respectfully followers of Ali. What is of significance to note is Khaki's purpose behind recording the dream which, according to him, was to impress upon

Muslims to desist from nursing ill-will against one another. Perhaps Khaki realised that the Shia-Sunni conflict had undermined the strength of Kashmiri society; this explains why he was particularly keen on making Muslims feel repentant over their past sins.[59] It is also against this background that Khaki's remark in praise of patriotism assumes relevance: *Hub-i watan az iman ast.*[60]

Thus the tolerance of the Rishis seems to have softened, if not completely changed, the attitude of the Suharwardis towards the Shias. If on the one hand, Khaki shows his concern over the besetting rancour of his Shia contemporaries against the *Ahl-i Sunnat wa Jama'*, on the other, he gives proof of his earnestness in seeking a change in their attitude in the best interests of creating stable social and religious conditions. Furthermore, Khaki was also concerned over the sectarian conflicts that raged round Kashmir in the sixteen century. His mysterious account of 'Ali's "displeasure" with his followers for reviling the three other companions of the Prophet and the *Ahl-i Sunna wa Jama'* may appear fanciful; nevertheless, we should not altogether ignore the social significance of the subtle manner in which Khaki sought to reconcile the two main groups among Muslims.

That the Suharwardis imbibed the spirit of religious tolerance from their association with the Rishis is also reflected in Khaki's eulogization of Sultan Yusuf Shah Chak. In his *Risala-i Gusl-i Yusuf Shahi*, he showers praise on the Shia ruler of Kashmir for his equitable justice, nobility of culture, promotion of learning and policy of non-interference in the religious life of his subjects.[61] Not only Yusuf Shah but also his father, Sultan 'Ali Shah, are praised by Khaki for their respect for the pious (*salihan*).[62] From Khaki's account it is also evident that the Rishis exercised considerable influence even on the religious attitudes of the Sultans. We are also told that both 'Ali Shah and Yusuf Shah paid personal visits to Hardi Rishi and sought his blessings.

The attitude of the Suharwardis towards the asceticism of the Rishis also deserves careful examination. Not only do they approve of their extreme ascetic habits such as retiring to secluded places and abstention from marriage and consuming meat, onion, leek (*gandana*) and garlic,[63] but they even offer an explanation for these convictions of the Rishis. In this context the purport of Khaki's arguments is expounded below:

1. The Rishis are always absorbed in meditation. Since garlic, onion and leek cause bad breath, the Rishis have to avoid such food as

may disturb their concentration on the remembrance of the names of God (*Asma-i Haqq*).[64]

2. Abstention from meat brings the pious closer to God through the development of certain spiritual values.[65]
3. The more one is in possession of the bounties of God, the more accountable does one become to the Creator in the performance of social obligations. Meat is essentially a costly food in contrast to the simple vegetarian diet of the poor. With the use of costly food one's responsibilities towards human beings are bound to increase; thus the Rishis gave up meat lest a terrible fate should await them in the Hereafter for their failure to fulfil social obligations.[66]
4. The Rishis did not violate the *Sharia* on account of their abstention from meat; actually, they did not declare taking of meat as unlawful, but simply avoided it for good reasons, both in spiritual and psychological terms. The giving up of meat was further justified if its use made one lustful and stone-hearted.[67] Khaki refers to *Kimiya-i Sa'dat,*[68] *Khazinat al-Jalali*[69] and *Targib al-Salat*[70] to substantiate his point. Even Makhdum-i Jahaniyan is quoted as advising some of his unmarried friends (*yaran-i mujarrad*) to abandon meat and instead eat bitter things for crushing their lust.[71]
5. The reasoning powers do not get impaired through the abandonment of meat. On the contrary, according to khaki, abstention from meat improves one's intellect.[72]
6. The asceticism (*zuhd*) of the Caliph Ali is also cited in favour of the Rishis' abstention from meat. It is amazing to find a Sufi scholar of Khaki's calibre putting forth a strange argument that so pronounced was the *zuhd* of Ali that he would not eat meat except the liver and bile of only such animals as were slaughtered on the eve of *Id al-Adha.*[73]
7. Various kinds of sacrifices are performed by human beings;[74] of these, making best use of one's material possessions for the public good is of supreme value. Caliph Uthman's personal sacrifice in terms of parting with wealth and property for the general good of the people is referred to in this regard.[75] This kind of sacrifice is not obligatory on the poor people like the Rishis.[76] Khaki sees no reason behind the unintelligent (*kam-fahman*) criticism of the Rishis' failure to sacrifice an animal on the eve of the *Id al-Adha.*[77] As against external sacrifices, he emphasizes the importance of

the sacrifice of *nafs-i batini* in relation to *martazan goshgir wa wasilan faqir.*[78] This kind of sacrifice requires the killing of one's carnal self (*nafs-i ammara*).[79] The men of God like Shaikh Nuruddin Rishi and some of his followers are credited with having superbly performed the sacrifice of subduing their *nafs-i ammara.*[80]

Viewed against the background of Khaki's defence of asceticism, it is not difficult to understand why Hamza Makhdum himself practised celibacy and even approved of the virtues of vegetarianism and seclusion for enabling his disciples to free themselves from the snares of the self. Interestingly, when Shahi Rishi became a disciple of Hamza Makhdum, he abandoned the practice of vegetarianism and instead started consuming non-vegetarian meals in great quantity. But the Suharwardi Sufi did not like gluttony on the part of his Rishi disciple; so he directed him not only to give up meat and fatty dishes, but also to resort to seclusion[81] in the true manner of the Rishis.[82] The fact is that Hamza Makhdum accepted the relatively disciplined asceticism of the Rishis which avoided the extremes of sensual indulgence and self-motification.

It is also remarkable that Khaki defended the Rishi practice of vegetarianism and their failure to perform ritual sacrifice from the standpoint of avoiding injury to the animals.[83] Verses from *Shahnama*,[84] *Miftah al-Jannah*[85] and Hafiz Shirazi's[86] works are quoted to give validity to the argument that the cultivation of the virtue of non-injury to the animals was a prerequisite for attaining God's favour. Even the killing of an ant was reprehensible[87] according to the author of *Shahnama*, since it too was struggling to exist in this world.[88] Khaki remarks that only the killing of such a soul is permissible in the *Sunna* as is likely to cause harm to human beings.[89] Undoubtedly Khaki testifies to the deep imprint of the Rishis' exemplary tolerance on his mind.

Another important development which took place in the religious attitudes of the Suharwardis in the natural environment of the Kashmir Valley was their growing belief in a closer affinity between the physical universe and the human condition. They interpreted the somewhat animistic beliefs of the Rishis as an organic or integral whole, endowed with a central meaning or ethos. Under the influence of the Rishis Khaki invested the springs with supernatural powers. Thus, according to him, the presence of the unbeliever was likely to cause offence and inconvenience to the springs and consequently they would occasionally put such visitors to trouble. However, the visit to the spring of a pious man for performing ablutions was interpreted as cementing the spiritual bonds between the two. We are told that the springs always looked forward to the visits of the pious for their own benefit and would even pray for them.[90] Khaki also gives assent to the folk beliefs of the Rishis that the springs could assume the form of human beings and snakes.[91] Hardi Rishi is quoted as saying that springs have their own spirits and that they would even visit him for seeking guidance. Khaki even testifies to the physical participation of one such spirit in the religious assemblies held at Hardi Rishi's home during the course of the recital of *Aurad-i Fathiyya*.[92]

Although Khaki does not refer to any religious source to support the Rishi viewpoint on the anthropomorphic attributes of the springs, he clearly lends credence to the ancient Hindu beliefs in their sacredness. Such beliefs, he himself observes, were current among the high (*khawas*) and the commoners (*'awam*).[93] Thus it would not be wrong to conclude that under the influence of the Rishis as well as through his belief in the sacredness of springs Khaki projected his own inner piety as a norm of universal applicability.

In fact, so strong was the impact of the Rishis on the Suharwardis that they were largely responsible for creating the cult of *pir-parast* in the Valley.[94] Khaki, for instance, was so impressed by the spirituality of Hardi Rishi that he even likened him to the prophets. For Khaki a man without a *pir* was likely to fall under the influence of the devil.[95]

چون رسول الله گفت پیر مانند نبی است   پس چنین تشبیه در وصفش نه لاف است و محال
هر کرا پیری نباشد پیر او شیطان بود   پس بود بی پیر در نوعی ز انواع ضلال

So enamoured were the Suharwardis of the spirituality of the Rishis that they even justified pilgrimages to their tombs from the standpoint of Islam.[96] Khaki quotes Hardi Rishi to give weight to the Suharwardi viewpoint on this issue.[97] Notwithstanding the spiritual solemnity with which the Suharwardis undertook visits to the tomb of Nuruddin Rishi, it cannot be denied that such visits encouraged the practice of tomb worship in the Valley, common even in our own days, which even prompted the celebrated poet philosopher, Sir Muhammad Iqbal,[98] to remark:

کشمیری کہ با بندگی خو گرفتہ
بتے می تراشد ز سنگِ مزارے

It would appear from the foregoing discussion that the Suharwardis too became the cultural mediators of local Islamic tradition, so much so that Khaki in spite of his being an illustrious *khalifa* of Hamza Makhdum, took pride in offering allegiance (*bait*) to Hardi Rishi. He describes Hardi Rishi as *Pir-i Suhabat*[99]; he even speaks of his initiation in the Rishi order as a blessing (*tabarruk*).[100]

A significant conclusion emerging from Khaki's eulogization of the Rishis is that the Suharwardi order itself, in due course, was assimilated and absorbed in the Rishi order. Khaki's own son, Shaikh Muhammad Sayeed, became the *khalifa* of Hardi Rishi and was buried at the latter's shrine in deference to public opinion on account of his popularity among the people of Islamabad.[101] Khaki's distinguished successor, Baba Nasibuddin Ghazi, and the latter's *khalifa*, Baba Daud Mishkati, were, indeed, true representatives of the period during which the Suharwardi and the Rishi traditions were gradually transformed by a process of mutual adjustment. It would, therefore, be useful to study how they sought to find a unity in the seemingly distinct trends as represented by the Suharwardis and the Rishis.

Baba Nasib, like his spiritual preceptor Khaki, was greatly influenced by the Rishi movement. Like Khaki, who mostly subsisted on wild vegetables, Nasib adopted vegetarianism and celibacy.[102] However, throughout his life, he remained socially active, moving from one village to another[103] in order to consolidate the foothold gained by Nuruddin among the folk. He went as far as Ladakh and Karna in the north-west and the Pirpanjal pass in the south. During his travels he also met the Rishis, and it was under their influence that he dedicated himself to the cause of the poor. The social work performed by him and his devoted followers, numbering three to four hundred throughout the length and breadth of the Valley, ultimately earned him the title of father of the poor, *Abul Fuqara.*[104] It is significant to note here that it was through Baba Nasib's interpretation of Nuruddin's sayings that the teachings of Islam spread down the social ladder. He is still remembered among the common folk for utilising the services of the *bhands* for the wider dissemination of Islamic teachings. The traditional performances of the *bhands* at the shrine of Baba Nasib on the eve of his anniversary not only remind us of their association with the saint but also of the broadening social horizon given to the process of Islamization by even a Suharwardi Sufi.[105]

A distinguished trait of Baba Nasib's social behaviour was his extremely tolerant attitude towards the non-Muslims. In spite of his *Shari'a*-mindedness,[105a] he visited the cremating places of the Hindus and offered prayers there for the departed souls. Such a practice did cause serious concern to his contemporaries. Thus while answering a question about his unique behaviour, he addressed his disciples with tearful eyes in words which are worth quoting:

> "Whatever I see is beyond your vision. Many souls of such persons as outwardly died Hindus appear to me as those of believers. And some of these souls even say (to me): 'Your blessings lessen our tortures': So, I feel pleasure in doing this beneficence."[106]

Daud Mishkati, himself a leading *faqih* of his time, while recording this anecdote, gives tacit approval to his preceptor's behaviour.[107] It would appear that Nasib, notwithstanding his *Shari'a*-consciousness, considered a faithful life of even a non-Muslim to be the best preparation for the next world.

Death was not interpreted as only a terror by Baba Nasib, but as an eye-opener for narrowing down the gulf between the rich and the poor. Were the wealthy, according to him, aware of the implications of death, they would cease to be instruments of social exploitation. Similarly, should the poor come to realise the meaning of death, they would be relieved of their wretchedness.[108] The idea of death was also bound to bring the believer closer to God. A moment's realization of the purpose of creation was better than a thousand years of worship.[109] One who really knew the truth was superior to lakhs of such *zahids* as merely resorted to extreme asceticism like subsisting on wild herbs, grass and leaves. Baba Nasib likened such ascetics to donkeys and cows. Similarly, men who only lived to eat rich food were denounced as belonging to the category of wild animals like wolves and leopards. Here Baba Nasib actually reflects his attitude towards the wealthy whom he thought unmindful of the interests of the poor. God recognition, according to Nasib, was thus beyond the reach of the exploiters of the weak, nor was the cognition of God a saleable commodity to lure rich men to purchase it in the market.[110] To live for the welfare of the poor was a virtue and the key to the realization of ultimate truth.

Thus, in the true manner of the Rishis, Baba Nasib himself wore ordinary clothes and even expressed his displeasure over his trusted disciple's act of carrying more than the required clothes with him during one of his travels. Nasib did not even touch the money which was offered to him by the people; instead, it was expended for charitable purposes including repairs of mosques, public baths and toilets. Once a person came to present some cash as *nazr* to Baba Nasib, but so averse was he to the idea of money for his personal comfort that he got annoyed with the visitor when in the course of shaking hands a coin touched his sleeves. He asked Daud Mishkati to bring some water and washed his hands, arms and sleeves. Sensing that his preceptor considered money to be impure, Mishkati, in a true juridical manner, questioned the belief of Baba Nasib, who quickly retorted: "For this *darwish* money is totally contaminated."[111]

We should not, however, misconstrue Baba Nasib's contempt for money as asceticism in its ordinary sense. The deeper social philosophy behind his disdain for money was that money was not the ultimate aim, but an instrument for higher ends. One who was in possession of money was required to make the best use of it so that good could be done to humanity. Under the influence of Nuruddin's teachings Baba Nasib urged the people to despise riches lest these should destroy their possessors. The verses of Nuruddin, mostly those sayings where he enjoins the believers to undertake public charities for the gratuitous relief of the distressed, find a prominent place in his *Numama*.[112] Loving kindness towards the poor, inspired no doubt by Nuruddin's verses, was the chief preoccupation of Baba Nasib. It was indeed his concern over the exploitation of the poor and the resultant concentration of money in fewer hands that determined his attitude towards the rich.

The influence of Nuruddin's poetry on the mind of Baba Nasib was such that he would often faint under the intoxicating spell of the verses,[113] pregnant with the words of *Shari'a*, *tariqa*, *ma'rifa* and *haqiqa*.[114] Since the verses of Nuruddin were also full of wit and wisdom, Baba Nasib quotes a *hadith* to support his contention that poetry is permissible in Islam.[115] Nasib seems to have been prompted to write in defence of poetry by the critical attitude of some *'Ulama* towards the mystical verses of Nuruddin. The central argument put forward by him was that for a beginner (*mubtadi*) in the path (*suluk*) indulgence in poetry is harmful since it is likely to detract his attention from true religion. Poetry for Nasib was, indeed, what it was to Wordsworth: "Poetry is most just to its divine origin, when it administers the comforts and breathes the thoughts of religion." The fact is that Baba Nasib regarded the poetry of a perfect Sufi like Nuruddin as not merely the utterance of deep and heart-felt truths but even an act of worship.[116]

It is not surprising, therefore, that to Baba Nasib goes the credit for being the first to render some of Nuruddin's verses into Persian. His purpose was to provide guidance to *saliks* and reveal to them the kind of beauty and truth which God had revealed to an illuminated soul like Nuruddin. Baba Nasib was also the first Kashmiri to compose a *manqabat* in the local dialect, which testifies to the veneration in which Nuruddin was held by the distinguished *khalifa* of the noted Suharwardi Sufi of Kashmir:

> Shaikh Nuruddin of Kaimuh
> The Prophet filled his breasts with his light (*Nur-i Muhammadi*).
> The Prophet will himself condescend to offer prayers at his grave;
> Such news has reached as far as Medina.[117]

A careful reading of Baba Nasib's *Nurnama* leaves us in no doubt about his earnest attempt to bring home to his readers that Nuruddin Rishi's words and deeds were rooted in the *Sunna* and the *Sharia*. Such an attempt should not be described as a deliberate distortion of the facts of history or the historical perspective. In reality, he makes his account of historical facts concerning the life of Nuruddin conform to the ideals of *Sunna* and the *Shari'a*, turning them into examples to be followed by *saliks* for whom the *Nurnama* was written. For understanding how an element of interpretation enters into every fact concerning the asceticism of Nuruddin and his followers, it is also important to know how Nasib himself argues the case in favour of the Rishis.

It is said that Nuruddin was once asked as to why he had violated the injunctions of the Quran by renouncing conjugal life. The Shaikh replied that whatever was ordained in the Quran and whatever the Prophet had said regarding the sanctity of marriage was incumbent on believers. But it is also true that the Almighty had created men mainly for the purpose of His worship. Thus it was expected of them to worship in seclusion for gaining the Lord's favour. Nuruddin considered the celebration of the marriage contract (*nikah*) to be obligatory (*wajib*); yet, according to Nasib, the Shaikh talks about the three categories of men. That is, marriage was *sunna* for those who could treat their wives equally; but men in possession of money and riches were lustful and prone to commit sin. So, for the second category, it was necessary to marry in order to save themselves from indulging in sin. However, men who lacked the capacity to fulfil the obligations of the conjugal life were sure to indulge in sin by making a mockery of such a sacred contract; for them, therefore, it was disapproved (*makru*).[118]

Even viewed strictly from the standpoint of Islamic ethics, Baba Nasib's defence of the celibacy of the Rishis admits of a satisfactory apologia. He nowhere insists on the practice of celibacy except for the Rishis who could not, on account of their weakness and disability consequent upon rigorous ascetic practices, fulfil the obligations of married life. According to Baba Nasib, *nikah* alone was not the *sunna*, there were many other sayings and deeds of the Prophet equally incumbent on believers. One who did not conform totally to the *sunna* was an apostate, continued Nasib, but one who gave up an act of the Prophet with the noble intention of soley devoting oneself to God was not guilty of committing a serious sin. Even the Prophet, remarks he, had approved of such an act.[119] It is also in this context that Nasib refers to the celibacy of Christ, Mary, Yahya (John the Baptist), Uways-i Qarni and Bibi Rabia. Thus while addressing the *saliks*, Nasib remarks: "O *darwish*, to keep away from women and children is the duty of men."[120] Like his preceptor, Baba Nasib wrote also in defence of vegetarianism,[121] but at the same time he strongly expressed his disapproval of the extreme aceticism of some Rishis. He even quotes Nuruddin's verses in his criticism of such Rishis as had retired to the jungle.[122] He wanted them to earn an honest living by the sweat of their brow. It is certain that the idea of leading a life of renunciation still found currency among certain men during his time; hence through undertaking various tours, he emphasized the significance of combining asceticism with social action. Hard labour in agricultural pursuits, combined with the concern for the poor and the needy was, in Baba Nasib's estimation, the prime virtue of true Rishis.

It would not be unreasonable to suggest that under the influence of Baba Nasib the Rishi movement entered a crucial phase in its history. Although Nasib never claimed to be a Rishi, in actual practice he seems to have chosen Nuruddin as a model of personal piety and conduct. It is of significance to note that not unlike Nuruddin he toured different parts of the Valley with the main purpose of creating *Shari'a*-consciousness[123] among people who, in spite of their professed faith in Islam, were wedded to the traditional religious culture. The undertaking of the repairs of the mosques and the bathrooms[124] and laying the foundation for mosques in several villages[125] were important steps in the direction of creating an Islamic ambience in a true sense.

Notwithstanding the vegetarianism and celibacy practised by some of the disciples of Baba Nasib, they played an effective role even as ascetics in the dissemination of Islamic teachings among the villagers.[126] Not only did most of them act as *imams* of mosques, but some of them even carried out proselytizing activities.[127] Even while living in a cave, Baba Salih, a disciple of Baba Nasib, considered it an act of piety to earn his livelihood by copying the Quran. The popularity of Baba Salih attracted the Mughal prince, Dara Shikouh to his cave.[128] Some of Nasib's disciples, like Haji Baba, Shaikh Nasir Bengali[129] Baba Abdullah[130] and Muhammad Amin Sofi[131] went from village to village enjoining people to follow the *Shari'a*. Among these, Baba Abdullah's activities deserve special notice. He is said to have attracted a number of people towards Islam.[131a] In fact, most of his time was spent among the illiterate villagers teaching them the fundamentals of Islam. Like Baba Nasib he toured the rural areas along with a host of his followers who, besides constructing mosques, public baths and toilets in the villages, also laid out gardens for the public. Baba Abdullah himself designed a garden in which he planted apricot trees.[132] Shaikh Haji Hasan, a disciple of Baba Nasib, practised celibacy and dedicated his life for the uplift of the poor.[133]

The most outstanding disciple of Baba Nasib was Baba Daud. It was on account of committing to memory a well-known book on *Hadith* that he was given the title of *Mishkati*.[134] Although Daud Mishkati was well-versed in *fiqh*, *hadith*, *tafsir* and allied fields, he did not deem it unworthy of an *'alim* to humble his pride by seeking the company of the Rishis. As a matter of fact, he accompanied his spiritual preceptor to the abodes of the Rishis.[135] It was under the influence of the Rishi movement that even as an *álim* he did not fail to explain the deeper meaning of Nuruddin's verses and sought to define the role of an *'alim* and an *'arif* as reflected therein. Nuruddin not only wanted an *'alim* to recognise his inner self, but also expected him to rise above the customary narrow grooves of his society. Mishkati was also conscious of the fact that Nuruddin had struck a balance by confining the role of an *'arif* within the bounds of the *Shari'a*.[136]

But the most marked feature of Mishkati's hagiography, like that of his forerunners in the field, was a genuine attempt at understanding the social roles of the Rishis through intellectual understanding or appreciation. This type of understanding was not merely sympathetically attuned to particular emotional responses; in fact, it was real in more than one important sense. The real understanding came about only when, as a standard-bearer of the *Shari'a*, Mishkati shared the beliefs of the Rishis and identified himself with them. And even from the standpoint of the *Shari'a*, Mishkati, like Baba Daud Khaki and Baba Nasib, did not fail to appreciate precisely what Islam meant to the Rishis.

The Kubrawi Response to the Rishi Movement

The influence of the Rishi movement on the Kubrawis of Kashmir can be gleaned from three sources: *Tarikh-i Kashmir*, of Sayyid 'Ali, a descendant of Sayyid Tajuddin;[137] *Khat-i Irshad*,[138] a document containing Sayyid Muhammad Hamadani's guidance for the founder of the Rishi order; and the *Fathat-i Kubrawiyya* of Abdul Wahab Nuri. Besides these main sources, the annual practice of the citizens of Srinagar of going in a grand procession to the shrine of Nuruddin under the leadership of the priests of the Khanqah-i Mu'alla, until very recent times,[139] also deserves some notice in view of its significance in a traditional society.

Although Sayyid 'Ali's work is a political chronicle, in actual fact it is rich in information in regard to the activities of the Sufis. The chief merit of the work, from our point of view, is that it not merely refers to the association of the Kubrawi Sufis with Nuruddin, but it also takes us into the deep recesses of the heart of a Kubrawi exposed to the radiant influence of the social philosophy of the Rishis. The deep influence of Nuruddin's mystical poetry on Sayyid 'Ali's writings is borne out by his unbounded praise for its ability to ennoble and uplift the human soul.[140] Not only does he testify to the social significance of Nuruddin's tomb as a centre of pilgrimage for all sections of the Kashmiri people,[141] but he even quotes approvingly the following verses of Khwaja Habibullah Naushahri, probably the first of their kind in Persian, in praise of Nuruddin:[142]

نورالدین ریشی است مرد بادشاه ریشاں　　اندرین کشمیر قبرش تیک دارد اشتهار

در ریاضت ثانیش نامد کسی در ملک ما　　چون نشانِ باطنش اندر کلامِ خوشگوار

بندگی باید پیمبر زادگی در کار نیست　　عبد رب است آنکه دارد جاگه قرب وجوار

هرکه اندر نسل نازد بے شک آنکس نادم است　　در قیامت پیش رب ذوالجلال قبح کار

اصل آدم خاک آمد زان سبب مرجع بخاک خاک را لایق نباشد در نسب کردا فتخار

نیست کس دم زدن اندر نسب جز آل او افتخار از نسل آدم یافت احمد ز انکسار

از نسب پرسش نمی باشد درون قبر تنگ از عمل پرسند آنجا دو ملایک نامدار

هر که گوید از کراهت نونده ریشی اصل نیست بے شک آنکس در جہنم جای دارد مرد کار

A close examination of Sayyid 'Ali's glorification of Nuruddin brings to light certain facts of history which have so far remained hidden for want of analysis.

The chronicler's admiration for the Rishi's devotion to God, besides testifying to the estimation in which Nuruddin was held in the Kubrawi circles just within a century after his death, points to the gradual absorption of the Kubrawis in the local Islamic identity. Not only in devotion but also in respect of esoteric knowledge, Sayyid Ali did not find any parallel to Nuruddin in Kashmir. This shows that Nuruddin had begun to wield greater influence among the Kashmiris than even Sayyid 'Ali Hamadani and Sayyid Muhammad Hamadani. And this explains the fact why he also came to be popularly known as *Shaikh al-'Alam*[143] in contrast to the title *Shah-i Hamadan*, bestowed by Kashmiris on Sayyid 'Ali Hamadani.

But more revelatory in the verses of Khawaja Habibullah Naushahri, himself a Kubrawi, is his criticism of the group of the Sayyids who, out of sheer vanity, claimed to be the descendants of the Prophet. So proud were they of their descent that they are said to have passed derogatory remarks about Nuruddin. The main reason for such unbecoming behaviour was their concern over the Rishi's extreme ascetic habits under the influence of Hindusim. It is however significant that the false pride of the Sayyids about their noble pedigree and their mistaken notions about Nuruddin's asceticism evoked criticism from even the Kubrawis themselves, who stressed that true nobility was derived not from birth but from devotion to God. Whosoever is proud of being a descendant of the Prophet's family, believes Sayyid 'Ali, will have to repent on the Day of Judgement. The main argument put foward to counter the claim of the Sayyids is that man is essentially made of clay; hence it does not behove a human to be proud of his origin. True, Sayyid Ali was conscious of the fact that none except the descendants of the Prophet (*Al-i Muhammad*) should be proud of their pedigree (*nasb*), but at the same time, it was his firm belief that among the sons of Adam, it is primarily Ahmad alone, who by virtue of his humility, deservedly earned the title of the Pride of Creation. Thus the Kubrawis even condemn such persons to hell as challenge the holiness of Nuruddin on grounds of his birth.[144] In other words, they considered it unworthy of the Sayyids to claim a high social position only because of their noble progenitor, and not to deserve it by living worthily, with the virtue of humility so dear to the Prophet Muhammad.

The attitude of the Kubrawis towards the Rishi movement is also exemplified in the discussion at a meeting Sayyid Muhammad Hamadani had with Nuruddin.[145] The circumstances leading to the meeting are laden with social meaning. After having stayed in Srinagar for a number of years with his companions as the guest of the Sultan, Sayyid Muhammad Hamadani heard about the popularity of Nuruddin among the rural folk. Thereupon he expressed his desire to see the Kashmiri saint, though his companions, the Sayyids, were unwilling to associate with someone they considered to be an illiterate man (*nadan marad*), practising austerities in the manner of the Hindu saints.[146] But the Sayyids had to eat humble pie when their leader set off to pay a personal visit to Nuruddin. The meeting between the Sayyids and the Kashmiri saint took place at Zalsu, about six miles on the road leading to the tomb of Nuruddin at Charar. From Sayyid 'Ali's description of the miracles performed at the meeting and the dialogue between the Kashmiri saint and the Kubrawi Sufi, some important conclusions emerge. His account is corroborated and supplemented by later sources which give added weight to these conclusions. First, the followers of Sayyid Muhammad Hamadani were convinced about the exalted status of the Rishi among the most perfect of the saints.[147] Second, the very presence of Nuruddin's two women disciples at the meeting namely Behat Bibi[148] and Dehat Bibi[149] was a pointer to the Sayyids that the isolation of women and segregating them from all social intercourse was not warranted by Islam. The purpose might also have been to show to the distinguished guests that there were also women elevated to the status of sainthood in the Rishi order in accordance with the teachings of Islam. Lastly, by offering formal allegiance to Sayyid Muhammad Hamadani, in spite of his high spiritual status,[150] Nuruddin not merely vindicated the honour of the Prophet's worthy descendant in the characteristic humility of a true Sufi, but he even acknowledged the debt of the Kashmiris to him and his father for their services to Islam in Kashmir as upholders of the *Shari'a*.

Not only the Persian chronicles, hagiographies, verses of Nuruddin, but also the *Khat-i Irshad*, an extant document preserved in the Khanqah-i Mu'alla, testify to the Kashmiri saint's final absorption in the Islamic identity. However, it should not be supposed that by acknowledging Sayyid Muhammad Hamadani as his preceptor Nuruddin lost his identity as a leader of the Rishis. As a matter of fact, his enrolment in the Kubrawi order took place just before Sayyid Muhammad Hamadani decided to leave Kashmir after staying there for seventeen years,[151] marking the successful fruition of the spadework done by the Kubrawis as religious teachers. What is of significance to remember is that in his *Khat-i Irshad* Sayyid Muhammad Hamadani used the term Rishi while referring to Nuruddin as a perfect *Wali*,[152] which also points to the Kubrawi Sufi's confidence in the Kashmiri saint in carrying on the mission of his predecessors. And by authorising Nuruddin to enrol disciples, the gifted son of Sayyid Ali Hamadani dispelled the false notion of his Sayyid companions that they alone, by virtue of their noble descent, were capable of providing religious leadership to Kashmiris. In fact, by investing a humble Kashmiri with the authority of guiding the people,[153] Muhammad Hamadani emphasized the importance of the basic Islamic teachings of primacy of human actions over any hereditary factor in determining an individual's social status. It is also worth noting that while Muhammad Hamadani entrusted the reigning Sultan to the guidance of his Sayyid companions,[154] considering the problem of language, the common man was left to the care of Nuruddin. This was because Nuruddin alone, with his local disciples, could prove an effective channel of communication between the Great Tradition of Islam and the Little Tradition of the peasant society. And this is particularly borne out by Nuruddin's innumerable verses in which he enjoins Kashmiris undergoing a process of Islamic acculturation to follow the *Shari'a*.[155]

It is also notable that Sayyid Muhammad Hamadani allowed Nuruddin to perform *chilas*,[156] thereby adapting to an Islamic framework[157] the Rishi's practice of meditating in the caves or in seclusion. Consequently the bonds of the Kubrawis and the Rishis were cemented in such a manner that in due course the Kubrawi order itself got absorbed in the Rishi order. In fact, no less a person than 'Abdul Wahab Nuri, the author of *Fathat-i Kubrawiyya* (the Triumphs of the Kubrawis) bears elaborate testmony to the influence exercised by the Rishi movement on the Kubrawis. Although Wahab's encomium on Nuruddin's miracles and poetry, saturated with didactic songs of *wahdat* and *m'arifa*,[158] is mainly based on the accounts of Nasib and Mishkati, he approvingly quotes the earlier hagiographers to prove the high position of Nuruddin in the hierarchy of the Sufis. Not only does Wahab applaud the social role of Nuruddin in guiding men to the right path[159] and protecting the interests of the weak against the strong,[160] but he even refers to the dreams of Baba Daud Khaki[161] and Maulana Jamaluddin in order to testify to the supremacy of Nuruddin among the *auliya.*[162]

Wahab reveals his *Shari'a*-mindedness when he shows his concern over the habit of certain Rishis who broke their fast with stones, earth and ashes. Such a practice, though looked at with disfavour by him from the viewpoint of the *Shari'a,*[163] did not prompt him to dub the Rishis as un-Islamic. Thus while writing about Baba Bamuddin, he remarks that, notwithstanding his habit of eating crushed stones, the Rishi lived as a Muslim.[164] Wahab even gave an 'orthodox' approval to Nuruddin's claim that the Prophet was the founder of the Rishi order; his main justification being that one who fought one's carnal desires was, according to the sayings of the Prophet, a faithful and virtuous Muslim.[165]

The foregoing discussion suggests that Wahab was in no small measure responsible for drawing the Kubrawis closer to the Rishis. Later, the custodians of the Kubrawi *Khanqah* at Srinagar kept alive the historic memory of their links with Nuruddin through the ingenious practice of holding a procession in order to avert an apprehended calamity. It seems that the Kubrawis perverted to local use the simple injunction of the Prophet for offering *salat al-istisqa*[166] during an imminent natural calamity, when they held public rogations and made a pilgrimage at the head of a procession to the shrine of Nuruddin. The procession would usually start from Khanqah-i Mu'alla and joined by men and even children on the way to Chrar, reach the tomb of the saint.

An interview conducted by the author with some old men in the city including the Imam of the Khanqah-i Mu'alla reveals that only the prayers of *istigfar* were recited loudly by the pilgrims in the procession. A keen observer of Kashmiri society, in the closing years of the last century, Walter Lawrence, recorded his impressions about the reverence which the shrine of Nuruddin commanded among the Kashmiris. As he remarks: "Musalmans from all parts of the Valley flock to Chrar Shariff and when scarcity is imminent, where calamities such as earthquake, cholera and drought occur, thousands gather there and sit silent on the hills around, confessing their sins and begging for pardon. This impressive ceremony is known as *Nafl.*"[167]

The Naqshbandi Attitude Towards the Rishis

Although the Naqshbandi order was introduced in Kashmir during the reign of Sultan Sikandar, it did not make any headway in the Valley until the advent of Khwaja Mahmud towards the close of the sixteenth century.[168]

The attitude of the Naqshbandis towards the Rishis is primarily reflected in *Tuhfat al-Fuqara* of Muhammad Murad Teng. A staunch follower of the Naqshbandi order,[169] Teng nevertheless does not fail to record the merits of the Rishis in his hagiography. He seems to have been a close friend of Nur Baba,[170] a disciple of Shaikh Daud *alias*, Batmaloo Sahib.[171] It was from Nur Baba that he learnt about the spiritual powers of the Batmaloo and his philanthropic activities.[172] Teng is full of praise for other contemporary Rishis of his time like Naji Baba [173] and Lal Baba.[174] Not only do the piety and abstemious habits of the Rishis seem to have captivated Teng but their sociability and popularity too prompted him to write about them. According to Teng, Lal Baba used to have frequent meetings with his father.[175] Teng also praises a contemporary Rishi, Mir Muhammad Sultan[176] for his simplicity, piety and service to the destitute and the needy.[177]

The Sufis of the Naqshbandi order do not seem to have left as great a mark on the Kashmiris as did the Rishis. In fact, the popularity of the latter among the masses even attracted the Naqshbandis to them. Thus the popularity of Ummi Rupi Rishi drew Teng to him.[178] Although Teng's conversation with the saint shows the concern of a Naqshbandi over the vegetarianism practised by the Rishis, he does not give the slightest indication of any disapproval of the practice. On the other hand, he makes no secret of the impact left by Ummi Rishi's respectful and friendly attitude to him. We are told that special non-vegetarian food was served to Teng by Ummi Rishi himself when he called at the Rishi's house. It was also on this occasion that the Naqshbandi saint entered into a dialogue with the Rishi on the latter's initiation in *suluk* and other matters. While answering a question as to why he had given up meat, Ummi Rupi Rishi, without entering into any argument, remarked that he was following the instructions of his *pir*, Baba Hardi Rishi.[179]

It would be seen that the Naqshbandis of Kashmir, like the Suharwardis, were influenced by the Rishi movement. True, they were able to enrol some Rishis as their disciples,[180] but they could not prevent such disciples from observing certain norms which were necessary for the cultivation of personal piety. Thus Mahdi Rishi Kakapuri, even after becoming the *khalifa* of Mir Muhammad Baqir Naqshbandi, subsisted on a vegetarian diet and continued to practise severe austerities.[181]

Conclusion

From the foregoing account, it is clear that the beliefs of the Rishis were not incompatible with Islam. While analysing the objective description of the way of life of the Rishis, as given by the hagiographers within the integrated framework of the spiritual and legal heritage of Islam, we have not allowed a misconception to enter our minds that the Rishi movement was somewhat outside the pale of the so-called "orthodox" Islam. Liturgical development among the Rishis was within the mainstream of Islam; in fact, the recital of *dhikr* was immensely valued as early as the foundation of the order by Shaikh Nuruddin along the lines of the Kubrawi, Suharwardi and Naqshbandi traditions. Thus the Rishis proved to be the cultural mediators of the Islamic tradition. They not only pulled down language barriers but also made the Islamic tradition more comprehensible to the common folk in meaningful rather than in outwardly syncretistic forms. It is true that the Rishis retained elements from the traditional Hindu-Buddhist religious culture, but it would be wrong to conclude on that reasoning that this development led to the growth of syncretistic religious sociology among Kashmiris. As a matter of fact, the evolution of the *Shari'a* bound structure of thought and the concomitant enfeeblement of such elements as celibacy, vegetarianism, extreme ascetic practices, and seclusion in caves is to be viewed as a natural sequel to the 'cult of saints'. The various nuances of this development can be fully understood against the background of the Quranic concept of civilisation, which values, within the bounds of its encompassing *Shari'a*, man's ongoing effort to establish an equilibrium between his need to give new forms of meaning to his experience and his desire to cling to the forms in which conventional wisdom lies. The fact is that the Rishis, while apparently accommodating local Hindu-Buddhist practices to the Islamic framework, gradually paved the way for the assimilation of the people in the Islamic identity. In the changed environment, the traditional religious scheme of thought was gradually abandoned, and no longer remained the basic frame of reference of the people, as they were swept by the wave of Islamic acculturation. It is indeed hard to escape the conclusion that the Rishis were largely responsible for influencing the environmental, institutional and linguistic forms which ultimately created conditions for the never-ending process of Islamization in both religious and social terms.

REFERENCES AND NOTES

1. The tombs of Baba 'Ali Raina, Baba Haidar Tulmuli and, particularly, Baba Nasibuddin Ghazi attract a considerable number of devotees on the *'Urs* days.
2. See Chapter III, "Socio-Religious Milieu of Nuruddin."
3. On his arrival in Kashmir during the reign of Zain al-'Abidin (1420-70), the Sayyid was coridally received by the Sultan and given a state grant for maintenance. See Sayyid 'Ali, *Tarikh-i Kashmir*, f. 29; Mulla Ahmad bin Sabur, *Khawariq al-Salikin*, f. 13.
4. See Chapter III, "Socio-Religious Milieu of Nuruddin."
5. Sabur, *op. cit.*, ff. 142b and 143a; Khaki, *Dastur al-Salikin*, pp. 65-67.
6. See Rizvi, *Sufism in India*, I. pp. 203, 277-78.
7. Nizami, *Some Aspects of Religion and politics in India in the Thirteenth Century*, pp. 255,256. See also Annemarie Schimmel, *Islam in the Indian Subcontinent*, p. 33.
8. It is situated in the district of Baramulla.
9. Sayyid Ali, *op. cit.*, p. 29a Mishkati, *Asrar al-Abrar*, f. 103b.
10. Mishkati, *op. cit.*, ff. 192-193a.
11. Khaki, *op. cit.*, p. 67.; *'Ulama-i Zahiri* is the name given to the wordly *Ulama* as against *Ulama-i Akhirat.* The first category of the *Ulama* was criticised by the latter on account of the cultivation of such habits of mind and heart, usually through their association with kings and rich people, as were inimical to the growth of higher spiritual and ethical values in Muslim society.
12. *Ibid.*, pp. 66-67.
13. Popularly known in the Valley as Makhdum Saheb, his shrine is situated on the picturesque slopes of the Hariparbat hillock in Srinagar. He was born in 1494 A.D. at Tujar, a village in the district of Baramulla. His father, 'Uthman Raina, was a patron of learning and is reported to have been one of the props of the seminary of Shaikh Ism'ail Kubrawi situated on the hillock. According to Baba Daud Khaki, it was an annual practice with 'Uthman Raina to donate one-tenth of his property (*'ushr*) to the seminary for its upkeep. See Khaki, *op. cit.*, f. 38.
14. His father had appointed Baba 'Ali Najar as his *khalifa*, who however became as Shia under the influence of Shamsuddin Iraqi. Consequently, the *khanqah* of Shaikh Isma'il Kubrawi was maintained by Fatullah for some time, though he was finally forced to emigrate to Sialkot by Kaji Chak. For the political role of Kaji Chak during the civil war in Kashmir. See Mohibbul Hasan, *Kashmir Under the Sultans*, pp. 111-112, 114-115, 117-118, 124, 128-135, 148, 153, 280, 297.
15. Shaikh Isma'il Kubrawi (d. 1510) lies buried near his own hospice at Hariparbat hillock in Srinagar. The *khanqah* maintained by him was once the great centre of Islamic learning attracting students from even Herat and Transoxiana. It was on account of his learning that Isma'il

Kubrawi was made *Shaikh al-Islam* by Sultan Hasan Shah (1472-84). See Sayyid 'Ali, *op. cit.*, f. 22b.

16. Khaki, *op. cit.*, p. 63.
17. *Ibid.*, p. 66.
18. It is interesting to note that Hamza Makhdum once took Rupi Rishi along with him for purposes of enjoying the beautiful landscape of the district of Lar. See Miram Bazaz, *Tadhkirat al-Murshidin* ff. 99ab.
19. Among these must be mentioned Shankar Rishi, Rupi Rishi and Hardi Rishi. See Khaki, *op. cit.*, ff. 178, 192b, 193a, 219a.
20. Hamza Makhdum offered *fatiha* at the tomb along with Rupi Rishi and his other disciples. Haidar Tulmuli, *Hidayat al-Mukhlisin*, f. 68a. According to Khaki (*op. cit.*, f. 177), Hamza Makhdum used to visit the tomb of the Rishis. See also Hasan Qari, *Rahat al-Talibin*, f. 12a.
21. 'Ali Raina, *Tadhkirat al-'Arifin*, f. 24b.
22. From Áli Raina's account, it appears that the custodians of the shrine of Nuruddin had begun to receive gifts from the visitors quite early. *Ibid.*
23. It is not merely on the authority of sources available to 'Ali Raina but also from an inner experience felt by him at the tomb of Nuruddin that he calls the founder of the Rishi order the spiritual preceptor (*murshid*), helper (*dastgir*) of a number of seekers (*taliban*) in the spiritual path, a perfect *wali* and above all *Qutb al-Aqtab*. *Ibid.*, ff. 31b, 33b; also 23a. Remarkably enough, the saint vouchsafed his vision to 'Ali Raina following the recital of *fatiha* and *Sura-i Yasin* by the seeker before going to sleep at the tomb for a night. See *Ibid.*, f. 24b.
24. *Ibid.*, ff. 262b-263a.
25. *Ibid*, f. 262b.
26. *Ibid.*, f. 263a.
27. The Quran 31/27; see also 18/109.

27a. 'Ali Raina, *op. cit.*, p. 263a.

28. *Ibid.*
29. *Ibid.*, f. 262b. Ishaq Qari remarks that before becoming the disciple of Hamza Makhdum, Hardi Rishi had received esoteric guidance from Christ, Moses, Khizr, Ilyas, Idris and 'Ali. (See *Chilchihat al-'Arifin*, f. 98b). Obviously, while quoting the long list of spiritual preceptors of Hardi Rishi before his initiation in the Suharwardi order, the purpose of the hagiographers seems to be clear. It was, in reality, to testify not only to the exalted status of the Rishi, but, also, more importantly, to that of Shaikh Hamza Makhdum who had the privilege of being the worldy (*zahiri*) guide of such an illuminated soul.
30. 'Ali Raina, *op. cit.*, f. 262b; also ff. 263b-264a.
31. *Ibid.*, ff. 264ab. Other disciples of Hamza Makhdum corroborate 'Ali Raina's information regarding the Suharwardi Sufi's personal visit to Hardi Rishi's house in order to initiate him in the Suharwardi order.

See Ishaq Qari, *op. cit.*, ff. 98b-99a; Haidar Tulmuli, *op. cit.*, ff. 43ab-45ab; Khawaja Miram Bazaz *op. cit.*, f. 30b.

32. Ali Raina, *op. cit.*, ff. 264ab.
33. See *Infra.*
34. Miram Bazaz, *op. cit.*, ff. 30b-31ab.
35. See Haidar Tulmuli, *op. cit.*, f. 44a, 45ab; Ishaq Qari, *op. cit.*, ff. 98ab-99a.
36. Miram Bazaz clearly writes that Hamza Makhdum advised Hardi Rishi not to eat meat and follow the way of the Rishis, *op. cit.*, ff. 31ab.
37. Haidar Tulmuli, *op. cit.*, f. 44a. Rupi Rishi was also honoured by Hamza Makhdum. The Suharwardi Sufi bestowed on the Rishi a patched frock (*khirqa*) cap (*kulah*) and a belt (*kamr band*). The Rishi was also authorised to popularise the order. *Ibid.*, f. 71b.
38. Hasan Qari's manuscript, available in the Research Library, Srinagar, comprises only twenty-three folios.
39. Haidar Tulmuli, *op. cit.*, f. 77b.
40. *Ibid.*, f. 72b.
41. *Ibid.*, ff. 77ab.
42. Ishaq Qari, *op. cit.*, f. 100b.
43. *Ibid.*, f. 100a.
44. 'Pole, axis', the highest member of the generally accepted hierarchy of Sufis around whom the world revolves.
45. 'Help' the title given to the most distinguished member of the hierarchy of Sufis; for instance, the celebrated Sufi 'Abdul Qadir Jilani is popularly known as 'Ghauth al-Azam'.
46. Ishaq Qari *op. cit.*, f. 101a.
47. See also Chapter VIII, "The Societal Dimensions of Miracles."
48. For his biography, see Pir Hasan, *Asrar al-Akhyar.* Urdu trans. under the title *Tarikh-i Auliya-i Kashmir*, pp. 175-179.
49. See also Khaki, *Dastur al-Salikin*, ff. 177b-178a, 192b-193a, 219a. For the importance of *Dastur al-Salikin*, see my student's unpublished M. Phil dissertation: Abdul Hamid Rather, *Historical Importance of Dastur al-Salikin of Baba Daud Khaki*, 1986, Dept. of History, Kashmir University.
50. Khaki, *Rishinama*, f. 16a.

    Ahl-i Sunna wa Jama' are 'the people of the community.' The expression is particularly used for the Sunnis who lay great stress on following the *Sunna*. "He who tires of my Sunna, does not belong to me." *Bukhari, Nikah* bab. I.
51. *Ibid.* ff. 32b. The Sufi practice of reciting *dhikr* aloud (*jali*) and mentally (*khafi*) has been mistakenly likened to *pranayama* by Tara Chand (*Influence of Islam on Indian Culture*, p. 82). Rizvi, *Sufism in India*, I, (pp. 272, 341, 351, 353) also believes that the Sufi practice of controlling their breath (*pas-i anfas*) was based on *pranayama*. Khaki, however,

leaves us in no doubt about the fact that *pas-i anfas* is a prerequisite for purifying the heart. It involves the practice of remembering God both aloud and inwardly or mentally, so that even a moment's forgetfulness does not sever the link between the Creator and the created. It is in this context that Khaki says that Hardi Rishi had a deep communion with God even while being part of the society he lived in. (*Tan ba khalq wa jan ba Khaliq dashtay zira ki ou: dam girifta dambadam maykard dhikray qalb wa bal*). *Rishinama*, f. 33a. Thus *pas-i anfas* was based on the Naqashbandi practice of *hosh-dar-dam* (social awareness even while breathing) and *khilwat dar anjuman* (spiritual awareness even in being as active member of society) rather than on the yogic *pranayama*. Khaki's explanation of the Naqshbandi practice of *dhikr* (*Ibid.*, p. 33a) in the context of Hardi Rishi is enough to dispel the misgiving that the Rishi's contemplative life was based on *pranayama*. See also Chapter II: "Historical Background of the Rishi Movement."

52. Khaki, *op. cit.*, ff. 20b, 22a.
53. *Ibid.*, ff. 15b, 16a, 20b.
54. Rafiqi's, (*op. cit.*, p. 23) account of the attitude of the Suharwardi's towards the Shias is mainly based on *Dastur al-Salikin*.
55. Khaki, *op. cit.*, f. 43b-44a.
56. Ishaq Khan, "Towards Understanding a Popular Muslim Ritual in the Kashmiri Environment," unpublished paper presented in the International Seminar on "New History" at India International Centre, New Delhi, February, 1988.
57. Khaki, *op. cit.*, ff. 43b-44a.
58. The forsakers of the truth.
59. Khaki, *op. cit.* ff. 43b-44a.
60. Khaki, *Qasida-i Gusl-i Yusuf Shahi*, f. 3a.
61. *Ibid*, ff. 4b-5ab.
62. Khaki, *Rishinama*, f. 121a.
63. Obviously the Rishis and Suharwardis were influenced by the Hindu-Buddhist environment, but what is of significance is that Khaki's basic frame of reference for justifying the asceticism of the Rishis remained the esoteric dimension of Islam.
64. *Ibid.*, f. 64b.
65. *Ibid.*, ff. 64b-65a.
66. *Ibid.*, ff. 65b-66ab.
67. *Ibid.*, f. 66b.
68. *Kimiya-i Sa'dat* is a well-known work of Imam Ahmed bin Ghazali (d. 1111 A.D.).
69. *Khazinat al-Jalali* is attributed to Makhdum-i Jahaninyan Jalauddin Bukhari. Its manuscript is preserved in the British Museum.
70. *Targhib al-Salat* was written by Muhammad bin Ahmad Zahid (d. 711 A.H/130-12 A.D.).
71. Khaki, *op. cit.*, ff. 66b-67ab.

72. *Ibid.*, f. 67b.
73. *Ibid.*, f. 68.
74. *Ibid.*, f. 69ab.
75. *Ibid.*, ff. 68-69a.
76. *Ibid.*, f. 69a.
77. *Ibid.*, f. 71a.
78. *Ibid.*, f. 70a.
79. In *Mirat al-Tabein* Sayyid 'Ali Hamadani remarks that one desirous of seeking God's favour should control one's ever-pestering cow-like self. Quoted in Khaki, *Rishinama* f. 69.
80. *Ibid.*, f. 70.
81. 'Ali Raina, *op. cit.*, ff. 45b-45a.
82. Shahi Rishi is said to have practised seclusion and vegetarianism for three years. *Ibid.*, f. 455a.
83. Khaki, *op. cit.*, f. 71a.
84. *Shahnama* is the work of the celebrated Persian poet, Firdausi.
85. *Miftah al-Jannah* was authored by Muhammad Mujair bin Wajiuddin (d. A.H. 770).
86. Hafiz Shirazi was the Persian poet well known for the odes in which he describes the joys of earthly and of divine love.
87. Khaki, *op. cit.*, f. 71a.
88. *Ibid.*, f. 71b.
89. *Ibid.*, f. 72b.
90. *Ibid.*, f. 83a.
91. *Ibid.*, f. 82b.
92. *Ibid.*, f. 83ab.
93. *Ibid.*, f. 82b.
94. See Ishaq Khan, *History of Srinagar, 1846-1947: A Study in Socio-Cultural Change*, pp. 104-105; see also Lawrence, *The Valley of Kashmir*, pp. 286-87.
95. Khaki, *op. cit.*, f. 97b. Shaikh Nizamuddin Auliya and Shaikh Nasiruddin Chirag also approvingly quote the *hadith* : he who has no *pir*, the devil is his *pir*. See Amir Hasan Sijzi, *Fawaid al-fuad* p. 175; Hamid Qalandar, Khyar *al-Majalis*, ed K.A. Nizami, p. 48.
96. Even the Ahl-i Hadith consider visits to graveyards to be the *Sunna*, though they do not approve of the visits undertaken with the sole purpose of invoking the help of the deceased.
97. Khaki, *op. cit.*, ff. 120ab.
98. Muhammad Iqbal, *Payam-i Mashriq*.
99. Most Sufis claimed several initiations and possessed a number of licences (*ijazas*). Trimingham dispels confusion and misunderstanding regarding upbringing (*Shaikh-at-tarbiya*) and discipleship (*Shaikh-as-Suhba*). See Trimingham, *The Sufi Orders of Islam*. p. 192.
100. Khaki, *op. cit.*, f. 55a.

101. The town is also known by its ancient name Anantnag. Situated in lat. 33° 44', long 75° 12', Islamabad is the second largest town in the Valley.
102. Pir Hasan, *op. cit.*, (Urdu tr.), p. 176; Diddamari, *Waqia't-i Kashmir*, ff. 99ab.
103. Diddamari, *op. cit.*, ff. 99ab.
104. Pir Hasan, *op. cit.*, p. 209; Khawaja Azam Diddamari remarks that Baba Nasib was a shelter for the poor and the destitute. See Diddamari, *op. cit.*, ff. 99ab.
105. It was through the courtesy of Mr. Abdul Rashid Lattoo of Bijbhera, presently in charge of the Library of the Department of History, Kashmir University that I was able to have a close view of the performances of *bhands* on the eve of the *Urs* in 1987.
105a. Wherever Baba Nasib went he preached the injunctions of the religious law (*ahkam-i Shar'a*). Diddamari, therefore, aptly remarks that the Baba, as a practical Muslim scholar, inspired men to seek true religious knowledge. Diddamari, *op. cit.*, ff. 99ab.
106. Hasan, *op. cit.*, p. 210.
107. *Ibid.*
108. *Ibid.*, p. 210.
109. *Ibid.*, pp. 210-211.
110. *Ibid.*, p. 211.
111. *Ibid.*, pp. 211-212.
112. See Baba Nasib, *Nurnama*, ff. 44ab, 61ab, 62b.
113. Baba Daud Mishkati, *Asrar al-Abrar*, f. 81b.
114. Nasib, *op. cit.*, f. 3a.
115. *Ibid.*, f. 3b.
116. *Ibid.*, f. 4a.
117. *Ibid.*, f. 5b.
118. *Ibid.*, ff. 88ab.
119. *Ibid.*, ff. 89ab.
120. *Ibid.*, f. 95b.
121. *Ibid.*, ff. 30ab.
122. *Ibid.*, f. 26b.
123. Diddamari, *op cit.*, ff. 99ab.
124. *Ibid.*
125. Diddamari, *op. cit.*, ff. 99ab.
126. See for details, Hasan, *op. cit.*, pp. 236-250.
127. Diddamari, *op. cit.*, f. 103b.
128. *Ibid.*, f. 104a.
129. Hasan, *op. cit.*, p. 241.
130. *Ibid.*, p. 245.
131. *Ibid.*, p. 249.
131a. Diddamari, *op. cit.*, ff. 156b-157a; Muhammad Murad Teng, *Tuhfat al-Fuqara*, f. 92b.

132. Hasan, *op. cit.*, pp. 245-246.
133. Diddamari, *op. cit.*, f. 103b.
134. According to Diddamari, the title was given to Baba Daud by his teacher Khawaja Haidar Charkhi. See *Ibid.*, f. 131b.
135. See Mishkati, *op. cit.*, f. 119a.
136. *Ibid.*, ff. 83ab-84ab.
137. See Appendix.
138. See Appendix.
139. Lawrence, *op. cit.*, p. 268.
140. Sayyid 'Ali, *op. cit.*, f. 33b.
141. *Ibid.*
142. *Ibid.*
143. The title Shaikh al-Alam appears first in Baba Nasib's *Nurnama*. See Nasib, *op. cit.*, f. 88a. Nasib also calls Nuruddin, 'Shaikh al-Arifin', *Ibid.*
144. Sayyid Ali, *op. cit.*, ff. 33b-34a.
145. *Ibid.*, ff. 34ab-35a; Wahab, *Fathat-i Kubrawiyya*, ff. 160b-162b.
146. Sayyid Ali, *op. cit.*, f. 34a.
147. *Ibid.*
148. Hasan, *op. cit.*, pp. 138-140; Miskin, *Tahaif al-Abrar*, p. 110.
149. *Ibid.*
150. For Mufti Jalauddin's views on Nuruddin's allegiance to Muhammad Hamadani, see "Uwaysiyyat aur Rishiyyat" in *Rishiyyat*, pp. 26-27.
151. Rafiqi wrongly states that Mir Muhammad left the Valley "after a stay of twelve years (808/1405)." Rafiqi, *op. cit.*, p. 103. See *Appendix*.
152. *Khat-i Irshad* is preserved in the Khanqah-i Mu'alla, Srinagar. It has been fully quoted in Wahab, *op. cit.*, ff. 163a-164b.
153. *Ibid.*
154. Sayyid Jalaluddin Bukhari was commanded by Mir Muhammad to guide Sultan Sikandar. Hasan, *op. cit.*, p. 27.
155. See Chapter V, "Religious Thought of Nuruddin."
156. Forty days seclusion, in which the novice or any Sufi completely secludes himself from the world in order to get absorbed in prayer and meditation.
157. See *Khat-i Irshad* (Appendix).
158. Wahab, *Fathat-i Kubrawiyya*, ff. 166a; also f. 145a.
159. *Ibid.*, f. 160a.
160. *Ibid.*
161. *Ibid.*, f. 166b.
162. Maulana Jamaluddin often visited the tomb of Nuruddin since he was told by the Prophet in a dream that nobody could reach the exalted status of the Kashmiri saint. *Ibid.*, f. 144a.
163. *Ibid.*, f. 169a.
164. *Ibid.*, f. 168b.
165. *Ibid.*, ff. 145ab.

166. Prayers for rain, consisting of two *rak'ah*, recited in the time of drought. *Mishkat*, IV, Chapter, III.
167. Lawrence, *op. cit.*, p. 288.
168. For a brief description of the history of the Naqshbandi order in Kashmir, see Rafiqi, *op. cit.*, pp. 125-29; Rizvi, *op. cit.*, II, p. 237-39.
169. Teng also authored *Hasnat al-Muqqarabin* in which wrote the history of Naqshbandis, beginning from Shaikh Ahmad Sirhindi to the days of his grand children. Teng's affiliation and abundant love for the Mujjaddi order is explicitly expressed at the beginning of the manuscript on the Sufis of Kashmir. See *Tuhfat al-Fuqara wa Auliya*. f. 1b.
170. Teng, *Tuhfat al-Fuqara*, f. 43b; also ff. 58ab.
171. Teng's account of Batamaloo Saheb is not only original but authentic. The later hagiographers have drawn upon *Tuhfat al-Fuqara* regarding the activities of Batmaloo Saheb.
172. See *Ibid.*, ff. 43ab-45ab.
173. Shah Jahan's Wazir, Sadullah Khan, paid a personal visit to Shaikh Najumuddin, *alias*, Naji Rishi Baba. The Baba was a true Rishi; he did not marry, nor did he ever touch meat, but remained engrossed in *dhikr* and *fikr*. He wore only one shirt throughout his life. Although the Rishi was popular among people for his aseticism, the visit of the Mughal dignitary is said to have further increased his popularity among the commoners. Naji Baba died in 1070 A.H. *Ibid.*, f. 46a.
174. *Ibid.*, f. 46b.
175. *Ibid.*, He died in 1105 A.H.
176. He was the *khalifa* of Teng's personal friend, Nur Muhammad Parwana. *Ibid.*, ff. 59ab.
177. *Ibid.*, f. 60a.
178. According to Hasan, Rupi Rishi was the resident of the village Lora in the *pargana* of Ular. Hasan, *op. cit.*, p. 145. But Teng describes Kocha Mulla in the same *pargana* as the habitat of the Rishi. Teng, *op. cit.*, ff. 61a-62a. Rupi Rishi had learnt by heart the verses of Nuruddin. Hasan, *op. cit.*, p. 146. Rupi Rishi was a contemporary of Batmaloo Saheb and enjoyed his company. He is not the same Rishi as Rupi Rishi of Shaikh Hamza's time.
179. Teng, *op. cit.*, f. 62.
180. Mulla Muhammad Fazil Kawausa gave up family life and resorted to seclusion after becoming the disciple of Naji Rishi Baba. But after coming in contact with the Mujjadid, Shaikh Ahmad Sirhindi, during the latter's visit to Kashmir, Kawausa denounced renuciation and thus came to be known as Nuruddin Thani. Teng, *op. cit.*, f. 85.
181. Even after becoming the *khalifa* of Mir Muhammad Baqir Naqshbandi, Mehdi Rishi secluded himself in a mosque at Kakpora for forty years. Hasan, *op. cit.* p. 146. According to Hasan, he lies buried in Kakapora (*Ibid*). But Teng who had personal relations with the Rishi writes that

he was buried at Kotapura near Amda Kadal in Srinagar. Interestingly enough, Teng also refers to the Rishi's ignorance about the act of touching the socks for purification, by drawing the three middle fingers over them (*masah*). But when the Rishi learnt about the practice of *masah* from Teng, he repented so much that he decided to repeat prayers, offered by him in the past in a state of ignorance, for two consecutive years. Teng, *op. cit.*, ff. 64b-65b, 66a.

CHAPTER VII

The Rishis and Conversion to Islam

The spread of Islam in the cultural context and historical circumstances of the Kashmir Valley—considerably different from those of sixth century Arabia—is a fascinating as well as intriguing topic. Earlier studies containing some information regarding conversion to Islam in Kashmir have laid great stress on the proselytizing role of Sufis from Central Asia and Persia. In particular, the role attributed to Sayyid Sharafuddin, Sayyid 'Ali Hamadani, Sayyid Muhammad Hamadani and a band of his followers is too well known to need repetition here.[1] While we do not deny the role of these Sufis in the spread of Islamic teachings in the Valley, it would be wrong to attribute the so-called 'mass conversions' of Kashmir to their miraculous exploits. Of course their activities led to certain individual conversions which must have been followed by group conversions. However, such a process of conversion took a long time to progress and mature, extending over centuries, largely owing to the persistence of the pre-Islamic customs and beliefs. 'Islamization' was thus a slow and a long process, involving initially the converts passive adherence to Islam, but ultimately a continuous progress towards bringing one's beliefs, attitudes or modes of conduct into harmony with the *Shari'a* This process is evident not only today but, as discussed before, is also reflected in the religious career of Nuruddin, whose attempt at the reconciliation of Hindu and Muslim practices actually paved the way for the gradual assimilation of the commoners in the Islamic identity.

Syncretism appears to be the key term in the study of early history of Islamization in Kashmir—a region which experienced a peaceful penetration of Islam long before the establishment of the Sultanate in 1320. As we shall see, Islamization in Kashmir was not a process of dramatic mass conversions secured by the Sufis through miracles, but what might be described as a gradual transmutation of the society, in which a considerable part of the population became Muslim, or was assumed to be Muslim, on its contact with the immigrant Muslim settlers, including the Sufis. A keen observer of Kashmiri society like Nuruddin was not oblivious of the changing pattern of the society he lived in. Having himself wandered in jungles and spent a good deal of time in meditation in a cave, Nuruddin ultimately realized, through his contact with the Kubrawi Sufis, the futility of following the path of renunciation. Thus in a number of verses he condemned asceticism and urged his followers to follow the Quran and the *Sunna*. But it remains a fact that in spite of Nuruddin's emphasis on strict adherence to the *Shari'a*, his early ascetic life and a number of his verses extolling renunciation had a popular appeal and, as a matter of reality, drew even the Hindu ascetics towards the Rishi movement. Nuruddin himself allowed his favourite disciples to retire to the caves and mountains in view of the popularity of the ascetics among the Kashmiri folk. Thus, if on the one hand he condemned renunciation, on the other it was used as a mode of conversion to attract the local people towards Islam.

Islam in fact became the religion of the great majority of rural Kashmir between the fifteenth and eighteenth centuries largely because, through the Rishis, it allowed the main configuration of pre-existing Kashmiri popular religion to adapt itself to the wider Islamic framework. The survival of pre-Islamic names,[2] particularly among the Rishis themselves, implies that Kashmiris experienced a gradual cultural and religious change. What makes this process of gradual change intelligible to us is also the fact that over the centuries the infiltration of Muslim ideas has had the effect of wearing down the temples: their properties dwindled and the spiritual and moral standards of their clergy declined. The corrupt practices of the cast-conscious Brahman priests must also have alienated the Kashmiris.[3] Nuruddin's condemnation of the caste system suggests that the members of low-castes must have been tempted to accept Islam in order to free themselves from the bondage of the Brahman.[4] Although their social position or family status did not improve or change radically after their entry into the Islamic fold, they could at least have the satisfaction of calling themselves members of the Islamic community. This sentiment is specially reflected in the *Rishinamas* of Chrar in which a conscious attempt has been made to present Islam as an egalitarian religion *vis-a-vis* the religious ethnocentrism of the Brahmanic faith.[5]

Islamization in Kashmir is thus not merely a religious question, but more importantly a subject of vital social importance. And in order to learn about it as a continuously evolving process of meaningful interaction between religion and society, we shall study Islamization at three levels: individual conversion, group conversion and acculturation. While the first category involves people embracing Islam voluntarily or as a matter of conviction or under the influence of Sufis and Rishis, the second category of 'converts' largely refers to people or groups of people who accepted Islam nominally in the wake of their tribal leader's conversion. Political and economic motives must also have made their nominal commitment to Islam possible. Under the third category, however, fall a large majority of commoners who experienced the gradual impact of Islamic acculturation on their social life through their contact with the peripatetic Rishis. Although the evolution of such a process had started much earlier through the creation of an Islamic ambience in the form of a few *khanqahs* and mosques, it gained momentum as a result of Nuruddin's visits to a number of villages in Kashmir which still preserve the tradition of his visits or sojourn in one form or the other.

What is striking about the pre-eminent position of Nuruddin in the history of Islam in Kashmir is the conversion of even prominent Hindu ascetics under his influence. Such conversions must have involved group conversions or initial adhesion to Islam. It is in the context of such situations that Nuruddin's verses in condemnation of polytheistic practices of the converts must have inspired.[6] Nuruddin's contribution to the gradual evolution of Kashmiri Muslim society had two dimensions: on the one hand he attempted to free Islam of its accretions; on the other his social behaviour—which was more in consonance with local practices than those of scholars, jurists or Sufi missionaries—influenced a considerable number of people to abstain from marriage and meat eating and subsist on dry bread or wild vegetables from the forest. The extreme asceticism, self-mortification, long fasts, sexual abstinence and seclusion, which marked the early life of Nuruddin, and indeed, the lives of his followers, must have weakened the contrast in the common mind between Islam and Hinduism or Buddhism thereby paving the way for the acceptance of the values of an alien system. This process of Islamic acculturation of the mass of Kashmiri people is made abundantly clear by certain important cases of individual conversions. Such conversions must have left a deep imprint on the illiterate folk living in a social milieu characterized by the potent belief in the spirituality of saints. It would, therefore, be necessary to examine the nature of certain cases of individual conversions in view of their significance in the medieval society.

Bhum Sadh's Conversion to Islam

During his travels in Anantnag, along with his disciple Baba Tajuddin, the Shaikh heard a group of people praising the miraculous feats of a prominent Brahman ascetic. Bhum Sadh, as he was known, was reputed to be accustomed to taking his daily bath, simultaneously at five places, namely, Chandanyar,[7] Shurahyar,[8] Chhatrayar,[9] Wullarnag,[10] and Khadanyar.[11] The ascetic had also gained celebrity for his seclusion in a cave at Bamzu[12] where he was absorbed in the adoration of hundreds of idols. The Shaikh, therefore, felt a keen desire to see the ascetic, not far from where he was travelling.[13]

On reaching Bamzu Nuruddin was involved in a lengthy discussion with the ascetic on several issues of religious and social importance, viz., the oneness of God, idol-worship, ritualistic practices evolved by the 'greedy' Brahmans, and above all, their social position as against that of the low-castes.[14] So vigorously did the Brahman ascetic defend his point of view to the last that no argument of the Shaikh could carry weight with him.[15] It was only when the ascetic asked the Shaikh to prove the authenticity of his statement that God was One that, through a miracle, the Rishi made the idols speak. Hearing his objects of veneration proclaiming the truth of the Oneness of God, Bhum Sadh willingly accepted Islam and entered the discipleship of the Shaikh.[16] The prominent convert to Islam was named Bamuddin.

The long conversation between the Shaikh and Bhum Sadh is recorded in verses attributed to both the saints. True, Baba Nasib's description of some of these verses is not without some value for understanding the social tensions inherent in Nuruddin's dialogue with the ascetic, but, significantly, in the later *Rishinamas*, innumerable verses concerning the discussion at Bamzu have been recorded assiduously. In the *Rishinamas* of Chrar, particularly, one cannot fail to detect interpolations in the verses attributed to Nuruddin. Such interpolations suggest a continual social discontent among the common folk against Brahmanic supremacy. They are also crucial to our understanding of the role of the converts themselves in perpetuating the memory of the greatness of Nuruddin, singling him out as the hope of the down-trodden and, therefore, a perpetual object of veneration. The popular perception of Nuruddin was not only that of a saint but also of a champion of the commoners, including even menials like sweepers and tanners, who prominently figured in the discussions with Bhum Sadh.[17] Thus not only the supposed supernatural spell cast by Nuruddin over Bhum Sadh but, more importantly, his denunciation of the caste system must have prompted the so-called low castes and the weaker sections of Kashmiri society to break off their ties with a caste-ridden social structure.[18] It is not unlikely that many lower-caste Hindus were attracted to Islam, though in stages, as the dialogue between Nuruddin and Bhum Sadh rapidly gained currency among the rural folk. As the process of Islamic acculturation advanced through the repetition of these dialogues at social gatherings like village festivals, the so-called low-born like the village dancers and acrobats (*bhands, dambael maets or faqirs*), played a significant role as transmitters of the values of the Rishis in the traditional rural society. Even now they make their presence felt at the shrines of the Rishis on anniversaries. Not long ago, these dancers would even visit peoples homes to remind them through their acrobatic performances about the historical role of the Rishis as upholders of human equality and brotherhood.

An important aspect of Bamuddin's twelve-year existence as a Muslim saint until his death was the reputation he earned as one who consumed crushed stones and water only, as his normal diet.[19] During this period he did not have a servant, nor did he maintain a proper kitchen. Such claims are bound to be treated with scepticism by the modern reasoning mind, but we find in them a certain degree of truth considering the complexities and mysteries associated with the mundane existence of some mystics.[20] Reason, indeed, can hardly explain how some mystics could have lived a long and healthy life on a diet of crushed stones.

While it is outside the domain of scientific history to emphasize such extraordinary feats, nonetheless, the persistence of such traditions even to our own day does not permit us to totally reject the evidence furnished by the hagiographers and chroniclers about the extreme nature of Bamuddin's asceticism. Such evidence testifies to the positive role that Nuruddin played as a seminal missionary rather than as a radical reformer making an open assault on existing practices. In allowing a die-hard Brahman ascetic like Bhum Sadh to resort to extreme practices near his traditional place of worship, in a locality sacred to the Brahmans,[21] Nuruddin seems to have kept alive among the common people the fame of Bamuddin more as an ascetic than as a zealous convert to Islam.

It is not to be wondered at, therefore, that the Rishi movement led to a gradual transformation of Kashmiri society, particularly in matters of beliefs. While in the pre-Muslim society, popular beliefs centred round the magical powers of Brahman ascetics, in the changed circumstances it became transformed or absorbed into an unswerving allegiance of the commoners to the Muslim Rishis. It would be wrong, however, to assume that the Muslim ascetics acquired an aura of holiness in the Hindu environment mainly because of the persistence of the local saint culture. Although the extreme asceticism of the Rishis attracted the commoners to them, it must be borne in mind that their personal piety and humaneness played no less a part in drawing people closer to them. In the dialogue attributed to Nuruddin and Bhum Sadh, while the Muslim saint emerges as an embodiment of human virtue, piety and compassion, the Brahman ascetic is made a butt of ridicule for propitiating the gods through ritual performances for which the common folk had to pay.[22] Even if we doubt, without much reason, the authenticity of the verses attributed to Nuruddin criticising the extravagant rituals of the Brahmans, the inescapable conclusion must be that the fact of the conversion of a renowned Brahman ascetic was turned by Nuruddin's followers into something relevant to the collective concerns of a people at the cross-roads, paving the way for their gradual adaptation to the Islamic pattern of social life.

Impact of Bhum Sadh's Conversion

Although the extant earlier sources do not directly refer to the impact of Bhum Sadh's conversion on the local people, the authors of later *Rishinamas* of Chrar furnish us with useful details in this regard. As a matter of fact, they were in a position of authority to record oral information transmitting from one generation to another about the reaction of various strata of Kashmiri society to Nuruddin's missionary role. However, in undertaking such an academic exercise the later Rishis seem to have taken great pains in recording even the minutest details preserved in the oral repertory. It is for this reason that we consider Baba Kamal and Baba Khalil's description of Tuli Raina's encounter with Nuruddin to be worthy of some analysis.

About 1200 Hindus under the leadership of Tuli Raina are reported to have met Nuruddin in exasperation in the wake of Bhum Sadh's conversion to Islam. The Shaikh was asked several questions of a metaphysical nature about the creation of the universe and is reported to have countered the beliefs of the Brahmans in this respect. However, it was only after a thorough discussion on divergent beliefs on various issues that Tuli Raina entered the fold of Islam along with his followers.[23]

Our examination, of the reported dialogue between the Shaikh and Tuli Raina, besides testifying to the vitality of the oral tradition, also attests to the persistence of pre-Muslim beliefs among the common folk, in spite of their adherence to Islam. However, in this context, the honesty of purpose of the Rishis is clearly reflected in their candid spirit of narrating the folk beliefs about creation that persisted among the converts. Not the least, the recorded conversation between the Shaikh and the tribal leader also helps us to understand how the memory of the conversion process, not recorded by the chroniclers, was not only preserved but even orchestrated by the common folk themselves. Although in transcribing such a process in black and white, the latter-day literary Rishi tradition was prone to adopt exaggerated overtones, the oral information collected through this source reveals how with the gradual spread of Islam the Kashmiri society articulated its own perception of the process of Islamization.

Conversion of Zia Singh

Zia Singh's ancestral home was in Kishtwar[24] where his father, a descendant of the rulers of that country, was put to death by his enemies. At a very young age Zia Singh fell ill. The critical condition of the young boy caused a great deal of anxiety to his mother. It was at this juncture that Nuruddin is reported to have made his appearance in mysterious circumstances. At the saint's command, the worried mother pledged to visit Kashmir on her son's recovery and also agreed to embrace Islam.[24a] Although Zia Singh recovered due to the benedictions of the saint, his mother did not keep her word. After some time the young boy was again taken ill, but when his mother was reminded by the Shaikh in a vision of her failure to fulfil the solemn pledge, she set off for Kashmir along with her son.[25]

Although most sources describe the conversion of Zia Singh to Islam against the background of the solemn promise taken from his mother by Nuruddin,[26] Khwaja Azam Diddamari attributes his acceptance of Islam at the hands of the saint to divine command.[27] Another source however states that since Zia Singh was looking for a *pir* he became a Muslim on seeing Nuruddin.[28]

Sayyid 'Ali's earliest account about the circumstances leading to Zia Singh's conversion, however, needs to be noted together with that of Baba Nasib, Daud Mishkati and others. True, Nuruddin's mystical appearance in Kishtwar may appear fantastic to the modern mind; but in the history of Sufism, such experiences have been the rule rather than the exception. Even in modern times we hear of some individuals having embraced Islam through the suasions of the Sufis in visions or dreams.[29] To reject such evidence merely on the grounds of 'reason' or one's own inability to fathom the mysteries of the Sufi's existence is therefore nothing short of sophistry. For an objective understanding of the religious transmutation of certain individuals we must be prepared to develop a vicarious experience of the world of the Sufis.

Zia Singh, who after his conversion to Islam came to be known as Zainuddin, undoubtedly held an eminent position among the disciples of Nuruddin. Significantly, he chose a cave on the top of the mountain, at 'Aishmuqam,[30] for purposes of worship. His piety and austerities impressed even his master, who extolled the saintliness of the disciple in the following verse:

> My Zaina is the fountain-head of nectar;
> Such is his devotion to God that he surpasses his preceptor.[31]

Although the many miracles attributed to Zainuddin testify to his distinguished position,[32] the veneration of the boatmen for the saint to this day, suggests that the Rishi's sphere of influence must have been widespread. So great seems to have been his influence on folk consciousness that even a rationalist like Abul Fazl lent a credulous ear to the stories current about the saint and wrote: "For twelve years he (Zainuddin) occupied this cell (at 'Aishmuqam) and towards the end (of his life) he closed its mouth with a huge stone and never went forth again and no one has even found trace of him."[33]

Such stories, together with the many miracles ascribed to Zainuddin also point to the enormous extent of the Islamic acculturation of commoners under the influence of the Rishis. Even a modern writer was struck by the links fostered between the commoner and the tomb of Zainuddin. "This shrine" writes Lawrence, "is much respected by the boatmen of Kashmir, who take their children (there) and cut off their first lock of hair. If this was done elsewhere the child would die or become blind."[34]

Conversion of Ladi Raina

Ladi Raina was the chief of Maru-Adavin[35] and before his conversion to Islam had enjoyed the company of Muslims.[36] It was during one of his visits to Srinagar that the idea of seeing Nuruddin struck him.[37] The dialogue[38] between the saint and Ladi Raina is worthy of note:

Nuruddin — What brings you here?
Ladi Raina — Your love and the longing to see you.

Nuruddin	—	Nothing is more false than a friendship without union of minds.
Ladi Raina	—	What is the true characteristic of a friend?
Nuruddin	—	Obedience to God's commands?
Ladi Raina	—	What does He command?
Nuruddin	—	Surrender unto Him and be His servant alone.
Ladi Raina	—	Since I serve my own Lord there is no need for me to serve your Lord.
Nuruddin	—	How do you reconcile your polytheistic practices with the belief that the Lord of the universe alone is your Sustainer?

Ladi Raina was impressed by the argument and then and there joined the brotherhood of the Rishis. Not only did he relinquish his post, he even distributed his wealth and property among the poor in deference to the wishes of Nuruddin.[39] It is interesting to note that during the course of his spiritual training Ladi Raina was again drawn into a discussion by his preceptor:[40]

Nuruddin	—	What was your main achievement before joining the Rishi order?
Ladi Raina	—	It was wealth.
Nuruddin	—	Was your father wealthy too?
Ladi Raina	—	Yes.
Nuruddin	—	To whom did he bequeath his wealth?
Ladi Raina	—	To me.
Nuruddin	—	Why didn't he take it with him?
Ladi Raina	—	It was not of value (after death).
Nuruddin	—	He (your father) was not sagacious enough to capitalize on his worldly fortune after his death. A sage is in constant search of something of an abiding value.

It follows that the main purpose of the Shaikh was to bring home to the new convert, renamed Latifuddin, that worldly wealth was the devil's bait to a traveller on his way of God. For an erstwhile chief now turned into a Rishi it was no longer a distinction to be rich, since according to his master's teaching wealth engendered selfishness, nurtured arrogance and above all damaged the nobler feelings and aspirations of the heart.[41] Baba Latifuddin's fame as a true Rishi, subsisting merely on wild vegetables, spread among the commoners. They are reported to have sought his blessings at Uttar[42] where he was sent by Nuruddin for popularising the Rishi order. But the heavy rush of the commoners to the saint's dwelling-place ultimately forced him to move to a forest named Poshkar[43] where the saint was buried. Poshkar is now a village,[44] where anniversary of Latifuddin is celebrated with traditional gaiety by the village people.

The Shaikh and the Brahmans

The vast and as yet unexplored documentation regarding the reaction of the Brahmans to Shaikh Nuruddin's popularity among the commoners deserves careful examination. Conversations of the Brahmans with the Shaikh bear testimony to the utmost contempt with which the lower sections of Kashmiri society were treated by the higher castes. Here we shall attempt to study not only the hostile reactions of the Brahmans, but also the leavening influence of the Shaikh's poetry in ennobling their minds. In fact, the importance of the genus of material examined below lies in the conversion of certain Brahmans more by personal precept, example and convincing arguments of the Shaikh rather than by charisma.

Once a Brahman visited Nuruddin and started rebuking him by asking how a thief and an ignoramus could claim to be an *'abid* and *zahid* by retiring to a corner. The Brahman also questioned his faith, arguing that a low-caste like him could not recognize God by professing to be a Muslim. Nuruddin, however, told the Brahman that it was through mental introspection of the natural environment that he was able to recognize the Ultimate Reality. It was while realising that the sky, earth, sun moon, water, fire, air and food cannot have their own origin, maintained Nuruddin, that the reality of God's existence slowly dawned upon him. But the Brahman did not appreciate the reply couched in allegorical terms. He started taunting him again, now with a different argument. To the Brahman's reproach that it was unbecoming of a self-styled Rishi like Nuruddin to take milk,[45] the latter's response was that even the Rishis of yore had tasted milk as it was the bliss (*ni'amat*) of God.[46]

Baba Nasib does not tell us whether the Brahman's conversation with Nuruddin bore any fruit, although a later source is categorical about his conversion.[47] Whatever may be the truth, the discussion between the two, recorded in the hagiographical literature, is of considerable value from the viewpoint of the social dimension of conversions to Islam. In the first place, the Brahman's argument that a man with a low origin could not recognize God reveals the particular paradox and tension that the Kashmiri society experienced as a result of Nuruddin's advocacy of virtues such as self-imposed poverty, identification with the poor and the down-trodden, and above all opposition to the caste system. Secondly, while explaining the abstract and deep spiritual meaning of God's reality through concrete and material forms, Nuruddin seems to have generated a new sense of awareness among the folk that it was not difficult, even for the under-priviledged, to throw off their traditional bonds with their priests by regarding nature as their guide. Nuruddin's teachings did not, however, imply that people should resign themselves with implicit obedience to the sacred commands of nature. In fact, he wanted his followers to study nature more so that, to use Milton's phraseology, "In contemplation of created things, by steps we may ascend to God."[48]

There is much evidence that Nuruddin felt deeply concerned over the caste distinctions that separated man from man. In his own humble way he seems to have made a bold attempt at eliminating such barriers by reference to mystical explanations of natural phenomena. The following account illustrates his approach and is worth objective analysis.

A group of Brahmans, understandably alarmed by Nuruddin's popularity among the commoners, subjected him to ridicule on the ground of his birth. But the Rishi sought to humble their pride through the analogy of a particular kind of grass abhorrent to animals like cows, horses, sheep and donkeys. Although the grass was worthless in the eyes of animals, the gardener tied a bouquet of flowers with the same grass to decorate the king's palaces. What enhanced the value of the grass was not only the gardener's practice, but, more importantly, the social usefulness of an apparently lowly thing.[49]

> The grass of a lower stock,
> Not swallowed by devouring animals,
> See: it reaches (even) the head of the king,
> How can animals recognize its true worth.[50]

It also follows from Nuruddin's mystical interpretation of even insignificant material objects that he wanted his followers to adopt a meliorist or pragmatic attitude towards the problems of society. For him it was not man's noble birth, but ultimately his actions that were of supreme importance in determining his social status.[51] How this persuasive mystico-social philosophy of Nuruddin influenced even men of piety among the Brahman families is also worth considering. In this respect, the role played by some Kashmiri Brahmans in popularising

Nuruddin's mystical poetry can hardly by ignored since they considered the act of copying his verses in the *Sharda* script to be a source of great personal comfort.[52] It is not unlikely that their families felt a gradual religious transmutation in due course. In order to understand how this process started it is necessary to mention in particular the seminal role of Kati Pandit.

A Brahman well-versed in the *Shastras* and having kept the company of various Hindu saints, Kati Pandit seems to have been cast in the typical mould of seekers after the truth. It was his fondness for Nuruddin's mystical poetry which drove him to the saint.[53] So struck was the inquisitive Brahman by the austerities of Nuruddin that he proclaimed in exultation the pre-eminence of the Rishi among all the saints he had seen. But reacting to the words of praise pouring forth from the mouth of the Brahman, Nuruddin remarked that he was conscious merely of his sins from his very birth.[54] Kati Pandit was so impressed by Nuruddin's sense of guilt and feeling of sin that he joined his discipleship. He was named Qutubuddin and, after his death, in view of his closeness to Nuruddin, was buried near his tomb.[55]

There is no doubt that the austerities and humility of Nuruddin prompted Kati Pandit to join the brotherhood of the Rishis. But in the course of the dialogue between Nuruddin and Kati Pandit, a cardinal virtue of the saint's personality seems also to have captivated the Brahman. This was the Brahman's ability to perceive in Nuruddin's humility a sorrow converted into action, a movement towards a new and better life. How this movement gained momentum in due course is amply borne out not only by Kati Pandit's practice of committing to writing Nuruddin's verses for posterity, but by the continuance of this tradition even among certain families of Brahmans. The persistence of this tradition as late as the seventeenth century also accounts for the gradual adaptation of such families to Islam.[56] It is significant that there are still certain Muslim families in the Valley in which the memory of their particular ancestor's voluntary conversion to Islam is still alive. And, indeed, it is they who have preserved the manuscripts of the verses of Nuruddin to this day.[57]

Nuruddin's criticism of the Brahmanic ritualistic practices is also worth examining to understand the impact which his compositions left on the common man. Such criticism seems to have been prompted more by his concern for the poor groaning under the weight of rituals rather than by his hostility to Hinduism. Evidence is not wanting to show how in his verses Nuruddin, while addressing the Hindus, tried to impress upon them the futility of propitiating Siva through the mere recital of his name or performance of rituals associated with his worship.[58] Here we consider it necessary to relate an account of his encounter with a group of Brahmans engaged in performing the ritual of *Shrad*.[59]

Once while going to the river bank for performing his ablutions Nuruddin saw some Brahmans throwing water with their hands to their left and right. On being asked to explain the purpose of this act, the Brahmans told the saint that these exercises were undertaken mainly for satiating the thirst and hunger of the departed souls. Nuruddin tried to convince the Brahmans that it was useless to perform such a practice in view of their indifferent attitude towards the problems of human beings living in abject poverty. He urged them to make every possible effort to seek the countenance of God by feeding the poor. And it was by such acts alone, emphasized the saint, that one could render some good to the deceased souls. The Brahmans were moved by the exhortations of Nuruddin and consequently, embraced Islam.[60]

Thus there is much evidence attesting to the influence exercised by Nuruddin over his contemporaries. But the gradual transmutation brought about by his compositions even in the lives of the Brahman ascetics is particularly worthy of notice. Such individuals apparently lived as Hindus, although, in their heart of hearts they seem to have accepted Islam. In the *pargana* of kamraj,[61] for instance, there lived a Brahman ascetic who spent most of his time in meditation near a spring at Andarhama.[62] Once while passing by the spring Nuruddin entered into an argument with the ascetic. Reacting to the ascetic's prating about the virtue of bathing seven times before prayers, Nuruddin remarked:

> "If seven times bathing were to bear any fruit,
> The fish and crocodile alike would behave.
> If God were gladdened when we famish with fasts;
> Never would the destitute put rice in the pot."[63]

Although the Brahman ascetic kept in close touch with Nuruddin, he never gave the impression of having felt any religious mutation on account of his association with the Rishi. However, as he lay dying, the ascetic instructed his followers to perform the death rites according to the Muslim rather than the Hindu custom. Consequently, remarks Baba Nasib, the Brahman ascetic's devotees were left with no alternative but to turn away from their religion in aversion[64] and to adjust to the Muslim pattern of social life. It is against the background of such unique cases of conversion that in later days the Rishis nurtured the concept of the life of a Brahman believer, to the extent that he was considered to be closer to God than a so-called Muslim.[65] A saying attributed to Nuruddin suggests that the converts themselves sought to reintegrate the men of piety among the Hindus into the fold of Islam.[66]

There is, then, little doubt about the contribution of Nuruddin in attracting non-Muslims to Islam. Even during the lifetime of the Shaikh his disciples embarked upon the task of proselytization. Sozan, a Muslim ascetic and originally a weaver by profession, gave up performing penances in the hollow of a tree when Nuruddin expressed disapprobation at his extreme asceticism. He was advised to be of some service to the people of Pran Bhavan,[67] a village inhabited by the Hindus. Subsequently, the inhabitants of the village accepted Islam as a result of the persuasions of Sozan.[68] In Rupvan,[69] Nuruddin enrolled a large number of disciples.[70] Earlier, during his travels in various villages of Kashmir, Nuruddin was able to enrol disciples even among the Hindu women, whose asceticism particularly attracted other female adherents. They were, no less than men, prepared to guide people, though in relative solitude and seclusion. It was on account of Nuruddin's teachings that the religious life of the Kashmiri women came to be held in high esteem, so that they were regarded as no less holy than men following the Sufi path. Among the prominent Hindu women converted by Nuruddin to Islam particular mention must be made of Behat Bibi,[71] Dehat Bibi,[72] Sham Ded,[73] and Shanga Bibi.[74] Of these, the elevation of the last to sainthhood was of great social significance, considering her low origin as a prostitute.[75]

It was thus not only the supreme excellence of Nuruddin among the contemporary mystics, but more importantly, his humanity that was seen as the significant feature of his religious career by Brahmans as well as by illiterate folk. His innumerable verses provide us with an understanding of various aspects of conversion. They seem especially to have acted as a source of spiritual comfort for the labouring classes. As pointed out earlier, Nuruddin pointed to a deep spiritual meaning in every detail of social life to impress upon the common man the value of the dignity of labour in the sight of God. He was thus able to draw the commoners towards Islam through the popularity of his songs.

Although conscious of the local people's belief in the holiness of ascetics, Nuruddin left no stone unturned in exposing the hypocrisy and the greed of the false ascetics of his time.[76] At the same time, however, he seems to have laid great stress on combining asceticism with social endeavour. This explains the fact that he especially entrusted the task of guiding people to the right path to his three prominent disciples of Hindu origin. And what inspired the innumerable devotees of these Rishis was Nuruddin's ability to create among them, through their own medium, a philosophical attitude towards the problems of life. Thus it is not surprising that even the disciples of the immediate *khalifas* of Nuruddin were able to draw the Brahman ascetics into their fold through intelligent discussions. Here it is worthwhile to allude to two such cases of conversion.

Before becoming a Rishi Shukuruddin, the celebrated disciple of Zainuddin, is said to have been a rich man. He gave up his material possessions to follow the path of the Rishis when the truth of reality dawned upon him.[77] It was through his personal example that Shukuruddin was able to draw Dariya Rishi,[78] Regi Rishi[79] and Bibi Sanga[80] to his fold.[81] Dariya Rishi, or Dhar Sadhu was formerly a revered Brahman ascetic. Although engrossed in the worship of idols in a temple near the spring, the Brahman was apparently fascinated by the asceticism of Shukuruddin and sought an interview with the Rishi which, at first, was not granted. The Rishi's refusal led to a discussion with his disciples. Describing Shukuruddin's attitude towards him as unwarranted, the Brahman impressed upon the saint's disciples that there was little difference between him and the Rishis. His main argument was that he too like the Rishis had dedicated himself to God after renouncing worldly possessions. Furthermore, the Brahman ascetic convincingly argued that it did not behove believers in one God to be uncharitable towards another. It was only after the arguments of Dhar Sadhu were conveyed to Shukuruddin that he directed his disciples to show the visitor in. During his discussions with the ascetic the Rishi was able to convince him of the futility of venerating idols, leading ultimately to his initiation in the Rishi order.[82]

A careful examination of the circumstances leading to Dhar Sadhu's conversion reminds one how important asceticism was in the religious life of Kashmiris in the medieval period. The very fact that even the wealthy Hindus, long before their entry into the Rishi order, had decided to renounce the world shows that it was not difficult for such men to join the brotherhood of the Rishis after coming into contact with them. In fact, it is primarily the ascetic orientation of the Hindu converts to Islam which explains why certain features of the old Hindu tradition were retained in the changed religious environment.

Another anecdote relates to the conversion of the Brahman priests of a temple in the village of Uttar[83] at the hands of Luda Mal, himself a convert, who is reputed to have selected the hollow of a chinar tree as his abode for a considerable time. He had as many as 3060 disciples[83a] whose lands he helped to bring under cultivation.[84] Although his spiritual powers are said to have caused many springs to gush forth,[85] his attitude towards his own brother, Lankar Mal, deserves special mention, in view of the ethical influence exercised by the Rishis on contemporary society.

Lankar Mal was said to have amassed a huge fortune through his oppressive acts. He had also gained notoriety for his licentiousness. Once the thought of paying a visit to his saintly brother occurred to him and in order to create a favourable impression on the saint he dressed himself like a *darwish*. On seeing his brother masquerading as a saint Luda Mal was so displeased that he refused to talk to him. Insulted at the indifference of the Rishi, Lankar Mal burst into anger but the disciples of Luda Mal calmed him down and advised him to discard the dress of the *darwish*. And, indeed, Lankar Mal received an affectionate welcome only after changing his dress. While replying to the saint's question about the purpose of his visit, Lankar Mal expressed his desire to offer *tauba*. Significantly, however, mere confession of sins did not earn Lankar Mal a discipleship in the Rishi order; instead, the saint impressed upon his brother that the best way to atone for his sins was to restore to the lawful owners what he had taken from them or restore its money equivalent. It was only after atoning for his sins in a practical manner that Lankar Mal was enrolled in the Rishi order. The real test for Lankar Mal in following the path of the Rishis, however, began when he was instructed by his master to perform extreme penance for his past sins by subsisting on ginger alone for forty days in seclusion.[86] So impressed was the wife of Lankar Mal, Bibi Ganga, by the austerities of her husband that she too joined the brotherhood of the Rishis and earned a name among the common folk for her indomitable will in overcoming desires of the flesh.[87] The extreme self-denial of Lankar Mal is even said to have led a Brahman ascetic to embrace Islam at his instance.[88]

The story of the conversion of Lankar Mal bears testimony to the deep influence of the idea of making amends expounded by Nuruddin and later by his followers even on men whose behaviour did not conform to the accepted patterns of conduct, consistent with principles of personal and social ethics. At the same time, it also shows that the Rishis attached a great deal of importance to the cultivation of inward piety in contrast to maintaining a semblance of reverence for God by wearing the garments of the Sufis. But what is of immense significance is that at every opportunity, the Rishis advocated the cause of the exploited and oppressed sections of the society. The very fact that the disciples of the saint accompanied Lankar Mal to ensure restitution on his part[89] testifies to the efforts of the Rishis to set right an unjust situation, if not to create a just social order in the modern sense. In fact, the asceticism of the Rishis needs to be understood not merely in terms of their aversion for the material comforts of life, but more as a protest against the tyrannies of an iniquitious social order. Even the long fasts observed by the Rishis seem to express their concern for the sufferings of the poor. The social philosophy behind observing such fasts would be clear only if we try to understand the circumstances leading even men of affluence to choose a life of poverty like the Rishis. The behavioural pattern of a number of wealthy men[90] studied by us, shows the development of a humane trait. Their action in choosing a life of self-imposed poverty sprang fundamentally from two considerations; first, a sense of guilt for being the instruments of social exploitation and, second, a concern not only for one's fate on the Day of Judgement, but also for the sufferings of the poor. In more than one important sense, the Rishis launched what may be termed a silent protest for the vindication of the rights of the poor.

Little wonder therefore, that the Rishis elicited admiration for their social role even from the *Shari'a*-minded hagiographers. Among them, Muhammad Murad Teng, a sufi of the Naqshbandi order,[91] deserves special mention. In his valuable work Teng not only testifies to the conversions of the Hindus under the influence of the Rishis as described in the other sources, but he even furnishes an eye-witness account of how the efforts of Rishis in bringing about a gradual transmutation in the lives of the Hindus continued unabated till the 18th century. For instance, a Hindu, who visited Shaikh Dau'd, popularly known as Batmaloo Sahib,[92] had expressed his intention of becoming a Muslim during the saint's lifetime. But it was only after the death of the saint that he affirmed his faith in Islam. He became a disciple of Nur Muhammad Parwana, one of the closest companions of the Batmaloo, and after his conversion, assumed the name of Shaikh Abdul Shukur.[93] Teng also refers to the conversion of another disciple of the Batmaloo who came to be known as Shaikh Wanta Puri.[94] What impressed Teng about the Shaikh after his enrolment in the Rishi order was his asceticism even while leading a married life.[95] Teng also refers to the conversion of Shaikh 'Abdul Rahim at the hands of Naji Baba, who too led a family life.[96] But the Naqshbandi hagiographer particularly extols the role of Baba 'Abdullah, a disciple of Naji Baba, for constructing mosques, bridges and baths. The extent to which Baba 'Abdullah was able to make his presence felt even among non-Muslims is shown by the conversion of the inhabitants of the village of Lari Bar at his hands.[97]

General Remarks

From the foregoing discussion it is evident that the Rishis enjoyed a distinguished position in the traditional Kashmiri society. The individual and certain cases of group conversions examined by us must have accelerated the process of Islamic acculturation of the commoners. This is also testified to by many a miracle attributed by the commoners to the Rishis. However, the popular belief of the commoners in the Rishis' spiritual powers or efficacy in holiness should not be misconstrued as an important factor in their gradual conversion to Islam. The accounts of the miraculous triumphs of the Rishis over the Hindu saints need to be understood in their social context and within a framework which explains conversion in terms of improving social relationship.[98] Notwithstanding the part played by the charismatic element of the saint's personality, the dynamic role of Nuruddin and his followers in making Islam comprehensible to the commoners through precept and example cannot be over-emphasized. Their criticism of the caste-system and the Brahmanic rituals and customs contributed a great deal to the loosening of the old social and religious ties. Judged from the converts' perception of the process of Islamization, as reflected in the oral literature, conversion to Islam meant a relative advance in their social status. Significantly, Nuruddin himself regarded Sayyid Husain Simnani,[99] Lal Ded,[100] Sayyid 'Ali Hamadani[101] and Sayyid Muhammad Hamadani[102] as deliverers. A careful reading of the Shaikh's verses enables us to appreciate how, through his creative effort, he was able to promote a fresh understanding of Islamic teachings in a different cultural milieu. The sentiments of respect and admiration for Islam and faith in its ultimate destiny are not only reflected in the innumerable verses of the Shaikh, but equally, in a number of euologistic verses, composed by the converts in honour of their 'national saint.'[103] It would not therefore be unreasonable to assume that the Islamic acculturation of the commoners ultimately meant a transition from a traditionally defined caste-ridden society to the community of the Prophet Muhammad (*Umma*). That is to say, having undergone a process of Islamic acculturation, the converts saw their identity in terms of the new religious community, of which they had become members, consciously or unconciously. It led to the development of a Kashmiri Muslim society in the medieval period in which social identity was normally defined in Islamic terms as opposed to caste.

It follows that during the period under review the most significant social change that took place was the gradual development of Islam as the focus of social identity among the commoners. How they were able to free themselves from the degrading oppression of their caste-conscious superiors and raise themselves and their descendants in the social scale is further borne out by their embroideries on Nuruddin's verses, transmitting from generation to generation as words of the exemplar of ideal Muslim behaviour. In fact, it was through a variety of didactic songs of Nuruddin that the commoners gradually adapted themselves to the Islamic way of life. It is relevant to examine here why the title 'Shaikh' was adopted by various communities exposed to the influence of the Rishis.[104] This title was actually used for Sufi masters of some social standing, but a convert who followed the example of his master also came to be known as a Shaikh, as for example, Shaikh Salaruddin, Shaikh Bamuddin, Shaikh Zainuddin, Shaikh Latifuddin, Shaikh Wanta Puri and so on. However, for the majority of people groaning under the weight of Brahmanic tyranny, the arrogation of the title, Shaikh, was not merely an important badge of identity but also a sign of religious solidarity. In order to distinguish themselves from their ancestors' position in the pre-Muslim society, the lower sections of the Hindu society, including even the scavengers, adopted the title of Shaikh, to the bewilderment of the Brahman. The title contains many nuances peculiar to a socially oppressed peoples' conception of themselves and of pre-Muslim society.[105]

The relative change in status of the converts in the social identification is further testified to by the performances of the folk dancers on the eve of the anniversaries of the Rishis. Their performances have a symbolic significance for assessing the role of the Rishis in drawing the peasants and farmers to their fold. But, more importantly, the conspicuous presence of the folk dancers on the eve of anniversaries and the villagers' age-long interest in them imply that it was a social rather than mere religious conversion that created the pressures for change which, in turn, also affected the course of Islamic religious development in the Valley. The issues raised by the folk dancers through their acts concern the relation of the individual believer to God, and equally important, contact between the ordinary believer and the saint, who is in direct contact with God. It was through such contacts that the use of the Kashmiri language as a religious vehicle was fostered and Islam opened up to people who were not educated in classical Arabic and Persian. The overall impact of the Rishi movement was that through the performances given by *bhands, dambel maets,* etc. Islam was brought to the masses in a meaningful way. Since at that time the only education for the illiterate folk was that which was transmitted orally, there arose groups of acrobats and singers who assumed the role of teachers. Thus it is not difficult to understand why the festive occasions at the shrines of the Rishi saints are days of rejoicing and thanksgiving. They commemorate the formative stage of conversion when the commoners entered the fold that proclaimed the equality of all men.

Although the above discussion suggests the existence in medieval Kashmir of a world of syncretism of beliefs and conduct, the ground paved by it for gradual conversion of the people to Islam should not be lost sight of. This is also reflected in the changing pattern of naming the people undergoing the process of Islamic acculturation. True, many converts retained the tribal *nisba* or occupational affiliation as a last name, but what is of interest is the immense popularity of names with strong religious connotation, e.g., 'Abul Rahman, Ghulam Ahmad, Ghulam Muhammad, Ghulam Hasan and so on. The assertion of ones identity by defining a relationship to Allah and the Prophet Muhammad through the assumption of distinctive Muslim names signified an important development in the conversion process. It is true that in spite of this development, the *domb, dambel maets, hanjis,* etc. continued to be discriminated against in marriage, but in contrast to their ancestors' position in the Hindu social structure they were not socially ostracised or reviled. It was this group however, that initially by its very existence, posed questions about the social character of Islam. Not only did Nuruddin's interest centre around social questions of critical importance, but even centuries after his death his followers continued the search for a just social order and eventually in their search they gave shape to such a structure.[106]

The emergence of Islam as a social religion among the rural masses was bound to give birth to institutions that eventually assumed pre-eminence in the developing Islamic society. What actually brought about the need to develop such institutions was the process of acculturation itself which influenced their growth, partly through conflict, but mainly through a peaceful and orderly evolution. Indeed, the emergence of social institutions like the *asthans* of the Rishis in every nook and corner of the Valley, covered a far broader horizon than the *asthapans* of the Hindus. In fact the unlettered folk began to see their community as socially distinct, complete with its own religious infrastructure in the form of mosques adajacent to the shrine. It is in the times of the later Rishis like Baba Nasib and some of his followers that we are able to understand how the converts spontaneously but cautiously acted upon this perception of being members of an Islamic community. Gradually the need for participating in congregational prayers, particularly on Fridays, began to be felt keenly by the converts—a practice which decisively separated the Muslim community from the Brahmanic. It was at the congregational prayers, through the loud recitation of *Aurad-i Fathiyya, durud, nats,* etc. that the universality of their religion was proclaimed by the converts in radical contrast to their ancestors' deification of the priest or an ascetic in the pre-Islamic cosmological structure. So deep was the influence of the all-encompassing power of the Most Beneficent and the Merciful Allah on the people that the practice of glorifying His Majesty and His last messenger aloud continues in the mosques and shrines of Kashmir to this day.

From a careful examination of the source material, including innumerable songs composed by the common folk in praise of the Prophet Muhammad, Nuruddin and a number of his followers, it would also appear that the Kashmiris themselves perceived their conversion more in terms of a social process than a sudden or a dramatic change felt by them in their lives. Of course, conversion of certain individuals in the latter sense did take place owing to their intimate contacts with the Sufis, but it would be unwise to propound a general theory of spectacular mass conversions on the basis of such exceptional cases. What seems more reasonable to suppose is that it was only in the wake of the construction of mosques that the preliterate people of an agrarian society were absorbed into the religious ideology of the expanding Islamic frontier. However, it needs to be emphasized that even in the mosques the *tadhkiras* of the Rishis and other Sufis remained the medium of instruction in the values of Kashmiri Muslim society. The reason why Kashmir has always had a weak foundation in theology may, among other factors, be explained in terms of the popularity of the mystic poetry of Nuruddin among the rural masses.

The Rishis thus had the role of exemplars thrust upon them. The convert population looked up to them as their role models as well as the custodians of their tombs and of their communal identity. What is of further significance is that the people, out of reverence for their saints, looked to these custodians as surrogate priests. Ultimately the product of this evolution was the accumulation of power and authority in the hands of an unappointed clergy, which was used mostly for petty, mundane interests. It is not to be wondered at, therefore, that the various dimensions and implications of the process of Islamization actually came to the fore in the paradox of the reform process started by the Ahl-i Hadith towards the close of the nineteenth century. For the latter the converts needed to be converted afresh in view of their adherence to and devotional focus on the shrines. Thus, in the recent past, the widespread network of mosques in the Valley with its emphasis on *tauhidic* universalism—mainly as a result of the activities of the Ahl-i Hadith—and the added emphasis upon preserving the unique character of the shrines as symbols of Kashmiri Muslim identity, may be seen as efforts at perfecting the process of conversion in the region.

To conclude, from the standpoint of history, the complete absorption of the masses in Islam can by no means be measured, though attempts to do so continue unabated. Looking at it even from the Quranic point of view, complete surrender to Allah, or faith in Islam, implies a meaningful interaction between religion and society, which in the ultimate analysis appears to us as an unending process in which one steers oneself out of the narrow waters of ethnocentrism into the broad sea of humanism and universalism.

REFERENCES AND NOTES

1. See Chapter III, "Socio-Religious Milleu."
2. Among these names may be mentioned Lacham Rishi, Diti Rishi, Behat Bibi, Sanga Bibi, Ratan Rishi, Sanghi Rishi, Regi Rishi, Rupi Rishi, Luda Mal, Lankar Mal, Ganga Bibi, Watur Thakur, Ludi Kutur, Shankar Rishi, Bangar Rishi, Shoga Rishi, Nimi Rishi, Rati Rishi, Zogi Rishi, Nuni Rishi, Sonti Rishi, etc.
3. Lal Ded's role in generating mass discontent against the Brahman clergy has already been discussed. See Chapter III, "Socio-Religious Milieu."
4. See *Infra.*
5. Baba Kamal, *Rishinama*, Baba Khalil, *Rauzat al-Riyazat.*
6. See Assadullah Aafaqi, *Ain-i Haqq*, pp. 216-217.
7. Chandanyar is perhaps Kalhana's Chandrabhaga. While referring to this stream the Kashmiri chroniclar remarks: "When he (Jayapida) was appropriating (the land of) *Tulamulya*, he heard, while on the bank of Chandrabhaga, that a hundred Brahmans less one had sought death in the water of that (stream)." *Rajatarangini* (Stein), I, V., 638. For the importance of the large spring of Tulmul as a popular pilgrimage centre among Kashmiri Brahmans, see *Ibid.*, I, p. 178, Note 638.

8. According to Baba Nasib, Shurahyar is situated at the foot of the Koh-i Sulaiman (Shankarcharya hillock) in Srinagar. See *Nurnama* f. 99a. Hasan calls it Shivapara. See *Asrar al-Akhyar* (Urdu tr.), p. 126.
9. According to Hasan, it is situated in Chattabal, a locality of Srinagar. See *Asrar al-Akhyar*, p. 126.
10. The reference is to the famous Wular Lake.
11. Khadanyar is situated in the district of Baramulla.
12. For the ancient history of Bamzu, See *Rajatarangini* (Stein), Vol. I, Part II, p. 165n; Part VI, Notes: 177-178, II, p. 465.
13. The village of Bamzu is situated at a distance of 10 miles from Anantnag (Islamabad).
14. Baba Nasib *op. cit.*, ff. 98a-108ab; Baba Kamal, *op. cit.*, pp. 75-87; Baba Khalil, *op. cit.*, pp. 270-294.
15. According to Baba Nasib (*op. cit.*, f. 103), the discussion between the Shaikh and the Brahman lasted seven days. Sayyid Ali's account (*Tarikh-i Kashmir*, ff. 32b-33a; 37b-38ab) of the meeting is also useful and is, undoubtedly, characterized by freshness and originality. Baba Nasib and the later writers viz., Baba Kamal and Baba Khalil give a detailed account of the discussion.
16. Sayyid Ali, *op. cit.*, ff. 38ab, Baba Nasib, *op. cit*, ff. 104b-105a; Mishkati, *Asrar al-Abrar*, ff. 85b-86a; Baba Kamal, *op. cit*, pp. 75-87; Baba Khalil, *op. cit*, pp 270-94.
17. Baba Khalil, *op. cit.*, pp. 270-94; Baba Kamal, *op cit.*, pp. 75-87.
18. An eighteenth century writer testifies to the social influence of Bamuddin on the masses (*khalq*) in the following verses:

    Hadi-i khalq shud bara-i Khuda
    Sakht bisyari ashanaya Khuda

    See Sa'dullah Shahabadi, *Bagh-i Suliaman*, f. 183.
19. Nasib, *op. cit.*, f. 126a; Mishkati, *op. cit*, f. 88a; Shahabadi, *op. cit.*, f; 107a; Wahab, *op. cit.*, f. 168b.
20. Although Sayyid Ali sounds more reliable than the later chroniclers and hagiographers in saying that Bamuddin would eat *vopalhak* (*dispsacus inermis*) and vegetables, nevertheless, he too refers to the saint's habit of eating stones. Sayyid 'Ali, *op. cit.*, f. 38b.
21. About one mile south of Bamzu lies the *tirtha* sacred to Martanda which has, from time immemorial to this day, "enjoyed a prominent position among the sacred sites of Kashmir. It is marked by a magnificent spring (traditionally represented as two, *Vimala and Kamala*) which an ancient legend connects with the birth of the sun-god Martanda. The *tirtha* is visited at frequent intervals by crowds of pilgrims and is well known also in India." The popular name of the *tirtha*, *Bavan*, is derived from Suk and means sacred habitation. The great king Lalitaditya (700-736 A.D.) constructed a temple 'in honour of the presiding deity of the *tirtha*'. The imposing ruins of the temple "are situated a little over a

mile to the south-east of 'Bavan' near the northern edge of the great Udar which stretches towards Anantnag." See *Rajatarangini* (Stein), Vol. II, pp. 465-66.

22. Baba Kamal, *op. cit.*, pp. 75-87; Baba Khalil, *op. cit.*, pp. 270-94.
23. Baba Kamal's description (*op. cit.*, pp. 87-88) of Tuli Raina's encounter with the Shaikh is brief. However, Baba Khalil describes at great length the discussion that reportedly took place between the Shaikh and the tribal leader. See Khalil, *op. cit.*, pp. 300-308.
24. To the south-east of Kashmir lies the Valley of Kishtwar on the upper Chinab. The rulers of Kishtwar entered into matrimonial ties with the Sultans of Kashmir, and usually accepted their suzerainty.
25. Bab Nasib, *op. cit.*, ff. 12ab; Mishkati, *op. cit.*, f. 90b. Sayyid Ali's version, (*op. cit.*, f. 35ab) regarding Ziya's Singh's conversion is slightly different. According to him Ziya's mother did not deem it expedient to renounce her ancestral faith in Kishtwar, but pledged to embrace Islam on her entry into the Kashmir Valley. *Ibid.*
26. See also Wahab, *op. cit.*, ff. 171b-172a.
27. Diddamari, *Waqi'at-i Kashmir*, p. 64.
28. Mulla Ahmad Sabur, *Khawariq al-Salikin*, f. 42a.
29. Dr. Muhammad Ramzan who lives in the author's vicinity at Magarmal Bagh in Srinagar writes about the conversion of an American lady, Mrs. Hugan, to Islam at the hands of his spiritual preceptor, Muhammad Amin Qureshi, in somewhat strange circumstances. See for details, Muhammad Ramzan, *Nur-i Irfan*, Srinagar, 1973, pp. 15-20.
30. The picturesque shrine of Zainuddin is situated on the top of a hillock in the Liddar Valley.
31. *Bruj-i Nur*, p. 258.
32. Sayyid 'Ali, *op. cit.*, ff. 36ab-37ab; Baba Nasib, *op. cit.*, ff. 133ab-140ab.
33. Abul Fazl, *Ain i Akbari*, II, pp. 172-73.
34. Walter Lawrence, The *Valley of Kashmir*, p. 288.
35. "The name of a long and narrow Valley lying to the south-east of Kashmir, from which it is separated by a lofty range of mountains; its direction is nearly north & sought, its length being about 40 miles, its average breadth not more than a quarter of mile; that fast lying between Maru and Wardwan being nearly a narrow defile, whose sides are very steep and covered with a jungle, chiefly of fir trees." *Gazetteer of Kashmir and Ladakh.*
36. See Nasib, *op. cit.*, f. 141a According to Sadullah Shahabadi, Ladi Raina used to serve *faqirs* even before his conversion. Shahabadi, *op. cit.*, ff. 108ab.
37. Hasan, *op. cit.*, p. 132; see also Nasib *op. cit.*, 141a.
38. Mishkati, *op. cit.*, f. 96a.
39. Baba Nasib, *op. cit.*, f. 141a.
40. Mishkati, *op. cit.*, f. 96a.
41. See Chapter V. "The Religious Thought of Nuruddin."

42. A *pargana* in the Kamraz division of the Valley.
43. Sayyid Ali, *op. cit.*, f. 40a; Baba Nasib, *op. cit.*, f. 141a; Mishkati, *op. cit.*, f. 97b; Diddamari, *op. cit.*, f. 25a; Shahabadi, *op. cit.*, ff. 108ab.
44. Poshkar is situated in the modern district of Badgam, and is not very far from the village of Beru.
45. There is considerable evidence to show that Nuruddin subsisted on milk for 12 years during his stay at the house of Sangi Ganai in Daryagam. See Sayyid 'Ali, *op. cit.*, f. 33a.
46. Baba Nasib, *op. cit.*, f. 44ab. See also Baba Khalil, *op. cit.*, pp. 321-24.
47. Baba Khalil, *op. cit.*, pp. 321-324.
48. See Chapter V "The Religious Thought of Nuruddin."
49. Baba Nasib, *op. cit.*, ff. 59b-60a.
50. *Ibid*; Anand Kaul Bamzai's literal translation of these verses is as follows:

    "The flower-seller's *dyul* (grass with which a bouquet is tied) is of low birth:
    Neither pony nor cattle, nor cow will eat it.
    When it reached the head of the king
    Where did it (then) appear of low birth?"

    The Indian Antiquary Vol. LIX, 1930, p. 28.
51. See Chapter V: "The Religious Thought of Nuruddin."
52. Dr. Triloki Nath Ganjoo perhaps deserves the unique privilege of being in possession of a valuable manuscript on Shaikh Nuruddin's mystical poetry. The manuscript is written in Sharda script and is about four centuries old. It was gifted to Dr. Ganjoo by a Muslim family when he was a school teacher in the village of Safapore in the early fifties of this century. The manuscript seems to have been copied by its scribe Pandit Krishan Razdan from an original source who, significantly enough, does not hide his inner feelings by saying that it was a great source of personal comfort and enlightenment for him to copy the verses of Nuruddin. The family which donated the manuscript, according to its recipient, still remembered the name of their ancestor who had embraced Islam out of conviction centuries ago.
53. Kati Pandit is said to have written the verses of Nuruddin on *awraq-i tuz*. Baba Khalil, op. *cit.*, p. 325.
54. Baba Kamal *op. cit.*, pp. 90-91; Baba Khalil *op. cit.*, pp. 324-25. See also Baba Nasib, *op. cit.*, ff. 53b-54a.
55. Baba Khalil, *op. cit.*, p. 325; Miskin, *Tahaif al-Abrar fi dhikr-i Auliya-i Akhyar*, p. 108.
56. See *Supra*.
57. Based on an empirical study conducted by the author in several Muslim families of the Valley as still retain the memory of their ancestors' conversion to Islam willingly.

58. *Kulliyat*, p. 47; see also Baba Khalil, *op. cit.*, p. 372.
59. The *shradh* service is performed for the deceased "upto the seventh generation." See for more details, Lawrence. *The Valley of Kashmir*, p. 63.
60. Baba Nasib, *op. cit.*, ff. 61b-62b; Baba Khalil, *op. cit.*, pp. 372-74.
61. Abul Fazl's table tends to indicate that in Akbar's time the old *parganas* of Uttar, Lolab, Hamal and Machipur were included in the large paragana of Kamraj. See *Ain-i Akbari*, p. 371.
62. Baba Nasib *op. cit.*, ff. 60b-61a, Khalil, *op. cit.*, p 467.
63. Parimoo, *Unity in Diversity*, p. 269-270.
64. Baba Nasib *op. cit.*, ff. 60b-61a.
65. For Baba Nasib's attitude towards the deceased Hindus, see Chapter VI, "The Attitudes of the Sufi Orders Towards the Rishi Movement."
66. *Kehn daed rethchi kehn daed yethehi.*
    Some (Pandits) were consigned to the funeral pyre for their alleged polytheism.
    (But) some were (actually) consumed by the fire of His love (at the funeral pyre).
67. It is the modern Bhavan situated in the district of Anantnag. See Bahauddin Mattu (*op. cit.*, pp. 157-59). The hagiographer's statement that the entire locality of Bhavan embraced Islam within a year under the influence of the saint actually points to the weaning of the folk from the Brahman priests. The fact is that Bhavan still continues to be the sacred place of Kashmiri Pandits.
68. Sa'dullah Shahabadi, *op. cit.*, ff. 99ab; Bahauddin Mattoo, *op. cit.*, pp. 157. 159; Khalil *op. cit.*, pp. 358-59. See also Baba Kamal, *op. cit.*, pp. 104-5.
69. It is situated at a distance of almost one mile from the tomb of Shaikh Nuruddin at Chrar-i Sheriff.
70. Sa'dullah Shabadi, *op. cit.*, ff. 102ab; Bahauddin Mattoo, *Rishinama*, p. 203., Khalil, *op. cit.*, p. 570. The Shaikh is said to have founded a mosque in Rupvan. *Ibid.*
71. See *Appendix*: "Women Sufis of Kashmir"; also Miskin, *op. cit.*, p. 110.
72. *Ibid.*
73. Miskin, *op. cit.*, p. 109. For the elegy of Shyam Ded on the death of the Shaikh, see *Appendix*.
74. Wahab, *op. cit.*, 158b-160a; Miskin, *op. cit.*, p. 110.
75. See for greater details, Chapter VIII, "The Societal Dimensions of Miracles."
76. *Kulliyat*, pp. 773, 94-95. See also Khalil, *op. cit.*, pp. 362-366.
77. Mishkati, *op. cit.*, ff. 106b-107a; Wahab, *op cit.*, f. 176b; Kamal, *op. cit.*, p. 295.
78. Sayyid 'Ali, *op. cit.*, f. 44a.
79. Sayyid 'Ali, *op. cit.*, f. 44b; Baba Nasib, *op. cit.*, f. 16a; Mishkati, *op. cit*, f. 108a.

80. Shahabadi, *op. cit.*, f. 111a; Wahab, *op. cit.*, f. 117a; Miskin, op. *cit.*, p. 118.
81. Wahab, *op. cit.*, ff. 176b-177a; Miskin, *op. cit.*, 118.
82. Baba Nasib, *op. cit.*, ff. 160ab. Rafiqi wrongly states that Mishkati "is not certain" about the conversion of Dhar Sadhu (*Sufism in Kashmir*, p. 192n). As matter of fact, Mishkati while corroborating Nasib on this matter, simply remarks that according to some Dhar Sadhu did not become a Muslim. See Mishkati, *op. cit.*, f. 107b. However, Sayyid Ali, the earliest source on the Rishis, clearly states that Dhar Sadhu was converted by Shukruddin. See Sayyid 'Ali, *op. cit.*, f. 44a. See also Sabur, *op. cit.*, f. 46b; Wahab, *op. cit.*, f. 177a; Khalil, *op. cit.*, pp. 788-89.
83. See *Supra*, n. 61.
83a. Baba Nasib, *op. cit.*, f. 166b; Miskhati (*op. cit.*, f. 110b) however, refers to 3030 disciples of Baba Luda Mal.
84. Mishkati, *op. cit.* f. 110b.
85. Baba Nasib (*op. cit.*, f. 166b.) and Mishkati (*op. cit.*, f. 11a) refer to only one spring, but Hasan's statement regarding a number of springs is an overstatement.
86. Baba Nasib, *op. cit.*, ff. 167ab; see also Baba Kamal, *op. cit.*, pp. 93-94; Baba Khalil, *op. cit.*, pp. 783-84.
87. Baba Nasib, *op. cit.*, ff. 167b-168a; Khalil, *op. cit.*, p. 785.
88. Baba Nasib, *op. cit.* ff. 168b-169a.
89. *Ibid.*, f. 167a.
90. Latifuddin, Payamuddin, Jogi Raina, Shukruddin and a number of other Rishis came from wealthy families.
91. For his biographical sketch, See *Asrar al-Akahyar* (Urdu tr.), pp. 298-99.
92. See for his life, *Dhikr-i Shaikh Daud* (anonymous), R-P-O No 2987.
93. Teng, *Tuhfat al-Fuqara*, f. 60a.
94. *Ibid.*, f. 61a.
95. *Ibid.*
96. *Ibid.*, ff. 89b-90a.
97. *Ibid.*, f. 92b.
98. See Chapter VII, "The Societal Dimensions of Miracles."
99. *Kulliyat*, pp. 22-23.
100. See Chapter III, "Socio-Religious Milieu."
101. *Kulliyat*, p. 36.
102. Wahab, *op. cit.*, f. 109b.
103. The term 'national saint' has been appropriately used by Sir Walter Lawrence for Nuruddin. See Lawrence, *op. cit.*, p. 287.
104. Walter Lawrence who, as the Settlement Commissioner, had an intimate knowledge of the Kashmir Valley very rightly points out that "the great mass of the village people" bearing the title Shaikh are "descendants of the original Hindus." And while writing about their social position towards the close of the last century, Lawrence remarks: "The Shekh

(Shaikh) Musalmans of the Valley may have retained for some time after their conversion to Islam some of the Hindu customs of endogamy within the caste and of exogamy outside the *gotra*. But there is no trace now of these customs, and different tribal names or *krams* are names and nothing more. There is no restriction on marriage, and a Musalman of the *Tantre kram* can either marry a *Tantre* girl or any other maiden of the village, provided she be one of the agricultural families." *Ibid.*, p. 306.

105. It is significant to note that even by the end of the last century "men of low occupation" were "arrogating (to themselves) high sounding names." *Ibid.* This is amply borne out by the fact that the boatmen of the Valley steadily assumed the *kram* of *Dar* "as a patent of respectability"; and this, much to the annoyance of the original Dammaras, the landed gentry, who were assimilated in the Muslim pattern of life during the formative stage of Islam in Kashmir.

106. Although Lawrence was unable to understand the deeper social implications of the process of Islamic acculturation, nonetheless, an intelligent observer like him did not fail to describe the "social system" of Kashmiri Muslims as "delightfully plastic." Thus he furnishes an eye-witness account of certain cases in which the boatmen, on taking to agriculture, could not only claim "equality with the agricultural families" but even enter into matrimonial alliances with them. Likewise, the accursed *domb*, exalted by Nuruddin in his verses, could arrogate the title of Pandit to himself (See Lawrence, *op. cit.*, p. 307) much to the outrage of the Brahman. The extent to which the social matrix has loosened in our times is now illustrated by the religious leadership provided to Kashmiri Muslims by some respectable men whose ancestors followed traditionally despised occupations such as bakery. In fact, the appropriation of the revered name 'Sufi' by Muslim bakers throughout the Kashmir Valley, further attests to the fact that conversion to Islam provided a means of escape for the lower sections of the society from a life of degradation in the village.

CHAPTER VIII

The Societal Dimensions of Miracles and Legends

Miracles usually refer to such individual events in the physical world as apparently contravene all known human or natural norms and are ascribed to a divine or supernatural cause. Although miracles are generally considered to have no "historic foundation," yet the eulogization of the supernatural gifts or qualities of the saints in medieval chronicles and hagiographies prompts us to conduct an enquiry into this least studied aspects of the human environment. The repeated emphasis on the occurrence of miracles has, through centuries, led to the formation of a particular structure of belief within whose boundaries the individual and collective behaviour of a group of people are confined. A distinctive characteristic of such minds is their emotional attitude towards Islam and its saints. Any attempt by the modern rational mind at deprecating the value of miracles is generally disdained by Muslims; as a matter of fact, such an exercise is often described as an attack on Islam and a sacrilege to its heroes. It is, therefore, against the background of the deep-rooted impact of the miracles on the Muslim mind that we shall seek to establish a purely historical view of the supposedly supernatural phenomena.

Two questions of a fundamental nature suggest themselves at once for analysis and observation: first, what exactly is the meaning of miracles in the religious history of Islam; and second did Islam owe its triumph in Kashmir to the miraculous feats of the Sufis.[1]

It is nowhere mentioned in the Quran that Islam owed its success to the miracles wrought by the Prophet Muhammad. In fact the Prophet never claimed the power of working miracles, nor did he intentionally work wonders to prove his prophethood. However, what has led a vast majority of the Muslim population to attribute miracles to the Prophet is his supernal personality to which the Quran itself hints at more than one place. Thus the cleaving of the moon,[2] the divine aid given to the Muslims at the battle of Badr,[3] Muhammad's ascension to heaven (mi'raj)[4] and above all, the revelation of the divine message (Quran) to the unlettered (*ummi*) Prophet are quoted as examples of powers far beyond the reach of human excellence. Besides, several traditions recorded in the authoritative works refer to miracles worked by the Prophet in the company of his people.[5]

In order to distinguish the miracles[6] of Muhammad and those of the prophets before him, Muslim theology categorised the miracles worked by prophets as *mu'jizat*, while those of the saints were called *karamat.* The deeply pious al-Ghazzali, who represents the climax of Ash'arite theology, superbly defended the ability of the saints to work miracles in elaborating the views of his teacher Imam al-Haramayn al-Juwayni on this subject. Subsequently, Fakhr al-Din al-Razi "developed a whole arsenal of arguments," based on some Quranic verses, "in which he found support for belief in the miraculous powers of saints."[7] Even the celebrated historian Ibn Khaldun did not lag behind theologians in devising arguments to persuade readers of the reality of *karamat.*[8]

Literally, *karamat* means "beneficence," but as a term it refers to the "wonders wrought by saints for the good of the people as well as in proof of their own saintship."[9] In order to explain the inner meaning of the term, it needs to be emphasized that *karamat* is not wholly a supernatural feat performed by the saint, but springs from human action through divine grace. Miracles attributed to saints need not be understood as supernatural phenomena, but ought to be studied within their temporal and situational framework. They then appear as a phenomenon in religious and social history, in view of their influence on the life of the Muslims. In two senses miracles come within the realm of historical literature: first, because they occur within the bounds of history, and second, because they arise directly or indirectly out of history. In other words, miracles arise out of human experience, and indeed, the mind cannot soar into the realm of fantasy unless it has at its source some human experience. It is in this respect that we have attempted to make historical sense of the miracles which abound in the hagiographical accounts.

But it must be explained that it is not always sufficient to interpret hagiological literature by historical analysis. One recurring theme in this type of literature is that of the spirituality of the Sufi. Miracles, dreams and various religious experiences of the Sufi are recorded by eye-witnesses. There seems to be a great deal of exaggeration in the narration of such experiences, but historians ought to, as a part of their investigations, give thoughtful consideration to "appearances," some of which are worthy of examination in view of their normative power. Such "appearances," as Henry Corbin remarks, are the "phenomenological truth."[10] The "truth" revealed to a Sufi in a dream, a vision, *muraqaba*,[12] etc., thus imposes an extra task on the historian to study the existential experience of the Sufi. This existential experience of the Sufi[13] is significant because of its power and influence on the collective consciousness of the people of the period we call medieval.

It is outside the domain of history to determine which of the miracles that are said to have occurred is true or false. However, considering the potent belief of the people in the miracles of saints, it would be hazardous to dismiss the occurrence of miracles purely on the basis of reason, for in so doing we are prone to commit a violence upon the forces of a strong tradition. Even from the standpoint of the French *Annales* school, which stands for understanding a whole society in every detail and in all its interrelations and activities,[14] it would be ahistorical to superimpose the intelligence of our logical analysis on the pervasive folk consciousness. As a matter of fact, at a particular period in history, miracle-mongering itself seems to have created and interpreted contemporary reality. The objective fact is that miracles intervened at a critical juncture in a society's history and, consequently, they were handed down to posterity as events. Medieval hagiographers and chroniclers were profoundly conscious of the ability of the saints to work miracles. They played an important role in making the tradition of belief in miracles useful for the discussion of contemporary issues. In the course of transmission, traditional belief in miracles became a dynamic and not a static process. In such a process the events described, the significance attributed to them or the interconnection established between them by the observer was not without value. Here a clear distinction ought to be made between the facts observed and the interpretation put upon them, which was also a social fact, though of another kind. This kind of interpretation provides evidence of how the initial informant about the miracle—and perhaps his contemporaries as well—interpreted or reacted to certain events. The useful purpose which a judicious use of miracles can thus serve for the historian is that they enable him to form a picture of contemporary reactions of different sections of society to the social role of the Sufis.

Our aim is neither to establish nor cast doubts on the authenticity of the miracles attributed to Nuruddin and some of the illustrious adherents of his order; it is to fathom the meaning or truth of an objective fact, lost in the labyrinth of supra-mundane events. In so doing our purpose is not only to correct a myopic oversight concerning the nature of miracles, but it is also to bring to light certain social facts which have until now remained hidden because of the historian's preoccupation with the 'actual', 'pure' or 'temporal' facts. We shall however restrict our study to the analysis of only such miracles of the Rishis as seem to have endowed the issues of the medieval age with a new meaning.

Stories depicting Nuruddin's spirituality and most of his authoritative verses, when examined carefully, seem to be strikingly interrelated. Although the possibility of such stories having been spun out of Nuruddin's sayings cannot be entirely ruled out, nonetheless, it is most unlikely that a saying or a miracle with no roots in the values of contemporary society and in the folk understanding of the universality of his message would be attributed to him. In this context, the anecdote regarding the entry of a rich man's son into the rishi order is revealing.

Nasruddin, suffering from dyspepsia, was brought by his wealthy parents before Nuruddin, since 'a body of *abdals*' had suggested to the young boy in a dream that the saint alone could cure his prolonged disease. On being asked by the saint what his name was, the young boy replied: "I am Nasr and my surname is Raothar." To this the Rishi remarked: "Do you live up to the reputation of your high-sounding title?" Nasruddin replied: "Should I have your favour, I would." Thereupon, Nuruddin directed one of his disciples to serve a plate of rice to the ailing boy which he ate to the full. No sooner had the young visitor finished his meal than he found a spiritual mutation in himself and bidding good-bye to his parents, remarked: "I have found my doctor."[15] Bewildered at the sudden change in their son's behaviour, the perturbed parents told Nasruddin that their life would be dreary without him. But he replied, "To make it (life) happy, be with God."[16] Nasruddin thus renounced the world and till the death of his spiritual preceptor remained his close companion.

The circumstances leading to the renunciation of Nasruddin need to be read together with a popular dialogue he is reputed to have had with his spiritual preceptor. The dialogue between Nuruddin and his wealthy disciple reveals the mores of fifteenth century Kashmiri society and the conflict inherent in social disparities. When the disciple wished to return to the worldly life even while undergoing a period of spiritual training the master responded thus:

"O Nasr destroy thy sleep;
For whom will the Lord turn sand into coins of gold?

Most people are hungry for food,
Only the good realize the state of suffering.
God ordained it so that some should take to penance,
Who can scratch out the writ of Fate?.[17]

Nasruddin could not understand the profundities of his preceptor's remark that suffering was the surest means of making one true to oneself. Failing to realise that affliction was a divine diet for the Rishis, the young disciple began to talk about the humiliations to which the poor were subjected to by the rich as well as their kith and kin. But while worldly possessions continued to haunt the mind of Nasruddin, the teacher left no stone unturned in dispelling the doubts of his student. He even reproved the inattentive student.[18]

"O Nasr, what shall I tell thee and what wouldst thou hear:
Awake, thou sleepy one, and listen:
When thou goest from here, thou wouldst hear it before thou comest;
If thou dost not hear it here, thou
wouldst (surely) hear it there."[19]

Again:

"A ram cannot bear the burden of a plough,
Nor can a falcon hunt like a hawk;
Water can't curdle by putting it in the sun,
Nor will a fool listen to words of wisdom."[20]

Being reproached for his neglect, Nasruddin ultimately realised the depths of the words of his preceptor. Beseeching the teacher's help, he said:

"O my Guru like a shady willow-grove art thou,
Do show me the way to ferry across (the ocean of life)."[21]

Nuruddin responded thus:

"He can ward off his own sins
Who listens to what Nunda-Sanz says;
Thou hast to ferry across abandoning
The duality of the doer and the deed."[22]

He also enjoined upon him to follow the *Shari'a*[23] through cultivation of virtues such as piety, humility and moderation. Pointing to Nasruddin's excessive eating habits, he remarked:

"Eat only as much as keeps thee fit;
Gluttony is sure to make thee sick;
The human body, full of defilements, is as delicate as a flower;
Look not upon it as a royal-deodar tree."[24]

Nuruddin's words had the desired effect on Nasurddin who, in order to curb the demands of his *nafs*, made the practice of fasting a regular habit, so much so that he distinguished himself as a Rishi of enviable qualities. The hagiographical literature is replete with incredible stories of his breaking fast with ashes mixed with water.[25] Later, on the advice of his preceptor, he seems to have subsisted on a moderate diet though the earliest recorded mention in a chronicle refers to a hundred grains of rice as his normal consumption.[26]

A close examination of such a tradition, arising obviously from the miracles attributed to Nuruddin, points to the fact of a certain collective understanding. Such facts do not stand outside time and history. Their actuality lies in the depths of the psyche of men living in the flux of history, whose dominant characteristic was to create, in hyperbolic terms, a classical model of human personality, i.e. a model of man's realization of himself as an individual and at the same time, as a member of his society. One should take the extravagant statements of the hagiographers regarding Nasruddin's unbelievable feats not literally but figuratively, as part of a complex psycho-historical process. Understanding it requires a close examination of medieval culture and ways of thinking which goes beyond the narrow methods of "traditional" cultural history.

The range of miracles credited to the Rishis is, of course, wider than discussed here. However, it needs to be explained that the growth and viability of the Rishi order were ensured not merely by the transmission of reports of miracles, but more importantly because of their relationship with the wider social situation. This process particularly involved an emphasis on the continuing relevance of the ethic and ideology of the group to what Karl Mannheim has called, the collective purpose of the time.[27]

Another miracle attributed to Nuruddin concerns a rich man who requested the saint to taste a sumptuous meal that he had specially prepared for him. Although the Rishi declined, the visitor persisted. Enraged, the Rishi cast his eyes on the food which turned into filth (*najasat*). The rich man was taken aback, but then, Nuruddin explained to him that it was not proper for a Rishi to touch anything that was acquired by unlawful means. On seeing the *karamat*, the rich man repented of his conduct in forefeiting the rights of others, and after offering *tauba* joined the discipleship of Nuruddin.[28]

The story cited above is an example of how an unadorned fact about Nuruddin's social teachings[29] blossomed into an elaborate legend or miracle within a short span of about 150 years after his death. Giving expression to a consecrated, sublimated image of a society steeped in the teachings of its spiritual leader, the hagiographers depicted Nuruddin as one of the foremost exemplars of human virtues, noted for his love of God, hatred of cruel men, kindness to the poor and, above all, a scrupulous abstention from consuming anything that might be even remotely unlawful.

It would be clear then, that the 'legendary' evidence will always be in danger of losing its social content, if it is not read between the lines. In this context, one may examine the story of a courtesan's entry into the Rishi order.

Once the Sultan of Kashmir went to see a pious Brahman saint who lived at Ishbar.[30] The Brahman refused to meet the distinguished visitor, whereupon the insulted Sultan sent Yawan Mach,[31] a courtesan of a renowned beauty, to humble the pride of the Brahman. The Brahman was at first unwilling to grant an interview to the courtesan; she pretended to become his disciple, and he ultimately fell a victim to her charms. The seduction of the venerated saint made his devotees the butt of ridicule. So, in order to avenge the wrong, they sought the services of the same courtesan to tarnish the image of Nuruddin. When Yawan Mach approached the Rishi, she was asked to go back. When she persisted, the infuriated Nuruddin, with a mere glance, turned her into an old woman of ninety.[32]

Leaving aside the question as to whether a *Shari'a-conscious* ruler like Sultan Sikandar or his son the celebrated Budshah would have resorted to such foul means, the story illustrates the fact that Islam brought tremendous social and ethical tensions within a society characterized by established notions of piety of the Brahman class. As a matter of fact the origin of the story seems to have been almost contemporaneous with Nuruddin's reforming missionary activities.

This is reflected in the admonitions of the saint to the courtesan in the following verses:

"Born wert thou last to thy mother,
That too by the grace of God:
With a cleansed body didst thou move about.
Thou shalt realise thy good, despite thy maddening youth."[33]

"To the backwood thou camest like a brute:
Much good will this bring unto thee:
Like a rope of grass hast thou become now.
Thou shall realise thy good, despite thy maddening youth."[34]

"Who were the wicked men to advise thee thus?
Leaders of the theatre ought they to be
Sunk deep (in sin), like a stone, hast thou
Thou shall realize (thy good) despite thy maddening youth."[35]

"So long as thou wert fit for society,
Not a penny didst thou earn for Hereafter;
Weighed on the fire-wood balance wilt thy skeleton be now."
Thou shall realize (thy good) despite thy maddening youth."[36]

"Thou dost not cherish the preceptor's word,
Why art thou transgressing so wilfully?
Pious deeds shalt thou do, when old
Thou shall realize (thy good) despite thy maddening youth."[37]

"They will bring thee weeping and crying,
Since to the woods hast thou come longingly;
How will thy lovers recognize thee then?
Thou shalt realize (thy good) despite thy maddening youth."[38]

"Walking with airs and graces of youth,
Thou camest here that I may desire too,
Alas: thou has robbed the Sadhu at Ishabar,
Realize thy good, thou drunk with youth."[39]

"Thou didst not mind whether it was day or night,
And the news reached us before thou camest.
So thou has robbed thyself.
Realize thy good thou drunk with youth."[40]

"What a pious saint has thou robbed.
On examination, thou shalt sound like bell-metal, There,
Now thou pursuest me, O wicked woman:
Thou shalt realize (thy good), despite thy maddening youth."[41]

"How many bridges of good deeds hast thou demolished?
And disturbed the minds of Rishis?
Thou shalt lose thy youth now,
And shalt realize (thy good), despite thy maddening youth."[42]

"Whose daughter thou art,
Have we come to know beforehand;
Why shouldst thou rob me, the poor me?
Realize thy good, thou maddened with youth."[43]

"Of thy condition, I am quite ignorant,
And reprove thee with all good will.
O God, save me in this *Kali-Yuga*.[44]
Realize thy good, thou maddened with youth."[45]

A question to which we might usefully apply ourselves is to what extent are these verses authentic?

The verses are characterized by a preponderance of Sanskrit words in their composition.[46] Among many such words, mention may particularly be made of *ambi* (*amba*, mother), *Hara* (*Shiva*, *God*), *kay* (body), *dayak* (communicating, counseller) *nayak* (*nayaka*, a guide, leader), *rangan* (*ranga*, theatre stage), *Sadha* (*Sadhu*, saint), *vitsiy* (*vichya*, examination), *duhit* (daughter), *sva-yetshiy* (*sva-iccha*) with good intentions. *Sva* is a prefix meaning good. It is the opposite of '*kva*': bad), *Bugi* (*Bhagwan*, God), *kalaki* (*kalika*, *Kaliyuga*), *gor* (*guru*, teacher), and *kreyi* (pious deeds). Significantly, these verses suggest no such embroideries as are commonplace in some didactic utterances of Nuruddin. That these verses seem to have retained their original sense is clear from the use of exceedingly small number of Persian and Arabic words such as *qvadratsay* (*qudrat*, the grace of God) and *halas* (*hal*, condition).

Baba Nasib's pioneering collection of a small number of Nuruddin's select verses also includes those concerning the saint's expostulatory address to the courtesan.[47] However, while examining the interpretations put on these verses by Baba Nasib we must distinguish between two levels of discourse: the events described, and the significance attributed to them or the interconnection established between them by the observer. His interpretation is also a historical event, but of another kind. It is significant that the simple fact of the conversion of a courtesan into a disciple of Nuruddin is described as nothing short of a miracle. Also, the repentance of the courtesan and her consequent elevation to sainthood in the hagiographical literature[48] suggest the overwhelming importance that was attached by the convert population themselves to Nuruddin as a mystic imbued with the mission of raising the social status of even the most despised sections of medieval Kashmiri society.

There is ample evidence in the sources to show that Nuruddin's reformatory role was not looked upon with favour by the Brahmans.

We are told that during the illness of Zain al-Abidin the Brahman astrologers tried to convince the Sultan that his ailment was due to the presence of a man in the kingdom who practised deception disguised as a Rishi. The caste-conscious Brahmans even deluded the Sultan into believing that he would recover from his illness once he issued orders for the execution of the culprit masquerading as an ascetic. The Sultan sent for Nuruddin. However, the saint came to know, through secret knowledge, of the conspiracy hatched against him by the Brahman advisers of the Sultan and presented himself voluntarily before the foot-soldiers sent to apprehend him. No sooner did Nuruddin reach the royal palace than the Sultan's condition began to improve. While the Sultan attributed his recovery to the saint's grace, the Brahmans did their best to persuade him to take action against the impostor 'Nand Rishi.' The salvation of the Sultan's ill-fated subjects, the Brahmans argued, lay in the death of the pretender. The Sultan however scorned the suggestion of the astrologers and remarked: "The world will feel wounded at heart at an offence caused to a single *darwish*."[49]

Nearly all the stories of miracles and legends of traditional Kashmiri society centre round questions of social significance rather than purely religious matters. It is also significant that in none do we find any communal bias, taking either a narrow view of Islam or looking at Hindusim with jaundiced eyes. It is certain that conversion of the lower sections of Kashmiri society to Islam was accomplished by way of discussion of issues concerning the common man. In fact, there is a strong undercurrent of hostility in the legends to the Brahmanic idea that a low-born person could not attain the status of a saint or a religious leader. We also see in the hagiological literature a tendency to represent Nuruddin as a champion of the sentiments and aspirations of the commoners. This is also evident in the embellishments put by the hagiographers on the conversion of Bhum Sadh to Islam.[50]

It is also worthwhile to examine a wide range of miracles attributed to Nuruddin during his meeting with a group of Sayyids led by Mir Muhammad Hamadani. Such miracles cannot be summarily rejected, considering that the evidence was furnished by a chronicler who had access to contemporary sources of Nuruddin. What is of further significance is that the chronicler was a Sayyid himself; yet he did not hesitate to produce a plethora of evidence to prove the spiritual excellence of Nuruddin *vis-a-vis* the Sayyids who had expressed serious doubts about his saintly position. Their main charge against Nuruddin was his illiteracy; and this they considered to be at the root of his renunciation in the manner of the Hindu ascetics. Although the leader of the Sayyids, Mir Muhammad, was convinced about the spirituality of the Rishi, yet in order to dispel the doubts of his disciples he deemed it proper to ask a few questions to the Kashmiri saint. Asked to write the Quranic verse, the Rishi responded by taking the coal from the *kangri* putting it in his mouth and then throwing it on the wall of the room. The Sayyids were struck with wonder to see the verses miraculously appear on the wall.[51] At another meeting with Nuruddin one of the Sayyids stood up to give the call for prayers (*azan*). But the Rishi stopped the *mu'azzin* from reciting *azan*; his contention was that the *mu'azzin's* action was not well timed and did not meet the demands of the time of prayer fixed at the *arsh*. Mir Muhammad then asked Nuruddin several questions about the esoteric knowledge with which he was gifted. Answering every question satisfactorily the Rishi was finally able to create a favourable impression on the Sayyids about his spirituality.[52]

The real purport of the miracles can also be understood in terms of the immense popularity that Nuruddin seems to have enjoyed for over a century after his death. Notwithstanding the supernatural elements in the miracles, it would be grievous error to separate these from the social structure and its dynamics. These miracles constitute a collective phenomenon which tell us much about the psychological background of the period: the interpenetration of the tangible and the supernatural worlds dispelling the false notions of high birth or long pedigree.

Many miracles are ascribed to the disciples of Nuruddin and the Rishis of succeeding generations. Although some of these are laden with social content, generally, they seem to have been designed by the common people to place the Rishis at the pinnacle of sanctity. Thus Zainuddin is credited with having made a stream gush forth;[53] on another occasion, his anger is supposed to have caused a canal to dry up. But he restored the water in the canal when the people living near Aishmuqam[54] begged him to do so.[55] Latifuddin is said to have given up eating green herbs after his disciple Pirbaz told him that the green herbs started bleeding and talking to him about his cruelty in uprooting them.[56] Thus, the message conveyed is suggestive of the Rishi's commitment to the philosophy of non-violence. Payamuddin,[57] a noble of the Sultan, is said to have become a Rishi after observing the behaviour of ants during one of his hunting expeditions. The ants' practice of storing grain brought home to him the urgency of making preparations for the Hereafter.[58]

Bamuddin is reputed to have turned wine into milk when asked by Shaukat Mir and Fakhruddin Mir[59] to play the role of the cup-bearer. Impressed by the spirituality of the saint, the merry makers gave up the life of ease and took to the life of the Rishis.[60] Hardi Rishi is also credited with having humanized the behaviour of the people in accordance with the ethical standards of the age. However, the hagiographers' accounts[61] regarding his powers in elevating even dogs to the status of *Qutbs*,[62] *Abdals*[63] and *Ghauth*[64] have only a symbolic meaning. The allegory is not about animals taking part in the human drama, but refers to the animal-like behaviour of certain individuals whose habits were reformed under the influence of the Rishi.

Above all, miracles attributed to the Rishis reflect the historical changes in the behaviour of a people at the crossroads. Miracles can be seen as stages or aspects in the discovery and development of man's basic qualities—moral, spiritual, and above all, social. Our study points to the eminently anthropocentric character of the pattern of historical development which consists both in the emergence of man as the central figure in the picture of the universe, and in the gradual enrichment of his multidimensional personality. The fact is that in the history of Sufism miracles, dreams, visions,[65] etc., have played an important part in constituting a means of communication between society and faith. Even in the contemporary social scene, the miraculous appearances of the saints in visions or dreams speak of the complexity and mystery of human existence—a phenomenon requiring a far deeper understanding than mere psychological skill or even empathy on the part of the historian of Sufism.

REFERENCES AND NOTES

1. For a preliminary discussion on this issue, see Ishaq Khan, "Islam in Kashmir: Historical analysis of some of its distinctive features", in *Islam in India* (ed. Troll). II, pp. 86-97; see also author's research paper, "Towards an analysis of a popular Muslim ritual in the Kashmiri environment," presented in the International Seminar on "New History," and organized by Jawaharlal Nehru University at the India International Centre, New Delhi, in February, 1988.
2. *The Quran*, S. 54: V. 1, 2.
3. *Ibid.*, S. 3, 123.
4. *Ibid.*, S. 17: V. 1.
5. See *Sahihu'l Bukhari.*
6. The only term used in the Quran for a miracle is *ayah* (pl. ayat), "a sign" or "signs." See the *Quran*, 13/27; 29/49. But what is worthy of

note here is that the Quran lays great stress on the fact that the Prophet Muhammad's mission was not to work miracles but guide mankind in the best traditions of the prophets sent before.

7. Goldziher, *Muslim Studies* (tr. Barber and Stem), II, p. 338.
8. See Ibn Khaldun, *Muqaddama* (Urdu translation by Maulana Ragib Rahman Delhavi, I, pp. 292, 294, 318-19). The great Arab historian remarks: "Among the Sufis some who are favoured by acts of divine grace are also able to exercise an influence upon worldly conditions. This, however, is not counted as a kind of sorcery. It is effected with divine support, because the attitude and approach (of these men) result from prophesy and are a consequence of it." See Ibn Khaldun (*Muqaddama*, tr. Rosenthal, II, p. 167).
9. Hughes, *Dictionary of Islam*, p. 350.
10 The main aim of Henry Corbin is to penetrate Sufism by way of the phenomenological method. By assuming the role of subjectivity as existing inseparably in all human knowledge (in the relation of inter-subjectivity), this method, besides allowing one to show respect for the thoughts of others, also enables one to enter into their intentions by understanding them from within. It is within the framework of this method that Corbin raises his legitimate protests against those who regard the world of imagination as an unreal world. According to him this world is undoubtedly real, and the visible world is only an appearance. The image and the inter-mundane sphere of imagination have an ontological reality. They belong to an intermediary realm, a place where "spirits become corporeal and bodies are spiritualized." This meeting of the spirit and the body is indeed the world of symbols and archetypal images (*mithal*). But it is the symbol and not what is symboished that is real. See Corbin, *Creative Imagination in the Sufism of Ibn 'Arabi* (Eng. tr. R. Manheim), Princeton, 1969.
It may be pointed out that our intention is not to penetrate into the intermundane sphere of the imagination by means 'of initiation into the secret of the gnostic (*'arif*) or mystic.' On the other hand, we have endeavoured to expound the in-depth meaning (*batin*) of the intermundane realm of imagination by way of reason, unfortunately devalued by Corbin in his illuminating discussion.
11. According to a *hadith*, "Good dreams are one of the parts of prophecy." See *Mishkat*, XXI, C. IV.
For the importance of dreams in the lives of Sufis, see Al-Hujwiri, *Kashaf Al-Mahjub* (Eng. tr. Nicholson), pp. 88, 91, 92, 93, 94, 100, 116, 129, 138, 145, 218, 321, 358, 359. See also *Infra*, 65n.
12. See for Sayyid Ali Hamadani's mystical experience, Chapter III, "Socio-Religious Milleu."
13. The age-long practice of reading *Aurad-i Fathiyya* aloud in the mosques and shrines of the Kashmir Valley may be ascribed to the impact that the mystical experience of Sayyid Ahmad Krimani has had on the vast

bulk of Kashmiri Muslim population. See *Ibid.* See also Ishaq Khan, "Toward an Analysis of a Popular Muslim Ritual in the Kashmiri Environment." *op. cit.*

14. See author's review of *French Studies in History* (ed. Maurice Aymard and Harbans Mukhia), Vol. I, in *The Indian Historical Review.*
15. Baba Nasib, *Nurnama*, f. 142b; see also Sayyid Ali, *Tarikh-i Kashmir*, f. 40b; Mishkati, *Asrar al-Abrar*, ff. 98ab; Wahab, *Fathat-i Kubrawiyya*, ff. 98ab; Diddamari, *Waqiat-i Kashmir*, ff. 25ab.
16. Mishkati, *op. cit.*, f. 98b. Wahab, op. cit., f. 182b.
17. Parmu, *Nund Rishi: Unity in Diversity*, p. 170.
18. The latter-day Rishis of Chrar have given a faithful description of lengthy dialogue between the Shaikh and Nasruddin. See Baba Khalil, *Rauzat al-Riyazat*, pp. 326-34.
19. Parmu, *op. cit.*, p. 186.
20. *Ibid.*, p. 187.
21. *Ibid.*, p. 201.
22. *Ibid.*, p. 202.
23. Khalil, *op. cit.*, p. 344.
24. Parmu, *op. cit.*, p. 203.
25. Sayyid Ali, *op. cit.*, ff. 40b-41a; Mishkati, *op. cit.*, f.99a.
26. Although Baba Nasib clearly remarks that Nasruddin accepted the advice of the Shaikh (*op. cit.*, f. 143b), yet the hagiographical accounts are full of the insignificant quantity of food consumed by the Rishi. While Mishkati (*op. cit.*, f. 99b) says that Nasruddin finally reduced the quantity of grains to eight only, Mattu (*Rishinama*, p. 118) puts the number at forty.
27. Mannheim contends that modes of thought "cannot be adequately understood as long as their social origins are obscured." The sociological point of view, in his opinion, must seek the genesis of meaning in the context of group life. "Knowledge is from the very beginning a cooperative process of group life, in which every one unfolds his knowledge within the framework of a common fate, a common activity, and the overcoming of difficulties." And he further adds "precisely because knowing is fundamentally collective knowing. . .it presupposes a community of knowing which grows primarily out of a community of experiencing prepared for in the subconscious." See Mannheim, *Ideology and Utopia*, pp. 2, 4, 24, 28.
28. Mulla Ali Raina, *Tadhkirat al-Arifin*, f. 32a.
29. See Chapter V, "The Religious Thought of Nuruddin."
30. Situated on the north-east shore of the famous Dal Lake, Ishbar is half a mile from the Nishat Bagh. It is an important place of pilgrimage for Kashmiri Pandits. The sacred spring, called Guptanganga, is the chief attraction for pilgrims.
31. Baba Nasib refers to her as both Loli and Yawan Mach. See Nasib, *op. cit.*, ff. 32b, 34b. The latter name definitely suggests that Loli was

popularly remembered as an enraptured soul after her entry into the Rishi order. According to Baba Khalil, after offering *tauba*, Loli was named Shanga Bibi. See Khalil, *op. cit.*, p. 456.

32. Nasib, *op. cit.*, ff. 32ab-37ab.
33. Parimoo, *op. cit.*, p. 256.
34. *Ibid.*
35. *Ibid.*, p. 257.
36. *Ibid.*
37. *Ibid*, p. 258.
38. *Ibid.*
39. *Ibid.*, p. 259.
40. *Ibid.*
41. *Ibid.*, p. 260.
42. *Ibid.* pp. 260-61.
43. *Ibid.*, p. 261.
44. It means the dark age. See Monier William, *A Sanskrit-English Dictionary* p. 262.
45. Parimoo, *op. cit.*, pp. 261-62.
46. *Ibid.*, pp. 256-262; *Kulliyat*, pp. 185-88.
47. Nasib, *op. cit.*, f. 34b.
48. Ibid., f. 39a. Miskin, *Tahaif al-Abrar fi dhikr-i Auliya-i Akhyar*, p. 110. Bahauddin Mattu (d. 1832) eulogized the courtesan's conversion to Islam in his poetical composition. See Mattu, *op. cit.*, pp. 132-133.
49. Nasib, *op. cit.*, ff. 63ab.
50. See Chapter VII, "The Rishis and Conversion to Islam."
51. Sayyid 'Ali, *op. cit.*, ff. 34ab.
52. *Ibid.* See also Sabur, *Khawariq al-Salikin*, ff. 33b-34a.
53. Nasib, *op. cit.*, ff. 134b-145ba, Mishkati, *op. cit.*, f. 93a.
54. Situated in the Liddar Valley.
55. Nasib, *op. cit.*, f. 136a. See also Sayyid Ali, *op. cit.*, f. 40a.
56. Nasib, *op. cit.*, ff. 141b-142a.
57. His tomb, situated in the neighbourhood of Tangmarg, attracts a large number of pilgrims including tourists to the Valley from different parts of India.
58. Sayyid Ali, *op. cit.*, f. 47a., Nasib, *op. cit.*, ff. 155ab; Mishkati, *op. cit.*, f. 110a; Sabur, *op. cit.*, ff. 43ab; Shahabadi, *Bagh-i Sulaiman*, f. 110b; Diddamari, *op. cit.*, f. 28b.
59. According to Baba Nasib, both of them were in royal service. See Nasib, *op. cit.*, f. 144a.
60. Ibid, Hasan, *Asrar al-Akhyar*, *op. cit.*, pp. 103-04.
61. Haidar Tulmuli, *Hidayat al-Mukhilisin*, f. 81a. Ali Raina, *Tadhkirat al-'Arifin*, ff. 267ab.
62. He is the pivot of the universe; therefore the highest member of the generally accepted hierarchy of Sufis. See Al-Hujwiri, *Kashaf al-Mahjub.* (Eng. tr. Nichlson), pp. 147, 206, 214, 228, 229.

63. About the degrees of sainthood, 'Ali bin 'Uthman al-Hujwiri writes: "But of those who have power to loose and to bind and are the officers of the Divine court there are three hundred called *Akhyar*, and forty called *Abdal* and seven called *Abrar*, and four called *Awtad*, and three called *Nuqaba* and one, called *Qutb* or *Ghauth*. All these know one another and cannot act save by mutual consent." See Hujwiri, *op. cit.*, p. 214.
64. The title is given to the most distinguished member of the hierarchy of Sufis.
65. Trimingham observes: "The importance of dreams and visions in the whole scheme of the Sufi path can hardly be overstressed; the literature of Sufism and the hagiographa (sic) in particular are full of them, and their significance in the life of individuals and society. Ibn al-'Arabi's *'Al-Futuhat al-Makkiyya* derives directly from such experience and he shows how the decisive stages of his life were marked by dreams. Visions of the Prophet and al-Khadir were the decisive point in the authorization of an illuminate to strike out along his own way. They were a convenient way of obtaining permission from long-dead Sufis to teach their doctrines and *award*, thus leading some people to assume the continuity of line from al-Junaid or another early Sufi," *op. cit.*, p. 190. For a discussion of the role of dreams in Sufism, see the relevant chapters in G.E. Von Grunebaum and Roger Caillois, *The Dream and Human Societies*, California, 1966; also A.J. Arberry, *Muslim Saints and Mystics*, London, 1966, pp. 40, 81 (about divine manifestation), pp. 93, 98, 179, 180, 203, 220, 246, 247, 254, 260 (appearance of the Prophet) and pp. 46, 51.

CHAPTER IX

Epilogue

Edward Said remarks: "To some writers of history Islam is a politics and a religion, to others it is a style of being; to others it is 'distinguishable from Muslim society'; to still others it is a mysteriously known essence, to all the authors Islam is a remote, tensionless thing, without much to teach us about the complexities of today's Muslims. Hanging over the whole disjointed enterprise which is *The Cambridge History of Islam* is the old orientalist truism that Islam is about texts, not about people."[1]

Taking a cue from Said's objective criticism of the Orientalist scholarship, we have attempted to understand Islam through an historically oriented cultural anthropology, not merely as a culture and civilisation in the manner of Orientalists.[2] Islam in this study has been interpreted both as a religion and a social reality. As a living religion, it is an aggregate of different people with a variety of interpretations concerning the course of Islamic development, rather than just the fundamentals of faith which demand unswerving belief in Allah, the Quran and the finality of the prophethood of Muhammad. As a social reality, Islam includes various Muslim ethnic groups or communities which, in spite of the persistence of local traditions in their cultural settings, maintain the universalism of Islam against internal and external challenges. Thus our study shows that whatever people have believed to be Islam is Islam, and what Orientalists generally describe as 'syncretism',[3] formal adhesion,[4] and so on does not have any special significance, considering that neither Islam nor the people who have professed it through centuries of Islamic acculturation were (or are) static.

The history of Islam is actually a history of Islamization; and the process of Islamization at the social level is a process of Islamic acculturation in which individuals and groups gradually break their ties with traditional religion or culture and eventually follow a path that ends with their adherence to the *Shari'a*-bound structure of Islam. The syncretism of Islamic beliefs and local practices is actually the beginning of a movement for the realisation of the ultimate, if not immediate, objectives of Islam at both the individual and social levels. Syncretism or, for that matter, even synthesis is not the culmination of the Islamization process. It is the never-ceasing battle against reprehensible innovations (*bid'a*), accretions, or a mass of strange superstitions and contradictions which distinguishes the Muslim society from other societies. Islam is thus a huge historical movement rather than a mere ontological phenomenon independent of life situations.

Unfortunately very little effort has so far been made to objectively analyse the true nature of the various dimensions of the societal responses that Islam evoked in its actual historical manifestations. However, while studying the Rishi movement in terms of people's response to the penetration of Islamic beliefs and practices in the Hindu-Buddhist environment, we have attempted to explain how Islam has been a distinctive kind of social experience in the geographical, linguistic and cultural setting of the Kashmir valley.

An important question to which this study has addressed itself is whether the Rishi movement was an integral component of the process of Islamization that started in Kashmir in the wake of the introduction of Sufi orders from Central Asia and Persia in the fourteenth century. True, the social behaviour of the Rishis bore the stamp of the local culture; but it would not be correct to say that Islam got diluted in Kashmir as a result of the Muslim Rishis' strict adherence to vegetarianism, celibacy, extreme asceticism, and above all non-violence. A superficial examination of some similarities in the social behaviour of Muslim and Hindu mystics tends to create an erroneous impression that syncretism was the dominant characteristic of the Rishi order. Bruce Lawrence, for instance, describes the Rishi Movement as "marginally Muslim" and compares it with the Bhakti Movement.[5] However, our study shows that the similarities between the Rishi and the *Bhakti* movements are often deceptive and that the "Rishi devotional language" unlike that of Bhakti did not lead to the emergence of religious sects in Kashmir. On the other hand Nuruddin's pervasive mystical poetry was one of the finest and systematic expositions of the *Tauhidic Weltanschauung* at the level of regional manifestation. What is, therefore, remarkable about Nuruddin's role as a Sufi reformer is that, in spite of being an apostle of Hindu-Muslim unity, he did not fail to visualise the risk of Islam being swamped by the ancient religion of Kashmiris, and took special care to urge them to mould their personal life in accordance with the *Shari'a.* The fact is that Nuruddin's poetry served as a spiritual guide to the personal ethics of the *Shari'a* for Kashmiris.

Nuruddin's rejection of renunciation in the characteristic style of a Sufi reformer was aimed at imparting a dynamism to his order which was closest to the tradition going back to the sober Junayd-i Baghdadi[6] (d. 910) and the later exponent of *Wahdat al-Shuhud*, Ala al-Dawla[7] Simnani (d. 1335). Nuruddin himself acknowledges his debt to the Kubrawi Sufis whose order gives priority to the "way of Junayd" as the centre of the novice's education. It was also in this context that, in spite of his being against renunciation, Nuruddin allowed his prominent disciples to resort to seclusion and asceticism. And by so doing he used the local beliefs in ascetics and the sacredness associated with nature, *i.e.*, the mountains and forests as modes of conversion, attracting the unlettered folk towards Islam. Another method of seeking the assimilation of the commoners in Islam was through the profuse use of vocabulary not only from the Quran, but from the traditional sources of the Hindus—the *Vedas* and the *Upanishads.* In his songs the Shaikh introduced many words in current use. However, he contrived to use them in such a way as to recast their meanings with the aim of anchoring Kashmiri society in the wider system of Islam.

No wonder, therefore, that the Rishi Movement did not become a cult like the Bhakti. True, through the Brahman ascetics' conversion Islam in Kasmir incorporated and welded together different spiritual insights; yet in this process of assimilation they were transformed and given a uniquely Islamic orientation. And although the Rishis were gifted with inward illumination, they never attempted to reduce intense personal experiences to the level of abstract thought where misunderstandings and misinterpretations become inevitable. The Kubrawis, the Suharwardis and the Naqshbandis were so impressed by the *Shari'a*-oriented asceticism of the Rishis that they perceived their movement to be a powerful instrument for generating a momentum of change, essentially from within, on the basis of Islamic teachings. The synthesis of the Rishi and the exogenous Islamic mystic traditions thus created conditions for the gradual eclipse of the local Hindu-Buddhist practices in Kashmir; by the end of the eighteenth century, we hear very little about the Rishis practising celibacy, abstinence from meat or even seclusion in caves, forests or on tops of the mountains.

This study ought to dispel any doubts that modern scholars may have about the role of Islam as an ideology of liberation *vis-a-vis* the

Brahmancial tyranny.[8] Muhammad Habib was the first historian to offer us an insight into the causes of the disintegration of the Rajput society in medieval India in the wake of the spread of the egalitarian message of Islam.[9] While the bold assumptions of the doyen of Indian historians have rarely been tested,[10] Islamization in India has generally been linked with the proselytizing[11] and sometimes the political role of Sufi missionaries.[12]

In this study, however, we have questioned the role of Sufis from Central Asia and Persia as being powerful channels of conversion, considering the language barrier which separated them from the masses. This is not to suggest that the Sufis did not influence society; as a matter of fact, as true representatives of Islamic ethical ideals, they gradually created a ferment in the society which was exposed to their radiant influence. It is against this background that we have studied the emergence of the mystic order of Muslim Rishis in Kashmir as the culmination of the mounting disaffection, tension and conflict generated in the course of time in a particular section of the people on their contact with Islam. The Rishi movement was thus not merely a movement of ascetics, but in reality, a manifestation of social protest against the caste taboos that cut at the very root of human dignity. Nuruddin's exaltation of manual labour, against the Brahmanic tradition of looking down on all forms of it had considerable influence. Among the Muslim Rishis the significance attached to manual labour was without parallel, whereas the Hindu ascetics considered it to be improper. The Brahmans' reaction to Nuruddin's liberating role reveals the paradox and tension that Kashmiri society experienced consequent to the Rishis' advocacy of virtues such as self-imposed poverty, their identification with the poor and above all their opposition to the caste system. Never lacking in social consciousness,[13] the unlettered masses did not take long to throw off their traditional bonds with the Brahman priests and to proclaim the Rishis as deliverers in their folk songs still sung with great fervour in the fields.

This study also examines why, under the influence of the Rishi movement, men of affluence and power willingly distributed their possessions among the needy and the poor after adopting the life of self-imposed poverty (*faqr*). In the conversions of Baba Latifuddin, Baba Payamuddin, Baba Shukruddin and Lankar Mal, for instance, we have attempted to show that self-imposed poverty was chosen by such wealthy men with a view to helping themselves to follow the Prophet's way towards identification with the poor. Although the continual fasts observed by the Rishis were motivated by spiritual desires, they also speak of their concern for the poor. That the Rishis launched a silent protest against the worldliness and inveterate materialism of both the Muslim rulers and the *'Ulama* is clearly shown by their aversion to the society of the affluent. So dear were the social and ethical ideals of Islam to the Rishis that they did not fail to vindicate the poor man's ego even before the rulers. Thus when Sultan Ali Shah visited Baba Bamuddin, he was cold shouldered and no sooner had the distinguished visitor left the Rishi's habitat than he advised his disciples to wash the mat on which the Sultan had seated himself.[14] Baba Zainuddin did not even care to talk to Sultan Zain al-Abidin when the latter visited him.[15]

In this study miracles attributed to the Rishis have been interpreted in a rational way so that it has not been difficult to find the human element in the supra-mundane affairs after separating the chaff from the grain. Our examination of miracles and legends points to the social nature of the process of conversion to Islam in Kashmir. Even miracles attest to the fact that conversion of the lower strata of Kashmiri society to Islam was achieved by way of discussion of issues which concerned the common man. The dominant characteristic of the hagiographies is to represent Nuruddin as a champion of the sentiments and aspirations of the commoners; and in fact, the Brahmanic myth that a low-born person could not attain sainthood or become a religious leader was exploded. In this context not only are the dialogues attributed to Nuruddin in his conversations with die-hard Brahmans revealing, but what is more remarkable is the great significance that was attached by the common folk to Nuruddin as a mystic imbued with the mission of elevating even the most degraded sections of Kashmiri society. Our analysis of legendary material thus points to the eminently anthropocentric character of historical development which consists in the emergence of man as the central figure in the picture of the universe.

Religious thought among the Rishis never developed a philosophy of religion; it was in essence a confirmation of the true spirit of the *Shari'a* by a harmonious blending of belief and practice. It is tempting to describe the Rishis as anti-*'Ulama*, but it would be a grave error to suppose that their movement was directed against the so-called "official" religion. The fact is that Nuruddin was more concerned to present the *Shari'a* as a moral code to the unlettered folk. This is amply borne out by his intuitive realisation that it was possible to accommodate certain elements of the warm, earthy, mystic religion of the Valley to the *Shari'a* without really distorting the latter. His disgust with the *'Ulama* was due to their deviation in a practice from the inner spirit of the *Shari'a*. In his role as the founder of a new mystic order, Nuruddin, while giving social authenticity to local traditions, made them respond to Islam in a creative spirit, so that the orientation of pre-Islamic traditions and practices in his order changed with the flowering of the resilient Islamic tradition of the Muslim Rishis.

It is worth asking whether the Rishi movement had anything in common with the Mahdawi movement[17] and the Shattari order of the Sufis which flourished in some parts of India in the sixteenth century.

Not unlike the Mahdawis, the Rishis showed an utter disregard for property and a life of ease and luxury, and were against exploitation of the weak by the strong. What is more, both Rishis and Mahadawis sought the confidence of the poor and some of them with all humility begged the forgiveness of those whom they had offended and insulted. While some Mahdawis disposed of the land received by them from the state for subsistence, most Rishis, formerly living in affluence, voluntarily bore poverty and starvation. Such was the influence of Rishis and Mahdawis that some sensitive souls deserted their households and joined the brotherhood in a passive vindication and affirmation of the rights of the poverty-stricken people.

But notwithstanding the social content in the role of the Mahdawis, their movement was for all practical purposes confined to a small section of society, and the mass of Indian Muslims did not come under their influence. That the Mahdawis, in spite of their concern for restoring the pristine purity of the *Shari'a*, were viewed with suspicion among Muslims is shown by their refusal to disown Sayyid Muhammad of Jaunpur as the promised Mahdi. No wonder the veneration of the followers of Sayyid Muhammad almost turned into disbelief, so much so that even Shaikh Ahmad Sirhindi[18] charged them with heresy. The Mahdawi movement thus turned into a sect while the Rishi movement proved to be the first potent and incisive expression of Muslim religious thought in India and a dynamic moral and social force.[19] In fact, the only Sufi order in India to doggedly oppose Brahmanism on the basis of the ethical and social ideals of the Quran and the *Sunna* was that of the Rishi.

It is interesting to note that the Sufi order of the *Shattari*[20a] bears close resemblance to the Rishis in certain respects. Like some Rishis, the Shattaris lived in fosests on a frugal diet of fruit and herbs, and subjected themselves to hard physical and spiritual exercises. The ten rules mentioned by Rizvi for the achievement of the Shattari goal viz., repentance, renunciation, trust in God, patience, satisfaction, *dhikr* and concentrated attention on God also guided the Rishis in their pursuit of the mystical truth.

However, the syncretical element was clearly discernible not only in the social behaviour of the Shattaris but even in their liturgical formulae.[21] Some Shattari Sufis even "recommended the sitting posture of jogis, and outlined several magical and mystical practices for achievement of supernatural powers."[22] The most illustrious representative of the Shattari order was the ascetic Muhammad Ghauth who was held in high esteem by Akbar in his youth. But unlike Nuruddin, Ghauth did not attempt to convert Hindu mystics whom he held in veneration and even composed *Bahr al-hayat*, the first treatise written by a Muslim in India on the practice of yoga. Thus in contrast to the indelible influence of the Rishis on the Islamization of Kashmir, the influence of the Shattaris on the population of rural Bihar and the interior of Gujrat notwithstanding their dentification with yogic practices, was infinitesimal.[23] Khaliq Ahmed Nizami seems to be nearer the truth when he says that "the Shattari *silsilah* was a spent bullet in the seventeenth century"[24] probably owing to the popularity of the Mujaddidi school which was very critical of the "pantheistic philosophy" and syncretistic ideas of the Shattaris. The Rishis, on the other hand, elicited the praise of the adherents of the Mujaddidi school in Kashmir like Muhammad Murad Teng, Khawaja Muhammad Azam Diddamari and Bahauddin Mattu.[25] The latter even composed *Rishinama* in which he versified the contribution of the Rishis to Islam in Kashmir.

Like the Chistis, the Rishis did not associate themselves with the government. Nor did they accept honours and wealth from the rulers or build their fortunes like the Suharwardi Sufis of Multan and Ucch.[26] However, like the Suharwardis, the Rishis seem to have rejected the public recital of music which prevailed among the Chistis in the form of *sama*. True, both the Rishis and the Chistis were influenced by the local religious environment; but the distinctive characteristic of the Rishi order was that while taking over indigenous practices from the yogis—extreme ascetic discipline, celibacy and vegetarianism—under their inspiring leadership, Islam did not simply tolerate what was local in origin, but sought to make the local traditions subservient to the *Shari'a*. A fundamental characteristic that distinguishes the shrines of the Rishis in Kashmir from those of the Chistis in India is that while the fomer are marked by pristine simplicity, the latter in their syncretistic form are scenes of religious interaction and confusion. The devotees at the shrines in the plains generally light candles around the Sufis tomb, offer flowers at the burial site of the Sufis and listen with devotional rapture to *qawwali* (often with musical instruments) in praise of the Sufi. Such practices, uncommon in Kashmir, bear a striking parallel to those of Hindu pilgrims at their shrines. But like their counterparts in the plains, some devotees of the shrines in Kashmir do observe circumambulation of the site and the touching of the grave and relics of the departed saint.

Nuruddin's role in the formation of a Kashmiri Islamic tradition bears some resemblance to that of Ahmad Ibn Ibrahim Ibn Ali (d. 1166) of Yasi, later called Turkistan.[27] Both in Turkistan and Kashmir Islam largely filtered down to the common folk through the poetic genius of their spiritual leaders. The *silsilah* of the Rishis like that of the Yasaviyya was a "tariqa of wanderers." In fact, a pilgrimage to the tombs of the Yasaviyya Shaikhs in Central Asia and to those of the Rishs in Kashmir became a permanent feature of Islam in these regions. Both in Turkistan and Kashmir local customs incorporated into ritual and practice gave an ethnic colouring to Islam. Kashmiri like Turkish was used in worship outside ritual prayer in the mosques and shrines. The Rishi tradition like the Yasivi tradition had many ramifications—religious, social and cultural. The two traditions played almost similar roles in the Islamization of the unlettered folk, in the adaptation of the social environment to Islam, and of course, in linguistic reconciliation through the popular poems of Nuruddin and Ahmad.

One may ask why the Rishis were generally styled as *babas* in Kashmir . In Sanskrit the term is a synonym of an ascetic (*sanyasi*), but in Persian chronicles and hagiographies of the Valley the specific use of *baba* for the Muslim Rishis had definitely the connotation of the wandering Turkish *darwish*, the *babas* of Central Asia. While the Turkish *babas* of the Ghazi states of Anatolia in the thirteenth and fourteenth centuries "accompanied, followed, and fortified the warriors,"[28] in the Hindu-Buddhist environment of peaceful existence, tolerance, and spiritual enquiry, the vagrant *babas* of Kashmir replaced the worldly *'Ulama* as the commenders of Islam, to both the learned Brahman and the unlettered folk. It is significant that although the Rishis were generally unlettered yet they produced a peoples movement which was able to penetrate and transform the consciousness of even the learned Suharwardi and Naqshbandi Sufis, whose traditions blended in time in loyalty to the common ideal and purpose of making all mystic traditions submit to the direction and conformity of the Quran and the *Sunna*.

The lack of literacy among the Rishis meant that their movement did not develop along the lines of the officially-sponsored *khanqahs* in the

Arab world.[29] Lacking official patronage the Rishi order did not develop aristocratic tendencies, nor did it become a 'wealthy corporation' at any stage in its history. In a sense, the habitats of the Rishis may be compared with the *zawiyas*;[30] they were small, modest establishments, centred around the Shaikh who was a 'shepherd of souls' rather than an officially appointed administrator as in the khanqah of Arab lands. Small wonder that these one-time places of retreat of the Rishis became self-perpetuating centres of their order in due course. Having acquired the character of *ziyarats* after the Rishis' death, these places became focal points of Islam in the Valley—not merely centres of spirituality, religious fervour, ascetic exercises and Sufi training, but more importantly, agencies for the diffusion of Islamic teaching among the rural population. Consequently, it was through the *ziyarats* of the Rishis that Islam gained a firm footing in the Valley. That it had come to stay was clearly shown by the network of mosques and *madrasas* which sprang up everywhere round the tombs of the Rishis.

Although most *ziyarat* establishments were conspicuous for their poverty, some of the abodes of the Rishis seem to have become self-sufficient institutions even during their lifetime. The habitats of Baba Hardi Rishi, Baba Daud (Batmaloo Saheb), Baba Gangi Rishi[31] and many others were self-sustaining institutions, thanks more to their active social roles than gifts and donations offered by the devotees for the maintenance of the public charity kitchens (*langar*). There is no evidence to show that the revenues of the *ziyarats* were expended by the immediate successors of the Rishis in rich living. However, in later times, the charge of the *ziyarats* assumed hereditary characteristics[32] with one or more social or occupational groups and gradually the *ziyarats* turned into breeding grounds for superstition and social exploitaion. Such a development not only sounded the death-knell of the Rishi movement, but at the same time it dealt a serious blow to their social role of rendering relief to the weaker sections of Kashmiri society. Since for barely four centuries the Rishis were much more than simply benefactors of the poor, it would be appropriate to evaluate the level of their social achievements in terms of the demands of the particular social, physical, environmental and in fact, political conditions of Kashmir during the seventeenth and eighteenth centuries.

Most Rishis considered service to humanity and even animals to be a way of reaching the truth. This is borne out both by their sayings[32a] and practice. Shaikh Daud, a petty salt dealer, on becoming a Rishi engaged himself in ploughing and earned the title of the Nourisher (the

Batmoul) for his regular practice of feeding the poor out of the produce of the land brought under cultivation by him.[33] Nuri Rishi, a disciple of Baba Latifuddin, earned his living through cultivation and utilized his income not only for satisfying the wants of the needy, but even for constructing *khanqahs* and bridges.[33a] The Rishi's philanthropic activities even drew the pious Suharwardi Sufis to his abode, and they were so charmed by his social role that they paid rich tributes to him in their hagiographies.[34] Baba Hardi Rishi was so particular about taking *halal*[35] food that, in spite of his exalted status among the Rishis of the sixteenth century and also the reverence he commanded in the Suharwardi circles, he did not hesitate to cultivate the land himself.[36] Ladi Katur, a disciple of Baba Latifuddin, maintained the *langar* for the comfort of the poor for twelve years.[37] Other disciples of Latifuddin, such as[38] Lacham Rishi[39] and Nauroz Rishi,[40] also dedicated themselves to the service of the poor. Baba Luda Mal, a companion of Baba Zainuddin, in spite of secluding himself in the hollow of a chinar tree, was able to bring home to his disciples the importance of manual labour. It was due to his inspiring leadership that hundreds of his disciples devoted themselves to agricultural pursuits for the public good.[41] Baba Hardi Rishi, a disciple of Baba Rajabuddin, and a successor of Baba Nauroz, himself worked hard in the fields and impressed upon his disciples the need to engage themselves in cultivation and learn some crafts to support themselves. The impact of his teachings and personal example was that as the custodian of the *ziyarat* of his preceptor for seven years he was able to turn the shrine into a self-supporting institution for the Rishis and the poor.[42]

So great was the influence of the Rishis' social role on the consciousness of the people that even women joined their ranks with a view to building up a healthy society on the ethical principles of the Quran. That the spirituality of Islam commits both men and women to an ethic of social action, is shown by the voluntary and affirmative behaviour of women in the Valley for bringing economic benefits to the community. A pious woman once donated a big piece of fertile land as *haqq-i mahr*[43] to Baba Nanda Rishi, a disciple of Baba Nauroz, to enable the Rishis to be self-supporting.[44] Another noble lady of the Rishi order who consecrated herself to the service of humanity and religion was Ganga Bibi. Even while observing continual fasts she founded mosques and constructed bridges with her hard-earned money.[45]

It is certain that as early as in Nuruddin's time, the Rishis' habitats had turned into close-knit communities of people sharing common ideals not only for their spiritual good, but more importantly, for the benefit of the poverty-stricken masses. Thus we hear of Baba Nasruddin, a favourite disciple of Nuruddin, maintaining a kitchen for the comfort of the inmates and the needy.[46] Nasruddin was able to bring about a great transformation in the life of Jogi Raina, a noble of the Sultan, noted for his riches, who renounced the world and succeeded to the office of the head of Rishis at Chrar after Nasruddin's death. It was due to the efforts of Jogi Raina that some Rishis, who had taken to begging—strongly disapproved by Nuruddin—chose instead to cultivate land for the common good. Jogi Raina himself took great pleasure in tilling the soil by hard labour so as to render help to the indigent.[47]

Baba Gangi Rishi was born with a silver spoon in his mouth; but he turned to asceticism in the prime of his youth.[48] He spent the rest of his life in relative seclusion and directed the qualities of his head and heart to the service of the commoners. Once while ploughing he found a large sum of money which he spent on the poor. His kindness to animals was well-known. He is also said to have planted a number of fruit trees in various villages and would repair bridges and mosques with his own hands.[49]

So great was the emphasis of the Rishis on combining asceticism with agricultural labour for the benefit of society that they even put novices on trial by directing them to do hard labour in order to atone for their past sins. Baba Nek Rishi, for example, asked Nauroz Rishi, a notorious person before becoming a Rishi, to engage himself in manual labour continuously for three days in order to repay a man the money he had deprived him of. The wicked person was granted discipleship in the Rishi order only after he gave exemplary proof of his resolve to follow the right path.[50]

Asceticism was thus for the Rishis the giving up of desires,[51] particularly selfish desires, for the common good. In order to achieve this objective they actively participated in the affairs of their society. Occasionally they were so determined to mould their society that they would adopt stern action in preference to passive resistance. Thus Ummi Rupi Rishi of Kocha Mula of pargana Ular took strong exception to the encroachment of public land by certain vested interests. He is reputed to have restored a graveyard to its original position when an attempt was made to bring it under cultivation for the personal benefit of a certain individual.[52] We have already seen how Luda Mal made his brother pay for his acts of tyranny.[53]

In the concluding pages we may also try to elucidate the philosophical and religious content of the behaviour of some Rishis, and situate them within a general conception of mysticism. Such behavioural patterns should not be read out of context, nor should we regard these as syncretism. Furthermore, it would be dangerous to assert—on the basis of the symbolic behaviour of the Rishis—that their movement did not fully fit in with the "Islamic prophetical structure." Like other Sufi movements in Islam, mistakenly supposed to exist parallel to it, the Rishi movement did not present a striking contrast to "the prophetic religion."[54] Thus on closely examining the evidence regarding Baba Zainuddin's symbolic act of reciting *fatiha* at the grave of a frog whom he had buried after having accidentally trampled it to death under his feet,[55] it will become clear that the Rishis realized, in the core of their being, a homogeneity between their own individual life-process and the rest of the cosmic order. For that matter even Baba Nasibuddin's symbolic act of prayer for the departed souls of non-Muslim believers points to the same fact.[56] This sense of homogeneity, we are tempted to believe, sprang from a deep-rooted realization of the oneness with the whole universe. The Rishis seem to have nursed in their minds a strong feeling that their human individuality was just a part of an all-absorbing entity, of which the whole universe was a manifestation in time and space. Both man and the world of man were comprehended by them as possessing unity in an integrated whole. The sense of homogeneity produced by the realization of unity was not without its roots in the ethical structure of the Quran.[57]

The Rishis' concept of non-violence had a life-affirming and universalistic value, rather than only other-worldly connotations. Islam, as understood by them, sought to subject the felicity of life on this planet to the norms of morality and of responsibility. Man therefore had to regulate the pattern of human life in such a way as confirmed the truth of the Islamic dictum: "Religion is indeed man's treatment of his fellows."[58] Thus the Rishis' aversion to causing injury to animate beings, including even plants, insects and animals; their concern for conserving forests,[59]; dissuading hunters from hunting *hangul*, the prized possession of the Valley's forests[60]; personal care of pets, tamed animals[61] and birds,[61a] planting trees throughout the length and breadth of Kashmir,[62] and above all, their insistence on bringing more and more land under cultivation—all point to the fact that the true religion for the Rishis was to conduct and order life on earth in a way intended by its Creator. The Rishis' spirituality was thus a dimension of earthly life; they realized and enjoyed it in full by living morally in God's Presence. *i.e.*, by their exemplary responsibility to nature, to themselves and to society. The anecdotes about some Rishis' proverbial friendships with wild animals[63] may not appear true, yet they bear testimony to the stature of Rishis as custodians of the Valley's forest culture and protectors of their country's natural beauty and wealth. Even while escaping temporarily from the bustle of life into the solitude of forests, or in certain cases permanently, the Rishis were not unmindful of the cares of worldly life. There was a dynamic interaction between their asceticism and the environment; in fact, their social impact, apart from meditative practices and strict ascetic discipline, was the measure of their spiritual manhood.

The Kashmir Valley thus constitutes a special area in the history of Islam. It may be true that the Muslim Rishis of Kashmir contributed little to the doctrines and methods of *tasawwuf*, but what is of significance from the viewpoint of history is that their movement, as a social phenomenon, not only dealt a vital blow to Brahmanism, but simultaneously, created an atmosphere of tolerance, faith, friendliness and fellow feeling for members of society. The strength of the Rishi movement lies not only in using the Sufi concept of self-realization for ennobling and humanizing social behaviour, it also lies in galvanizing human action for the betterment of society. The movement also gave birth to institutions that were peculiarly Islamic, viz. *ziyarats* and mosques; and the gradual process of assimilation of the rural masses in Islam through these institutions suggests that conversions to Islam in the Valley were secured through a peaceful and orderly evolution. The social nature of the conversion process, notwithstanding certain individual cases of conversion in the strict religious sense, fostered fraternal forms of social organization. This is attested to not only by the joint efforts of the Rishis in bringing large areas of land under cultivation to meet the ordinary requirements of the hungry and the needy, but also by the degree of social respectability the unlettered folk gained by becoming members of the Islamic community. This they did through their participation in congregational ritual prayers, ceremonies associated with the *Urs* celebrations and above all by singing together poems composed in the local dialect in praise of the Rishis and the universality of the Prophet Muhammad's message.

The *ziyarats* of Rishis continue to remind the faithful of both spiritual realities and social obligations. Despite the criticism of local practices by the Ahl-i Hadith, a vast majority of villagers celebrate the anniversaries of their saints in the traditional manner. They continue to practise vegetarianism on festive occasions when they invite relatives and friends to taste the modest vegetarian food as a mark of respect to the disciplined soul of the Rishis. In certain areas austerity is practised in the true manner of their patron saints;[64] relics of the Rishis such as their dress, wooden clogs, cups, turbans, staff, etc., are exhibited on festive occasions when devotees invoke the intercession of the Rishis in the presence of these relics.

All said and done, it would not be proper to be unduly critical of the cultural side of Islam in the Valley; the objective reality is that while the tombs of the Rishis are cultural symbols of Islam in Kashmir, the mosques adjacent to their premises are true symbols of a universal faith in the strictest religious sense. The dualism between high culture and the popular culture can be seen as a misleading formulation ordained by Western scholarship, once we are able to take an empathic view of the visitations of the faithful on Fridays and festival days. Such visits, which continue to be the highlights of the religious life of the masses, give them an opportunity to display their communal solidarity by participation in ritual prayers.[65] At the saints' tombs, even women, notwithstanding their practice of making offerings, petitionings, or even communion with the spirits of the tombs, continue to offer congregational prayers, thereby disproving the Orientalist notion that there exists a dualism between male and female religion. The local Islamic tradition of singing hymns aloud in praise of Allah, the Prophet Muhammad and local saints in the mosques and shrines of the Valley is anathema to the Ahl-i Hadith; but notwithstanding the reformist role[66] of the latter in the religious history of modern Kashmir, the essential fact which needs to be grasped and treated with sensitivity, is that the Kashmiri way of reciting *dhikr, aurad, durud, manqabat* and *na't* aloud was a well-thought-out way through which the unlettered folk learnt the fundamentals of faith during long centuries of Islamic acculturation.

It follows that Islam and society are not distinct identities, but closely interrelated variables in creative tensions with each other. In this significant dialectical relationship, Muslim societies have generally been characterized by the ongoing process of Islamization of their little traditions. And indeed, in the context of the present study, the process of Islamization repeatedly makes itself intelligible as a unifying socioreligious and moral force radiating significance to life and thought in Muslim societies.

REFERENCES AND NOTES

1. Edward Said, *Orientalism*, p. 305
2. See Grunebaum, "An Analysis of Islamic Civilization and Cultural Anthropology", Chapter III of the author's *Modern Islam: The Search for Cultural Identity*, 1962, also Chapter I, "Introduction" and 30n.
3. Orientalists are prone to exaggerate the importance of "syncretic devotionalism," of the commoners *vis-a-vis* the misconceived and misapplied notion of the "orthodoxy" of the *'Ulama*. See for example, Eaton, *Sufis of Bijapur*, idem, "Sufi Folk Literature and the Expansion of Indian Islam", *History of Religion*, No. 14: 2 Nov., 1974, pp. 117–27; also Asim Roy, *The Islamic Syncretistic Tradition in Bengal*, Princeton, 1983.
4. See Chapter I, "Introduction" and 28n.
5. Bruce Lawrence, "Lectures on Sufism", *Studies in Islam*, Vol. XVIII, Nos. 3–4, July/October, 1981, p. 139.
6. Nuruddin, like Junayd, described the drunkeness of a Sufi as a passing phase. The evolution of his mystical career confirms the view of Junayd that "the perfected saint would go beyond it to a state of sobriety in which his awareness of God would make him a more complete human being in complete self-possession." It may not, therefore, sound strange that Junayd's pupil, al-Hallaj, was executed for describing the mystical experience under the spell of intoxication.
7. Born in 1261 in the Khurasanian village of Simnan into a family with a civil service tradition, he turned a Sufi during the period of his service of the Buddhist Ilkhan Agrghun (reg. A. D. 1284–91). After being initiated into the Kubrawi *silsilah*, he raised his voice against the existing corruption (*bid'a*) in Sufi thought. In particular, he attempted to dispel doubts about the supposed theosophical theories of Ibn al-Arabi, emphasizing that the world is a reflection, not an emanation, of Reality. He stood for strict conformity to the *Shari'a* as the very basis for progress along the Sufi path of seeking the countenance of God. He did not merely advocate a literal interpretation of the Quran, but popularised *dhikr* practices in consonance with its essential spirit.
8. Richard Eaton rejects the "religion of social liberation" theory on three flimsy grounds: first, "Are we to assume that before their contact with Muslims the untouchables of India possessed, as though they were familiar with the writing of Rousseau or Jefferson, some innate notion of the fundamental equality of all men denied them by an oppressive Brahmanical tyranny?" Second, "Muslim intellectuals did not stress the Islamic ideal of social equality as opposed to Hindu caste," and third, "the converted Hindu communities failed," to improve their status in the social hierarchy and that, on the contrary, they singly carried over into Muslim society the same practice of birth-ascribed rank that they had had in Hindu Society." See Eaton, "Approaches to the Study of

Conversion" *Approaches to Islam in Religious Studies*, p. 110. Although our findings have subjected Eaton's view to some serious qualifications, here it will suffice to say that the politics of the Muslim elite, coupled with the widerspread illiteracy and economic backwardness of the Hindu converts to Islam has largely been responsible for the latter's supposed lower status in the Muslim Society. In contemporary history, however, there is no dearth of evidence to testify to the upward mobility in the lower strata of Muslim society consequent to the relative improvement of their educational and economic standards.

9. Elliot and Dowson, *History of India as Told by its own Historians* (Revised ed. Habib, Rashid and Nizami), II, p. 52.
10. Irfan Habib's view (see his article "Economic History of the Delhi Sultanate", *The Indian Historical Review*, Jan, 1978, Vol. IV, No. 2, p. 297) that there is no evidence of any direct assault from. . ."the Muslims upon the caste system: nor even any revolt from within. . ." is not justifiable in the set of circumstances or facts that surrounded the history of conversions to Islam in Kashmir.
11. Thomas W. Arnold. *The Preaching of Islam*, London. 1913, pp. 154–93.
12. In a highly controversial article which reached me through the courtesy of Prof. Iqtidar Husain Siddiqi of Aligarh Muslim University, Aziz Ahmad's "Conversions to Islam in the Valley of Kashmir," *Central Asiatique Journal* ascribes the conversions to Islam in Kashmir to "the Great Tradition represented by the Hamadani mosque and *Khanqah*" and the efforts of the militant Bayhaqi Sayyids. And while attributing the "religious and social transformation" of Kashmir in Sikandar's reign to the influence of Sayyid Ali Hamadani's political ideas on the Sultan, the author inadvertently lends credence to the theory of dramatic and forcible conversions. Being not well conversant with the sources, the noted scholar deprecates the role of the Rishis in the history of Islam in Kashmir as compared to the Kubrawis. It is also amazing to nôte that Aziz Ahmad describes Kashmiri Muslims' zealousness and fanaticism as also leading to conversions in the Valley.
13. These findings may also be read in the context of the brazen-faced cultural superiority and some form of intellectual prejudice that characterizes Eaton's remark that the Westerners alone had "some innate notion of fundamental equality of all men. . ."See *Supra.*
14. The Rishi is said to have been angry with the Sultan since he had not discarded the royal dress (Baba Nasib, *Nurnama*, f. 128a; Mishkati, *Asrar al-Abrar*, ff. 89ab; *Wahab, Fathat-i Kubrawiyya*, f. 169b) while visiting the friend of the poor.
15. Nasib, *op. cit.*, f. 137a; Wahab, *op. cit.*, f. 173b. Mishkati, *op. cit.*, f. 94a.
16. See Chapter I, "Introduction", 32n.

17. For the History of the Mahdawi Movement, see Mujeeb, *Indian Muslims*; Qamar-ud-Din, *The Mahdawi Movement*.
18. For a perceptive analysis of his historical role, see Aziz Ahmad, *op. cit.*, pp. 182–90.
19. Mujeeb wrongly holds the same view about the Mahdawis. See Mujeeb, *Op. cit.*
20. For the History of the Shattari order in India, see Nizami, "The Shattari saints and the their attitude towards the state" *Medieval India Quarterly*, I, No. 2; *Rizvi, Sufism in India*, II, pp. 151–173.
21. Aziz Ahmad, *Islamic Culture in the Indian Environment*, p. 137.
22. Rizvi, *Sufism in India*, II, p: 156.
23. Ishaq Khan, "Sufism in Indian History", *Muslim Shrines in India ed.* Christan W. Troll, pp. 273–91.
24. Nizami, "The Shattari saints and their attitude towards the State," *op, cit.*, I, No. 2, p. 67.
25. Bahauddin Mattu was affiliated to the Kubrawi order, but the very fact that he also eulogized the activities of the Naqshbandis in a long verse shows his *Sharia*-mindedness. Even Pir Ghulam Hasan testifies to Mattu's adherence to the *Sharia* in personal life, See Hasan, *Asrar al-Akhyar* (Urdu, tr. p. 338).
26. See for greater details, Nizami, *Some Aspects of Religion and Politics in India in the Thirteeth Century*.
27. For the role of the Yasaviyya order in Central Asia, see Spencer Trimingham, *Sufi Orders in Islam*, pp. 58–60.
28. *Ibid.*, pp. 68, 24.
29. Trimingham observes that in Arab lands "*Khanqahs* which from the beginning had been defined and regulated by the state," had to pay a heavy price for "official recognition and patronage." *Ibid*, p. 69. For the organization of *khanqah* life, see *Ibid.*, pp. 169–72; also Nizami, "Khanqah Life in Medieval India", *Studia Islamica*, VIII, 1957, pp. 51–69.
30. Trimingham, *op. cit.*, pp. 168, 171–73, 176–77; Nizami explains well the difference between *khanqah*, *jama'at khanqah*, *zawiyas* and *daerahs* in the Indian context (Some *Aspects of Religion and Politics in India During the Thirteenth Century*, p. 175n). However, the learned scholar's view that the inmates of *zawiya* "did not aim at establishing any vital contact with the outside world" does not seem to be tenable with regard to Kashmir.
31. Nasib, *op. cit.*, ff. 161ab.
32. Hasan, *op. cit.*, p. 131.

32a. Ladi Katur, a disciple of Latifuddin, is reported to have stressed that service to the needy and the poor bring men closer to God. Mishkati, *op. cit.*, f. 117a.

33. According to a near contemporary Naqshbandi source (*Teng, Tuhfat al-Fuqara* f. 43ab), Shaikh Daud devoted himself to the cultivation of land under the influence of the hadith:

اطلبوالرزق من خبایاالارض

33a. Mishkati, *op. cit.*, ff. 118b–119a; Diddamari, *Waqiat-iKashmir*, ff. 32ab.
34. Mishkati, *op. cit.*, ff. 118b–119a.
35. That which is lawful, *i.e.* earnings through hard labour. *Halal* is distinguished from *haram*, or that which is unlawful.
36. Baba Daud Khaki bears an elaborate testimony to Hardi Rishi's arduous agricultural labour in this verse.

کردن کشت و زراعت بوده اکثر کار او

احتیاط او بسی بوداست در اکل حلال

See Khaki, *Rishinama* f. 58a; also Mishkati, *op. cit.*, f 101a.
37. Mishkati, *op. cit.*, f. 117a.
38. All hagiographies are replete with information regarding the social roles of the disciples of Latifuddin.
39. Mishkati, *op. cit.*, f. 118a; Sabur, *op. cit.*, f. 39b; 157b; Wahab, *op. cit.*, f. 39b; Khalil, *op. cit.*, p. 816; Kamal, *op. cit.*, pp. 318–19.
40. Nasib, *op, cit.*, f. 157b; Wahab, *op. cit.*, f. 180b–181a.
41. Mishkati, *op. cit.*, f. 110ab; Khalil, *op. cit.*, p. 780.
42. Nasib, *op. cit.*, f. 148a; Wahab, *op. cit.*, f. 171a; Mishkati, *op. cit.*, f. 104a; Sabur, *Khawariq al-Salikin*, f. 53b; Khalil, *Rawzat al-Riyazat*, p. 697; Kamal, *Rishinama*, p. 258.
43. The dower or settlement of money or property on the wife, without which no marriage contract (*nikah*) is legal.
44. Kamal, *op. cit.*, pp. 258–60; Khalil, *op. cit.*, pp. 699–700; Hasan, *op. cit.*, pp. 106–07.
45. Wahab, *op. cit.*, f. 178b; Khalil, *op. cit.*, p. 785; Kamal, *op. cit.*, p. 301.
46. Mishkati, *op. cit.*, f. 99a.
47. Kamal, *op. cit.*, pp. 334–35; Wahab, *op. cit.*, f. 182b; Khalil, *op. cit.*, pp. 714–15.
48. Hasan, *op. cit.*, pp. 138–39.
49. Nasib, *op. cit.*, ff. 161ab; Sabur, *op. cit.*, f. 38a; Khalil, *op. cit.*, pp. 821–23.
50. Nasib, *op. cit.*, f. 157b.
51. Mishkati, *op. cit.*, f. 114a.
52. Teng, *op. cit.*, f. 62b.
53. Nasib, *op. cit.*, f. 166b. See Chapter VII, "The Rishis and Conversion to Islam."

54. The Orientalists are at pains to prove polarity between the "Islamic prophetical structure" and Sufism. Triminghan boldly claims: "We have shown that Sufism could never be fully accommodated into the Islamic prophetical structure, but was allowed to exist parallel to it. . . "*op. cit.*, p. 143. Annemarie Schimmel also points to "two constantly interacting strands of Islamic attitudes in India," which she describes as "mystico-syncretistic" and "prophetic-separatistic." See Schimmel, "Reflections on popular Muslim Poetry", *Contribution to Asian Studies*, Vol. XVII, p. 18.
55. Nasib, *op. cit.*, f. 136b.
56. Hasan, *op. cit.*, p. 210. See also Chapter VI: "The Attitude of Sufi orders towards the Rishis."
57. "No animal that creeps on earth or flies in the air but belongs to a community like you (and stands under the commandments of God). God's imperatives are relevant to all beings, to all things without exception. All will have ultimatley to reckon with God." *Quran* S. 6. V. 38. "In our pride we may exclude animals from our purview,"observes Abdullah Yusuf 'Ali, "but they all live a life, social and individual, like overselves, all life is subject to the plan and will of God. . .They are all answerable in their several degrees to His Plan ("Shall be gathered to their Lord in the end"). This is not pantheism; it is ascribing all life, activity, and existence to the Will and Plan of God." See Yusuf Ali, *The Meaning of the Glorious Quran*, Vol. I, p. 298, 859n.
58. إنّما الدّين المعاملة see *SeeSahi al-Bukhari* ; *Muslim*.
59. Shaikh Nuruddin is reputed to have said:

ان پوشہ تیلہ یلہ ون پوشہ

Food will last as long as forests last.
60. Ali Raina, *Tazkirat al-Arifin*, f. 35a.
61. Baba Nasib, *op. cit.*, f. 161b; Diddamari, *op. cit.*, f. 43a; 65a; Khalil, *op. cit.*, p. 796.
61a. Khalil, *op. cit.*, p. 796; Diddarmari, *op. cit.*, f. 43a; Kamal, *op. cit.*, p. 302.
62. Kamal, *op. cit.*, p. 302.
63. Nasib, *op. cit.*, f. 156ab, 168a;Khalil, *op. cit.*, p. 721.
64. Nishat Sultanpuri, "Zamana hal maen Rishiyyat kay Naqush", *Rishiyyat*, pp. 173–187.
65. Many a devout Muslim have repeatedly told the present author that they are attracted towards shrines not merely by the spirituality of the

Sufis, but also by the idea of offering the prescribed prayers in congregation in accordance with the spirit of the Quran and the Prophet's *Sunna*.

66. In their reformist zeal, however, the Ahl-i Hadith create the false impression that Sufism is opposed to Islam. This fact alone accounts for their inability to exercise greater influence on the large majority of Muslims in the subcontinent wedded to the shrines for certain historical reasons. The Ahl-i Hadiths' hostility to Sufism is, in fact, mostly based on the persistence of the misconception that Ibn Taimiya (d. 1328) was opposed to Sufism. In a brilliant article, based on M. Henri Laoust's researches on Ibn Taimiya, George Makidisi dispels the false notion about the great Egyptian reformer's hostility to Sufism. Not only does Makdisi refer to Taimiya's affinity with Sufism, but he even testifies to the latter's "admiration for the works of the Sufis. ..." See Makdisi, "The Hanbali School and Sufism", *Humaniora Islamica*, ed. Swartz, Waardenburg. etc. Vol. II 1974, pp. 61–72.

APPENDIX—A

Genealogy of Shaikh Nuruddin

An element of mystery surrounds the family history of Nuruddin. While two earlier Persian sources do not claim any noble ancestry for Nuruddin,[1] the latter-day sources consider his father to be a descendant of the rulers of Kishtwar.[2] The main source for this view is the Shaikh's poetry itself.

It is significant that the lineage of the Shaikh has been preserved in the folk consciousness even to this day by some illiterate Kashmiri villagers of saintly qualities and widsom. An encounter of the present author with one such gifted man, from a very remote forest area at Daryagam, was revealing in several respects. At the persistent request of the author, the villager was able to recite many Sanskritised verses of the Shaikh from his enviable oral repertory. What is of significance to note here is that the pious villager's oral recitation of Nuruddin's verses in regard to the latter's ancestry, place of birth, association of his parents with Sayyid Hussain Simnani, etc., were in strict conformity with the verses recorded in the *Rishinamas* of Chrar.

True, there exists a strong tradition about Nuruddin's familial links with the rulers of Kishtwar, but it seems that during centuries of intense social tension in the Valley the rural folk took special care to preserve and perpetuate the memory of the Shaikh's high birth in order to counter the argument of some caste-conscious Brahmans as to how the son of a shepherd and a bandit could rise to the pinnacle of sainthood.[3]

In the following verses the Shaikh refers to his lineage:

> (My) forefather's name was Ogra Sanz;
> who was killed in the battlefield;
> His kin called him Gurza Sang;
> And he bore but few offspring;
> Drupta Sanz was one born to him;
> And Drupta Sanz's children were: Salat and Solu;

One of the sons, Salat Sanz, was my inspirer;
(He) Embraced Islam willingly;
His Guru was Husain Simnani;
Who was a close relative of Haidar of Kulgam.[4]

REFERENCES AND NOTES

1. See Sayyid Ali, *Tarikh-i Kashmir*. Baba Nasib clearly remarks that Nuruddin belonged to the tribe of village watchmen (*pasban*). See Nasib, *Nurnama*, f. 2b.
2. Bahauddin Mattu, *Rishinama*; Hasan, *Asrar al-Akhyar*.
3. See Chapter VI, "The Rishis and Conversion to Islam."
4. Translated from *Kulliyat-i Shaikh al-ʿAlam*.

APPENDIX—B

Genealogy of Sayyid Ali

An error has inadvertently crept into some modern works that Sayyid Ali, author of *Tarikh-i Kashmir*, was of Kashmiri ancestry. This is the reason why sometimes the Kashmiri tribal name of Magre[1] has been used as his surname. The author was actually a descendant of Sayyid Tajuddin, a cousin of Sayyid 'Ali Hamadani, who entered Kashmir in 762 A.H. The very fact that the author's grandfather was the *mutwalli*[2] of Khanqah-i Mu'alla shows that the chronicler was connected with the family of the Kubrawi Sufis. It was mainly because of his noble descent that Sayyid Ali had an easy access to the earliest sources relating to the Kubrawi *silsila*. Significantly, the chronicler abruptly begins his narrative with the advent of his ancestor, Sayyid Tajuddin, though he does not himself claim to be a man of piety and noble birth like other Sayyids. On the other hand, he makes a brief reference to his mother who was the daughter of Sultan Nazuk Shah (1529–30).[3] The genealogical table of the chronicler, based on Persian sources, is given below:

Sayyid Tajuddin
|
Sayyid Hasan Bahadur
|
Sayyid Kamalauddin
|
Sayyid Jamaluddin
|
Sayyid Ni'amatullah
|
Sayyid Shamsuddin
|
Sayyid 'Ali
|
Sayyid Muhammad
↓ ↓
Sayyid 'Ali — Sayyid Ahmad

REFERENCES AND NOTES

1. During the Sultanate period in Kashmir, the head of such families as Magres, Chaks, Rainas, Dars and Bats formed the nobility of the Sultans. For the role of Magres, see Mohibbul Hasan, *Kashmir Under the Sultans*, pp. 119–22, 129, 130, 146, 208, 210.
2. Mulla Ahmad bin Sabur, *Khawariq al-Salikin*, p. 7.
3. Sayyid Ali, *Tarikh-i Kashmir*, f. 27b, 4. Sabur *op. cit.*, p. 7.

APPENDIX—C

Women Sufis of Kashmir

Kashmir is the only region in the sub-continent which has a deep-rooted tradition about the spirituality of women. The elevation of Lal Ded to 'Maryam-i Makani', 'Rabi'a Thani', 'Arifa' and so on in the Persian hagiographical literature explodes the myth about the lower status of women in Islam. Furthermore, most female Sufis of the Valley were converts to Islam. Their glorification in the Persian sources, in fact, points to the estimation in which they were held by the folk. Unlike Bibi Jamal and Jahan Ara Begum—the only known female Sufis during the Mughal period[1]—the Kashmiri women Sufis were able to develop close contacts with the commoners. It would, therefore, be worthwhile to give a brief sketch of their role in the history of Islam in Kashmir.

Behat Bibi and Dehat Bibi

The hagiographers give conflicting accounts regarding the enrolment of the two Hindu sisters, Behat Bibi and Dehat Bibi, in the Rishi *silsila*. Whatever be the truth, it is certain that both of them were disciples of Shaikh Nuruddin.

One might doubt the ability of Behat Bibi and Dehat Bibi to converse with a Sufi like Sayyid Muhammad Hamadani in the Persian language. However, strong documentary evidence as also the tomb of the two women at Zalsu—the place which to this day commemorates the historic meeting between Shaikh Nuruddin and the Sayyids—support the ability of the disciples of Nuruddin to communicate with the leader of the Sayyids. Besides, both sisters were daughters of a *patwari* who also embraced Islam at the hands of Nuruddin. Being daughters of a Persian-knowing father, it is most likely that both sisters were familiar with the language which had begun to be popular among the Kashmiri Brahmans.[2] It is possible that Sayyid Muhammad Hamadani himself, as a conscious missionary, was able to understand the Kashmiri language during his long stay in the Valley extending from 796/1393 to 814/1410. The meeting between the Sayyid and the Shaikh took place in the later part of the Sayyid's long stay in the Valley. By that time, the Sayyid must have also been able to speak broken Kashmiri.

The sayings[3] attributed to Behat Bibi and Dehat Bibi are revelatory of their intuitive grasp to fathom the deep mystical truths under the care of Nuruddin. Some of these sayings are worthy of note here.

Sayings of Behat Bibi

1. The biggest veil between the Master and the servant is the existence of the human being.
2. To imagine that every human action reaches its ultimate end due to the efforts of the self is the greatest *shirk.*
3. One who destroys one's ego is relieved of the sorrows of one's existence.
4. Salvation from hope and fear lies in annihitating the self.
5. Were not the Shaikh (Nuruddin) my *pir,* Allah Himself would have been my Guide.

Dialogue between Sayyid Muhammad Hamadani and Dehat Bibi

Sayyid Muhammad Hamadani first posed a question to the Shaikh; no sooner did the latter answer the question than Dehat Bibi began to argue with the distinguished guest:

Sayyid Muhammad Hamadani: Why have you weakened the horse (pointing at him)?

Shaikh Nuruddin: Being an inexperienced rider, I cannot afford to give rich food to the horse. If he is not kept under control, he may become unruly and cause me trouble (while reaching the goal).

As a close disciple of Nuruddin, Dehat Bibi was profoundly aware of the spiritual attainments of her preceptor. Perhaps, sensing that the humility of the Shaikh might not create a favourable impression upon some arrogant companions of Sayyid Muhammad Hamadani, she intervened:

Dehat Bibi: Those who have (already) reached the goal do not need either conveyance (horse) or a whip.

Sayyid Muhammad Hamadani: Who have attained the goal ?

Dehat Bibi: Those who have liberated themselves from (the snares of) the self.
Sayyid Muhammad Hamadani: Have you freed yourself from the self?
Dehat Bibi: But for annihilating my self, I would not have dared sit in this solemn meeting and shared secrets (with you).
Sayyid Muhammad Hamadani: Are you a daughter or a son?
Dehat Bibi: If I am non-existent (*neest*), then I am neither a girl nor a boy; but if I am existent (*hast*) then I am nothing.
Sayyid Muhammad Hamadani: How have you gained this?
Dehat Bibi: After having attained salvation from the death of the spirit.

Dehat Bibi and Behat Bibi are popularily known as Chhat Kori, *i.e.*, daughters trained under the spiritual care of Shaikh Nuruddin.

Shanga Bibi alias Yawan Maech

We have already referred to Shanga Bibi's initiation in the Rishi order under the influence of Nuruddin.[5] She was a courtesan of enticing beauty who was apparently asked by some Brahmans of the city to seduce the Shaikh. The Shaikh admonished the alluring courtesan so convincingly that she felt ashamed and after offering *tauba* gained entry in the Rishi order. By virtue of her devotion and austerities, Shanga Bibi was even granted the unique privilege of acting as a *mujawir* at her spiritual preceptor's tomb. That a courtesan, after clothing herself with the robe of faith and humble repentance, could be elevated to sainthood bears elaborate testimony to the egalitarian appeal that Islam had for the commoners in the Valley.

Shanga Bibi lies buried near the tomb of Shaikh Nuruddin at Chrar-i Shariff.

Deta Bibi

Nothing is known about Deta Bibi beyond the fact that she was a devoted disciple of Nuruddin. Her burial place is at Mukhta Phokri near Naushahr in Srinagar.

Sala Bibi I and Sala Bibi II

Both women received the guidance of the Shaikh. Because of their devotion, meditation and asceticism, the hagiographers call them gnostics. Their graves are at Chrar-i Shariff near the Shaikh's tomb.

Sham Ded

We have already referred to the Shaikh's conversations with peasant girls during his sojourn at Hunchipura in the *pargana* of Beru. The girl who was prompt in responding to the Shaikh's taunts[6] was Sham Ded. Baba Kamal and Baba Khalil who give us a useful account of the dialogue pay rich tributes to her poetic genius. So distressed was Sham Ded at the death of Nuruddin that she composed an elegy as a token of her intense love for and deep devotion to her spiritual preceptor.[7] The elegy is the first of its kind in the history of Kashmiri literature, and indeed, the credit for composing such a unique literary piece goes to the female disciple of Shaikh Nuruddin.

Sham Ded, like most Rishis, subsisted on wild vegetables from the forest. After the death of Nuruddin she travelled in every nook and corner of the Valley in the manner of her preceptor. She finally settled in Poshkar near the habitat of Baba Latifuddin whom she served for a considerable time. It seems that during her travels Sham Ded popularised the mystical poetry of Nuruddin among the folk. Perhaps this is the reason why some old Kashmiri women still carry on the tradition of preserving the heritage of Nuruddin and Sham Ded by committing to memory mystical verses and precepts of both the teacher and the taught. Some of the sayings of Sham Ded are reproduced below:

1. The teacher is the fountain-head of nectar. One who drinks deep at this fountain will never die.
2. Divulging the secrets of God is worse than shedding the blood of a thousand innocent men.
3. In this world the status of man is higher (than woman); but in *malakut* the status is dependent on courage. And a man characterized by cowardice is worse than a woman. But (indeed) a courageous woman is better than a man.
4. In (seeking) union with God, I was intoxicated (unmindful of my own puny existence); but while recognizing my own self I was saturated with the knowledge (*m'arifa*) of His Presence.

Many other words of mystical wisdom are ascribed to Sham Ded.

Sanga Bibi

She was a seeker after the truth from her very childhood, but she earned reputation as a Sufi only after her initiation in the Rishi order at the hands of Baba Shukruddin. Although her ancestral home was in the *pargana* of Hamal, she secluded herself on the top of a mountain in the village Buthu of Kuihama at the command of her spiritual preceptor. She observed continual fasts and spent sleepless nights in deep meditation. Even as an ascetic, however, she did not lose touch with society. Her disciples were many and whatever was offered by them in *nazrana* was expended for the poor. Her *khalifa*, Baba Neki Rishi, proved to be a true disciple of the noble lady by his philanthropic activities. He even distributed the domestic animals, belonging to the fraternity of the Rishis, among the needy and the poor.[8]

Ganga Bibi

Ganga Bibi became a Rishi after her husband, Lankar Mal, joined the *silsila* of Rishis under the influence of Baba Luda Mal. The Bibi observed continued fasts and in spite of her austerities, did not shirk hard manual work. Whatever little she earned by the sweat of her brow she donated for making bridges and mosques. When Baba Lankar Mal secluded himself in the forest of Dandakvan, Ganga Bibi proved her mettle as a devoted wife. She would bring her husband water for his ablutions. And it is said that whenever she came across wild animals while carrying water they would take to their heels on seeing her.[9]

REFERENCES AND NOTES

1. For a very brief account of these female Sufis, See Rizvi, *Sufism in India*, II, Appendix B, pp. 480–81.
2. So popular was Persian with the Kashmiri Brahmans that they composed even hymns to their deities in this language. See Ishaq Khan, "Persian Influences in Kashmir in the Sultanate Period", *Islamic Culture*, January, 1977, pp. 1–9.
3. Based on Baba Kamal's and Baba Khalil's accounts. Pir Hasan Shah has also recorded some of these sayings in his *Tadhkira-i Auliya-i Kashmir*.
4. See *Ibid.*
5. See Chapter VIII, "The Societal Dimensions of Miracles."
6. See Chapter V, "Religious Thought of Shaikh Nuruddin."
7. See Appendix G.
8. See Mishkati, *Asrar al-Abrar*; Diddamari, *Waqiat-i Kashmir*; Wahab, *Fathat-i Kubrawiyya*; Baba Kamal, *Rishinama*; Baba Khalil, *Rauzat al-Riyazat*.
9. *Ibid.*

APPENDIX—D

A Note on *Risala-i Lahmiyya*[1]

The author of *Risala-i Lahmiyya*, Shaikh Ahmad Trali, belonged to the occupational group of oil-pressers (*telis*). From his childhood, he took lessons in *tasawwuf* from Mufti Ghulamuddin Jami. Later, he was initiated in the Kubrawi *silsila* by Sidique Khan, a disciple of Shaikh Muhammad Munnawar Hatbi. He also enjoyed the company of some other Sufis from whom he learnt a great deal about *tasawwuf*. Ahmad Trali's penchant for learning drove him to Delhi where he learnt *Ilm al-Hadith* from Maulvi Ishaq. He also performed Hajj and died in 1296H.

For a greater part of his life in the nineteenth century, Shaikh Ahmad Trali led a crusade against the existing *bid'a* in his home town. But he himself admits that he was not liked by the people for his attacks on their cherished false beliefs (*batil 'aqaid*).

In his *Risala-i Lahmiyya*, the author attempts to dispel the misgivings of the people about the Rishis' abstention from meat. He severely criticises the popular belief that the Rishis disliked meat and that it was their aversion for non-vegetarian food that involved some people in trouble. Ahmad Trali feels particularly concerned over the belief of the people that Baba Hardi Rishi felt offended if someone visited his *ziyarat* after eating meat. So persistent was this belief that a person's natural death or if someone's house caught fire, was attributed by the folk to the sacrilege caused by that person to the shrine of Hardi Rishi. Contrary to this belief, Ahmad Trali argued in the light of the Quran and *Hadith* that it was inconceivable that Hardi Rishi would punish his devotees if they visited his tomb after eating *halal* food.

The main reason given by Ahmad Trali for the Rishis' abstinence from meat is not their dislike for *halal* food but their determination to subdue the self (*nafs*) to seek the countenance of God. For the Rishis meat eating was a luxury, and since they abstained from rich food purely for spiritual reasons, they regarded the practice of curbing the ordinary demands of the self as *Jihad-i Akbar.*

Shaikh Ahmad Trali was undoubtedly one of the ablest Kashmiri Muslims of the nineteenth century who felt concerned over the beliefs of a people not completely absorbed in the *Shari'a*-oriented system of Islam. This is not to suggest that people who nourished false beliefs were not Muslims; the fact is that owing to mass illiteracy and the mundane interests of the illiterate *mullahs* and custodians of the shrines, the common folk remained steeped in superstition, darkness and ignorance. For this reason alone, Shaikh Ahmad Trali's efforts in bringing the social behaviour of the folk in conformity with the *Sunna* did not bear fruit in his own time. Nonetheless, Ahmad Trali was, in certain respects, the precursor of the Ahl-i Hadith movement which gained momentum in Srinagar with the dawn of the present century.[2]

REFERENCES

1. Copies of the manuscript are preserved in the Research Library (Kashmir University) and the Cultural Academy, Srinagar.
2. For the Ahl-i Hadith movement, see my student's theses: Bashir Ahmad Khan, *Ahl-i Hadith Movement in Kashmir* (M. Phil thesis); idem, *Ahl-i Hadith Movement in Northern India*, (Ph.D thesis). Iqbal Library, Kashmir University.

خطِ ارشاد

وَاعْلَمْ اَنَّ الْبَیْعَةَ مِنْ سُنَنِ الْاَنْبِیَاءِ عَلَیْهِمُ السَّلَامُ وَمِنَ الْخُلَفَاءِ الرَّاشِدِیْنَ الْمَهْدِیِّیْنَ وَهِیَ بَاقٍ اِلٰی یَوْمِ الْقِیٰمَةِ بِلَا نَکِیْرٍ فَلَا یَجُوْزُ لِاَحَدٍ مِنَ الْاَوْلِیَاءِ الْعُلَمَاءِ اِدِّعَاءُ الْخِلَافَةِ بِلَا الرُّخْصَةِ وَالْبَیْعَةِ بِاخْتِیَارِهٖ اِلَّا اَنْ یَکُوْنَ لَهُ الرُّخْصَةُ مِنَ الشَّیْخِ الَّذِیْ یَکُوْنُ مَاذُوْنًا وَّمُرَخَّصًا بِالتَّحْقِیْقِ مِنَ الشَّیْخِ الْعَامِلِ الْکَامِلِ اِلٰی نَبِیِّنَا صَلَّی اللّٰهُ عَلَیْهِ وَسَلَّمَ

بِسْمِ اللّٰهِ الرَّحْمٰنِ الرَّحِیْمِ

اَلْحَمْدُ لِلّٰهِ الَّذِیْ وَفَّقَنَا وَسَائِرَ الْعِبَادِ بِاتِّبَاعِ طَرِیْقِ الْهُدٰی وَحَفِظَنَا وَجَمِیْعِ الْاَخْیَارِ الْاَبْرَارِ مِنِ اقْتِدَاءِ اَهْلِ الْبِدَعِ وَالْهَوٰی وَبَلَّغَنَا وَطَوَائِفَ الْمُخْلِصِیْنَ الْمُحِبِّیْنَ اِلٰی اَقْصَی الْمَرَاتِبِ هِیَ الْمَعْرِفَةُ الْکُبْرٰی وَالصَّلٰوةُ وَالسَّلَامُ

على رسوله و نبيه و صفيه محمد ن المصطفى و على اله الذين

محبتهم وسيلة للسعادة العظمى و الدولة الاعلى و اصحابه

الذين كالنجوم بايهم اقتدينا اهتدينا فيقول العبد الضعيف

النحيف الجانى كثير التقصير و التوانى محمد بن على ابن

شهاب الدين الهمدانى عفى الله عنه بالفيض الصمدانى

اعلم ان المقصود من خلقة الانسان معرفة الله تعالى سبحانه

كما تشهد بعض الايات الكريمة و الاحاديث القدسية و

الاخبار الشريفة و الاثار اللطيفة فالواجب على كل فرد

من افراد انسان ان يسعى لما خلق له و الطرق الى الله

تعالى منها لا تعد و لا تحصى لقوله عليه افضل الصلوة

و اكمل التحيات الطرق الى الله تعالى بعدد انفاس

الخلائق و من اقربها طريق العلية العالية الشريفة

الكبروية الهمدانية الحسينية الذهبية الذى

دل على و الدى على الهمدانى قدس الله سره السبحانى

كما دل و هدى عليه المشائخ الذين اجازوه

بالارشاد وهم ثلثة وثلثون كلهم من اكابرهم

و بعد فان الاخ الصالح العارف الكاشف المجاهد

المشاهد المسمّى بنور الدين ريشي الكشميري الزاهد

العابد اصلحه الله كما اصلح الصالحين العارفين

و احسنه الله كما احسن الواصلين الكاملين

فلما جاوز عن حد الالحاح و عجز كثيرا بلسانه ان

يدخل فى السلسلة العاشقين الكاملين المكملين

كما ادخل اسوة جماهير المبتدعين و المنتهيين

فاجزته بنوبة المريدين و بيعتهم و ترغيب

الطالبين السالكين و تربيتهم و تعليم الاذكار

كاذيع الضروب لتصقيل القلب عن كدورات

المكائد و الكروب و اخذ النذورات و الفتوحات و

جلوس الخلوات الدائم كالاربعينات القائم

و سائر ما يجب و يستحب فى هذا الطريق العالية

السادات و سبيله ان لا ينسانى فى الاوقات الشريفة

المرجوة بالدعوات بعد الاقوال والاشغال قد
حررت هذا فی لیلة الجمعة خامس عشر من شهر رجب المرجب
سنة اربع عشر و ثمان مأة فی بلدة الکشمیر صانها
الله تعالی مع سکانها عن الآفات و التدمیر -

مهر محمد همدانی

APPENDIX—E

Khat-i Irshad of Sayyid Muhammad Hamadani

Realise that allegiance (*bait*) is the *Sunna* of the prophets and *khulafa* and this *Sunna* will remain unchanged until the Day of Judgement. Thus it is not permissible for any one among the protege of Allah (*aulia*) and *'Ulama* to claim for himself vicegerency of Allah without authorisation and so long as he has a permission from a perfect teacher and guide, himself owing allegiance to such an order as is continuously connected with the Prophet Muhammad (Peace of Allah on him).

In the Name of Allah who has graced us and all (pious) servants to follow the right Path and, besides, saved us and all noble and dignified servants from emulating *Ahl-i bid'a* and *Ahl-i hawa* and, besides, elevated us, the group of sincere and friendly (believers), to such exalted ranks as are marked by the *m'arifa* of Allah. And praise and salutations upon His messenger and His *nabi* and his chosen one Hazrat Muhammad Mustafa and upon his progeny whose love is a passport for gaining virtuosity and exalted power (*daula*) and upon such of his companions as are the shining stars of the spiritual kingdom, and in following them we have received guidance. And then the one who is weak, feeble and defective is Muhammad bin 'Ali bin Shihabuddin Hamadani. May Allah grant him His special favours. (And) he says: Realise that the meaning and purpose of creation is to arrive at an understanding of Allah (*m'arifa*) as some verses of the Quran, *ahadis-i-Qudsiyya*, sayings of the prophets and pious history bear testimony to it. Thus it is obligatory on everyone among human kind to struggle towards that goal for which he has been created. And since there are innumerable ways leading towards Allah (and) as the Prophet (Peace of Allah on him) has said: "The ways guiding towards Allah are equivalent to the breath of (whole) creation." And among these the nearest path (*tariqa*) is the exalted *madhab* of

Kubrawiyya, Hamadaniyya and Husainiyya led by my father 'Ali Hamadani as in this path he was guided by such *mashaikh* as had granted him permission of *irshad* and the number of such dignitaries is thirty three. And then my brother Nuruddin Rishi Kashmiri who is pious, gnostic, man gifted with *kashf, mujahida* and *mushahida* and is also a *zahid* and '*abid.* May Allah guide him like *salihin* and '*arifin* and shower on him His grace like those who are perfect in piety and nearest to Allah. He not only insisted on his entry into the circle of Allah's lovers and perfectly pious souls but implored for it with every fibre of his being. Hence I granted him permission to make seekers (after the Truth) repentful and take allegiance from them. And may guide and train those seeking guidance in the Path. And may teach them *dhikr-i chahar zarab* which will cleanse their heart from the dirt of its snares and (other) obstacles. (Besides) may accept *nazr* and *hidaya* and resort to seclusion, looked with favour in the exalted *tariqa* of *Sa'dat,* and it is an integral part of *tariqa* that he may not forget me at occasions solemnized by the grant of prayers. I have written this (treatise) on the night following Friday on the 15th of the month of Rajab, 814 Hijra in the capital of Kashmir.

May Allah save Kashmir and its inhabitants against calamities and destruction!

Mir Muhammad Hamadani

Note: Although I have translated the *Khat-i Irshad* from Urdu into English (*Bruj-i Nur*, pp. 85–86), its original version in Arabic has also been kept in view.

شامہ بی (رندآہم صُدی)

حضرتِ شیخس پیٹھ

۱ نندہ سُنز گو سۆرگس ماتو
۲ نندہ سُنز گو سۆرگس ماتو

اسہ سُنز گو سۆرگس ماتو
〃 〃 〃 〃 〃 〃

نندہ سُنزک سُنزی یانہ
مِیُلّ ژرِیہ رۆس چھُپنہ زیبا نہ

للہ یانہ بو وۓ کا لو
نندہ سُنز گو سۆرگس ماتو

نندہ سُنزک سُنزی رلیشہ
بیہ میلو پنہ نے دلیشہ

دہ دہ دلیشہ بو گارت کا لو
〃 〃 〃 〃 〃 〃

حضرت امیرہ سُندہ ژالوٹ
پھٹرت ولہ ویر پننہ گالوٹ

اوسک کُستور ژھٹہ والو
〃 〃 〃 〃

ڑوپہ وُتس حقس وڑنگ
تو لچھ لوکہ ویپائک؟

تنہ خلقت خبرا گاییتو
〃 〃 〃 〃 〃

چھی مومن فاتحس پرارانْ
آک وست یوت ژار پرارانْ

حق تعالیٰ خاطرس والو
〃 〃 〃 〃 〃

جون خرقہ کھڑاو تہ عاصہ
کت کرایت بیر واتسہ ساسہ

سُتھ بیہ کُس شوبان آسو
〃 〃 〃 〃 〃 〃

بیہ لعلاہ کُنٹھ اتھ تراوو
یوہے منطق اسہ نشر دراوو

کیا براوو وہ زینی کاکو
〃 〃 〃 〃 〃 〃 〃

ژاٹہ کورلو میّہ وڈ ودی شامے
وندہ بُل وت آسم شامے

گارک پیڑہ شامے کارلو
نندہ سُنز گو سۆرگس ماتو

APPENDIX—F

Elegy of Shyam Ded

Nunda Sanz (Nuruddin Rishi) has left for his heavenly abode
Nunda Sanz has left for heaven's eternal sphere
Our Nunda has left for his heavenly abode
Nunda Sanz has left for heaven's eternal sphere
O worthy and righteous Nunda! without you our presence does not have radiating impressiveness.
How long shall I cry my heart out?
Nunda Sanz has left for his heavenly abode
Nunda Sanz was a Rishi of mettle
We shall join together in the eternal home.
How long shall I wander around for our reunion?
We shall join in the eternal home.
O disciple of Hazrat Amir (Muhammad Hamadani)!
The sublimity of your wisdom captivated boon companions and die-hards
O flying thrush! your melodious notes permeated the environment
The sublimity of your wisdom captivated boon companions and die-hards.
While vindicating the Truth at Rupavan,
Many souls were brightened to all eternity
There (at Rupavan) people recognised the Truth
Whose souls were brightened to all eternity.
Believers have been praying for you
Ever since you were entombed at Chrar
Your cloak, wooden slippers and staff (adorn Chrar)
Can one attain to such heights in a thousand years (to come)?
No one looks so graceful as yourself
Can one attain to such heights in a thousand years (to come)?
How can I part companv with such a brightest jewel?

This logical reasoning is the outcome of our spiritual association.
O brother Zain (Zainuddin)! shouldn't we be proud of such a glorious association?
This logical reasoning is the outcome of our spiritual association.
Your women disciples have been wailing for you;
The light has dimmed; who will brighten our souls!

Note: Translated into English by the present author from original Kashmiri verses reproduced in Mohiuddin Hajini, *Koe: Shir Shoe: Yiree*, New Delhi, 1960.

Glossary

abdal — "substitutes", certain Sufis of whom, it is said "God continues the world in existence. When one dies another takes his place, being so appointed by God."

'abid — a devotee, one who intensely adores God.

abjad — the Arabic alphabet in the traditional arrangement, in which the letters denote the numbers as used for chronograms: a=1, b=2, t=400, th=500.

abrar — a state of being well pleased. 'Ali bin 'Uthman al-Hujwiri writes: "But of those who have power to loose and to bind and are the officers of the Divine court there are three hundred, called *Akhyar*, and forty, called *Abdal*, and seven, called *Abrar*, and four, called *Awtad*, and three, called *Nuqaba*, and one, called *Qutb or Ghawth*. All these know one another and cannot act save by mutual consent." *Kashf al-Mahjub*, tr. Nicholson, p. 214.

Abul Fuqara — father of the poor; the title of Baba Nasibuddin Ghazi.

Advaita tatva — a distinctive system of Kashmiri Saivite philosophy based on the principle of idealistic monism (*advaita)*. In this philosophy the knowledge of the 'basal truths', or 'fundamental and general factors of which the apparent universe consists (*tatva*)' is a pre-requisite for attaining union with the Supreme Self or *Parama Siva.*

ahankar — pride.

ahl-i qalam — 'men of pen'. In olden days the Kashmiri Pandits were also known by this title.

ahkam	sg of *hukm*, injunctions, instructions, regulations.
ahkam-i Shar'a	injunctions of the religious law.
Ahl-i Hadith	the followers of the Prophetic tradition. Muslims are generally followers of the Prophetic tradition in one way or the other. However, in the context of history, the people who call themselves *Ahl-i Hadith*, or the people of Tradition, take special care to adhere to the Quran and *hadith*. They speak of themselves as *Muwahhid*, or "Unitarians', and severely condemn visit to the shrines, *'Urs* ceremonies, holding of gatherings in which the help of saints is invoked and any such practice as did not exist in the time of the Prophet. The *Ahl-i Hadith* do not form any sect of Islam, but they are essentially Muslim reformists; and in their religious zeal they have hurt the susceptibilities of the devotees of the shrines to such an extent that they have been misunderstood as anti-Sufi.
Ahl-i Sunna wa Jam'a	'the people of the community.' The expression especially used for the Sunnis who lay great stress on following the *Sunn'a*—'He who tires of my *Sunna*, does not belong to me'. *Bukhari*.
Ahl-i bait	the people of the house. A term used in the Quran (33/33), and in the *Hadith* (Mishkat XXIV-21), for the household of Muhammad.
akhyar	see *abrar*.
aksar	most.
Allah	the name of the Creator of the universe in the Quran.
'alam al-mithal	'the world of analogies'; the world of the spiritual powers between the human (*nasut*) and the divine (*malakut*) spheres; there the advanced Sufi can see such events related to both the past and the future as are beyond ordinary description.
alif	first letter of the Arabic alphabet; symbol of Allah; numerical value 1.
'alim	a scholar learned in religious sciences; a member of the *'ulama* class.
'alam al-mulk wa *shahada*	see nasut.

'alam al-Ghaib	the (uncreated) world of mystery.
Al-i Muhammad	the offspring of the Prophet Muhammad.
amana	turban.
amba	mother.
ambi	mother.
am	plebian; the common people.
amr	command.
ana al-Haqq	'I am the Creative Truth', uttered by al-Hallaj (exec. in 922 in Bhagdad). Superficially interpreted as 'I am God' but, in its deeper meaning, affirmation of the existential unity of the Creator and the created.
anubhava jnana	'direct experience, active participation in the eternal truth, is distinguished from the indirect and passive participation in religious knowledge by belief. . . This is *jnana*, the most perfect union between God and man.' S. Radhakrishanan, *Recovery of Faith*, p. 139.
'aql	intellect.
'aqida-i Sunniya	belief of the large majority of Muslims acknowledging the first four *khalifas* to have been the rightful successors of the Prophet Muhammad, "and who receive the *Kutub's Sittah*, or "six authentic books of tradition, and who belong to one of the four schools of jurisprudence founded by Imam Ahmed ibn Hambal." The word Sunni with its plural Sunniyan is the Persian equivalent of the Arabic Ahlu's-Sunnah, "the people of the Path." The Shias who also claim to follow the traditions of the Prophet, have, however, allowed the Sunnis to claim the title of traditionalists.
'arif	the gnostic, advanced mystic, he who possesses true knowledge gained by contemplation, meditation, and so on.
'arsh	the throne of Allah.
Asma-i Haqq	Names or Attributes of Allah.
Asmau'l hasna	most beautiful Names or Attributes of Allah.
'ashiq	a lover.
'ashiqan	pl. of *'ashiqan*, lovers.

asthan	abode; shrine; place of pilgrimage.
attahiyat	'greetings. The adorations (i.e., *attahiyyatu)* which are part of the daily prayers of Muslims throughout the world are for 'Allah, and also of the body and of alms-giveing. Peace be on thee, O Prophet, with the mercy of Allah and His blessing. Peace be upon us, and upon Allah's righteous servants.'
aurad	invocatory prayer.
'auraq-i tuz	leaves of the thin bark of a species of birch for writing upon, in lieu of paper.
avatar	incarnation of a deity.
'awam	commoners.
awtad	props or pillars; in *tasawwuf* the term is used for the four saints, 'by whom the four corners of the world are said to be supported.' See *abrar.*
ayah	sign, index or evidence of God. pl. *ayat.*
azan	announcement; the call or summons to public prayers proclaimed by the crier *(muazzin).*
Baba	In Sanskrit the term is a synonym of an ascetic (*sanyasi*), but in the Persian chronicles and hagiographies of the Valley of Kashmir the specific use of *baba* for the Muslim Rishis has certainly the connotation of the wandering Turkish *darwish*, the *babas* of Central Asia.
bait	allegiance; pledge of allegiance of a Sufi novice to his initiating spiritual preceptor by grasping his right hand. The vow binds the disciple to his master in spiritual matters.
bakshish	present; gift; reward; beneficence.
baraka	blessing, power of blessing inherent in saintly persons or sacred objects.
batin	inner; hidden; the antonym of *zahir*, q.v. The 'inner learning (*al-'ilm al-batin*),' meaning esoteric or Sufic learning. It is "depth" learning, hence distinguished from the exoteric learning (*al-'ilm az-zahir*) of such an *'alim* as does not care to delve deep into the depth meaning (*batin*) of the Quran under the guidance of a *murshid.* Al-Batin, 'The Inner', is one of the Names of Allah in the Quran.

bhakti	popular mystical current in medieval Hinduism in which the relationship between man and his deity is described in terms of love.
bhand	the strolling players; 'the minstrels of Kashmir'.
bhakta	a person who practices selfless devotion (*bhakti*) as a means of reaching Brahman.
Bhagwat	Name of a philosophic poem (an episode of Mahabharata) held in high esteem by the Vaishnavas.
Bhagavad Gita	a portion of the Mahabharata, 'having the form of a dialogue between the hero Arjuna and his charioteer, the avatar Krishna, in which a doctrine combining Brahmanical and other elements is evolved.'
Bhugi	derivative of *Bhagwan*, God. Shaikh Nuruddin invariably uses the term in his poetry.
bid'a	a reprehensible innovation; something added to or deviant from the Prophetic tradition.
buddhi	perception; intelligence; understanding; sense; intellect; wisdom.
Budshah	the Great King; the title of Sultan Zain al-'Abidin.
Chour Alam	four worlds or four gradations of existence.
Chilla	forty day's seclusion, in which the novice or a Sufi is completely detached from the world and engrossed only in prayer and meditation.
dambael	dance.
dambael maet	ecstatic dancers.
dammaras	feudal landowners of medieval Kashmir who destroyed the power of the Tantrins.
darwish	a Persian word derived from *dar*, "a door", *i.e.*, those who go from door to door. The term is generally used for a Sufi who practises *faqr*.
dastgir	helper.
dayak	communicating; counseller.
dev	monster.
dharma	righteousness; religious ordinances; rules of conduct; peculiar duties of the individual, while the *Dharmasastra* is a collection of legal aphorisms.

dhikr — remembrance of God by the repetition of Divine Names or religious formulae.

dhikr-i chahar zarb — see *makhfi chahar zarb*

dhikr-i khafi — remembrance of the Creator in the heart and mentally. Shaikh Nuruddin emphasizes the recitation of *dhikr* inwardly as well as mentally (*dhikr saethi ratun malay fikr saethi tarus pan*).

dhikr-i jali — repetition of Divine Names or religious formulae in a loud voice. God's Names or religious formulae contained in the *Aurad-i Fathiyya* are still recited aloud in a rythmic manner in the mosques and shrines of the Kashmir Valley.

dhikr-i jahri — see *dhikr-i jali*

dhyan — contemplation; profound religious meditation.

doha — an old and popular Prakrit and Hindi metre; a couplet, distich the two verses of which rhyme, each verse consisting of 24 matras.

duhi — daughter.

dumbs — village watchmen in Kashmir.

durud — a benediction; recitation of blessing for the Prophet Muhammad in *namaz* and every prayer of the faithful.

dyul — grass with which a bouqet is tied.

dwija/divija — the twice born; according to Hinduism, everyone is a Sudra by birth and is eligible to a higher status only after performing certain rites. Brahmans, Kshatriyas and Vaisyas are said to be twice born, the first being natural birth and the other religious when initiation takes place.

falah — excellence in the deed.

faqir — poor; general name for the Sufi; a Sufi having attained the state of ecstatic rapture; also used for religious mendicants.

faqih — expert of jurisprudence (*fiqh*).

faqr — poverty; indigence; the ideal or the quality of the Prophet Muhammad who claimed that it was his pride; hence also the ideal of the Sufis both in the sense of not possessing anything in this world and not to be possessed by anything. The Quran (35/16) states: "Oh you men! you are the

	poor (*fuqara*) in relation to God, and it is He who is The Independent, The Glorious."
fikr	thought; reflection.
fiqh	jurisprudence.
fatiha	the first chapter of the Quran, repeated in *namaz* and almost at every religious occasion; in special *fatiha* ceremonies in the Valley of Kashmir the *fatiha* is recited over saltish Kashmiri tea for the benefit of a deceased person.
fuqara	pl. of *faqir.*
Furqan	one of the names of the Quran, meaning 'a discrimination'.
gandana	leek.
ghazi	a warrior, especially one who fights for the cause of Islam.
gongal	a ceremony observed in the villages of Kashmir on the eve of spring.
gor	a spiritual teacher or preceptor.
gotra	tribal divisions of Kashmiri Pandits.
Ghauth	'Help'. The title is given to the most distinguished member of the hierarchy of Sufis; for instance, the celebrated Sufi Abdul Qadir Jilani is popularly known as 'Ghauth al-Azam'.
habs-i dam	hold one's breath for a long time during the *dhikr;* breath control. Shaikh Nuruddin remarks: *dhikr-i Haqq par zev dith talas,* i.e., remember God while keeping the tongue pressed against the roof of your mouth, your lips and teeth firmly shut, and hold your breath.
hadith	saying of the Prophet Muhammad based on the authority of a chain of transmitters. The Prophet uttered his words of wisdom at a given situation. His sayings (*ahadith*) form the very basis of Muslim life. The most authentic sayings were collected in six volumes in the second half of the 9th century; among them, those of Bukhari (d. 870) and Muslim (d.875), called *Sahihain,* are of particular significance.
hajj	pilgrimage to Mecca, obligatory on every Muslim once in his life, if he has the means to perform it.

hal — condition to which a devotee of Allah is transferred by purifying his *nafs;* spiritual state.

hangul — the Kashmiri stag.

Hara — a name of Mahadev or Siva and of Agni. Nuruddin has also used the name Hara (Har) in his poetry for the dissemination of Islamic teachings among the unlettered folk.

haqiqa — mystic truth; reality; the main goal of a Sufi is to reach the stage of the divine reality which is possible only by following the *Shari'a.*

haqq-i mahr — a marriage-portion, or gift, settled upon the husband before marriage; dower.

Haqq — truth or reality, according to the Quran (18/29) "The truth is from your Lord"; in other words, God alone is the Reality of realities. The essential reality of a Sufi is that his every action is determined by *ihsan.* The Prophet's saying: *likulli dhi haqqin haqiqah,* 'to every real thing there corresponds a divine reality (or truth)' also needs to be read in this context.

Hazrat — presence; majesty; highness; or the modes of divine presence in contemplation.

hikma — wisdom; prudence; it may consist of practical knowledge or of intuition concerning the divine essence and Names.

hosh dar dam — social awareness even while breathing; the Sufis of the Naqshbandi order were mentally alert even while controlling their breath.

Id al-Adha — the feast of sacrifice.

ihsan — doing everything as beautifully as possible; perfection in spiritual terms which consists in worshipping God "as if your were seeing Him, for if you do not see Him, He sees you."

ijaza — licence; most Sufis claimed several initiations and possessed a number of licences (*ijazas*).

ikhlas — sincerity; purity of intention; title of the 112th chapter of the Quran.

imam — one who leads the ritual prayers at a mosque; among Shias the leader of the community who is the descendant of the Prophet's son-in-law, Ali, and his daughter Fatima.

iman	faith; the inward aspects of Islam.
Islami masawat	the Islamic concept of equality.
istighfar	seeking forgiveness of God; the Prophet is reputed to have remarked: 'I swear by Allah that I ask pardon of Allah, and repent before Him more than seventy times daily."
izn	permission; leave.
Jabarut	the world of Omnipotence, *i.e.* of the divine Names and Attributes; manifestation beyond form.
jali	aloud.
janbaz	one who gives up one's life; Sayyid Muhammad Isfahani earned the title of 'Janbaz' for his extreme ascetic practices.
jihad	'hold war' against the tyranny, oppression and ethnocentrism of the infidels; in terms of the depth meaning of the Quran, *jihad* connotes an incessant struggle against one's base instincts (*nafs-i ammara*).
jizya	capitation tax (based on Sura 9/29) realised from the *ahl al-kitab;* theoretically, the payment of *jizya* ensures the protection of non-Muslims in an Islamic state and earns them exemption from military service. Sultan Zain al-Abidin abolished *jizya.*
kaya	the body; appearance.
kalika	relating to time; temporal; periodical.
kalima	word; the profession of faith in Islam.
kaliyuga	a world which is full of evil and wickedness.
kam-fahman	unintelligent.
kamar band	belt.
kangri	a portable earthenware bowl, covered with a frame of wicker work; Kashmiris put hot embers into the bowl for keeping themselves warm during the winter and the cold season; usually *kangri* (actually called *kangar*) is kept under a long loose-wrapper (*pheran)* or a blanket.
karma	moral conduct; religious observance; work; act.
karamat	a miracle attributed to a Sufi.
kaula	race; tribe; family; noble birth.

kaval	see *kaula*
khas	distinguished from common people; high; noble.
khawas	plural of *khas*; distinguished persons; privileged.
khafi	mentally.
khalq	creation; mankind; people.
khalifa	viceregent; successor of a spiritual leader; a Sufi usually had one or more *khalifas* who were authorised to induct others, into the order. According to the Quran (Sura 2/31), God made Adam his *khalifa*, his viceregent on earth, which shows man's exalted status among the creatures.
khanqah	the humble structure in which a Sufi lived; spiritual training was given in the *khanqah* and usually a public kitchen and other facilities were attached to it.
kharwar	an ass's load, equivalent to 177lbs. For centuries past it has remained the standard weight in the Valley.
Khat-i Irshad	see Appendix.
khilwat dar anjuman	spiritual awarencess even in being an active member of society.
khirqa	the patched frock worn by Sufis, generally gifted by a spiritual preceptor to a *khalifa* to symbolise the latter's succession or legitimise his authority to guide people.
khwaja	master; teacher; title of the pioneers of the Naqshbandi order.
Koshur Wa'iz	Kashmiri preacher.
kitab	book.
kram	family appellation.
kreyi (kriya)	an action; especially pious deeds, an act of devotion; act of worship; a holy action.
krav	to strive in God's way.
kriya	see *kreyi.*
krodh	anger.
kulah	cap.
lahut	the world of Godhead; indescribable world of unity, though erroneously defined as a stage in which human identity (*nasut)* is absorbed in 'timeless unicity'.

lam — letter of the Arabic alphabet; numerical value forty; a mystic symbol.

la makan — to go beyond the limits of space

libas-i fakhira jamal — a costly and beautiful dress.

libas-i taqwa — the dress of piety.

lobh — lust; cupidity; greed; according to the Saivite philosophy, *lobh* is the chief of the six enemies or sins which create impediments in uniting the individual self with the Supreme. The six are: sexual desire (*kama)*, wrath (*krodh*) desire (*lobh*), arrogance (*mada*), delusion of mind (*moha*) and jealousy (*matsara*). Shaikh Nuruddin repeatedly uses these words in order to impart Islamic teachings to the folk.

maet or mut — wandering *faqirs;* religious mendicants.

magfirat — pardon for sins on the part of Allah. "Satan enjoins upon you the works of shame and sin. Allah promises you His mercy, forgiveness and bounty." *Quran*, 2/268.

Magh — name of the tenth Hindu month (corresponding to January-February), the full moon of which is near the constellation of *Magha* or a Leonis (Regulus).

makhfi chahar zarb — a particular method of glorifying God by the constant repetition of His Names, by rhythmic breathing either mentally (*dhikr-i khafi*) or aloud (*dhikr-i jali or jahri*). This practice which was specially adopted by the Suharwardis also seems to have been popularised by Nuruddin.

makru — disapproved.

Malakut — the invisible, spiritual or angelic world.

malch — derivative of *mleccha;* the earliest colony of Muslims in the Valley was in Srinagar and this place is still known as Malchmar.

manqabat — anything in which a man glories or which confers on him prominence; glory; ability; accomplishment

mantra — a religious formula enabling a Hindu mystic to attain unity with the Supreme.

maqamat — pl. of *maqam* or stage.

maratib-i wujud four spheres of existence.

ma'arifah knowledge; gnosis.

maruf good works. "You are the best *ummah* brought forth unto mankind, enjoining the good works, prohibiting the evil, and putting your faith in God." *Quran,* 3/110.

martazan goshgir *wa wasilan faqir* hermits in communion (with God).

masah to wet one's hair, neck and sometimes toes, covered by socks during ablutions.

matlub the desired goal.

mim letter of the Arabic alphabet, numerical value forty, symbol of Muhammad; a popular tradition makes God say: "*ana Ahmad bila mim,* 'I am Ahmad (honorific name of Muhammad) without a m,' meaning thereby *Ahad,* 'One'. In the Sufi literature allusions to this well known tradition are actually made to emphasize the Creator's love for the most perfect of human beings *i.e.* the Prophet. Hence, one who strictly adheres to the *Sunna* of Muhammad endears oneself to God.

mi'raj ascension.

mithal a key term in the Quran, which means learning not by logical but analogical method. "It is simply the Access to the parable and not the parable or any idea that the 'metaphor' equals its interpretation. It has no specificity. *Mithal* is grasped 'on the wing' so to speak. It cannot be explored or analysed or extended. That is to say, it must not be approached rationally but empathetically with direct and clear seeing-into."

moksa earthly existence.

mouk other.

mu'amalat juridical and political obligations; the major portion of the corpus of Islamic law belongs to *mu'amalat* which is evidently social in its content. "Only a tiny section of the law of Islam has to do with rituals and worship and strictly personal ethics; the large part of the law deals

	with the social order. "see Ismail Raji al-Faruqi. *Tawhid: Its Implications for Thought and Life*, p. 99. Nuruddin Rishi regards performance of rituals as a necessary prerequisite for the establishment of a peaceful and stable social order. Indeed, in his thought, even the personal aspects of the law, the rituals themselves, acquire a social dimension.
mubtadi	beginner.
mujaddid	renovator; he is supposed to appear at the beginning of every century in Islam. Shaikh Ahmad Sirhindi (d. 1624), who made his mark at the beginning of the second millenium *hijri* is popularly known as *Mujaddid-i alf-i thani*, 'renovator of the second millenium."
mu'jizat	pl. of *mu'jizah;* "making weak or feeble", that which renders the adversaries of the truth weak and feeble.
Mulla	a Persian form used for the Arabic *Maulawi;* a learned man; a scholar.
muminun	pl. of mumin; believer; faithful.
munajat	fervent prayer (often chanted).
munkar	the evil; the sinful acts. "Let there be of you an *ummah* which calls for the good, which enjoins the good works and prohibits the works of evil. Those are truly felicitous." *Quran.* 3/104.
muraqaba	meditation. an act of contemplation, especially performed by the Sufis.
murid	a disciple; a novice
murshid	the spiritual preceptor; literally: he who leads straight.
nadan marad	an illiterate man.
nafl	a work of supererogation.
nafs	the lower self; the lower instincts; the soul.
nafs-i ammara	the soul that, according to the Quran (Sura 12/ 59), is inclined to evil.
nafs-i lawwama	the soul that, according to the Quran (Sura 65/ 2), is self-reproaching and seeks God's grace and pardon after repentance and tries to amend.
nafs-i mutma'inna	the soul that, according to the Quran (Sura 79/

	27), is at peace. The Sufi's soul returns to its Lord in an exalted state, *i.e.* it is at peace.
nahi-munkar	prohibiting the evil: "You are the best *ummah* brought forth unto mankind, enjoining the good works, prohibiting the evil, and putting your faith in God. "The *Quran*, 3/110.
najasat	filth.
nama	a letter; epsitle; a record; treatise; history; a deed.
nasb	pedigree.
namaz	the Persian term for liturgical prayer (*salat*); the term is also used in Urdu and Kashmiri for the prayer at appointed times and also for supererogatory prayer.
nasut	human nature; human identity; the mundane or phenomenal world, described by Ghazzali as *'Alam al-mulk we Shahada.*
n'at	poetry in praise of the Prophet; the tradition of reciting *n'at* aloud in chorus still exits in the mosques and shrines of the Valley.
nayaka	a guide; leader.
nazrana	a gift or present.
ni'amat	bliss.
nikah	marriage contract.
Nirguna	God is one and unqualified; the noumenal, without constituents; in Hindu mysticism, the Absolute finally comes out of darkness into light, of the unconscious into the conscious, and of *nirguna* into *saguna*; when the Absolute becomes the subject and object of all thought; the noumenal becomes the phenomenal. In Hinduism, the divinity is generally known through its names and attributes (*saguna*); the emergence of various sects in the history of Hinduism with their distinctive modes of worship for propitiating their personal deities (Siva, Vishnu, Brahma, Agni, Lakshmi, Krishna, Hari, Ganesh, Ram. Kali, etc.).
nundaen	righteous people; pl. of *nund.*
nuqaba	see *abrar.*
Nur-i Muhammadi	"The Light of Muhammad"; the original essence

of Muhammad, known in Arabic as the *Haqiqat al-Muhammadiyah*, which is believed to have been created before all things.

ouk — one.

pap — a sin; a sinful act.

pargana — the most important administrative unit in which the officials came into direct contact with the cultivators.

Parama-Siva — the supreme Siva; according to the Saivite philosophy of Kashmir, all that exists is but the Siva or the Supreme in one or other of His manifestations. When therefore, one is ignorant of the unity of self and all creation with the Supreme self, and thinks that there is a difference between contemplation and its object, it is really the Supreme, temporarily blinded by His own illusive power, who is lost in this forgetfulness.

pasban — village watchman.

pas-i anfas — the Sufi practice of controlling breath intrinsically different from the yogic *pranayama*. While controlling their breath the Sufis are able to remember God either aloud and inwardly or mentally so that even a moment's forgetfulness does not sever the link between the Creator and the created.

patwari — village accountant.

pheran — a long loose-wrapper worn by Kashmiris to protect themselves against cold.

pir — Persian equivalent of the Arabic *Shaikh*; old man; venerable leader; the spiritual guide; the mystic leader.

pir parast — worshipper of the spiritual preceptor.

pir-i suhabat — see *Shaikh al-Suhba;*

Pirwaer — the Valley of spiritual leaders or Sufis; Kashmir is also called *pirwaer* by a large number of the devotees of the shrines of Sufis and Rishis.

pranayama — the practice of controlling breath in order to obtain *yoga*, or union with the Supreme.

Pratyabhijna — intrinsically a philosophical system; also known as 'Kashmir Saivism'.

pul-i sirat	the bridge across the infernal fire, 'which is described as finer than a hair and sharper than a sword, and is beset on each side with briars and hooked thorns; on the Day of Judgement, the pious alone can pass over this bridge on their way to heaven while the wicked will fall into the fire of hell.'
pun	a sin; a sinful act'.
purusa	the soul or spirit; the active principle in creation as distinct from nature or matter (the passive: *prakriti*).
qabila-i pasban	tribe of watchmen.
qawwali	musical concerts of a religious nature, though music is prohibited in Islam.
qudrat	the creation; the universe; nature; omnipotence.
Qulhu Allah	say, 'He is Allah'; the first verse of *Surat al-Ikhlas,* 112th chapter of the Quran.
Qutb al-Aqtab	the title given by Mulla Ali Raina to Shaikh Nuruddin; pl. of *Qutb* is *aqtab.*
Qutb	pole; axis; in *tasawwuf:* 'the pole of spiritual hierarchy'. The pole of a period is also spoken of; this highest member of the hierarchy of Sufis is often unknown to even the most spiritual of men.
sabad	word.
sadhu	a wandering devotee; an ascetic.
sadha	Kashmiri form of the Sanskrit *siddh*; a respected saint who has attained one of the stages of beatitude.
saguna	the sphere of divinity with distinctive attributes.
salat	the liturgical form of prayer recited five times a day; see also *namaz.*
rahib	ascetic.
rakah	from *ruku,* to bend, incline towards; during *namaz* the faithful, while making an inclination of the head and body and placing the hands upon the knees, separating the fingers a little says: "I extol the Holiness of my Lord, the Great."
Ramadan	the month of fasting in the Muslim calendar.

rangan or ranga	theatre; stage.
ratna mani	hidden jewel.
rida	acquiescence; satisfaction.
riyazat	to train; to discipline, religious exercise; devotion.
Rawafiz	dissenters; nickname for Shias. However, it is no longer in use in Kashmir, thanks to the development of a better religious understanding between Shias and Sunnis.
Rishwaer	the Valley of Rishis.
Rishivatika	the garden-house of Rishis.
roubkhana	grand drawing rooms
salat al-istisqa	prayers recited in times of dearth, especially rain; see *Sahi 'ul Bukhari.*
salik	a traveller on the Sufi path.
salihan	pl. of *salih,* the pious.
sanad	credential; testimonial; certificate; proof; authority.
sangan	unity; derivative of the Sanskrit term *sang.*
Sastras	a code of laws; institutes of Hindu religion; Hindu holy writ or learning in general.
Shaikh	a title of respect given to various Sufis, or elderly Muslims in general; a Muslim professing Arab descent. While converts to Islam generally assumed this title, it is also significant to note that, generally, every Kashmiri Muslim addresses the Muslim scavenger by the title of Shaikh. In fact, the community of scavengers and cobblers in the Valley has, since its assimilation in Islam, been known as "the Shaikh community." What is more, there exists a strong tradition in Kashmir that the *Qutb* is a cobbler or a scavenger by virtue of his profession, the humblest of all. Stories about the most exalted rank of an unknown cobbler, because of his piety and humility, still current in certain circles, actually point to the spirited societal response that Islam evoked in the caste-ridden Brahmanic society.
Shaikh al-Islam	title of the highest religious official.

Shaf'at intercession; recommendation.

Sharda a name of Sarasvati (q.v) and of Durga.

Sharia the Revealed Law; every Divine messenger (*rasul*) brought a new *Shari'a*, emphasizes the Quran, but that revealed to Muhammad is the final one since it consists of the totality of Allah's commands regulating the life of every Muslim in relation to God and his fellow beings.

shirk associating anything with God; polytheism; paganism; idolatory.

Shrad a kind of funeral rite or ceremony in honour of the departed spirits of deceased relatives observed at various fixed periods. It consists of offerings with water and fire to the gods and manes, and of food and gifts to the relatives present and to the Brahmans assisting.

shruk term used for the quatrains of Nuruddin.

shuniya void; emptiness; "The thing which is really nothing is the apparent material existence—the material world or the consciousness of the material world. With the acquirement of true knowledge, its unreality is recognized, and the apparent reality disappears in the transcendental Void." (See George Grierson, *Lalla-Vakyani,* p. 201). For how 'a void became merged in the Void', see *Ibid.*, pp. 200–201; also Chatterjee, *Kashmir Shaivism,* pp. 62ff.

silsilah the chain; in *tasawwuf* connotes the continuity of spiritual descent which goes from a Sufi master to the Prophet.

sirat way.

siratu'l mustaqim right way; in each *namaz* a Muslim prays to Allah for guiding him to the 'right way'.

Siva the Supreme Deity, absorption in whom is final emancipation.

slok a hymn of praise; a saying; a distich. verse. stanza (esp. the epic stanza, consisting of two verses, each of sixteen syllables).

suluk journey; road; path.

suffa	a kind of vestibule or portico for shade and shelter, open in front.
sunna	the tradition of the Prophet, his manner of life according to which the faithful should act.
sura	each of the 114 chapters of the Quran.
Sura-i Yasin	the 36th *sura* or chapter of the Quran, called 'the heart of the Quran', recited also for a dying or deceased person.
tabarruk	blessing.
tafsir	commentary; paraphrase.
taffakur	contemplation.
tajjali-i ruh	enlightenment of soul.
taklif	obligation; accountability.
talab	a state of quest.
taliban	pl. of *talib*, seekers in the spiritual path.
tariqa	path; Sufi order; religious brotherhood. All Sufi orders follow the path of Muhammad.
tasawwuf	Sufism.
tasfiya-i qalab	refinement of heart.
taqwa	piety; abstinence; continence; preserving or guarding oneself from the snares of the self through the observance of fasts.
tauba	the turning of the heart from sin; repentance; contrition.
Tauhid	'to declare that God is One'; monotheism; consciousness of one's oneness with God in the Sharia-structured relationship; in this oneness the seeker is profoundly conscious of his servantship (*'ubudiyyat*).
tadhkira	literally "mentionings"; a collection of biographical accounts, compiled from both written and oral traditions.
tazkiya-i nafs	purification of the self.
tirtha (tirath)	a shrine or sacred place of pilgrimage.
Trika	trinity; Kashmir Saivism consists of several trinities and therefore it is also named 'Trika philosophy'. "The first trinity of the system is that of its basic scriptures. This system is based on (1) *Siddha Tantra*, (2) *Malini Tantra* and (3) *Namaka Tantra*. The system teaches a practice

	of yoga which is analysed into three major categories named *Sambhava, Sakta* and *Anava.* This is the second trinity of this system." For details, see B.N. Pandit. *Aspects of Kashmir Saivism,* p. 201-202.
'ubud	humble servants; pl. of *'abd.*
'ubudiyyat	servantship: when God mentions the Prophet Muhammad, He refers to his 'servantship' and says: "He revealed to His servant that which He revealed." *Quran,* 53/10.
'ulama	pl. of alim; scholar-jurists upon whom the interpretation of the *Shari'a* rests.
'ulama-i akhirat	the *'ulama* whose interest is mostly directed towards the Otherworld.
'ulama-i zahiri	the worldly *'ulama* who associated themselves with the government and complied with a ruler's wishes, even if the latter flouted the religious law; usually cultivated such habits of mind and heart through their association with kings and rich people as were inimical to the growth of higher spiritual and ethical values in Muslim society.
umma	community.
ummi	unlettered.
Upanishads	philosophical tratises, from the Vedas, forming the basis of the monistic school of thought.
'ushr	pl. *ushur.* A tenth or tithe given to the public treasury of a Muslim state (Baitu'l-Mal).
vaakh	a word; *vaakh* is equivalent of the Sanskrit *vakya, i.e.* Lal Ded's sayings *(Lalla-Vakyani),* or the verses composed and recited by her.
Vedas	the sacred scriptures of the Hindus; name of a certain system of philosophy and theology based particularly on the Upanishads.
Vedanta	one of six systems of Hindu philosophy.
vela	time.
velu	corrupt form of *vela;* time.
vichaya	examination.
vopalhak	*dispsacus inermis.*
wahdat	unity; oneness.

wahdat al-shuhud	unity-in-experience, implying that Allah and His seeker are joined together but their individuality is preserved. In this unity the seeker is profoundly aware not only of his human individuality but, more importantly, of His beloved's unique individuality.
wahdat al-wujud	unity of being; it is experienced by an inflamed Sufi who believes that 'Everything is He'. That is how Ibn 'Arabi's ideas on the mystical experience were summarised in later mystical poetry, particularly in Iran, Turkey and India. The term has generally however been misunderstood and misinterpreted.
wajh	face; the words "Face of God" and "His Face" occur in the Quran in an appropriate signification in each place. *The Quran,* chapters 2/115;6/52;18/28.
wajib	obligatory.
wali	protégé of God; saint; protector.
wali-i madarzad	a born friend or protégé of God.
wazifa	a term used for regular repetition of the Quran or a portion from it or for repeating certain prayers preserved in various religious compilations; any religious duty stipulated or agreed upon; a pension, a stipend.
wow	sow
yaran-i mujarrad	unmarried friends.
yagya or yajna	sacrifice; offering; oblation.
yaqin	belief; true faith.
yavanas	the Greeks generally, but the term was loosely used to denote any non-Hindu, particularly Muslims.
yoga	the power of devotion, the power or strength derived from continued abstract meditation.
yogi	one who practises penance by undergoing all sorts of physical mortification; one well-versed in the practice of *yoga* in particular.
zahid	ascetic.
zahir	external; apparent; opposite of batin; *Az-Zahir,* The External, or, The Apparent, is one of the Names of God in the Quran.

zahiri	worldly.
zali-dab	balcony.
zawiya	small modest establishments, centred around the Shaikh.
Zeth	the second month of the Hindu calendar (corresponding to May-June).
ziyarat	visit to a shrine, often the shrine itself; in the Valley of Kashmir it also denotes a glimpse of the relics of the Sufis caught by the visitors to the shrines on special occasions. The shrine of Hazratbal in Srinagar is famous for being the repository of the Prophet's sacred hair which is exhibited on special occasions.
zuhd	asceticism.

Bibliography

I. Persian Manuscript Sources

Aba Rafi'uddin — *Nawadir al-Akhbar*, B.M. Add. 24029

Abdul Wahhab Nuri — *Fathat-i Kubrawiyya*, R.P.D. 50.

Abdul Wahhab Sha'iq — *Riyaz al-Islam*, C.A. 449.

Amin Ahmad Razi — *Haft Iqlim* (a) R.P.D. 1216.
(b) A.S.B. 282.

Baba Da'ud Khaki —
I. *Qasida-i Lamiyya*, R.P.D. 28; 805.
II. *Qasida-i Gusul-i Yusuf Shahi*, R.P.D. 1914.
III. *Rishinama*. (I have widely used the manuscript in possession of Pir Ghulam Muhammad Khaki, Naibasti, Islamabad, though occasionally, R.P.D. No. 1822 has also been referred to.)
IV. *Dastur al-Salikin*, R.P.D. 741 and 1108.

Baba Da'ud Mishkati — *Asrar al-Abrar*, R.P.D. 5.

Baba Haidar Tulmuli — *Hidayat al-Mukhlisin*, R.P.D. 497.

Baba Kamal — *Rishinama*, C.A. 24.

Baba Khalil — *Rauzat al-Riyazat*, C.A. 31.

Baba Nasib'uddin Ghazi — *Nurnama*, R.P.D. 795.

Birbal Kachru — *Majmu'a al-Tawarikh*, R.P.D. 935.

Dhikr-i Shaikh Daud R.P.D. 2987.
(Anonymous)

Haidar Badakshi — *Manqabat al-Jawahir*, R.P.D., 3269.

Haidar Malik Chadura — *Tarikh-i Kashmir*, (a) R.P.D. 1856.

(b) I.O. 510, (c) Bib. Nationale, Blochet, I, 626.

Hasan b. 'Ali Kashmiri — *Tarikh-i Kashmir*, Bodleian, 315.

Jafar Badakshi — *Khulasat al-Manaqib*, R.P.D.

Khwaja Hasan Qari — *Rahat al-Talibin*, R.P.D. 501.

Khwaja Ishaq Qari — *Chilchihat al-'Arifin*. R.P.D. 500.

Khwaja Miram Bazaz — *Tadhkirat al-Murshidin*, R.P.D. 503.

Khwaja Muhammad Azam Diddamari — *Waqi'at-i Kashmir*, (a) A.S.B. 41 (b) R.P.D. 1843.

Majmu'a dar Ansab Masha'ikh-i Kashmir, Anonymous, A.S.B. 79, (Quoted in Mohibbul Hasan, *Kashmir Under the Sultans*).

Malfuzat-i Timuri, A.S.B. 85.

Mirza Haidar Dughlat — *Tarikh-i Rashidi*, A.S.B. 210.

Mulla Ahmad b. Subur — *Khawariq al-Salikin*, R.P.D. 230.

Mulla Ali Raina — *Tadhkirat al-'Arifin*, R.P.D. 592.

Mulla Baha'uddin Mattu — *Rishinama*, R.P.D. 48.

Muhammad Aslam Mun'ami — *Gauhar-i Alam*. R.P.D.

Muhammad Murad Teng — *Tuhfat al-Fuqara*, R.P.D. 19.

Naryan Kaul Ajiz — *Muntakhab-ut-Tawarikh*, R.P.D. 1193.

Nuruddin Ja'far Badakshi — *Khulasat al-Manaqib*, R.P.D. 658.

Risala-i Mulaqat Hazrat Mir Muhammad Hamadani ba Hazrat Nund Rishi, R.P.D. 3176.

Sadullah Shahabadi — *Bag-i Sulaiman*, R.P.D. 1059.

Sayyid 'Ali — *Tarikh-i Kashmir*, R.P.D. 739.

Sayyid 'Ali Hamadani —
I. *Dhakirat al-Muluk*,
II. *Rasail*, R.P.D. 1600, 1966. also entitled *Maktubat*, R.P.D. 1979, 2490.
III. *Risala-i Uqbat* (quoted in Muhammad Riyaz. *Ahwal-u Asar wa Ash'ar Mir Sayyid Ali Hamadani*.
IV. *Risala-i Dah Qa'ida* Ali Hamadani, R.P.D.
V. *Aurad-i Fathiyya*, R.P.D. 1348.

Shaikh Ahmad Trali — *Risala-i Lahmiyya*, R.P.D., 1056.

Tahir — *Baharistan-i Shahi*, I.O. 509

(Anonymous) — *Tuhfat al-Ahbab* R.P.D., 551.

II. *Kashmiri Manuscript Collections and Published Sources*

Kalam-i Shaikh al-Alam, R.P.D.1756, 2993, 3184, 3279.
Kalam-i Hazrat-i Shaikh al-Alam Shaikh Nuruddin Nurani, R.P.D., 2993.
Malfuzat-i Kashmiri, R.P.D., 639.
Kalam-i Shaikh al-Alm (compiled by Mir Abdullah), R.P.D. 45.
Gongal Nama, R.P.D. 3192.

NOTE:—The manuscripts mentioned above have not been referred to in the text; however, their abundant use has helped me in checking the authenticity of the following compilations on Nuruddin's poetry:

Kulliyat-i Shaikh al-Alam, compiled by Moti Lal Saqi, 2 Vols, C.A.P. 1979, 1981, respectively.
Kulliyat-i Shaikh al-Alam, compiled by Moti Lal Saqi, C.A.P. 1985.
A'in-i Haqq, compiled by Asadullah Afaqi, Chrar-i Sharif, 1958.
Rishinama, Urdu, tr. of Nuruddin's poetry by Taus Banihali, Islamabad (Pakistan), 1980.
Guldasta-i Shaikh Al-Alam, Urdu tr. of Nuruddin's poetry by Abul Ashraf Qari Saifuddin, Srinagar, 1988.
Nund Rishi: Unity in Diversity, Eng. tr. of Nuruddin's poetry based mainly on Mir Abdullah's compilation; *Kalam-i Shaikh al-Alam*, C.A.P. Srinagar, 1984.
Mirat al-Haqq, poetry of Nuruddin Rishi compiled by Ghulam Nabi Shah (published by Farooq and Co. Srinagar, n.d.)

III. Printed Persian, Sanskrit and Arabic Sources

Abul Fazl, *Akbar-nama*, tr. H. Beveridge, 3 Vols, Bib. India, Calcutta, 1897–1939.
A'in-i Akbari, Vol. I, tr. Blochmann, Bb. Ind. Calcutta, 1927, Vol. II and III, tr. Jarret, Second ed. J.N. Sarkar, Bib., Ind, Calcutta, 1948–49.
Afif Shams Siraj, *Tarikh-i Firuz Shahi*, ed. Maulvi Wilayat Husain, Bib., India, Calcutta, 1890.
Ahmad bin Mahmud Uwaysi, *Lataif-i Nafisiyya dar Fazail-i Uwaysiyya*, Urdu tr. Sayid Manzur Hasan Rizvi Chisti Nizami Ashrafi Dehlavi, Delhi, 1940.
Baba Daud Khaki, *Sharh-i Qasida-i Lamiyya*, Published by Master Asadullah Rishi, Naibasti, Khanbal, Kashmir, 1979.
Baha'uddin Mattu, *Rishinama*, (ed. Muhammad Asadullah Wani &

Masud Samu), C.A.P., Srinagar, 1982.
Al-Bukhari, Abu Abullah Muhammad, *Sahih al-Bukhari*, an abstract of 1044 *ahadis* in original Arabic with Urdu translation given in *Muqaddima Tajrid al-Bukhari*, Malik Muhammad Din and Sons, Lahore, 1936.
Al Ghazzali, Abu Hamid Muhammad, *Kimiya-i Sa'adat*, Urdu trans, under the title *Ikseer-i Hidayat*, 20th ed. Newal Kishore, Lucknow, 1976.
Hujwiri, 'Ali, *al-Kashf al-Mahjub, Eng.* tr. R.A. Nicholson, Reprint, 1982, New Delhi.
Jonraja, Pandit, *Rajatarangini of Jonaraja*, ed. Srikanth Kaul Hoshiarpur, 1967; Eng. tr. J.C. Dutt under the title *Kings of Kashmiria*, Vol. III, Calcutta, 1879–98, pp. 1–98.
Jahangir, Emperor, *Tuzk-i Jahangiri*, 2 Vols, Eng. tr. by A. Rogers and H. Beveridge, London, 1909–14.
Kalhana, Pandit, *Rajatarangini*, Eng. tr. Sir Aurel Stein, 2 Vols, London, Westminster, 1900; Indian Edition, Delhi, 1964. Also Eng. tr. R.S. Pandit, Allahabad, 1985.
Khusrau, Amir, *Nuh Siphr*, ed. Wahid Mirza, Oxford, Calcutta, 1948.
Miskin, Muhi'uddin, *Tahaif al-Abrar fi zikr-i Auliya-i Akhyar*,
Mirza Haidar, *Tarikhi Rashidi*, Eng. tr. Denison Ross, London, 1895.
Pir Hasan Shah, *Tarikh-i Hasan*, 4 Vols, Ist, 2nd and 4th volumes published by Research Library, Srinagar; Urdu translation of Vol. II (Political) and Vol. III (on *Aulia-i Kashmir*) also referred to in the book.
Qalandar, Hamid, *Khayr al-Majalis*, ed. K.A. Nizami, Aligarh, 1959.
Razi, A.A. *Haft Iqlim*, Ed. E.D. Ross, etc. Vol. I, Bib. India., Calcutta, 1939.
Sayyid Ali Hamadani, *Aurad-i-Fathiyya*, Urdu tr. with commentary by Assadullah Shah Dawarki under the title *Tafhim al-Aurad*, n.d. Lahore.
Sharaf'uddin Ali Yazdi, *Zafar-nama*, II, ed. Maulvi Muhammad Illahadad, Bib. India, Calcutta, 1855–88.
Sijzi, Amir Hasan, *Fawaid al-Fuad*, Newal Kishore, Kanpur, 1885.
Srivara, Pandit, *Rajatarangini*, Eng. tr. J.C. Dutt, under the title *Kings of Kashmira*, Vol. III, pp. 98–336, Calcutta 1935. (b) ed. P. Peterson, Bombay, 1896.
Suka, Pandit and Prajabhata, *Rajatarangini*, Eng. tr. J.C. Dutt *op. cit.*, Vol. III, pp. 337–427, Calcutta, 1935.

IV Traveller's Account

Lathan, Ronald *Travels of Marco Polo* (ed. and tr.) Penguin, 1958.

V Secondary Works (Persian and Urdu)

Azad, 'Abdul Ahad — *Kashmiri Zuban aur Sha'iri*, 3 Vols, Srinagar, 1959.

Cultural Academy — (i) *Rishiyyat*, Srinagar, 1978.
(ii) *Sham al-Arifin*, Proceedings of a Seminar on *Shaikh al-alam* 1978.
(iii) *Bruj-i Nur*, Srinagar, 1981.
(iv) *Shiraza*, Shaikh al-alam, No. Vol. 17, No. 303, 1978.
(v) *Shiraza*, Lal Ded, No. Vol. 18, No. 7–8, Srinagar, November-December, 1979.
(vi) *Nund Reush*, Vol. 15, No. 2, special No. of *Shiraza*, Srinagar 1978.

Hasan Pir Ghulam — *Asrar al-Akhyar*, Urdu trans. under the title *Tadhkira-i Aulia-i* Kashmir, Srinagar, 1960.

Ikram, Shaikh Muhammad — *Ab-i Kawthar*, seventh printing, Lahore, 1968.

— *Rud-i Kawthar* n.d; *Mauj-i Kawthar*, Lahore 1950.

Mihr, Ghulam Rasul — *Sayyid Ahmad Shahid*, Lahore, 1952.

Miskin, Haji Muhiuddin — *Tahaif al-Abrar fi dhikr-i Aualiya-i Akhyar*, Lahore.

Thanvi, Maulana Ashraf Ali — *Shari'at wa-Tariqat*, Delhi, n.d.

Riyaz, Muhammad — *Ahwal-u Athār wa Ash'ar Mir Sayyid 'Ali Hamadani*, Islamabad (Pakistan), 1985.

Zafar, Sayyida Ashraf — *Sayyid Mir Ali Hamadani*, (Indian Reprint), Delhi, 1987.

VI Secondary Works (English)

Ahmad Aziz — *Studies in Islamic Culture in the Indian Environment*, Oxford, 1969.

Arberry, A.J. — *Muslim Saints and Mystics*, London, 1966.

Arnold, T.W. — *The Preaching of Islam*, London, 1913.

Carr, E.H. — *What is History?*, Penguin Books, 1968.

Cassirer, E — *The Philosophy of Symbolic Forms*, Vol. I (tr. Mannheim). New York & London, Yale, 1953.

Carrithers, Michael — *The Buddha*, Oxford, reprint, 1986.

Chatterji, J.C. — *Kashmir Saivism*, Srinagar (reprint), 1962.

Corbin, Henry — *Creative Imagination in the Sufism of Ibn Arabi*, Eng. tr. R. Manheim, Princeton, 1969.

Dasgupta — *A History of Indian Philosophy*, II, III. London, 1932–40.
Hindu Mysticism, New York, 1959.

Dhar, K.N. — *Nund Rishi* : a Rosary of Hundred Beads, CAP, 1981.

Eaton, Richard Maxwell — *Sufis of Bijapur*, 1300–1700: *Social Role of Sufis in Medieval India*, Princeton, 1978.

Elliot and Dowson — *History of India as Told by its own Historians* (Revised ed. M. Habib, Ab. Rashid and K.A. Nizami), II, Aligarh 1952.

Elliot, Sir Henry — *Appendix to the Arabs in Sind*, Vol. 3, Part I of the *Historians of India*, Cape Town, 1853.

al Faruqi, Ismail Raji — *Tawhid: Its Implications for Thought and Life*, Pennsylvania, 1982.

Francke, A.H. — *Antiquities of Indian Tibet*, 2 Vols, Calcutta, 1914–26.

Geertz, Clifford — *Islam Observed*, New Haven, 1968.
The Interpretation of Cultures, New York, 1973.

Goldziher, I — *Muslim Studies* (trans. Barber and Stern), New York, Vol. I, 1967, Vol. II, 1971.

Grierson, Sir George and Barnett, Lionel D. — *Lalla-Vakyani, or, the Wise Sayings of Lal Ded : A mystic poetess of Kashmir*, London, 1920.

Grunebaum, Gustave Von — *Modern Islam: The Seach for Cultural Identity, New York*, 1964.

Habib, Muhammad — *Sultan Mahmud of Ghaznavi*, 2nd ed., New Delhi, 1967.

Habibullah, A.B.M — *The Foundation of Muslim Rule in India*, Lahore, 1945.

Hamadani, Agha Husain Shah — *The Life and works of Sayyid Ali Hamadani* (A.D. 1314–1385) Islamabad (Pakistan), 1984.

Karim, Abdul — *Social History of the Muslims of Bengal*, Dacca, 1959.

Kaul, Jayalal — *Lal Ded*, Sahitya Akademi, New Delhi, 1973.

Kaul, Gawashlal — *Kashmir Through the Ages.*

Kerr, M.H. *Islamic Studies : A Tradition and its Problems*, California, 1980.

Khaldun, Ibn — *The Muqaddimah*, Eng. tr. by F. Rosenthel, 3Vols. New York, 1958.

Muqaddimah-i-Ibn Khaldun, Urdu tr. by Maulana Ragib Rehmani Dehlavi, 2 Vols., New Delhi, 1987.

Khan, Mohammad Ishaq — *History of Srinagar* 1846–1947: *a study in socio-cultural change*, Srinagar 1978.

Perspectives on Kashmir: Historical Dimensions, Srinagar, 1983.

Khan, Yusuf Husain — *Glimpses of Medieval Indian Culture*, New Delhi, reprint, 1973.

Lawrence, Bruce — *Notes from a Distant Flute : The Extant Literature of pre-Mughal Indian Sufism*, Tehran.

Lawrence, Walter — *The Valley of Kashmir*, Srinagar, 1967.

Malik, Hafeez *Poet Philoosopher of Pakistan* (ed), Columbia, 1971

Malik, S.C. — *Indian Movement: Some Aspects of Dissent, Protest and Reform*, Simla, 1978.

Madan, T.N. — *Family ad Kinship*, Bombay, 1965.

Mannheim, Karl — *Ideology and Uptopia*, Eng. tr. L. Wirth and E. Shils, London, 1972.

Martin, Richard C. — *Approaches to Islam in Religious Studies*, Tuscon, 1985.

Massignon, Louis — *The Passion of Hallaj.* A Vols, Eng. Tr. from the French with a biographical foreword by Herbet Mason. (Bollingen Series, 98), Princeton, 1982.

Maurice, Aymard and Mukhia, Harbans (ed.) — *French Studies in History. The Inheritance*, Vol. I, New Delhi, 1988.

Mohibbul Hasan — *Kashmir Under the Sultans*, 2nd ed., 1974, Srinagar.

Muir, J. — *The Origin of Castes in the Vedic Age*, Delhi, 1972.

Mujib, Mohammad — *Indian Muslims*, Montreal, London, 1969.

Nizami, K.A. — *Some Aspects of Religion and Politics in India during the Thirteenth Century*. Reprint, 1978, Delhi.

Tarikh-i Mashaikh-i Chisht. Delhi, 1980.

Studies in Medieval Indian Society. Aligarh, 1956.

State and Culture in Medieval India, New Delhi, 1985.

Olivelle, Patrick — *Renunciation in Hinduism: A Medieval Debate*, Vol. I, Vienna, 1986.

Pandey, R.K. — *The Concept of Avatars* (with special reference to Gita) Delhi, 1979.

Pandit. B.N. — *Aspects of Kashmir Saivism*, 1977, Srinagar.

Parimoo, B.N. — *Nund Rishi: Unity in Diversity*, Srinagar, 1984.

Parimoo, B.N. — *The Ascent of Self*, Delhi, 1978.

Parmu, R.K. — *History of Muslim Rule in Kashmir*, Delhi, 1969.

Qamaruddin — *The Mahdavi Movement in India*, Delhi, 1985.

Qureshi, I.H. — *The Muslim Community of the Indo-Pak Subcontinent* (1610–1947), 1st Indian ed., Delhi, 1985.

Rafiqi, A.Q. — *Sufism in Kashmir*, Delhi, n.d.

Ramzan, Muhammad *Nur-i Irfan*, Srinagar, 1973.

Ray, S.C. — *Early History and Culture of Kashmir*, Calcutta, 1957.

Redfield, Robert — *Peasant Society and Culture*, Chicago, 1956.

Rizvi, S. Athar Abbas — *A History of Sufism in India*, Vol. I, New Delhi, 1978, Vol. II, 1983.

Rowse, A.L. — *The Use of History*, London, 1963.

Roy, Asim — *The Islamic Syncretistic Tradition in Bengal*, Princeton, 1983.

Said, Edward — *Orientalism*, London, 1978.

Schimmel, Annemarie — *Islam in the Indian sub-continent*. Leiden, 1980.

Sufi, G.M.D — *Kashir*, 2 vols. Lahore, 1948–49.

Tara Chand — *Influence of Islam on Indian Culture*, 2nd ed., Allahabad, 1963.

Tarafdar, Momtazur Rahman — *Husain Shahi Bengal*, Decca, 1965.

Titus, Murray — *Indian Islam*, London, 1930.

Trimingham, Spencer — *The Sufi Orders in Islam*, Oxford, 1971.

Troeltsch, E. — *The Social Teachings of Christian Churches*, London, 1956.

Troll, Christian W. (ed.) — *Islam in India*, Vol. II, New Delhi, 1985; *Muslim Shrines in India*, Vol. IV of Islam in India Series, Oxford, 1989.

Varsina, Jan — *Oral Tradition: A study in Historical Methodology*, tr. from French by H.H. Wright, London, 1965.

Weber, Max. — *The Protestant Ethic and the Spirit of Capitalism*, New York, 1959.

Zutshi, N.K. — *Sultan Zain-ul-Abidin of Kashmir*, Lucknow, 1976.

VII. Select Research Articles in Learned Journals and Publications

Aziz Ahmad — "Conversions to Islam in the Valley of Kashmir" *Central Asiatique Journal*, Vol. XXIII, No. 1–2, 1979.

Bamzai, A.K. — "Life of Nund Rishi", *The Indian Antiquary* Vol. 58; 1929, Vol. 59; 1930.

Eaton, Richard Maxwell — "Approaches to the Study of Conversion," *Approaches to Islam in Religious Studies*, (ed. Richard C. Martin), Tuscon, 1985.

"Folk Literature and the Expansion of Indian Islam", *History of Religions*, 14 No. 2 Nov, 1974, pp 117–27.

Evans, Pritchard — "Social Anthropology: Past and Present", *Man*, 1950, Vol. 198, pp. 118–124.

Habib Muhmmad — "The Arabic Conquest by Sindh", *Islamic Culture*, October, 1929.

Habib, Irfan — "Economic History of the Delhi Sultanate", *The Indian Historical Review* January 1978, Vol. IV, No. 2.

Hardy, Peter — "Modern European and Muslim Explanation of Conversion to Islam in South Asia: A Preliminary Survey of the Literature", *Journal of the Royal Asiatic Society*, 1977, No. 2.

Kaw, R.K. — "Compendium of Pratyabhijna Philosophy of Kashmir", *Research Biannual*, Vol. I, No. II, pp. 4–14.

Khan, Mohammad Ishaq — "Persian Influences in Kashmir in the Sultanate Period, 1320–1585", *Islamic Culture*, 1977.

"The Impact of Islam on Kashmir in the Sultanate Period, 1320–1586", *The Indian Economic and Social History Review*, 23, 2 (1986).

"Kashmiri Response to Islam, A.D. 1320–1586", *Islamic Culture*, January, 1987.

"Islam in Kashmir: Historical Analysis of its Distinctive Features", *Islam in India*, Vol. II, ed. Christian W. Troll Delhi, 1985.

"Sufism in Indian History", *Muslim Shrines in India*, ed., Christian W. Troll, Vol. IV, Oxford, 1989.

"The Significance of the Dargah of Hazratbal in the Socio-Religious and Political Life of Kashmiri Muslims", *Muslim Shrines in India, op. cit.*

"The Mystical Career and Poetry of Nuruddin Rishi Kashmiri", *Studies in Islam*, January/April, 1982.

"The Societal Dimensions of the Mystical Philosophy of Nuruddin Rishi Kashmiri", *Proceedings of the Indian History Congress*, Srinagar session, 1986.

Lawrence, Bruce – "Sufism and the History of Religions",

Studies in Islam, Vol. XVIII, Nos 3–4, July/October, 1981.
"Islam in India: The Function of Institutional Sufism in the Islamization of Rajasthan, Gujarat and Kashmir", *Contributions to Asian Studies*, Vol. XVII, Leiden, E.J. Brill, 1982.

Makdisi, George — "The Hanbli School and Sufism", *Humaniora Islamica*, (ed. Swartz), Vol. II, The Hague, Paris, 1974.

Newal, D.J.F. — "Some Account of the Rishis or Hermits of Kashmir", *J.A.S.R.*, 1870, XIX, 265–70.

Nizami, K.A. — (i) "The Shattari saints and their attitude towards the state", *Medieval India Quarterly*, I, No. 2.
(ii) "Khanqah in Madieval India", *Studies Islamica*; VIII, 1957.
"The Impact of Ibn Taimiyya on South Asia", *Journal of Islamic Studies*, I, Oxford, 1990.

Schimmel, A. — "Mystic Impact of Hallaj", in Hafeez Malik, *Poet Philosopher of Pakistan*, ed. Columbia, 1971.
"Reflections on Popular Muslim Poetry", *Contributions to Asian Studies*, Vol. XVII Leiden, E.J. Brill, 1982.

VIII Reference Works

Grierson Sir George — *A Dictionary of the Kashmiri Language*, Calcutta, 1932.

Hughes, Thomas Patrick — *Dictionary of Islam*, reprint, Oriental Books Reprint Corporation, New Delhi, 1976.

Knowles, J.H. — *A Dictionary of Kashmiri Proverbs and Sayings*, London, 1885.

Monier-Williams — *A Sanskrit-English Dictionary*, new ed., enlarged in collaboration with E. Leumann, C. Capeller and others, 1899; reprint, Oxford, 1964.

Platts, John T. — *A Dictionary of Urdu, Classical Hindi and English*, London: Oxford University Press, 1968.

Steingass, F.A. — *A Comprehensive Persian-English Dictionary*, Beirut: Librarie du Liban, 1970.

Arabic-English Dictionary, reprint, Cosmo Publications, New Delhi, 1985.

Storey, G.A. — *Persian Literature: A Bio-Bioliographical Survey*, 2 Vols. London; Luzac and Co., 1927–71.

Gazetteer of Kashmir and Ladakh, complied under the direction of the Quarter Master General of India in the Intelligence Branch, first published in 1890, by the Government Printing Press, Calcutta.

IX Translations of the Qur'an

'Ali, A. Yusuf — *The Koran : Text, Translations and Commentary*, Washington, D.C., 1946.

Arberry, A.J. — *The Koran Interpreted*, London, 1953; New York, 1964.

Pickthall, M.M. — *The Meaning of the Glorious Koran*, New York : New American Library and Mentor Books, n.d.

Shafi, Mufti Muhammad — *Ma'arif al-Quran*, 8 vols., Indian edition, Deoband, U.P., n.d.

Index